Spatial Representations and the Jacobean Stage

Spatial Representations and the Jacobean Stage

From Shakespeare to Webster

Russell West
Professor of English
University of Lüneburg
Germany

First published 2002 by
PALGRAVE
Houndmills, Basingstoke, Hampshire RG21 6XS and
175 Fifth Avenue, New York, N. Y. 10010
Companies and representatives throughout the world

PALGRAVE is the new global academic imprint of
St. Martin's Press LLC Scholarly and Reference Division and
Palgrave Publishers Ltd (formerly Macmillan Press Ltd).

ISBN 0–333–97373–9

This book is printed on paper suitable for recycling and
made from fully managed and sustained forest sources.

A catalogue record for this book is available
from the British Library

Library of Congress Cataloging-in-Publication Data
West, Russell, 1964–
Spatial representations and the Jacobean stage: from Shakespeare to
Webster / Russell West.
    p. cm.
Includes bibliographical references and index.
ISBN 0–333–97373–9
    1. English drama—Early modern and Elizabethan, 1500–1600—History
and criticism. 2. Shakespeare, William, 1564–1616—Stage history—To 1625.
3. Webster, John, 1580?–1625?—Stage history—To 1625. 4. English
drama—17th century—History and criticism. 5. Shakespeare, William,
1564–1616—Technique. 6. Theater—England—History—17th century.
7. Webster, John, 1580?–1625?—Technique. 8. Space and time in literature.
9. Setting (Literature) I. Title.

PR658.S59 W47 2001
792′.09′031–dc21   2001036885

10   9   8   7   6   5   4   3   2   1
11   10   09   08   07   06   05   04   03   02

Printed and bound in Great Britain by
Antony Rowe Ltd, Chippenham, Wiltshire

Contents

List of Illustrations

Acknowledgements

Utrecht University Library, the Provost and Fellows of Worcester College Oxford, and the British Library kindly granted permission to reproduce illustrations.

Helmut Bonheim's generous sponsorship facilitated the award of the one-year Hertz Fellowship which allowed me to undertake the preliminary work for this book in the English Department of the University of Cologne. Many thanks also to Adrian Poole, who kindly supported the application at such short notice.

I wish to thank the members of the panel who enthusiastically supported an earlier version of this book as a post-doctoral qualifying thesis in Cologne: Beate Neumeier, Hubert Wurmbach, Heinz Antor, Rainer Zaiser, and Helmut Bonheim.

I am grateful to Richard Aczel, Frank Lay and Tilman Höss, who were (and still are) faithful friends and colleagues always ready to give advice and encouragement. Manfred Jahn and Helmut Bonheim were thorough readers of the manuscript who gave me valuable critical feedback.

And much more than thanks to Kristina Reiss, who has witnessed the evolution of this project from its conception in Cardiff to its conclusion in Cologne and Lüneburg. This is for her with love.

Play Editions Used

Arden of Faversham, in *Three Elizabethan Domestic Tragedies*, ed. Keith Sturgess (Harmondsworth: Penguin, 1969).

[Beaumont, Francis?] and John Fletcher, *Beggar's Bush*, in *The Works of Beaumont and Fletcher*, ed. Alexander Dyce (London: Edward Moxon, 1845), vol. IX.

Beaumont, Francis and John Fletcher, *The Knight of the Burning Pestle*, in *The Works of Beaumont and Fletcher*, ed. Alexander Dyce (London: Edward Moxon, 1843), vol. II.

Beaumont, Francis and John Fletcher, *The Sea Voyage*, in *Three Renaissance Travel Plays*, ed. Anthony Parr (Manchester: Manchester University Press, 1995).

Brome, Richard, *The Antipodes*, in *Three Renaissance Travel Plays*, ed. Anthony Parr (Manchester: Manchester University Press, 1995).

Campion, Thomas, *The Lord Hay's Masque* in *Court Masques: Jacobean and Caroline Entertainments 1605–1640*, ed. David Lindley (Oxford: Clarendon Press, 1995).

Chapman, George, *The Memorable Masque* in *Court Masques: Jacobean and Caroline Entertainments 1605–1640*, ed. David Lindley (Oxford: Clarendon Press, 1995).

Daborne, Robert, *A Christian turn'd Turk*, ed. A. E. H. Swaen, in *Anglia* 20 (*NF* 8) (1898), 188–256.

Daborne, Robert, *A Christian turn'd Turk: Or, The Tragicall Liues and Deaths of the two Famous Pyrates, Ward and Dansiker* (London, 1612).

Daniel, Samuel, *Tethys' Festival* in *Court Masques: Jacobean and Caroline Entertainments 1605–1640*, ed. David Lindley (Oxford: Clarendon Press, 1995).

Day, John, William Rowley and George Wilkins, *The Travels of the Three English Brothers*, in *Three Renaissance Travel Plays*, ed. Anthony Parr (Manchester: Manchester University Press, 1995).

Ford, John, *'Tis Pity She's a Whore*, in *Three Plays*, ed. Keith Sturgess (Harmondsworth: Penguin, 1985).

Greene, Robert and Thomas Lodge, *A Looking-Glasse for London and England*, in *The Life and Complete Works in Prose and Verse of Robert Greene M. A.*, ed. Alexander Grossart (New York: Russell & Russell, 1964).

Heywood, Thomas, *The Fair Maid of the West (Part 1)*, in *The Dramatic Works of Thomas Heywood* (New York: Russell and Russell, 1964), vol. II.

Jonson, Ben, *Eastward Ho!* in *Ben Jonson*, eds C. H. Herford, and Percy and Evelyn Simpson (Oxford: Clarendon Press, 1932), vol. IV.

Jonson, Ben, *Every Man Out of his Humour*, in *Ben Jonson*, eds C. H. Herford, and Percy and Evelyn Simpson (Oxford: Clarendon Press, 1927), vol. III.

Jonson, Ben, *For the Honour of Wales*; *The Fortunate Isles*; *The Golden Age Restor'd*; *The Masques of Blackness and of Beauty*; *The Masque of Queens*; *Mercvrie Vindicated from the Alchemists at Covrt*; *Neptune's Triumph for the Return of Albion*; *Newes from the New World Discover'd in the Moone*; *Oberon: The Faery Prince*; *Pleasure Reconcild to Vertue*; *The Speeches at Prince Henry's Barriers*; *The Vision of Delight*; all in *The Sad Shepherd/The Fall of Mortimer/Masques and Entertainments*, in *Ben Jonson*, eds C. H. Herford, and Percy and Evelyn Simpson (Oxford: Clarendon Press, 1941), vol. VII.

Jonson, Ben, *The Alchemist; Bartholemew Fair; Volpone*; in *Three Comedies*, ed. Michael Jamieson (Harmondsworth: Penguin, 1974).

Middleton, Thomas and William Rowley, *The Changeling*, in *Three Jacobean Tragedies*, ed. Gamini Salgado (Harmondsworth: Penguin, 1969).

Middleton, Thomas, *A Chaste Maid in Cheapside*, ed. Alan Brissenden (London: Ernest Benn, 1968).

Middleton, Thomas, *A Mad World, My Masters; Michaelmas Term; No Wit, No Help Like a Woman's; A Trick to Catch the Old One*; all in *A Mad World, My Masters and Other Plays*, ed. Michael Taylor (Oxford: OUP World's Classics, 1995).

Philip Massinger, *The City Madam*, in *The Plays and Poems of Philip Massinger*, eds Philip Edwards and Colin Gibson (Oxford: Clarendon Press, 1976), vol. IV.

Shakespeare, William, *The Comical History of the Merchant of Venice, As You Like It, The Tragedy of Hamlet, Twelfth Night, Troilus and Cressida, The Tragedy of Othello, The Life of Timon of Athens, The History of King Lear, The Tragedy of Antony and Cleopatra, The Tragedy of Coriolanius, Cymbeline*; all in *The Complete Works*, eds Stanley Wells and Gary Taylor (Oxford: Clarendon Press/Oxford University Press, 1988).

Tourneur, Cyril, *The Revenger's Tragedy* in *Three Jacobean Tragedies*, ed. Gamini Salgado (Harmondsworth: Penguin, 1969).

Webster, John, *A Cure for a Cuckold*, in *The Complete Works of John Webster*, ed. F. L. Lucas (London: Chatto and Windus, 1927), vol. III.

Webster, John, *The Duchess of Malfi*, in *Three Plays*, ed. David Gunby (Harmondsworth: Penguin, 1972).

Webster, John, *The White Devil*, in *Three Jacobean Tragedies*, ed. Gamini Salgado (Harmondsworth: Penguin, 1969).

Introduction: Staging Space

Two experiences of theatre were formative in the genesis of this book. The first was a passing visit to a former monastery cloister in Compiègne, France, just after I had completed my undergraduate degree. I was there on a summer evening at the right moment to witness a medieval mystery play performed in such a way as to integrate the imposing old cloisters. The second experience was an equally casual visit, almost ten years later, to the just-completed New Globe Theatre on the Bankside in Southwark, London. Again, the visit was hasty, with time only to see part of a performance of a Shakespearean history play. But as in Compiègne, the tangible sense of the spatial dynamics of performance in such a setting made a deep impression. I was left with an exciting feeling that the full resonance of a performance involved exploiting the potential of the performance space, a space in turn embedded in a historical place with its own attendant spatial networks. Both experiences started me wondering about the ways in which the place of performance gives form to the virtual dynamics of the dramatic text, and the ways in which the text may perhaps only be adequately understood when it is read back into its original spatial context.

Such an effort of understanding is demanded by Antony's grand statement, 'Here is my space', at the beginning of Shakespeare's *Antony and Cleopatra*. Antony's words constitute the 'deictic' statement *par excellence* – pointing to the pragmatic context in which dialogue is anchored,[1] indicating the speaker's place on the stage, grounding the dramatic action in the here-and-now of performance.

Such an ostentatious appropriation of place is, within this play, an act which is inherently antagonistic. For in the same breath Antony suggests that 'Kingdoms are clay': 'Let Rome in Tiber melt, and the wide arch | Of the ranged empire fall' (1.1.35–7). The play sets Egypt against

1

Rome, private romance against public obligation, pleasure against duty. In the very act of their enunciation, moreover, Antony's words also set the power of dramatic discourse against the existence of the Roman state, fantasy against reality: 'Kingdoms are clay.' By extension, the actor's declaration also implicitly opposes the privileged enclave of theatrical spectacle to the pragmatic urban setting in which it is inserted. In these series of oppositions the shadow of the antagonistic relationship between the City and the Liberties, between the City fathers and the theatres, between 'playing' and civic virtue, can perhaps also be glimpsed.

Yet the whole movement of the play suggests that the stability of such oppositions can only ever be provisional. The barriers Antony erects are merely temporary; the action of *Antony and Cleopatra* shows that there can be no private realm hidden from the imperatives of political feuds. Likewise, the distinction between theatrical fiction and the real context of the theatre may be equally illusory. Indeed, the polyvalent resonances of 'Here is my space' in the mouths of Roman Antony and English actor make it a statement referring both to the fabric of performance *text* and to the *context* of performance, such that the notion of 'my space' allows no absolutely hermetic separation between the fictive world enacted on the stage and the social context in which the stage is inserted.

Antony's delineation of 'his space' marks it off from other spaces, making the domain of artistic performance distinct from other parts of the world he occupies. But at the same time, by the deictic force of an emphatic verbal indication, his words intensify the concrete materiality of the place he occupies, in a way which cannot but bring back to the audience's awareness the stage as a distinct site in the early modern social fabric. When Antony stakes his claim upon a corner of the classical world, or upon a corner of the Jacobean stage, we are confronted with an example of the stereoscopic vision which, I will suggest, is typical of the early modern theatre.

On the one hand, the 'apartness' attributed here to theatrical performance is crucial to the work of art, for it is the aloofness of the artistic product which delineates it from other objects made by human labour and allows it to gain an additional value and meaning over and above its material existence, to 'speak' about the world rather than merely serving a pragmatic purpose. Yet the capacity to stand back from its context and to speak about that context also implies the very opposite of autotelic isolation. For the self-reflexivity of the work of art, by gesturing towards itself as a thing made, also raises the question of its materiality, of its production within a network of supply and demand – in other words, of its 'worldliness', to take a term coined by Edward Said.[2] To examine the self-reflexivity of art is, in the final analysis, to situate the work of art in a place. It was the theatre's striking otherness, and at the same time, its intensely vibrant presence in the here-and-now, which came home to me so forcefully in my epiphanic experiences in Compiègne and Southwark.

In this book, I will try to outline some of the ways in which the Jacobean theatre, as an ostentatiously spatial art-form, interacts with the context of early modern society. During the period from the death of Elizabeth I (1603) to the end of the reign of James I (1625), many of the controversial social and political questions in debate were issues of space: questions of enclosure, of rural unemployment and vagrancy, of social mobility, of relationships between court, country and city. These spatial tensions can be seen as being constituted variously by the polarized desires for mobility and flexibility, and, conversely, for fixity and static social structures. Distinct groups of social actors had varying and conflicting degrees of interest in forms of social, geographical or political mobility or fixity. These interests were constantly alluded to in the theatre of the day, making it an important semiotic mode of intervention in the spatial debates of the period.

However, not only the themes dealt with by the Jacobean drama were concerned with spatial aspects of early modern existence. More importantly, the drama itself was a spatial art-form, determined in the last instance by the various stages upon which the plays were produced. Theatre is now commonly acknowledged to be not just a verbal and temporal mode of artistic creation, but also a spatial artistic form, an aspect of drama which was particularly prominent in the large open stage of the English Renaissance. That drama frequently drew attention to its own spatial characteristics, and to its place within the society which produced and consumed it. The material existence of the theatre – not only the much discussed question of stage design, but the more fundamental one of the inherently spatial character of theatre as an art-form – mediated between the larger space of social reality in its most concrete aspects, and the plays with their thematic treatment of issues of spatiality. In a society which was highly conscious of social and cosmic hierarchies, much articulation of social relations and debate about spatial problems was couched in explicitly spatial terms. Thus the form of theatrical art foregrounded space as a major theme of the drama of the time, thereby constituting a 'spatial signifier' for the 'cultural signified'.[3] The theatre was therefore both an integral part of social processes, and offered a means of articulating and understanding those same processes. The theatre thereby occupied an ambivalent position, both participatory and critical, within the dynamism of social transformation.

Recent years have seen a re-emergence of interest in spatial aspects of social existence almost prominent enough to constitute a 'spatial turn' in contemporary culture. Following a dynamic impulse given by French philosophers after the Second World War – Bachelard, Lefebvre, Foucault[4] – spatial enquiry has enveloped almost every aspect of the human sciences. Up until the beginning of the twentieth century, 'space' was conceived of as a sort of a container into which things were inserted. It was regarded as stable, homogenous, empty and neutral. However, the stability and homogeneity of space were cast into question by the theory of relativity. Notions of the emptiness and neutrality of space were also irreversibly shaken by a wide range of social sciences in the course of the twentieth century. There is now a broad consensus in the human sciences that space does not pre-exist social formations; rather, it is constituted by them, so that every change within a given social formation is accompanied by a change of its spatial characteristics. Conversely, changes in spatial structures also influence the social structures of the given group. According to Lefebvre, each historical period, characterized by particular social forms, particular modes of production, and particular political conflicts, expresses these social structures in corresponding spatial configurations of private dwellings, public spaces, buildings, or the spatial movements of its subjects; changes in social modes of production engender new spatial arrangements.[5] Some critics have expressed concern that this attention to space signifies the neglect of historical transformation, but, as Foucault pointed out, spatial processes and their transformations are necessarily historical processes, and spatial forms of social life have their own particular histories.[6] Space is thus the context, the defining condition, the object and the result of social action and interaction in history. Space is increasingly regarded as an aspect of almost every aspect of social activity, coterminous with the material texture of existence. It is a facet of being so all-pervasive as to be virtually invisible until made the focus of critical enquiry.

There has been a veritable explosion of research on every possible imaginable area of spatial life in recent years. Beyond the geographical, urban and architectural aspects of spatial organization, postmodern concepts of space include the spatial characteristics of power relations (hierarchies, exclusion), of social relations (proximity and distance), of bodily experience (spatial orientation, the body as a boundary for the self), or of gender (public and private spaces, sexual dichotomy). Even quite abstract or intangible areas of human activity, such as language, thought or economic exchange, are increasingly being conceptualized in terms of space; they are often structured in spatial terms, both in their logic and the meta-discourses about them, and work powerfully upon more concrete spatial phenomena.[7]

Critics have objected that space has come to be such an all-pervasive concept in the contemporary human sciences that it may be asked whether the term 'space' has any meaning at all, or have criticized the excessively metaphorical use of the term.[8] The problem, however, is not merely one of careless or inadequate definition, but rather that the aspects of human life to which space pertains are potentially limitless. This means that the notion of space has so many domains of application that the term inevitably takes on a broad spectrum of meanings. New definitions of space are needed for each specific domain of application, in order to reveal the many aspects of space in various areas of social existence. In this book, I shall endeavour to make the notion of space concrete by situating it in quite specific areas of historical social practice, thereby avoiding the perils of excessive metaphoricity, while maintaining the conceptual flexibility inevitably necessary to deal with very diverse aspects of human action. Thus I will talk about spaces of exchange (business partnerships, market places, exchange as replacement of one entity by another), spaces of social mobility (class structures, aristocratic houses), demographic mobility (itinerant populations), geographical spaces (home and away, the familiar and the foreign and movement between them) and spaces of thought (universal-abstract and local-empirical thought). A single definition of space will not be applied exclusively through the book; rather, the spatial aspects of quite distinct areas of social existence will determine the usage of the notion of space in the respective chapters. In this way, I hope to be able to do justice to the variety of human existence and its representation on the early modern stage, rather than locking that variety into the restricted bounds of a narrow definition.

Obviously, one constant aspect of spatial practice none the less traverses the various aspects of space explored in this book. That is spatial signifying practice in the art-form which most insistently and dynamically exploits space – the theatre. Theatre, by virtue of its spatial dynamism, forces the spatial aspects of semiotic practice into the limelight. In the theatre we are confronted with a practice which, in accord with the insights gained by recent spatial theory, appropriates space, moulds it so as to create a micro-system of social relationships and practices, underpinned by a dense, multi-layered network of overdetermined messages issued to the audience.

The workings of spatial signification in drama have been given very close scholarly attention since the work of the Prague structuralist theatre analysts, showing that far beyond 'location' or 'verbal scenery', theatre is a complex process of spatial semiosis utilizing a diverse range of spatial codes.[9] Almost everything on the stage – stage design, scenery, lighting, actor positioning with respect to the audience and with respect to other actors, gesture and mime, voice projection, costuming – can be seen to participate in the spatial aspect of theatre. Even the verbal text of drama, whose traditional prominence in theatrical criticism tended to elide the concrete spatiality of performance, is replete with spatial indicators.

Spatial signs have a vital role in organizing the production of theatrical meaning. The theatre confronts the spectator with a 'primary sign-system' of 'iconic' stage-signs which imitate gestures, words, objects and spaces in the non-theatrical world; this barrage of iconic signs, however, cannot take on meaning for the audience until it is made coherent by a secondary system of signification which creates connections and meaningful links between the elements of the first order of signification. Such second-order explicatory work is principally done by indexical signs, signs which, following Peirce's famous definition, create relationships of causality.[10] This notion is explained by Aston and Savona, when they note that

> Ideally, theatrical signs should combine (a) to transmit clear messages and (b) to hierarchise the messages sent. In the case of film ... the 'eye' of the camera helps to direct meaning. It selects the subject(s) to be viewed, thereby focusing our attention and directing the meaning-creating processes. In theatre, there is no such mediating device. Everything is put before us and we have a panoramic as opposed to a partial and pre-selected view of the stage. Signs operating within the theatrical framework need to be hierarchised in such a way as to help 'fix' meaning. Like language, theatre can foreground or 'make strange' specific elements of staging as a means to creating difference or significance.[11]

The theatre creates meaning by a process of selection and foregrounding, that is, making prominent in an imminently spatial sense, be it by means of lighting or by placing at the centre or the front of the stage. Elam comments: 'Despite its origin as a linguistic concept, foregrounding is essentially a spatial concept and thus well adapted to the theatrical text. It is of course possible for those devices which serve to defamiliarize the linguistic utterance in other contexts also to operate in the drama.'[12]

Foregrounding (*aktualisace*) was originally a linguistic term developed by the Prague school of formalists, designating the process whereby perception was 'deautomatized', such that the receiver was forced to take note of utterance itself rather than of its supposed 'content'. Seen more broadly as an art-form in a social context, the theatre functions not according to the Aristotelian operation of 'diegesis', that is, telling, but according to 'mimesis', showing the world as it is, a process Elam names 'ostention'. The relation of global theatrical sign to referent is an 'indexical' one, that is, once again following Peirce's definition, based on the function of designation or spatial contiguity.[13]

But these theoretical insights appear to have had little influence on Renaissance theatre studies until now. Following partly on a growing interest in the role of space in literary texts, but probably more as a result of the fruitful innovations of North American New Historicism and British Cultural Materialism, pioneering work has been done in recent years on the role of space in English Renaissance literature.[14] Such studies have been supplemented by very interesting research looking at broader aspects of spatial experience in the early modern era such as the rise of cartography.[15] However, it is surprising, given the close connections of space and time in drama, even more prominent on the stage than in other literary forms, that there has been little attention given to the role of space on the Renaissance stage.[16]

The few exceptions, such as Mullaney's much acclaimed *The Place of the Stage* and Sullivan's *The Drama of Landscape*, unfortunately include no analysis of the theatrical space of performance, or of the marking of space in dramatic texts, thus neglecting the manner in which stage performance may have addressed the spatial and thus political location of their performance.[17] These writers display no interest in the plays as spatial artefacts, whether at the textual or at the performance level. While displaying careful and erudite attention to the material *context* of the plays, there is no acknowledgement of the material *texture* of the plays themselves, as theatre or as drama, thus paradoxically rendering them static, abstract and *spaceless*. Whence a central task of this book: to describe the internal functioning of the dramatic space of Jacobean plays. It should become clear that the dynamics of the drama on stage is a response to the larger context of spatial thought and spatial experience motivating the theatrical production.

A spatial analysis of Renaissance drama cognizant of the spatial forms of the theatre and the spatial structuring of social and political existence would, implicitly, take up de Saussure's founding assumption regarding the materiality of the sign. His concept implies that signification, far from transparently communicating reality, has its own substance and consistence, its own rules of operation; signification is a material practice which is no less productive than the worldly processes which it 'mediates' and thus makes available for reception by perceiving subjects. It is this awareness of the materiality of spatial signifying practices which furnishes the central theoretical tenet of this book: in so far as signifying practices share the materiality of the world they signify, it can be assumed that they also participate in the spatiality of the world of practice. To that extent, my analysis can be seen as addressing an as-yet-unresolved question of theatre semiotics, that of articulating the material processes of semiosis on the stage upon the thematic and narrative content of the drama on the one hand, and the context of production on the other. The issue of space in its triple manifestation as an essential component of theatrical semiosis, as a frequent theme of dramatic narratives, and as the context of performance (both as the place of theatrical production, and as the object of contestation of so much contemporary social and political discourse), allows the formulation of a comprehensive answer to this thorny theoretical problem.

The possibility, albeit limited, of reconstructing the spatial element in a cultural history of the theatre (complicated by the paucity of performance records of early modern drama, or the scarcity of stage directions in Shakespeare, but compensated by a plethora of spatial indices in dramatic dialogue itself[18]) implies that spatially oriented readings of Renaissance culture are not merely anachronistic projections of postmodern preoccupations upon the helplessly mute actors of the past. On the contrary, the achievements of recent theorization of spatial experience can render us more sensitive to spatial aspects of Renaissance theatre. Thus an analysis of the spatial structures and techniques of the theatre can be correlated with a broad range of other varieties of textual evidence which suggests that spatial concerns were widespread through different sectors of society and across many domains of cultural production. If spatial representation has come into the limelight in recent studies of Renaissance culture it is in large part because our modern experience has allowed us to recognize a crucial aspect of early modern formulations of knowledge and experience, until recently obscured by paradigms of interpretation which often foregrounded history and progress rather than the spatial dimension of social practice – just as contemporary 'steps forward or breakthroughs' in theatre production 'turn out to be (unwitting) rediscoveries of techniques taken for granted by Elizabethan audiences (the open stage, the mixing of viewers, extempore improvizations based upon suggestions from the audience).'[19]

The first chapter of the book sets out to curtail the possible dangers of a one-sided projection of contemporary critical interest in questions of space by demonstrating that Renaissance culture was acutely aware of the spatial dimension of social life, and in particular of the transformations of perceptions of the world, to which that culture was a witness. In particular, the early modern theatre was an art-form whose referential functioning dedicated it to symbolic intervention in its immediate social and political context.

Following on from this prefatory chapter, the remainder of the study explores representations of space on the Jacobean stage in specific areas of social life in early modern England. A recurring aspect of my argumentation will be the ambivalent position of the theatre in its context. In a society constantly torn between conservative notions of stability and the inevitable disruptions and turbulence produced by accelerating forces of historical change, the theatre was both part of the powerful currents of mobility, and equally a vehicle for discourses of stability.

Chapter 2 looks at the court masque as a dramatic form inherently concerned with the shape of the universe, but hostile to all forms of change and instability. It constructed a complex of idealist images of the court and monarch, creating a mythical version of the realm which was increasingly vulnerable to the pressure of social realities beyond the court.

The fundamental force for historical transformation in the early modern era was the emergent money economy. Chapter 3 explores the all-pervasive spatial mobility and acceleration provoked by the incipient rise of capitalism, and then scrutinizes the intimate imbrication of the stage itself in the very economic processes to which it owed its existence – processes which, like other modes of traditionalist discourse, it so often decried. The theatre was a profit-driven art-form only partly willing to admit the forces to which it owed its success.

The new money economy propelled new forms of social mobility, with a concomitant fluctuation of the signs of social status. In Chapter 4, the performance of social mobility in the Jacobean drama is examined under three categories of social identity in descending scale of magnitude: starting with changes in relationships of land ownership, via changes within the identity of the aristocratic family, and culminating at the point where the theatre foregrounded its own mode of functioning, namely, in changes in the sartorial marking of individuals' social rank.

The acquisition of wealth and its status symbols for some meant expropriation and poverty for others. Chapter 5 explores the connection commonly made, in the context of increasing demographic mobility as a result of changing economic conditions and rural dispossession, between the threatening groups of 'masterless men' who roamed the highways of England and congregated in the suburbs of London, and the common players. Once again, the stage both dramatized its own association with the forces of social mobility, in this context that of vagrancy, and attempted to defuse the threat which it embodied in its power to magnetically attract companies of 'masterless men'.

The desire for rapid wealth was one of the principal motivations for early modern mobility in its most glamorous form, overseas travel. In Chapter 6, the travel drama is analysed as the genre *par excellence* which, tangibly and visually, performs the topos of geographical transgression, in the act of departure and in the confrontation with cultural alterity, so as to comment recursively upon the culture in which the theatre is embedded. The transgression of boundaries enacted within the Jacobean travel drama was sometimes neutralized within the plays' limits, in which case transgression acted as a foil for the confirmation of cultural value; conversely, however, transgression could also be allowed to unfold its subversive consequences for the source culture.

The same greed for novelty which drove early modern travel was also at work at home. Chapter 7 describes the emergence of a new mode of subjectivity arising out of localized, empirical thought at odds with and yet co-existing with prior notions of an hierarchic and pre-ordained order of things in which human beings had their rightful place. The new mode of subjectivity was operative, pragmatic and Machiavellian, finding in theatrical play-acting a concrete metaphor of its own deviousness and duplicity. It is this 'histrionic' duplicity, with its concomitant mode of knowledge, which was responsible for producing a new subjectivity, one whose mode of insertion into the social world was that of acquisitive appropriation of social space.

After an inaugural analysis of the self-vitiating idealism of the court masque, this book focuses upon various nodes of early modern spatial social existence as they were explored on the intensely worldly Jacobean public and private stages. Whereas the court masque endeavoured to keep the spatial transformations of early modern English society at arm's length, the public and private theatres were interested in all the domains of spatial dynamism and novelty of their times: money as a catalyst for spatial transformation, social mobility, demographic mobility, sea travel, and the formation of interior spaces of subjectivity through the force of operative thought. In each of these domains, it was the attainment of novelty – through the appropriation of new social, political, geographical or subjective spaces – which constantly drove the representations of social existence on the Jacobean stage. Thus the acquisitive drive so prominent in the emergent money economy provides the pattern underlying the subsequent forms of spatial transformation analysed in their stage manifestations. In all these domains of social existence, the drama hovered between involvement in new forms of mobility and critical distance; between celebration of the very forces of transformation which brought the theatre into being and anxious gestures of control. The playwrights constantly introduced braking mechanisms to tie in the consequences of their tangible explorations of the spatial possibilities of a new acquisitive sensibility. Yet in the last analysis, the theatre with its profit-driven portrayal of new spaces and spatial consciousness, was founded upon and could not but be part of this greedy reaching out for new experiences which determined it.

1

Stage-space in the Jacobean Age

Early modern conceptions of space

In the opening scene of Shakespeare's *Cymbeline* a gentleman claims that one would have to search the whole earth to find an equal to the banished Posthumus, one of the protagonists of the play. The speaker's companion demures at this assessment: 'You speak him far.' To which the first speaker ripostes, 'I do extend him, sir, within himself; | Crush him together rather than unfold | His measure duly' (1.1.24–7). The homage offered to the unfortunate Posthumus is given as concise, compacted eloquence rather than as elaborate, overblown rhetoric, such that communication attains the status of topological activity. In a play which is about place and displacement in the definition of national identity, it is not by chance that public reputation and its propagation by verbal discourse are conceived of in spatial terms. Renaissance discourse, whether concerned with social life in general, or scrutinized more narrowly as a specific use of language, entailed a strong sense of spatial imagery quite unfamiliar to us today.

Early modern modes of codifying knowledge emphasized tangible, concrete qualities of experience, often fixing upon the spatial dimensions of existence. Even more, social ruptures and transformations abruptly cast spatial structures into question, making them more particularly the focus of discursive attention. The task of this chapter is to demonstrate in detail that spatial categories characterized common modes of articulating social experience in early modern England – at least in so far as those modes of experience can be reconstructed through textual evidence. Thought, speech, communication, social identity, all appear to have been conceptualized by early modern thinkers and writers in strikingly spatial language. It comes as no surprise, then, to find that in a similar manner the theatre was also understood by contemporaries as a primarily spatial art-form. Consequently, discussions of the theatre were couched in a spatial language which assumed that performance space was social space.

Processes of thought were commonly imagined in spatial terms in the early modern period. Drawing upon a heritage in which knowledge had been encoded verbally rather than in writing, the Renaissance possessed a plethora of mnemonic techniques which used mental images of buildings or rooms to systematize and categorize knowledge spatially, thus making memorized knowledge 'visually' available for retrieval; real buildings or places would be employed as a physical support for the categorization of information to be retained for future reference.[1] John Willis described a typical spatialized mnemonic method: 'The Art of Memorie, so farre foorth as it dependeth upon Places & Idea's, consisteth of two parts: *Reposition,* and *Deposition.* ... A *Repositorie* is an imaginary house or building' which 'we prefixe before the eyes of our mind, as often as we intend to commit things to memory'; 'A Place (as it is considered in this art) is a Roome determined in the *Repositorie* [set?] for receiuing the Idea's or formes of things thereinto.'[2]

In Renaissance thought, the mind participated in the objective order of things, within an epistemological configuration in which subject and object of knowledge were not fully distinct from one another. Donne's claim in his fifth *Holy Sonnet*, 'I am a little world made cunningly | Of Elements', enacts that very porosity of the self as knower of its environment.[3] Human beings made up a Microcosm which reflected the grand Macrocosm of the universe. The person was a 'little world' which epitomized the 'great world', and whose substance and life forms, both physical and spiritual, repeated in miniature the structures of the universe of which it was a constituent part.[4] The microcosm of the mental world was a spatial analogy of the macrocosm of reality, but it was precisely the concreteness of space which allowed a more physical and consequently fluid interconnection than simply one of 'mere' analogy as a metaphorical structure. The links of resemblance and correspondence between different levels of the universe defied the establishment of clearly defined boundaries between the various spheres, such that thought was always a concretely spatialized activity. Were these spatial images for mental processes perhaps merely metaphorical, as one would expect for spatial imagery transferred to the mental world in modern usage?[5] Early modern people, working as they did with a macro- or microcosmic view of the universe, appear not to have thought in terms of the separation presupposed by a transfer process and consequent metaphorization of space, but would have understood these usages more or less literally.

Likewise, speech and communication appear to have been understood during the Renaissance as spatial practices. Language itself could be spatialized, so that Richard Mulcaster's *First Part of the Elementary* (1582) aimed to facilitate 'the entrie to language', or Sanford's Spanish textbook offered *An Entrance to the Spanish Language*.[6] When Montaigne travelled south through Tyrol, he thought of himself as entering not Italy but 'the Italian language'.[7] The form of language often reflected the spatial themes addressed. Philip Jones's 1589 translation of Albrecht Meier's guide for 'Gentlemen, Merchants, Students, Souldiers, mariners, &c. Employed in Seruices Abrode' anatomizes the various details of the geography, chorography and topography of foreign lands to be noted by the careful observer, moving methodically from the scale of the world down to the individual dwellings of the notables of particular cities; the treatise offers a breakdown of the categories of memory under the heading 'The general sections, or places of this discourse.' Similarly, Sir Thomas Palmer, in his *Essay of the meanes how to make our Trauailes … the more profitable*, tabularized the myriad possible forms and motivations of travel in a tentacular and expansive tree diagram offering the reader almost a hundred conceptual routes to explore, in anticipation of the real journey where the typography of curiosity would be realized in empirical observation. Gerard Malynes divided his treatise on *The Center of the Circle of Commerce* into 'fiue Chapters or Zones' stretching from the 'Articke circle' via the 'Tropicke of Cancer', the 'Equinoctiall', the 'Tropicke of Capricorne' to the 'Antarticke circle'. Likewise, John Barlow, in a work of pietistic theology envisaged his discourse as a carefully managed surface of production, the 'ground, than I intend to scatter with good grain' or 'that peece of cloth, I purpose … to make up into a garment', imagining discourse as a place where the speaker works a trade.[8]

Fertilizing this receptivity for the spatial imagery and structures of speech was the acute 'verbal imagination' which the Elizabethans and Jacobeans seem to have possessed.[9] Rhetoric, so important in the early modern age, is an inherently spatial operation upon language, a 'tourning' from one usage of language to another, as primers of rhetoric usually pointed out in their opening definitions. The very titles of such primers (*A Garden of Eloquence, The Arcadian of Rhetoric*) underlined the spatial nature of work with language.[10] It is significant that the teaching of rhetoric and public speaking in the Renaissance proceeded by visual and therefore spatial means. The theatre in particular was a privileged locus of rhetorical speech. Renaissance speakers' acute sensitivity for spatiality in language is unfortunately as unfamiliar today as the early modern sense of the dynamism of language which George Steiner claims we have irretrievably lost.[11]

Underlying these conceptions was a notion of social organization which was often presented in strongly spatial ways. It is no coincidence that the term 'place' referred to a person's position in the social hierarchy, a clearly structured and easily visualizable ladder of rank. The Church of England homily on order encapsulated and propagated early modern conceptions of social hierarchy:

> Almightie God hath created & appointed al thynges, in heauen, yearth, and waters in a most excellent and perfect ordre.... Euery degree of people, in the vocacion, callyng, & office, hath appoynted to them, their duetie and ordre. Some are in high degree, some in lowe, some kynges & princes, some inferiors and subiectes, priestes and laimen, masters and seruantes, fathers and children, husbandes & wifes, rich and poore, and euery one hath nede of other, so that in al thinges, it is to be lauded & praised ye goodly ordre of God, without ye whiche, no house, no cite no common-wealth, can continue & endure.[12]

This passage, regularly read in church, was familiar to every Englishman and -woman and deeply ingrained in the collective consciousness of hierarchical social structures.

The visual hierarchies embodied in vertical structures were also embodied in easily understood topographies. In early modern society, demarcations of social status were clearly visible in the structures of towns, with the Hearth Taxes reflecting a rich nucleus and impoverished peripheries.[13] Similarly, attainment of the status of landowner is expressed in a vividly imagined scenario by Middleton's Quomodo in *Michaelmas Term*: 'Now I begin to set one foot upon the land. Methinks I am felling of trees already; we shall have some Essex logs yet to keep Christmas with' (2.3.331–3). Quomodo's imaginative geographical simile makes concrete the change in social status brought about by Easy's relinquishment of his estate.

The highly visual and spatialized character of images describing Jacobean society logically produced concepts of identity which were predominantly organized by spatial schemas. As late as 1700, Richard Gough, writing the history of the Shropshire parish of Myddle, could complete his study with 'Observations concerning the seates in Myddle and the familyes to which they belong', using this centrally visible spatial hierarchy – the seating in the parish church – as the structure around which to recount life histories of notable individuals in the parish. It was place, rather than identity in the modern sense, which was the subject of dispute in arguments that might erupt upon the decease of a husband, rendering doubtful the right of the widow, particularly when she remarried, to retain her 'place' in the status-bound arrangement of church-pew seating.[14] Early modern language reflected the connections of possession, status, hierarchy, in words such as 'propriety', which in seventeenth-century English signified both *property* and *knowing one's place*.[15] Identity was a matter of place.

Such identities were determined less by inward characteristics, as modern sensibility would dictate, than by outward relationships, whence the enormous importance of clothing as a means of making visible social place. Elizabeth had passed sumptuary legislation in 1553 fixing particular articles of clothing as appropriate for particular social groups, and issued 10 proclamations during her reign enforcing this legislation. The sumptuary laws were repealed in 1603, but even as late as 1636, Charles I forbade the selling and wearing of imitation jewellery. In an intensely heterogeneous social environment such as London, dress played a major role in permitting people to locate their fellows in the social hierarchy.[16]

One salient example of the spatialization of social identity is the aristocratic family manifesting a collective rather than individualized identity, and with its seat in a country residence sometimes bearing the family name and embodying reputation, lineage or genealogy, property, rank – all those social statuses being gathered together in the early modern term 'house'.[17] Thus, in Shakespeare's *Romeo and Juliet* social life is spatialized from the very outset with the mention, in the opening words of the Prologue, of 'Two households'. The centre of the aristocratic kinship clan was the country house, with its many retainers and surrounding estates and hierarchical relationships of dependency and lordship, its reciprocal relations of duty and responsibility. The house itself symbolized a certain form of hospitality reflected in the welcome offered to guests, and the material care for an entire body of subordinate personnel.

The very architecture of early modern aristocratic dwellings embodied this spatialized family structure: rather than organizing individual rooms along the central axis of a long corridor, a design for interior space which started to appear from the mid-seventeenth century onward, the interior organization of early modern buildings consisted of an aggregate of rooms linked together by multiple interconnecting doorways. The later structure of the monadic spaces of the private room separately linked to a central trunk of the passageway had yet to supersede the network of rooms through which it was necessary to proceed to reach any other room. The plethora of interconnecting doors made a house a network of discrete but thoroughly interlinked rooms, in which there was no real distinction between the way through a house and the living spaces contained in it. The house thus constituted a sort of permeable honeycomb-space, in which the numerous members of the household passed through the matrix of rooms where day-to-day life was conducted.[18]

The architecture of the aristocratic house provides a concrete image of spatialized and tentacular family or household structures, providing individual identity by embedding it within a network of relationships rather than decking it out with a set of interiorized, privatized personal traits. Historians have spoken of the 'porosity' of the aristocratic family, characterizing it as an institution with weak boundaries separating it from other social spaces, an institution lodged in wider network of relationships, linked to kin by ties of dependence, loyalty and reciprocity.[19] Sir Bounteous Progress says in *A Mad World, My Masters* upon the occasion of a feast given at his manor: 'Every jack has his friend today, this cousin and that cousin puts in for a dish of meat' (5.1.3–4). Relations of hospitality are spatialized in Sir Bounteous's capacious greeting to Follywit, 'Your honour is most spaciously welcome' (2.1.93).

Recently, social historians of the early modern period have queried the prevalence of such extended families, providing evidence that the majority of English households consisted of simple, nuclear families, whether in towns or in the country alike; they suggest that the pre-industrial extended family appears to have been a myth. At the same time, however, these revisionist historians have also demonstrated that the majority of families, with the probable exception of the labouring poor, were generally extended by the presence of servants, usually regarded as members of the family. Moreover, the family, if not always porous in the sense of embodying a tentacular social network, remained, in an early modern society characterized by the absence of privacy, a social unit in which the individual existed as a public entity, as a very visible part of collective existence: whence the prevalence of defamation disputes in a 'face-to-face' society where people were constantly on show, and where the 'symbolic capital' or 'credit' of a person was of prime importance.[20]

Thus the phenomenon of the aristocratic family, if it perhaps did not reflect a generalizable historical reality, none the less symbolically bore out the ineluctably public character of social and collective identity in the early modern world, and offered a culturally visible embodiment of early modern social consciousness. Perhaps the most interesting evidence of the significance of spatialized aristocratic social identity is to be found in the transgression of this form of identity. In Jonson's *Volpone*, Mosca reveals to Bonario the latter's father's plan to disinherit his son, to 'thrust you forth | As a mere stranger to his blood' (3.2.44–5). Both belonging to and exclusion from the kinship structure are expressed in spatial terms. Similarly, this spatial configuration of the aristocratic family is open to ironical manipulation by reversal: the Courtesan in *A Mad World, My Masters* describes her relationship with Sir Bounteous Progress in terms of a manor park which is not carefully guarded, allowing her, as his game, to escape from the confines of the aristocratic domain to offer her sexual services to other clients (1.1.127–33). That the imagery of the noble house was subject to ironic contestation demonstrates to what extent it was present as a significant topos in the cultural imagination of the Jacobeans.

It is not by chance that society was often figured by the image of the organic household unity. Social categories were frequently described as rooms in a larger unified structure, allowing society to be imagined as a clan-family entity organized around rights, duties and responsibilities along a vertical axis. James announced in *Basilikon Doron* that he would speak of the king's duties to society once he had arrived, in the second part of his treatise, at 'the owne roome'. When the Elector of the Palatinate accepted the crown of Bohemia, thus symbolically questioning the sacredness of monarchy and confirming a disturbing suspicion that subjects might dispossess their kings, James accused the Elector's envoy of spreading seditious ideas among the English people, so 'that my subjects may drive me away, and place another in my room'. Likewise, Stow's anatomy of London referred to the humblest inhabitants of the city, 'hyrelings', as occupying 'the lowest room' in the domestic analogy for social hierarchy.[21] Even the perverse image of social harmony embodied in Subtle's and Face's misappropriation of the house in Blackfriars relies upon the domicile as an image of organic social unity. Face makes the house available to Subtle as a venue for his alchemical practices in return for Subtle's sublimation of Face into a richer form of villain. When the two tricksters quarrel, endangering the parasitical society they have set up in the squat, Dol Common accuses them of self-destructive strife, explicitly mentioning 'civil war' (*The Alchemist*, 1.1.82).

It is evident from *The Alchemist*'s setting in the house at Blackfriars that even subversion or questioning of the visual and spatial paradigms of the hierarchy of social rank occurred within the terms of extant spatialized social conceptions. Such modes of questioning exemplified by virtue of this recursive operation what Greimas calls a spatial 'contestatory metadiscourse' which works to loosen the established, consensual links between spatial signifier and cultural signified.[22] Thus the disintegration of the sentiment of a coherent social body was described in the spatial terminology of the very order under attack; the erosion of notions of 'rightful place', under pressure from the accelerated mobility of individual destinies, could only be expressed in a tangible spatial language soon to be superseded by more abstract modes of representation. Thus the manifold transformations of early modern English society occurring in this period were understood as spatial and thus visually perceptible transformations.

Follywit's opening declaration in Middleton's *A Mad World, My Masters* exemplifies the tremendous energy of social transformation in play in the Jacobean era: 'I was as well given till I fell to be wicked, my grandsire had hope of me; I went all in black, swore but o'Sundays, never came home drunk but upon fasting nights to cleanse my stomach; 'slid, now I'm quite altered, blown into light colours, let out oaths by th'minute, sit up late till it be early, drink drunk till I am sober, sink down dead in a tavern, and rise in a tobacco shop. Here's a transformation' (1.1.11–18). The satirical mode pushes against all forms of traditional constraint and custom; the norms of discipline are travestied by 'alteration' and 'transformation', by 'sinking down' and 'rising again' in a different place, by the force of mutability and mobility. The entire action of the drama is driven by transgressive energy, an energy only just contained by the neat closure of the final scenes of the play.

Such centrifugal energies within the social order were widely commented. The very parameters of the cosmos were cast into question by Galileo's refutation of the Ptolemaic conception of the universe, sending reverberations through English literary culture, from Donne's lament in *The First Anniversarie* ('And new Philosophy calls all in doubt, | The Element of fire is quite put out; ... 'Tis all in peeces, all cohaerence gone; | All just supply, and all Relation'), to allusions to Galileo in Fletcher's *The Elder Brother* and Webster's *Duchess of Malfi* (2.4.17).[23]

The Jacobean drama mirrored all these trends. Spatialized modes of knowledge and intellection are widespread on the stage. In Middleton's *The Changeling*, we are told of the fools and madmen imprisoned by doctor Albius, the 'scholars in the upper room | Are out of order' (3.3.116–17). Here the mind and its functioning is given expression according to an internal architecture of the intellect. The stage direction at 3.3.197 clearly gives spatial form to the undisciplined action of the unhinged intellect: '[*Enter*] *madmen above, some as birds, some as beasts.*' The projection of the deranged activity of the mind onto the spatial structure of the theatre (the space 'above' signifying the work of intellection) evinces the capacity to situate the processes of thought both within the space of a still porous, not yet fully differentiated individual subjectivity, *and* to project such processes onto the immediate environment of that subjectivity. The very name of the Globe theatre hardly needs comment as an instance of theatre understood as a microcosmic version of the larger world.

In the theatre, the sense of the speaker occupying discourse as a place, as a topos, was very strong. In Middleton's *Michaelmas Term*, Shortyard can say to Easy, clarifying a misunderstanding in their conversation, 'I thought you had been in London', meaning: I thought you had been talking about London (3.3.43). This sense of the speaker being situated in a discursive place took on a particularly dynamic quality on the stage. In *The Changeling*, the Warder of an asylum, Lollio, asks the newly-arrived inmate complicated questions to ascertain the degree of his derangement. When not understood the first time, he recasts his question in clearly spatial terms: 'I come to you again, cousin Tony' (1.2.163). The act of communication is seen as a spatial movement, a bodily interrogation.

Elizabethan players may have been more intensely conscious than modern ones of the rhetorical, and thus spatial structure of their discourse, emphasizing the twists and turns of argumentation clearly marked in their speeches.[24] Not only the actors, but also the educated members of the audience would have been sensitive to the spatial features of dramatic language, as well as other spectators who had not benefited from a classical education but were none the less attuned to the shape and configuration of artful speech. Much visual imaginative power on the part of early modern theatregoers would have been triggered by the skilful manipulation of spatial constructs in the actors' language.

The theatre itself was no exception to the highly visible structuring of social classes. In the public theatres, differing entry prices corresponded to distinctive audience areas clearly visible in the daylight space of the theatres: in the 'Lords' Rooms', the private boxes adjacent to the stage, a seat cost a shilling; seats in the protected galleries were threepence and twopence respectively, while the rest of the audience stood in the pit, exposed to the elements, for a penny. The private theatres, located within the City precincts, accommodated in closed houses, and catering to a more select clientele, were more expensive again. The theatre was a place to be seen, and where social status was clearly displayed; this was most true for none other than the King. For the imported theatrical performances at court, the king was not only the most important spectator, but indeed, the object of the other spectators' attention. At a performance at Oxford in 1605, the King's position had to be shifted, in order to render him more visible for the audience, with the result that he himself could hardly see the play – this latter disadvantage of his position was however not thought to be of great consequence.[25]

In the theatre as elsewhere, societal role was indicated by costume: a crown for a king, particular robes for doctors and lawyers, and so on. Dramatic character was thus constructed differently to our modern conception of identity as the result of an inward personality: the important role of costume underlined the overwhelming significance of 'exterior shape', to quote John Marston, by which social identity was created by appearance, by the outward signs of belonging to a particular social site rather than possessing a unique set of individual characteristics. Thus dramatic dialogue was a product of social role rather than of subjective interiority. If the character, by virtue of the costume worn, embodied not a set of personal characteristics but rather a clearly delineated role within the social organism, then the soliloquy would have taken on a quite different dimension to that with which we are familiar. Rather than the character talking 'to himself' within the privacy of an inward subjectivity, the soliloquy must be understood as a public discourse which is 'intimately' conducted between one character and the audience.[26] The audience was confronted with a speaking costume type, as it were, rather than a speaking personality.

A similar employment of social place rather than individual identity can be seen at work in the distribution of roles in the players' company. Actors would often take two or three parts so that a company of 11 or 12 players could cover the 20 or more characters of a play. In the quarto text of *The Fair Maid of the Exchange* of 1607, for example, some of the cast of 11 are allotted up to four parts. This arrangement would sometimes leave the players only the briefest of intervals to change costumes in order to take on another role. Plot constraints could even mean that a player occasionally found himself acting two characters who were simultaneously on stage at the same moment – in which case, another actor would temporarily step in to take over the doubled part.[27] This apparently confusing doubling of character was probably less of a problem for audience perception than we would expect, the costume as a marker of social identity and social place being a more important dramatic factor than the person wearing it. Identity on the stage was defined more clearly through costume than through its bearer. Further, the portrayal of social place on the stage in turn determined geographical place. Often, the locality of a scene could be indicated by the presence of typified characters, whose costumes or accessories provided the necessary cues for the spectator – soldiers, for instance, indicated that the scene was that of a battlefield, a shepherd that of a pastoral meadow.[28] Here geographical place on the stage was entirely a function of social place as indicated by easily identifiable visual markers in the form of costume.

Thus identity, in so far as a proto-modern form of individualized subjectivity can be seen to emerge on the Jacobean stage, is also cast in terms of place. In Jonson's *Alchemist*, Dol Common is described by the two tricksters of the play as 'our Dol, our castle, our Cinque Port, | Our Dover Pier, our what thou wilt', embodying a geography of social location, aside from the commodification of woman as a form of desirable property (3.3.17–19). The spatiality of identity becomes most clear in the plays of the Jacobean era by virtue of the striking mobility performed on stage. When Shortyard in *Michaelmas Term*, having abandoned his former identity as Master Blastfield, can say: 'I am glad I am where I am', he is not referring to his safe physical distance from Andrew Lethe who seeks to give him a revengeful beating for earlier confidence tricks suffered at the hands of Blastfield (3.5.58) – for Lethe and Shortyard appear together on stage at this very moment. Rather, Shortyard occupies a different 'place' to the extent that he possesses a different identity, and it is this new position in the social fabric that keeps him out of harm's way. In *The Alchemist* Face declares: 'I must to my Captainship again then' (4.2.3); the play is constructed around the mutability of identity as a visible social function that can be assumed, even 'donned' at will (whence the importance of the Captain's uniform), or even more, a place or site 'to' which the character repairs.

Thus the stage, with its constant meditation upon social identity, foregrounded in the figure of the actor's mutability, can be seen as a laboratory for new versions of identity. The statement of a character such as Iago, when he declares, ' 'Tis in ourselves that we are thus or thus. Our bodies are gardens, to the which our wills are gardeners', exemplifies such conceptual experiments (*Othello* 1.3.319–21). Iago's metaphor indicates that a change is underway: the self is described here both as a place, locatable within a social landscape, and in contrast, as one which possesses clear boundaries and an interior space. Bruster suggests that there is a noticeable shift between Elizabethan drama and Jacobean drama, one of whose characteristics is in the description of objects by means of their location to their description in terms of composition and interiority.[29] Iago's self-characterization highlights the theatre's exploration of shifts in the texture of subjectivity; he is on the cusp between conceptions of self as location and self as enclosure.

Theatre as space

The stage portrayed the organization of Jacobean society in strongly spatial terms, and was itself, not surprisingly, perceived by contemporaries as a spatial art-form. A frequent and widespread approach to theatre has been to view it as a primarily verbal art-form, as a mode of writing relying almost entirely upon direct discourse: 'the dramatic work is carried by words, is determined by the verbal function, and is nothing but that function.'[30] This one-sided and impoverishing attitude to theatre was not one for which early modern dramatists would have had much sympathy. The inherent spatiality of the theatre was something of which the Jacobeans and even their successors, judging by their references to the theatre, were acutely aware. In the Argument of Jonson's *Volpone*, we are informed that the protagonist's 'Parasite ... | ... weaves | Other cross-plots, which ope themselves, are told' (3–6). Middleton's Follywit expatiates on the 'plots' he will 'cast into form' with his loyal henchmen, thus stressing the spatialization of dramatic narrative, an apposite pun given that the action of the play turns around his foray into the country to trick his uncle into ceding the young man's rightfully owned lands (*A Mad World, My Masters*, 1.1.5). The Jacobeans clearly had no difficulty envisaging the theatrical undertaking as a dynamic spatial process. A little later, Sir William Davenant's 'play recipe' proposed, following upon acts one and two, a third act which 'makes a visible correspondence in the underwalks (or lesser intrigues) of persons; and ends with an ample turn of the main design, and expectations of a new [turn]. The fourth (ever having occasion to be the longest) gives a notorious turn to all the underwalks, and a counterturn to that main design which turned in the third. The fifth begins with an entire diversion of the main and dependent plots.'[31] The play's action is conceived of as a network of interwoven itineraries and paths whose intertwining contributes to the dramatic tension and suspense of the performance.

The physical movements of the actors on the stage are often reflected in the dramatic dialogue. The actor can generally find all the necessary guides to performance in the lines of the Folio Shakespeare, or in the dialogue of other dramatists. The movements of actors upon the large

Renaissance stage will often be verbally duplicated in the dialogue, thereby directing the audience's attention to developments at one of the multiple places on the stage where action may be focused.[32] Thus Tybalt announces Romeo's progress downstage, possibly hesitating, from the upstage door with the deictic statement: 'Well, peace be with you, sir. Here comes my man' (*Romeo and Juliet*, 3.1.55). His words break off his conversation with Mercutio and Benvolio, and direct his gaze, and that of the audience, towards the figure advancing downstage. In this way the actors' movements are 'ostended' or highlighted by verbal discourse, which in turn gives us vital hints regarding the dynamic performance of the belligerent alliances of the play.

Spatial modalities are evinced not only in the language of the actors, but in the visual and positional techniques of performance. The open stage with its daylight performances and raucous audiences would have been dependent upon clear visual marking to convey the substance of the dramas performed.[33] Thus the German Johannes Rheanus, in England in 1611, reported that 'even the most eminent actors have to allow themselves to be *taught their places* by the Dramatists, which arrangement gives life and ornament to a well-written play.'[34] The opening stage direction in Act 5, Scene 6 of *'Tis Pity She's a Whore* has the characters 'take their places', which may refer to seats set out on the stage for the banquet, but also alludes to the general placing of the actors on the stage. The broad narrative outlines of a scene were often sketched out by a dumb show, the element of redundancy being a necessary compensation for communicational interference of audience participation in what was, to all intents and purposes, an open-air theatre. Not all spectators had an equally close view of the action, so that communicational redundancy also worked to overcome auditorium distance. A common feature of open or public performance spaces is the inflation of redundant paralinguistic factors such as enunciation, volume and gestural stress.[35] This was probably another function fulfilled by the Elizabethan dumb show, closely connected with the easy readability of emblematic devices or heraldic designs derived from jousting tournaments.[36]

Indeed, the entire culture appears to have been oriented towards clear emblematic messages of public spectacle: the court was based on the visibility of spectacle, and public executions typified the spectacle character of royal revenge upon criminal transgression.[37] James I, as he travelled south from Scotland to accede to the English throne, orchestrated several public executions as performances of the monarch's power, that is, as exercises in royal public relations.[38] Traces of such spectacle are also to be found in the drama. When Jonson's Celia refuses to prostitute herself to Volpone in the interests of her husband Corvino's wealth, the latter threatens bodily mutilation of the most brutal and, more significantly, *readable* kind:

> And at my window hang you forth, devising
> Some monstrous crime, which I, in capital letters,
> Will eat into thy flesh with aquafortis,
> And burning cor'sives, on this stubborn breast.
>
> (3.7.102–5)

The open space of the Elizabethan and Jacobean stage partook of the culture of highly visible spectacle indicated here (albeit usually in less macabre ways, though there were exceptions) and for clearly practical reasons.

Within the context of early modern spectacle, theatrical meaning was constantly constituted by spatial means. From a very pragmatic point of view, the actor was forced to occupy a stage space such as that of the Globe with energetic movement and clearly visible gestures, otherwise risking being dwarfed by it; this mode of utilization of space would account, for instance, for the spread-out dimensions and expansive, emblematic gestures and postures of the actors in the de Witt drawing of the Swan Theatre (see Figure 1).[39] Symmetrical tableaux entailing bold moves and clear gestures easily visible on the large stage were a frequent feature of the drama. For those in the galleries, who looked down on the stage from above, players' moves up- or downstage would have been far more significant than in modern theatre, where such 'vertical' movements are flattened by the distance created by the proscenium stage.[40] Such tableaux or spatial configurations of the players can sometimes be gleaned from stage directions. The second scene of Middleton's *A Trick to Catch the Old One* opens with the direction: 'Enter at one door, Witgood, at the other, Host.' This symmetry gives concrete visual form to the agreement they are about to reach: Host lends horses and rides up to London with Witgood in the hope of 'prosperity' derived from Witgood's promised 'conjuror's trick' (1.2.16, 12–13). The stage is a place of transactions which are enacted spatially. The next scene opens with a more explicit example of the same semanticization of spatial configurations: the stage direction specifies: 'Enter at several doors, old Hoard, old Lucre, [with] Gentlemen … coming between them, to pacify 'em.' Once again, the stage directions provide clear spatialization of human relations. This time it is not the bargain which is spatialized by

Figure 1 Johnannes de Witt's sketch of the Swan Theatre, about 1596.
(University Library, University of Utrecht, Hs. 842, f. 132r)

the symmetrical patterning, but conflict between two individuals, where only the median position of the other gentlemen is able to keep them apart. The middle position conveys, visually, both mediation and eventually intervention: 'Nay, gentlemen, then we must divide you perforce', says Spitchcock (1.3.53).

More complex signifying processes can also be performed by the semanticization of stage space and configurations. *Troilus and Cressida* furnishes an interesting example of the spatial performance of conflicts of points of view. Achilles is off stage, refusing to emerge from his tent to speak with the Greek commanders; observing this petulant withdrawal from sight, Ajax chides Achilles for his bad-tempered, elitist absence. But Ulysses, Nestor and Agamemnon doubt the validity of Ajax's verbal attempt to elevate himself above the sulking Achilles:

> *Ajax*: A paltry insolent fellow.
> *Nestor*: (*aside*) How he describes himself!
> *Ajax*: Can he not be sociable?
> *Ulysses*: (*aside*) The raven chides blackness.
> *Ajax*: I'll let his humour's blood.
> *Agamemnon*: (*aside*) He will be the physician that should be the
>   patient.
>
> (2.3.205–11)

Thus the statements made by one character at one position on the stage are relativized and modified by a larger vision encompassing several other characters' positions, a vision which condemns Ajax to membership of that (offstage) group from which he believes himself apart. The distance separating onstage/offstage, which constitutes the mechanism spatializing the disjunctive relationship of moral superiority assumed by Ajax, is cast into question by the statements of the other characters on the stage, thereby undermining Ajax's claims and countering them with the assertion of a tacit bond linking Ajax to the absent Achilles. Thus the onstage/offstage distinction which gives physical body to Ajax's superiority complex is eliminated by Nestor, Ulysses and Agamemnon's perspective; by the same token, their mode of address to the audience creates a larger space of collective communication which expels Ajax from the mass of the Greeks no less effectively than Achilles' own self-imposed isolation.

At times the theatre actively reflects upon its own spatial mode of representing significant relationships. The false idiot Antonio in *The Changeling* persists in not understanding Lollio's complicated riddle: 'A fool before a knave, a fool behind a knave, between every two fools a knave. – How many fools, how many knaves?' Albius objects: 'Thou putt'st too hard questions to him, Lollio'; to which Lollio rejoins: 'I'll make him understand it easily; cousin, stand there. ... Master, stand you next the fool. ... Here's my place: mark now, Tony, there a fool before a knave. ... Here's a fool behind a knave, that's I; and between us, two fools, there's a knave, that's my master; 'tis but we three, that's all' (1.2.187–204). Thus Lollio demonstrates the question by placing himself, his master Albius and Antonio in the appropriate stage positions so as to show that all three of them are knaves or fools. The visible spatiality of stage positions is explicitly glossed by meta-spatial language so as to concretize, albeit to comic ends, the identity of characters on the stage and their relations to each other. In terms of theatrical semiosis, one theatrical code refers here to another – the diegetic (verbal) refers to the mimetic (spatial).[41] Thus Middleton has the drama meta-theatrically indicate (in the literal sense of indexicality, showing, pointing) its own process of signification through spatial relationships.

Middleton's comic scene foregrounds the spatial orientation of audience attention towards certain parts of the stage, towards certain characters, and towards relationships between the characters, a process which constitutes the concrete signifying processes of the Jacobean theatre. Modern stage lighting tends to obscure these techniques of tableaux-grouping, eliding the interrelationships between equally illuminated figures and their respective positions on the stage. In the absence of lighting techniques, the spatial movements of the players would have served to focus audience attention where required, another form of spatial 'ostention'.[42]

Meaning is certainly produced by the elaborate verbal art of Elizabethan and Jacobean drama, but equally by the theatrical space in which that verbal art is situated. Peter Brook has famously declared: 'I can take an empty space and call it a bare stage. A man walks across this empty space whilst someone else is watching him, and this is all that is needed for an act of theatre to be engaged.'[43] Brook is both right and wrong in his renowned statement. It is true that theatre can be made to happen anywhere, and is constituted by the entrance of an actor in front of a spectator. But it does not depend upon a pre-existing 'empty' space. Much recent theorization of spatiality has criticized the Cartesian notion of space as an vacant container in which objects are inserted like fish in a fishbowl, a notion Brook employs when suggesting that his relational theatre is simply inserted into an 'empty space'. But the very principle that he applies to theatre – the notion that theatre is a social phenomenon, that it emerges out of a set of human relationships which it most definitely does not pre-exist – is of cardinal importance for the space in which the 'act of theatre' is played out. That space is constructed and given meaning by the set of relationships and human interactions which constitute it. The spatial configurations of the Jacobean theatre suggest that space is made to signify, becomes meaningful, by the ways it is constituted in the very act of performance.

The constitution of meaning in single spatial tableaux can be supplemented by a more complex notion of the entire dramatic action as the interaction of various spaces. As noted above, geographical place was established in Renaissance theatre not so much by the imposition of a specific locality, but was often signalled by actors and their costumes or accessories.[44] This gave the theatre a certain degree of economy: if locality was a function of characterization, rather than a specific site into which characters were inserted, the stage could become, geographically speaking, extraordinarily flexible. The rapid scene changes in Marlowe's plays, often without stage-clearing to signal breaks between episodes, frequently draws the attention of modern critics.[45] The scene changes were signalled not so much by a location, as modern editions often misleadingly suggest, as by changing constellations of actors. Locations were social before they were geographical, and the action emerged from these sites of social interaction. Thus, as Styan wittily observes, when a character, having identified a location by his presence on stage, makes his exit, the location exits with him.[46]

The mobility of character-bound place is analogous to the mobility of character-bound perspectives upon the world. Subtle, in *The Alchemist*, says of Dapper, one of the victims of the tricksters' scheming, 'Conduct him forth by the back way', Dapper then being led out the back door while the next client is ushered in through the front door (1.2.163). Here, the theatre uses spatial means to perform the apparently contiguous and non-overlapping, fictional worlds (in reality belonging to a larger unity), that are specific to satirical comedy, and which Hayden White has categorized under the trope of synecdoche.[47] In Act 3, Scene 5, the comic effect of parallel but discrete worlds is heightened by the danger of the separate worlds actually merging with each other: Sir Epicure Mammon arrives before Dapper has been dispatched, with the result that the latter personage finds himself locked up in the evil-reeking privy until the coast is clear.

The most prominent spatial trope governing the plot structures of Jacobean drama (and the characters' plotting within the plays) is chiasmus. The logic of inversion is a constant in the dramas' vision of social existence. Whence the prevalence of characters' scheming proving their own downfall. In *Hamlet*, the eponymous hero declares of his erstwhile friends Rosencrantz and Guildenstern: 'Their defeat | Doth by their own insinuation grow' (5.2.59–60). Likewise, Laertes states: 'I am justly killed with mine own treachery' (5.2.260). And finally, Horatio summarizes: 'And, in this upshot, purposes mistook | Fall'n on th'inventors' heads' (5.2.338–9). In the closing scenes of *Volpone* (5.10, 5.11, 5.12), the spectators are confronted with a rapid and vertiginous series of reversals of fortune as Voltore confesses his guilt; then Volpone arrives and contrives to have the Avocatore abruptly feign madness in an attempt to recuperate a last chance of inheritance; Mosca enters the stage, re-asserting Volpone's death and his own status as heir, at the cost of Volpone; and finally Volpone reveals his identity in a last-ditch attempt to prevent Mosca from carrying away his master's booty, though this last confession seals Volpone's own fate. The instability of situation which drives these sudden reversals of the plot, and the corresponding abrupt changes of domination and subjection on the part of the warring characters, is pithily summarized by the abrupt inversion embodied in a judgement uttered by one of the Avocatori: 'These possess wealth as sick men possess fevers | Which truelier may be said to possess them' (5.12.101–2). The diachronic progression of the two halves of the sentence is a performance of the dynamic which drives the events of the closing scenes of the play; the ironic reversals of relations of domination between money and a newly emergent capitalist subject are performed, once again, through the dizzying scene-changes of the final sections of the drama.

Such reversals are in part possible because the characters are not aware that the attainability of any given position of power from a position of powerlessness automatically implies and makes possible its opposite; the mutability of positions on the social hierarchy, that is, the convertibility of subjection into domination, assumes that conversion in the opposite direction is equally possible. Each new move presents a completely different point of view on the affair, to the extent that the judges are reduced to frequent exclamations of perplexity. Significantly, one of the judges declares, 'This same's a labyrinth' (5.10.42) – that is to say, a *synecdochic* space and emplotment, one based on a problematic contiguity in which the relations of the parts to the whole are obscured from the sight of a given observer. At first glance, it appears that there are only partial truths, all of them mutually exclusive and equally contradictory. There is of course a larger truth, one that the audience, along with Mosca and Volpone, sees, but the comic effect comes from the rapid alternation between the various partial truths, the 'plays' within the play. Even the audience, however, does not have a total view of this fictional universe, for the diachronic line of the plot is only revealed to the audience step by step as the action of the drama progresses. The audience also shares the perplexity of many of the characters, and like them is captive in a partial sector of the play's emplotment which is connected to the whole by relationships invisible to the viewer. Thus *Volpone* is in part about the conflict between, on the one hand, the ubiquity of mutually interchangeable and, in the last analysis, virtually undifferentiated positions of power and subjection; and on the other, the actors' merely partial perception of their respective places within this larger geography of social struggle.

The prevalence of structural techniques based upon spatial stage techniques is so great that one is almost tempted to say, in imitation of the Russian Formalists' deliberately provocative claim, that rather than the theatrical form reinforcing the message of the dramatic text, the message is merely the logical reflection of the spatial structures of performance. *The Changeling* provides an example of a play entirely driven by spatial concerns. The play lodges a protest against all forms of imprisonment: its cast includes madmen locked up, women trapped in the rigid expectations of their parents, impostors caught in their roles, lower-class servants deprived of their right to self-determination by an aristocratic mistress. The play continually harps upon *place*, doubtless because such spaces could no longer be contained by traditional social structures in a mobile and mutable world. Diaphanta is flattered to be asked to take 'The bride's [Beatrice's] *place*' on the wedding night (4.1.127); Tomazo, speaking of his brother's disappearance in Vermarandero's castle, menaces 'This is the *place* must yield account for him' (4.2.20–1). The ersatz husband, Alsemero, is greeted by Tomazo, the brother of the murdered predecessor: 'I should have a brother in your *place*; | How treachery and malice have disposed of him, | I'm bound to enquire' (4.2.70–4; my emphases). Given that the theatres' place in the urban fabric, the social place of the actors, and the architectural form of the theatres were the result of new historical forces (as will be shown in more detail in subsequent chapters) it could plausibly be argued that the spatial form of the theatre, in the broadest sense, determined the themes of the drama.

This apparent primacy of spatial performance structures over the thematic content of the dramas results in a mode of signification closely woven into the material fabric of the problems it addressed. As an instance of this tangible, emblematic mode of thought, one could cite Dr John Caius' three gates at Gonville and Caius College, Cambridge, standing for Humility, Virtue and Honour, and embodying the student's progress through his course of studies in the college, and by implication, through the corresponding stages of maturity.[48] Every time the student passed through the college precincts, entering via one gate, crossing several courts and exiting by another gate, he became a bodily emblem of his own progression through a course of study, the performance being carried out on the very site of that pedagogic undertaking. Here we see a vignette of the Jacobean theatre and its functioning, to cite Artaud, as a 'concrete place demanding to have its concrete language brought to speech.'[49]

To adapt a felicitous expression of Jameson, the Jacobean drama is constantly in the throes of thinking through spatial problems in spatial terms. It is an example of what Jameson, following Deleuze, describes as a concrete mode of cognition, as concrete philosophizing: not just the (secondary) visual illustration of philosophical concepts or social processes, but rather, a (spatial) attempt to think a material thought.[50] The notion of material thought accounts for what has been termed the 'pre-scientific concrete perspective' in Shakespeare, handed down from the Middle Ages – a perspective in which, for example, things are in the foreground of the stage space when significant, and occupy the background if less important, a mode of understanding which probably characterized the concrete categories of thought familiar to an early modern public.[51] A similar analogy is furnished by Freud's concept of 'dream-work', in which the psyche has recourse to the spatial operations of condensation and contiguity to create meaning-bearing relationships between dream elements in a mode of representation deprived of more sophisticated means of portraying logical connections.[52]

Lévi-Strauss's concept of 'primitive thought' in his book of the same title provides an even more apposite avenue for theorizing the conjunction of a spatial form and the spatial content articulated by that theatrical form. 'Primitive' thought, significantly referred to in the title of Lévi-Strauss's opening chapter as 'the science of the concrete', is characterized by a remarkable resourcefulness in employing the 'material at hand' to make meanings; whereas modern thought steps outside its environment to solve problems of meaning, 'primitive' thought remains within the boundaries of the problem to be articulated.[53] In the same way, spatial dynamics within the social world are articulated in the Jacobean theatre by using the very same material as the problems to be addressed, that of space and mobility.

These modern and postmodern theoretical concepts may appear anachronistic in the context of Jacobean drama. Such concepts, however, were developed implicitly in reaction to the excessive idealism of modern thought, and in order to explore less intellectualized modes of meaning-making. They have the merit of allowing us to think through the functioning of early modern drama – in the last analysis an exceedingly down-to-earth and tangible set of operations – as an art-form which addressed the social processes contemporary spectators were confronted with in their own times.

Referentiality in drama

If the theatre of the Jacobean era can indeed be understood as a process of concrete signification, we need to examine more closely not just the workings of its signifying operations, but also the object of its referentiality. In this way it is possible not only to gain an idea of the 'how' of the theatrical process of meaning-making, but also of the 'what' about which the theatre spoke – or in the spatial frame of reference utilized here, of the 'where' in which it intervened.

Various technical aspects of the early modern open stage are helpful in gauging the relationships between the theatrical sign and its referent. Crucial to modern expositions of the functioning of theatrical performance is the notion of framing, by virtue of which the work of art is set off from reality, and is marked as having a fictional status, indeed, as being 'art'. The theatrical frame functions to govern the spectators' expectations of the kinds of reality involved in the performance, and the place of the audience, which is generally that of a privileged 'onlooker' gazing into a fictional world. Examples of framing devices are clear spatial and temporal brackets such as the stage boundaries or a prologue, which demarcate what is to be included and what is to be excluded from the fiction, both in terms of space and of time.[54] Paradoxically, even as they operate to set the work apart, frames must be ignored by the spectator, thus being excluded from the semantic field of the work of art.[55]

In theatre semiotics, it is the more or less visible division between audience and actor spaces which is deemed to constitute this frame, typically concretized in the bourgeois theatre of the nineteenth and twentieth centuries by the proscenium arch and the footlights, and less clearly marked by degrees in various forms of avant-garde or experimental theatre, disappearing altogether in the happening (so much so that some critics deem the happening no longer to constitute theatre, as the division between reality and fiction has been erased altogether.[56]) This audience/actor division was already being called into question in some quarters during its nineteenth-century heyday, but the validity of the distinction has none the less remained a commonplace of theatre theory and a crucial aspect of theatre practice to the present day.[57] James Agate, writing in the early years of the twentieth century, claimed that 'It is vital to the art of the actor that he *keep his frame*, and that there shall be no point of contact between him and the spectator.'[58]

In the context of the Jacobean theatre, the marking of the actor/audience division appears to have been less clear than is generally deemed necessary for the theatrical function to operate. It would be foolish to claim that such a division was not present, but I will suggest that it was more porous than modern conceptions of theatricality would generally assume, and that this porosity has important consequences for the operation of theatrical referentiality on the Jacobean stage.

One example of this partial erasure of audience–actor divisions can be seen in the conventions of royal processions in early modern England, a form of public performance crucial to the political life of the society. The royal visitors were confronted with a lavish spectacle of the city with which they had deigned to grace their presence, but upon which they were also dependent for political and financial loyalty. The city, in turn, was presented with the spectacle of royal majesty. Finally, the citizens of the city, themselves arranged according to rank, were presented with an image of their own identity, based upon a double loyalty to civic and national communities. Moreover, such spectacles were customarily held at a site of symbolic social significance, a conduit or a city gate, thus articulating in concrete form a set of social relations. Thus all three groups were part of a performance of political and civic relationships anchored in a local place, a place in which the rights and obligations of the three groups met and intersected, necessarily precluding any non-active role, one reduced to mere spectatorship, in the proceedings. All groups were simultaneously actors in and spectators of the performance.[59] Strong vestiges of this actor–spectator continuum in civic performances can be seen in Renaissance theatre in its more specific sense.

One of several important factors influencing the porosity of the audience/actor division was the dominance, in Renaissance thought, of the conception of correspondence between the macro- and micro-dimensions of the universe already mentioned above. The dominant, though increasingly contested, conceptions of microcosm and macrocosm meant that all signifying practices could be understood as analogies concretely linking the meaning of related phenomena from the smallest to the largest dimensions of existence. From the human body through to the cosmic bodies, each element was laden with significance, and referred to all others in a dense network of allusive meaning.[60] The meaning of a phenomenon, on the stage as in the world, was not contained in one side of a subject/object divide, but could penetrate and encompass the domain of the observer as well as that of the observable phenomenon. Such correspondences of meaning were of course compounded by the name of a theatre such as the Globe, whose circular form mimicked that of the larger universe; it was not uncommon to play upon the analogy between the theatre and the world, as in Jaques' famous 'All the world's a stage' (*As You Like It* 2.7.139) or Antonio's 'I hold the world but as the world ... – | A stage where every man must play a part' (*Merchant of Venice* 1.1.77–8), or Heywood's verses:

> The World's a Theater, the earth a Stage,
> Which God, and nature doth with Actors fill,
> Kings have their entrance in due equipage,
> And some there parts play well and others ill.[61]

Contemporaries clearly thought of themselves in some way as participating in a dramatic process which made their position part of the same experiential fabric as that of the actors upon the stage.

The establishment of such correspondences transgressing the boundaries of the stage space was reinforced by the visibility of the theatrical process. The undifferentiated illumination of the daylight theatre created a sense of continuity between the stage and the auditorium, between actors and their environment. The audience was visible to itself; spectators in the galleries would gaze across the stage space to their opposite numbers on the other side of the interior of the building, whether round or rectangular, given the wrap-around arrangement of audience space in almost all the theatres of the Jacobean era, whether public or private. The fact that audience members could see each other across the stage and all around it in the pit created an strong sense of the direct interaction of stage world and audience world.[62]

No significant distance separated the actors from the audience, particularly those standing in the yard. Indeed, when playing at the front of the stage, the actors were effectively surrounded on three sides by spectators at close proximity. Recent experiences at the reconstructed Globe theatre in Southwark have revealed the way in which the thrust stage tends to draw the actor forcefully into the middle of the crowd. Actors 'talk of feeling as if an invisible hand is pushing them forcefully out from the rear doors towards the audience.'[63] Moreover, the de Witt drawing's use of the double term 'planities sive arena' ('flatness or arena') for the yard in front of the stage has led several critics to suggest that the players may also have used the yard as a part of the performance space (see Figure 1). Once again, recent experiences at the new Southwark Globe have shown that the yard lends itself well to actor–audience interaction – thought not all actors are entirely at ease with such experiments, some feeling, for example, that they overly 'diffuse' the theatrical action.[64]

Moreover, this 'diffusion of the action' caused by the transgression of the stage space functioned in the opposite direction as well. A small number of spectators actually sat on the stage, paying extra to turn the theatrical performance into an advertisement of their own social status, gallants who preened themselves on the stage, getting in the way of the play's action and slipping in and out of the tiring house.[65] Jonson in *Every Man Out of His Humour* advised, 'sit o'the stage and flout, provided you have a good suit.'[66] Dekker told his gallant to 'cast vp a reckoning, what large cummings-in are pursd vp by sitting on the Stage. First a conspicuous *Eminince* is gotten;...the Stage, like time, will bring you to most perfect light.'[67] It has been suggested that the presence of spectators on the stage would simply be blocked out by the other spectators, as belonging to the 'frame' of the performance.[68] But this is difficult to believe in the Jacobean context, given the disruptive behaviour of the stage-spectators; Chambers quotes the prologue from *All Fools* (c. 1604): 'if our other audience see | You on the stage depart before we end, | Our wits go with you all and we are fools'[69] – such was the despair of actors in competition for audience attention with the antics of the stage gallants. In this case, there was a physical transgression of the stage space by the audience, and a blurring of the distinction between actors and audience: the gallant on the stage was clearly not part of the drama, but in so far as he was clearly orchestrating a performance of his own, he may be said, in a queer way, to have become one of the actors, when not always working in harmony with them. When the discontented citizen springs onto the stage at the beginning of *The Knight of the Burning Pestle*, and then invites his wife and his apprentice Ralph to join him, the theatre itself performs the disruptive transgression of its own stage boundaries.[70] The co-optation of stage-sitters could on occasions function quite smoothly: they may have been incorporated, for example, into the onstage players of the wedding banquet scene in *'Tis Pity She's a Whore*.[71]

An even clearer instance of this physical penetration of the stage space is given by the Restoration theatre commentator Edmund Gayton, who wittily remarked that 'it is good policy to amaze those violent spirits with some tearing tragedy full of fights and skirmishes ... which commonly ends in six acts, the spectators mounting the stage and making a more bloody Catastrophe among themselves than the players did.'[72] Presumably the physical barriers inherent in the stage boundaries – the stage was raised to the height of about two metres, and in some instances may have had railings around it – were intended in part as a deterrent against such incidents; but these pragmatic forms of separation of audience and actors merely underline the essential porosity of the audience/actor division. Whether we are to take such occurrences as happening frequently is difficult to say. None the less, they illustrate the strong sense of the audience/stage division of being transgressible, the sense that the fictions of the theatre were not hermetically sealed off from the reality of the audience space.

This transgression, or at least weakening or blurring, of the actor/audience boundary casts into question the concept of a clearly delineated space of fiction which is the logical consequence of the notion of the framing of the work of art. Weimann has employed the distinction between the *platea* and the *locus* of the medieval stage as representing degrees of proximity to an ostensibly plebeian audience, thus producing a similar blurring of actor/spectator divisions to the one I am positing. Yet Weimann's portrayal of a stage/audience continuity serves the purpose of supporting his thesis of the continuing existence of a popular theatre tradition of 'realistic' drama, one in which actors' social commentary is immediately accessible to the people not only in terms of its place of enunciation but also in its non-symbolic (and thus socially realistic) representational form.[73] The limitations of this argument can easily be demonstrated by the example of the court drama, where the blurring of actor/auditorium boundaries manifestly did not produce a mode of socially realistic theatre (as will be suggested in the following chapter).

In what follows, I shall argue that the space of the stage does not necessarily generate an immediate and unequivocal 'mimetic' reproduction of social reality, as Weimann claims, but one whose referential mode is more sinuous and complex. There are marvellous stories, for instance, of an audience said to have fled at the sight of an actor impersonating the devil, where the boundaries of the fiction appear to have been blurred by the possibility of the devil's influence contaminating the audience space.[74] The notions of influence and contamination describe most accurately the mode of reference which this porous mode of stage-signification appears to have possessed in the early modern period. The space of fiction is only weakly separated from the here and now of audience space, so much so that fiction appears in some cases not to have been perceived as such by audiences; but clearly this did not make the mode of referentiality of the stage 'realistic' or 'mimetic' in our modern sense of the word.

What then are the consequences of this at least partial erasure of a distinct demarcation between actor and audience space for the mode of reference of the theatre? The habitual assumption is that because the theatre portrays fictional characters by means of real actors, or imaginary events by means of the direct performance of those events, that theatrical art has a mimetic or iconic relationship to the world of the spectators, though there is some variation in critics' uses of these terms.[75] For Alter, the theatre employs a 'primary sign-system' of iconic signs, which however, can only make sense for the audience when embedded within and interpreted by a secondary system of causal, indexical signification.[76] Following Alter's formulation, I would suggest that it is less than certain that the relationship of spatial representation to its referent in the Jacobean theatre was a merely iconic relationship, but rather, one which complicates iconicity by having it alternate with other referential modes.

Certainly the plays themselves appear to doubt the adequacy of the mimetic process towards which their performances aspire. In comparison with the street-theatre tradition upon which the early public theatres followed, in which dramatic performance occupied a public space not physically distinguishable from it by clear demarcation, the new theatres may have left actors with an impoverishing sense of separation from a context hitherto capable of being assimilated into the fictional world and of carrying its symbolic meanings.[77] The armed Prologue-actor in *Troilus and Cressida* introduces the play with the apologetic announcement that

> our play
> Leaps o'er the vaunt and firstlings of those broils,
> Beginning in the middle, starting thence away
> To what may be digested in a play.
>
> (Prologue 26–9)

The limits of performance, albeit an agile one, necessitate short-cuts and accelerated entry into the matter so as to adapt the disproportionately constricted dimensions of the performance-*sujet* to the massive geographical dimensions of the play's *fabula*-action.

The most succinct formulation of this problem is to be found in Day, Rowley and Wilkins' *The Travels of the Three English Brothers*, which 'entreats' the audience to 'think | By this [time] hath borne our worthy traveller | Toward Christendom as far as Russia', then admitting that 'Our story then so large, we cannot give | All things in acts' (4.2–4, 9–10). The famous Prologue to *Henry V* has a similar task, and is exemplary in this respect:

> Can this cockpit hold
> The vasty fields of France? Or may we cram
> Within this wooden O the very casques
> That did affright the air at Agincourt?
> O pardon: since a crookèd figure may
> Attest in little place a million,
> And let us, ciphers to this great account,
> On your imaginary forces work.
>
> (Prologue, 11–18)

The prologue sets the boundaries of the theatrical experience, marking it off from the world, closing it within a 'wooden O'. By the same token, it opens up the realm of theatrical illusion to its exterior, for, by drawing attention to those boundaries it shows that the theatre is not a total world as it would aim to be. Thus the dramatic discourse underlines the inadequacy of that theatrical illusion to compete with reality.[78] The theatre clearly declares its problematic and definitely non-mimetic relationship ('a crookèd figure [which] may | Attest in little place a million'; 'ciphers to this great account') to a larger panoramic historical narrative.

The relationship of theatrical representation to the things represented is not one of adequate one-to-one correspondence, but rather, of inadequate gestures towards real events which the theatre attempts, by means of a remarkable economy of theatrical signification, to signify through a limited but versatile repertory of signifiers.[79] In order to allay the inadequacy of the means of stage representation, the spectator is often shown not the action itself, a shipwreck or a battle, but merely the results or the effects of the action; costume can display the results of actions not performed onstage, hair let down signalling a recent rape, or loose garments signalling psychic disorder, as in Hamlet's hanging garters; and onstage performance is frequently complemented in Shakespeare by the narration of offstage events, combining 'mimetic' with 'diegetic' semiotic functions.[80]

These theatrical signifiers are all of an *indexical* nature, based on a relationship of 'pointing', of spatial contiguity or of causal connection. An *iconic* relationship on the stage, functioning as a mode of 'expression', tends to stress the identity of referent and icon, suggesting the adhesion of the one with the other (and thereby suppressing the interval which necessarily separates icon and referent, without which, of course, the icon would *be* its referent). In contrast, relations of contiguity, of connection, of causality, that is, indexical relations, underline the spatial nature of stage signs, and of the context in which they are produced through performance. Thus the problematic character of iconicity in the Jacobean stage is not merely a sign of inadequacy, but an important and distinctive aspect of the theatre's semiotic operations.

Indeed, some dramatic situations are entirely dependent upon indexical signification. In Act 3, Scene 2 of *A Mad World, My Masters*, Mistress Harebrain is not where her eavesdropping husband thinks she is: he assumes she is closeted behind the curtains of the Courtesan Frank Gullman's bed, for he can hear one half of a dialogue ostensibly being carried on with his wife by the Courtesan; in actual fact, his wife is in the next room, equally invisible, equally quiet, making love with Penitent Brothel. Harebrain interprets the indexical signs (the Courtesan's replies to an imaginary Mistress Harebrain) as evidence of her presence; his interpretation, however, is false, for the interval between index and referent is somewhat wider than he realizes; Mistress Harebrain is embarked upon a different variety of intercourse, further away than he suspects. He greets his wife, as she re-enters the Courtesan's bedroom, where Harebrain has been eavesdropping, with the words 'Never was hour spent better.' 'Why, were you within the hearing, sir?' enquires his wife. 'Ay, that I was i'faith, to my great comfort' replies Harebrain (3.2.235–8) – on the one hand, mistakenly, in that he has, in fact, heard nothing of his wife, but merely the stage replies of the Courtesan; on the other hand, correctly, in that he has detected a series of indexical signs which pointed to his wife's presence, and which he has simply interpreted with an excess of optimism.

The crucial factor here is distance: the fictional signs emitted by the Courtesan plausibly signify proximity, and the success of the scheme depends upon Harebrain failing to verify the actual degree of proximity. The distance is in fact greater than he realizes, his wife having already escaped from the orbit of his jealous surveillance. What is essential in this scene is the coexistence of two separate but contiguous worlds. Theatrical space, in so far as it employs such signifying operations, is far from being an iconic space. Where the icon tends to obliterate that for which it stands, an index or metonymy, in contrast, leaves the referent intact, thus allowing inference and links to be made between the two – in the case of the above scene, erroneously. The more insistently iconic the sign's functioning, the more powerfully it tends to replace the thing itself, generating a 'reality effect', such that we tend to forget the existence of the 'real world'. In contrast, the more explicitly indexical the sign, the more the context of production and/or reception remains perceptible for the spectator.

But when, for instance, two armies are represented on the stage by four swords and bucklers, in Philip Sidney's mocking parody,[81] or in *Coriolanus* 'two Officers, … lay cushions, *as it were in the Capitol*' (2.2.1, s.d., my emphasis), the relation of sign to referent is not just one of cause and effect, but also one of part to whole. *Troilus and Cressida* explicitly names the indexical mechanisms of theatrical performance and its additional synecdochic function. Ulysses has just expressed his unease over Achilles' player-like parodies of his superiors in the Greek army; he then goes on to compare Achilles' prospective combat with the Trojan Hector also with play-acting:

> Though't be a sportful combat,
> Yet in this trial much opinion dwells,
> For here the Trojans taste our dear'st repute
> With their fin'st palate …
> … for the sucess,
> Although particular, shall give a scantling
> Of good and bad unto the general –
> And in such indices, although small pricks
> To their subsequent volumes, there is seen
> The baby figure of the giant mass
> Of things to come at large.
>
> (1.3.329–40)

Nestor speaks of what he believes will transpire to be an exemplary combat between Hector and Achilles, one which will point to the larger outcome of the Trojan war. This one episode he describes as a 'scantling', a specimen or sample which points to the nature of the larger entity. Thus his use of the term 'indices' is entirely justified, as these specimen moments, parts from which one can extrapolate the character of the whole, provide synecdochic figures of the larger course of events in which they are embedded. The 'sportful combat', in other words, the *play*, entertains an indexical relationship, both synecdochic and causal, with the drama of war of which it is but one scene. Likewise, the prologue to *Henry V* advertises the play as 'ciphers to this great account', the same passage drawing attention to the eminently spatial character of indexical signification. The prologue denies creating a miniature world which replaces reality for the duration of the performance; on the contrary, it declares itself theatre *in* the world, separated from the outer environment by a mere wall of half-timber and limed lathes, constantly porous to the outside because inadequate to 'hold' that larger reality – but simultaneously, being carried by that larger world, or rather, by the spectators' capacity to read 'ciphers' as belonging to the 'great account'.

The limited space of stage representation necessarily demands extension through the employment of noises, or verbal references, to indicate an 'off stage', a 'space without', thus deictically embedding the stage scene in a larger fabric.[82] By virtue of this extension the supposedly iconic spatial signifiers on the stage become not only indexical and metonymic, but also function as synecdoches of the larger space of which they are a part. The stage is both mimesis of reality, and part of that selfsame reality.[83] In this way, the theatre signifies that which it *is* not, but *in* which it is implanted: its own exterior, the world which surrounds it. Curiously, metonymy becomes, once again, metaphor, for what is mimed, iconically, concretely, in the relationship of onstage and offstage, is the relationship of inside to outside, of theatre to world. The theatrical icon here is an icon of the theatre's relations of contiguity to the world in which it is placed.

The most striking evidence of this, as mentioned above, was the disruptive presence of the gallants on stage, intruding into the play to upstage the actors with their own performance of social brilliance, parasitically absorbing the theatre into their own ostentatious social posing and social climbing. The permeability of worldly theatre and theatre in the world is further exemplified by accusations that the gallants stole lines from the plays to be used when dining out, or that Ben Jonson had merely lifted dramatic dialogue from what he heard in their company.[84] What is performed on the stage is the constant interlinking of theatrical and non-theatrical worlds – fiction and reality are terms of little utility here – and the transfer of elements from the one to the other, in both directions. Theatrical metaphoricity (iconicity) is not dissolved, but rather assimilated to metonymy – and vice versa.

But these relations of integration and distance are not constantly present. Many modern artistic texts display a productive tension between the maintenance of frames and their elimination.[85] On the stage, there appears to be an intermittent, never constant fusion of the real space of performance of the dramatic story (here and now in real space and time) and the fictional space of the story itself (necessarily situated somewhere else or at some other point in time).[86] This oscillation is frequently visible in the Jacobean theatre. The action of *Twelfth Night*, for instance, takes place in the fictional world of Illyria, created on the stage for the space of the performance; yet when the shipwrecked Sebastian and Antonio are cast up on the shores of Illyria, Sebastian advises his master to put up 'In the south suburbs at the Elephant' (3.3.39), referring to a real tavern not far from the Globe Theatre on the Bankside, so that fictional place of the tale and the real context of performance are superimposed upon each other, to the point where the boundary between the two threatens to dissolve.[87] When Subtle in *The Alchemist* refers to 'Your master's worship's house here in the Friars' (1.1.17) there is a blurring of the demarcation between reference to the fictional place performed on the stage, that of a house in the Blackfriars quarter, and reference to the real place of performance, Blackfriars theatre. Fictional and real locality are condensed so as to refer simultaneously to two ostensibly mutually exclusive levels of spatial localization. The play repeatedly employs an isomorphism in which the inside of the house where Subtle and Face carry out their profitable villainy (fictional world) displays the same spatial contours as the inside of theatre space (real world); this entails a further isomorphism of the real performance space at Blackfriars or the Globe in its functioning as a financially profitable place for creating fiction, with the no less profitable 'performance space' of the fictional house in Blackfriars: 'On with your tire', says Face to Dol Common, ushering her off into the literal tiring house (3.3.78). In *Bartholomew Fair*, Jonson plays even more consciously with this oscillation of incongruence and congruence of performance space and fictional space: 'though the fair be not kept in the same region that some here, perhaps, would have it, yet think that therein that the author hath observed a special decorum, the place being as dirty as Smithfield, and as stinking every whit' (Induction, 140–4) – though the Hope theatre is not Smithfield, it none the less smells exactly like it, thus wafting the spectators directly to the fictional location of the action.

The Jacobean stage thus produces an overlapping of two modes of spatial reference, a sort of 'double consciousness' encompassing normally mutually exclusive modes of representation (referential and fictional).[88] The spectators are obliged to participate in a form of double vision, being simultaneously conscious of the fictional world as an intact entity convincing enough to displace the real, and of the stage as a manifestly limited performance space which butts up against other spaces, those of the audience, and of the position of the theatre in a real quarter of London. Shklovsky spoke of a 'flickering' quality produced by the alternation between reality and illusion on the stage, while Barthes described a similar oscillation between 'fascination' with the screen/ stage image and an abrupt 'disengagement' and consciousness of the 'situation' of performance.[89] The stage fiction can only be created by demarcating it from its context, but at the same time, the larger world is recurrently alluded to as the situation of performance, and thus is drawn back into the compass of the theatre so as to become the referent of the spatial signs of the stage.

Pfister's analysis of theatrical space opens with a distinction between inner and outer communicative systems, that is, between two forms of space, that of the fictive world of the drama, and that of the real world of the performance where this fictive world is produced before the eyes of an audience.[90] The crossing of the two communicative systems allows the spatial message to signify not only within the inner communicative system of the fictional world, but also in the outer communicative system of the place of performance, which can in turn be extended to encompass not only the stage–audience space, but, as Mullaney has emphasized, the 'place of the stage' in society. If content belongs to the inner communicative system, and form to the outer or transmitting communicative system, then a meta-linguistic statement is the process by which one communicative system comments upon another. When the theatrical space of one communicative system reflects upon a another communicative system, we have a meta-spatial statement. In this respect, Jacobean theatre repeatedly mobilized meta-spatial communication by means of indexical and synecdochic modes of reference.

It is of course necessary to introduce a degree of differentiation into this picture of the referential oscillation at work in the Jacobean theatre. Certain differences between the public and private theatres need to be taken into account in order to qualify somewhat the claims made above. Inigo Jones's drawing for an unnamed playhouse – probably Beeston's Cockpit/Phoenix conversion of 1616 – shows a shallow stage surrounded by audience seating on three sides, in two galleries, both with stepped seating, and semicircular auditorium in front of the stage running parallel down the sides of the stage (see Figure 2). Even at the court, Inigo Jones's designs maintained, despite a more elaborate classicism of the façade, a non-scenic, open stage with audience seating on three sides. Thus the private and even the court theatre displayed a large degree of continuity with the staging configurations in the public play-houses. Available plans of the private theatres militate against the previously popular notion that the indoor theatres provided players and playwrights with the opportunity to avail themselves of scenic innovations developed in the court masque. Moreover, regular transfers of plays by some companies such as the King's Men, from public to private houses and to the Cockpit-in-Court would have produced a degree of standardization in staging practice. Poor lighting in the indoor private theatres may have reduced audience awareness of its own presence in comparison to the daylight theatres, but at the same time, the spectators were closer to the stage, perhaps diminishing the necessity for actors to use large gestures and clearly visible tableaux, though this may not necessarily have led to an increased naturalism of acting technique. Thus the style of acting probably retained a large degree of continuity, whereas the spatial dimensions, if not the broad spatial structures, changed, inevitably entailing some transformation of the representation of social space.

The theatrical experience of the public and private theatres would have differed to the extent that in the public theatres the spectators formed an unruly crowd, whereas in the private theatres they made up a smaller, compact audience, probably validating the material more by appreciation than by raucous participation.[91] There may have been a changed sense of the audience's own sense of itself, if diminished lighting made for less awareness of the audience as a collective entity, occupying less of a 'sociopetal' than a 'sociofugal' space splitting an audience into individual spectators enjoying a private experience.[92] There was also a significant change in the actor's position as the actor moved upstage in the private theatres, which despite the continued use of a protruding open stage, replaced the virtually complete circular audience space with a rectangular auditorium form and thus gathered more of the audience in front of the stage; the actor would thus have assumed a more face-on acting technique, which would probably have diminished the employment of visible spatial configurations. Certainly this was one of the effects of the introduction of perspective scenery, albeit limited to the Court until after the Restoration: perspective scenery implies a specific and individualized spectator position, and one that was clearly distanced from the action observed, whereas the early open stage broke down distance and offered multiple views of the action.[93] Differences between the public, private and court theatres in Jacobean London thus evince, against the background of a dominant open stage without a proscenium arch or perspective scenery, a gradual shift from the visibility of the

(a)

Figure 2(a)

Figure 2(b)

Figure 2   Drawings by Inigo Jones, about 1616, probably of the Cockpit or Phoenix Theatre, Drury Lane (a) the plan; (b) stage façade (the Provost and Fellows, Worcester College, Oxford)

entire theatrical space towards the individualization of spectator space, and a diminishment of the large spatial means of representation in favour of a 'flatter', more 'iconic' rather than 'indexical' mode of acting, particularly as the private theatres gradually superseded the public theatres in the 1620s and 1630s. None the less, these gradual changes did not yet, in the Jacobean period, substantially cast into question the general spatial parameters of the theatrical referentiality. Up until the closure of the theatres in 1642, the theatre persisted in drawing attention to its place in the world, and did this by means of spatial signification.

What are the epistemological conclusions to be drawn from the concrete function of theatrical space during the Jacobean era? Lefebvre's distinction between spaces of domination and spaces of appropriation, and the corresponding conceptual pair, spaces of representation (institutionalized tools of power) and representation of space (the representational practices developed by the users of space) is helpful in articulating the implications for modes of knowledge inherent in the spatial operations of the Jacobean theatre. Lefebvre concludes that the theatrical space is neither a space of representation nor a representation of space – and both at the same time.[94] In other words, it takes signifiers of the social and institutional spaces of which it is a part, and reworks them in fictive forms on the stage, alluding all the while to the spaces whose signifiers it has transmuted by means of artistic craft, spaces which continue to exist around about it. This dual practice (reworking and dissolution of the signs of the real *and* simultaneous allusion to their uninterrupted existence) can be seen at work in the mode of synecdoche discussed above.

According to Elam, synecdochic replacement of part for whole characterizes every aspect of dramatic representation because objects on stage function semiotically to the extent that they are based on a synecdoche of the kind 'member standing for its class'.[95] The process of synecdochic allusion depends, however, on a previous operation, that of 'ostention', that of *showing* things to the audience rather than *describing* them; in other words, of highlighting or isolating something in order to show it as a being a *representative* member of a larger class. Thus the operation of synecdoche involves two subsidiary spatial operations: first, a distancing, isolating movement, and secondly, a return to the larger context briefly departed from. To show the space of the stage as a synecdoche of the larger social space in which theatre occurs thus necessitates cordoning off the stage-space as an 'ostended', privileged, framed domain in which the functioning of social space is displayed in dramatic, performative form. This operation of distance and separation is necessary to the modelling function of art outlined by Lotman, a function to which the frame is crucial. Yet the counterpoised movement of synecdoche is equally necessary to the modelling function; for without a synecdochic relationship, the epistemological operation of modelling would lose its pragmatic function, that is, setting at distance in order to facilitate knowledge and reform of what surrounds the model. It has been suggested that it is the separation between the empirical space of performance situation and the dramaturgical space with its utopian possible world which allows the emergence of a model in critical relation to the audience's dominant social construction of reality.[96] We should, however, qualify this notion of separation and emphasize alternation as the crucial basis of the modelling function.

In a suggestive meditation upon the functioning of 'play' – the theatrical connotations of the term have useful resonances here – Bateson claims that this activity simulates or denotes a set of actions in the real world, but is set apart from the *real-world* denotations of such actions, and from their concrete consequences. An example of this can be found in Shakespeare's *Cymbeline*, when Posthumus meets Lord Cloten in combat. Posthumus 'rather *played* than fought, | And had no help of anger', thus averting a mortal outcome to the duel (1.1.163; my emphasis). The relation between real actions and played actions, Bateson suggests, can be compared to the relations between a territory and the map which describes it. In play, however, the 'discrimination between map and territory is always liable to break down.' In an illuminating comparison with psychotherapy, Bateson shows that the alternation of discrimination and lack of discrimination between territory and map, the oscillation between the presence and absence of a 'frame'/'context' distinction, constitutes a model of reality which allows a modification of real-world conditions.[97]

Likewise, in the oscillation between implication in and distance from society characteristic of the Jacobean stage, spectators would have been able to reflect upon the society of which they were active, participating members. In other words, the situation of the stage as a part of a whole is the precondition for and trigger of the critical process of distancing; the whole is the place to which critical thought returns once new knowledge has been gained via the distancing process. Space, Merleau-Ponty has suggested in a seemingly tautological formulation, is always produced by an active engagement with space.[98] This appears to be the mode of production of knowledge of the Jacobean theatre, reworking representations of social space without ever definitively setting itself up as distinctly apart from that selfsame social space, and thereby always able to speak *about* and *in* social space.

The theatre was intimately involved with the social, political and above all the economic life of Jacobean England. The emergence of the theatre was part and parcel with London's rise to prominence as the largest city in western Europe. Indeed, the tensions which characterized theatrical representation epitomized the economic context of the theatre's emergence. In the manifest dilemma of dramatists of how best to represent historical events set in an ever-expanding world, within the cramped confines of the playhouse, is revealed a conflict between contraction of the space of representation, based upon a more careful mode of control of the delimitation of audience boundaries, and the spatial phenomenon which accompanies it – that of an expansion of commercial activity both towards widening world horizons and in novel spaces of production and consumption such as the new public theatres. The theatres were clearly a salient aspect of London's busy economic existence. The Liberties, where the public theatres were predominantly situated, were an integral part of the City's economic domain, albeit subject to other forms of regulation.[99] The theatre was intensely involved in that economic dynamism, its fluidity and mobility. The dramatists shifted their production from one theatre to another, sometimes collaborating with other dramatists, sometimes working alone, alternating between genres, companies, audiences. The plays themselves went where the markets were, not being fixed at the Globe, as the contemporary Shakespeare heritage cult would have it, but circulating constantly between numerous other venues, such as Middle Temple, Queens College Cambridge and Penshurst Place.[100] It is in this extraordinary dynamism and fluidity that the theatres were situated and which, indeed, provided their conditions of possibility. Given the theatre's close involvement in the economic and social context, it is hardly surprising that theatrical modes of significance were so constantly oriented towards the social place in which the theatres arose.

Yet by the same token, the theatre made reality strange, set itself apart from the events of the day. For if the theatrical product it offered had not been substantially different from everyday life, it would not have been attractive to the paying public. Thus, by virtue of its enclosed circular building, the absence of any attempt to 'naturalize' the fictions presented upon its stage, and the corrosive, mocking or romantic transformation of reality achieved by its dramas, the theatre also remained clearly distinct from its world.

Perhaps the most expressive spatial simile for the oscillating mode of knowledge mobilized by the Jacobean theatre is furnished by Mullaney's notion of the marginal 'place of the stage'. Mullaney's study has been criticized by for its one-sided view of theatre as oppositional, subversive and marginal, whereas in fact the theatre was clearly inserted in the dynamics of a market which caused it to be oriented primarily *towards* the desires of the public, rather than *against* the authorities, although these two motivations of the content of theatre may occasionally have overlapped so as to effectively produce a political oppositional theatre.[101] Spatially, it would be more accurate to stress the *simultaneous* geographical marginality and economic integration of the

Figure 3 Detail of Hollar's *Long View of London from the Bankside*, 1647 (the labels of the Beargarden and the Globe are reversed) (British Library Maps Room)

theatres, their spatial ambivalence forming an emblem of their partly subversive and partly participatory place within the society; not so much marginal, but *liminoid*, on the threshold – as Mullaney stresses for the places where the theatres were built, the Liberties.[102] Thus the situation of the theatres was both within and without; both distanced from, but also participating in the economic and political processes of the period. As Carlson has cogently remarked of the theatres, these 'freestanding and distinctive structures … were quite obvious urban elements, as may be readily seen in the various Renaissance engraved "views" of the city; yet despite this distinctiveness they were not really landmarks … since they were not, properly speaking, a part of the urban configuration' (see Figure 3).[103] This concretely spatial simile encapsulates the functioning of theatrical referentiality on the Jacobean stage, at once implicated in and distanced from the context which produced it, and thus constantly able to offer its audiences a double perspective on their own society.

The influence of the stage

The theatre's power to revise representations of social space without ever losing contact with that space perfectly describes the theatre's mode of insertion in the society of the day. The oscillation summarized above, between critical distance and intimate participation in social processes, meant that the theatre was regarded as a potent influence for social stability or unrest. Certainly contemporaries saw the theatre as possessing a real – and for some, dangerous – degree of agency within the society of which it was a part. In a society where the majority of subjects were illiterate, drama possessed a persuasive aura of 'objectivity' which rendered it immensely powerful as a means of influencing the political climate; the theatre's persuasive agency has been demonstrated by Jerzy Limon in his study of the theatre as a mode of propaganda during the political crisis which followed upon Charles's and Buckingham's return to England after the failure of marriage negotiations with the Spanish Infanta in 1623–4.[104]

There were frequent assertions of the dangerous influence of the theatre, and equally frequent counter-claims of the beneficent virtues of stage plays. A petition of 1597 execrated the plays for 'conteining nothinge but prophane fables, lascivious matters, cozeininge devises, & scurrilus beehaviours, which are so set forth as that they move wholie to imitation & not to the avoidynge of those faults & vices which they represent.'[105] Thomas Nash said virtually the same thing in *Pierce*

Peniless, but simply inverted the topos: 'In Playes, all cozenages, all cunning drifts overguylded with outward holinesse, all stratagems of warre, all the canker-wormes that breed on the rust of peace, are most lively anatomiz'd: they shew the ill successe of treason, the fall of hasty climbers, the wretched end of usurpers, the miserie of civil dissention, and how just God is evermore in punishing of murthers. ... What should I say more: they are sower pills of reprehension wrapt up in sweete words.'[106] This symmetrical inversion of claims for the salutary or dangerous effects of theatre can be seen in the plays themselves. Webster's *White Devil* shows such maleficent influence at work in Act 2, Scene 2, when a dumb show performing Camillo's murder precedes the subsequent usurpation: drama suggests, indeed triggers, routes of action leading towards social unrest – though the actors may have meant this multiple layering of representations of regicide, and the consequent avoidance of showing the actual murder itself, as a form of protective self-censorship, in anticipation, precisely, of potential accusations of incitement to treason.

Several metaphors, particularly those of 'impression' and of 'contagion', attempted to explain the potent influence of the stage. The topos of mental 'impression' expressed one mode of maleficent educative influence thought to be inherent in theatre. Hamlet's demand that his players 'hold as 'twere a mirror up to nature' is explained as showing 'the very age and body of the time his form and pressure' (3.2.22–4). An aghast Viola in *Twelfth Night*, realizing that her assumed identity has captivated Olivia, muses: 'Disguise, I see thou art a wickedness | ... How easy it is for the proper false | In women's waxen hearts to set their forms' (2.2.27–30). Falsity, when convincingly presented, leaves a dangerously deep imprint in spectators' consciousness. Hamlet remembers that spectators 'sitting at a play | Have by the very cunning of the scene | Been struck so to the soul' (2.2.591–3). In this context, it is significant that the word 'strike' could connote the operation of a mould, the working of a printing press, the minting of a coin or the inscription of a mark.[107] Stubbes, in his *Anatomie of Abuses*, wrote that 'such is our grosse & dull nature, that what thing we see opposite before our eyes, do pearce further and printe deeper in our harts and minds, than that thing which is hard onely with the eares.'[108] Stephen Gosson remarked that 'the divel is not ignorant how mightely these outward spectacles effeminate and soften the hearts of men, vice is learned by beholding, senses is tickled, desire is pricked, and those impressions of mind are secretly conueyed over to the gazers, which the plaiers do counterfeit on stage.'[109] Bacon also used imagery of impression in employing an extended theatrical metaphor, explaining that 'the *Idols of the Theatre* are not innate ... but are plainly impressed and received into the mind from the play-books of philosophical systems.'[110] The theatres were regarded by the authorities as dangerous multipliers of disease, and were closed during outbreaks of the plague.[111] The same threatening imagery of contagion also lent itself ideally to descriptions of the theatre's transmission of 'influence'. John Northbrooke thundered against 'players of enterludes', 'sith they are so noysome a pestilence to infect a common wealth.'[112] A Lord Mayor complained that London's youth was being 'greatly corrupted & their manners infected with many evil and ungodly qualities, by reason of the wanton and profane divices represented on the stages of the sayd players', and in William Rankins' *Mirrour of Monsters* (1587) the author expatiated upon 'the manifold vices, and spotted enormities, that can be caused by the infectious sight of Playes.'[113] *Troilus and Cressida* explicitly links theatrical performance to the idea of disease, when Nestor complains that Achilles and Patroclus indulge themselves with 'slandrous' 'imitation', theatrical parodies of their senior officers: 'And in the imitation of these twain [Achilles and Patroclus] | Who ... opinion crowns | With an imperial voice, many are infect' (1.3.185–7). The 'actors'' impudent imitation of authority is in turn imitated by the spectators, in a chain of dangerously infectious transmission. Theatre is conceived as something which spreads contagious disrespect and insubordination through the rank and file, awarding authority to the upstart players who imitate the real figures of authority. It is significant that this metaphor directly follows a long speech made by Ulysses where social unrest and the rejection of hierarchy and degree are described as 'sickness' and 'fever' which destroys the body politic (1.3.85–137). Jonson, in the Induction of *Bartholomew Fair*, forbids 'censure by contagion', by which he means censure of the play itself by the audience (Induction, 89); but it is not difficult to imagine the same collective critical consensus being directed at the characters portrayed upon the stage, and by extension, to the public figures of authority to whom they might have alluded – a scenario evoked by Gervase Markham's allusion to 'the manie headed Monster opinion, euer then readie to be delivered from the wombe of common multitude.'[114] All these metaphors of the influence of the stage attempted to describe its disturbing agency, what Melrose has called a 'building up' of social energy generated by the powerful somatic event of theatrical performance.[115]

The power of theatrical influence also represented a dangerous appropriation of royal spectacle, itself an important instrument of power for the English monarchs, who depended upon the maintenance of good public relations for their popular support, in the absence of a powerful army and administrative system. 'We princes are set upon stages in sight and view of all the world,' Elizabeth told Parliament in 1586, and skilfully wielded the resources of spectacle to her own political advantage.[116] James I would repeat the remark: 'It is a true olde saying, That a King is as one set on a skaffold, whoese smallest actions & gestures al the people gazingly do behold: and therefore although a King be never so precise in the dischargeing of his office, the people who seeth but the outwarde parte, will ever judge of the substance by the circumstances.'[117] (James prudently replaced *scaffold* by *stages* in later editions of *Basilikon Doron*.) The royal simile was impudently appropriated by the players themselves. Heywood's defence of the acting profession included the assumption of a similar stance to that of the monarch's prominence: 'for as we [actors] are men that stand in the broad eye of the world, so should our manners, gestures and behaviours, favour of such government and modesty, to deserve the good thoughts and reports of all men.'[118] It is precisely the visibility of the theatre which appears to have unsettled the authorities. In a simile symptomatic of this dread of vulnerable visibility, Shakespeare in *Antony and Cleopatra* has the Egyptian queen apprehensive at the thought of public humiliation by the Roman actors:

> The quick comedians
> Extemporally will stage us, and present
> Our Alexandrian revels. Antony
> Shall be brought drunken forth, and I shall see
> Some squeaking Cleopatra boy my greatness
> I'th' posture of a whore.
>
> (5.2.212–17)

The theatre upstages the most prominent public figure of the realm, and travesties the representative authority of that figure.

It was this powerful representative capacity within society, its ability to intervene in social reality, which was grasped by contemporary writers as the explanation for drama's influence. Heywood recounts several hyperbolic stories of theatre having brought good to the community; two women have been moved by quite separate performances in Lin in Norfolk and in Amsterdam, to declare their murders of their respective spouses, one by the sight of the 'ghost of her husband', the other upon being confronted by the spectacle of a husband having a nail driven through his forehead; a party of invading Spaniards in Perin in Cornwall has been put to rout by a battle played on stage, thus betraying their hostile presence in the town and facilitating their defeat.[119] Shakespeare's Hamlet reports, in the passage already alluded to above, having 'heard that guilty creatures sitting at a play | Have by the very cunning of the scene | Been struck so to the soul that presently | They have proclaimed their malefactions' (2.2.591–4). Drama on the stage is perceived as taking effect upon and within reality. Other forms of spectacle clearly functioned in this way: when, in December 1596, Presbyterian ministers preached against James using the biblical story of Mordecai and Haman, members of the congregation subsequently took up arms and were soon battering the doors of the Edinburgh Toolbooth (where James was ensconced) shouting 'Bring out the wicked Haman.'[120] From preaching as a form of spectacle, to real revolt, and from dramatic biblical analogy to literal identification, the transition could be rapid and barely controllable.

In this notion of theatrical influence, the boundaries between stage and world are porous, allowing the drama to perform the ethical role attributed to it by writers such as Heywood. His examples have a thoroughly apocryphal air to them, but they confirm the assumption which both defenders and opponents of the theatre shared: namely, that the theatre was not a 'merely' aesthetic phenomenon, but rather, that it exerted a powerful influence upon audiences and made an impact upon the society of which it was a part. It was precisely the constitutive tension between participatory knowledge and distanced reflection which made the theatre's influence so dangerous. Its 'imitation' of its world was a distorting imitation which could exhort the populace to similar exercises in critical, usurping imitation.

The study of representations of social space on the Jacobean stage thus needs to combine several aspects of early modern performance: first, the concrete place of the theatre; second, the form of the theatre, crucial in determining its modes of referentiality; and third, the thematic content of the plays themselves, to which the substantive chapters of this study will pay closer attention.

These three aspects converge in the *performance* of place, form and thematics, as can be illustrated by two brief examples from *The Alchemist*. 'D' you think that I dare move him?' Face asks, mediating between his master Subtle and the client Dapper. Conversely, the wily Surly challenges the villains: 'I would not willingly be gulled. Your Stone | Cannot transmute me' (1.2.93; 2.1.78–9). In both instances the debate is a meta-linguistic one concerning the power of language as a rhetorical and thus spatial activity (tropes 'turn' language from the straight and narrow of correct referentiality) to change the position of the opponent, to set him on a certain path of action. What drives this coercive undertaking is the desirable mobility of wealth, symbolized in the transmutations of the philosopher's stone, a mobility which the tricksters hope to maximize by pure deception rather than the progressive steps of productive transformation of raw materials. The action of *The Alchemist* itself depends upon this essentially spatial dynamic and no less upon the predictable resistance it generates in some characters.

Here it is helpful to recall Lotman's suggestion to the effect that narrative is fundamentally driven by a transgression of semantic fields which provides the motor for the act of narration (*sujet*). A transgression of the unquestionable, given schemas of the world – most frequently encoded in the form of spatial binary oppositions – creates a *sujet*-laden text bearing information-rich events which make up the *sujet*-chain.[121] Thus a spatial movement (transgression of binary oppositions) generates noteworthy, narratable events, which in turn create a temporal movement of narration of events. Similarly, Elam has suggested that dramatic narrative is propelled by changes of the relations between distinct possible worlds; dramatic events are kinks in space. Characters identify themselves by deictic operations situating them in a particular possible world, and each change in the state of affairs is caused by a new deictic orientation.[122]

In *The Alchemist* it is the plague which forces the master out of town, in turn allowing Subtle and Face's occupation of the house; every further crossing of the threshold by their clients re-triggers the narrative of transgression of legal limits; these transgressions are motivated by attempts to change the deictic mode of being of the characters on stage, to control the subjective space of the other by cunning manipulation of one's own space: 'D' you think that I dare move him?' asks Face. The stage space is thus heavily semanticized as a generator of narrative, but also as a generator of power or wealth, both operations being essentially spatially structured. Issues as diverse as the disturbing mobility of London's underworld population, the disquieting analogies between actors and confidence-men, and London itself as an inhuman but dynamic entity no longer under the control of its inhabitants (Middleton calls it 'This man-devouring city' in *Michaelmas Term* – 2.2.21), are all addressed by Jonson's play. Thus the questions of the place of performance ('Our scene is London' – Prologue, 5), of theatrical space on the stage, and of spatial themes relevant to contemporary spectators can be seen to converge on the Jacobean stage.

Material stage configurations, the plays as the attempted articulation of problematic spatial issues, and the larger social context of expansion and mobility (economic, geographic, demographic) exist in multiple and overdetermined relations of mediation with one another. The arena of theatrical practice needs to be seen not as inert but rather as highly productive of spatial signs which should be read in connection with the linguistic content of the plays, their thematic and metaphorical functioning, and the larger issues of spatial power relations addressed by the drama. Thus Bruster's comment misses the mark completely when he says 'that the concept of *place*, once crucial to a social analysis of the plays, is ultimately less important in Renaissance drama than a concern with material life which underlies the themes and structures, a concern I call the materialist vision.'[123] This is a fallacious distinction. In the context of the Jacobean theatre, space is that which underlies and supports material life, it is the very site of material life, and is formed by material life. Bruster is disputing an outmoded concept of place, one concerned with 'locality' as an inert setting for scenes in a drama, or as the defining characteristic of a particular form of stage satire ('city comedy'), rather than the productive and produced fabric of material life. This perspective will structure the subsequent discussion of space in Jacobean drama. The succeeding chapters endeavour to show concretely the various ways in which the stage was a product of social, economic and political life in the Jacobean era, and conversely, the manner in which the theatres also employed spatial modes of representation to intervene within questions of the changing configurations of social space during the period.

2
The Sun King: James I and the Court Masque

Royal creations

The spatial semiosis of the theatre creates a fictional universe on the stage, in implicit opposition to the given realities of social space. The full presumption of such an artistic undertaking was at the centre of the massive projects of political image-making carried out in Jacobean England in the form of the court masques. In the manual of kingship composed for his son Charles, James I famously wrote: 'God gives not Kings the style of Gods in vaine, | For on his throne his Scepter do they swey.'[1] One integral part of the aura of divinity with which James clad his person was the masque. Other monarchs before him, notably Elizabeth, had utilized court entertainments as part of their repertoire of royal propaganda, but James's court spectacles far surpassed their forerunners in their sumptuous splendour, their technical sophistication under the innovative direction of Inigo Jones and Ben Jonson – and their exorbitant cost. The court masques of the Jacobean era, starting with Samuel Daniel's *Vision of the Twelve Goddesses* (1604) and culminating in Jones's and Jonson's *Fortunate Isles* (1625), implicitly attributed to James the creative elan they evinced, underlining in tangible, visible form the quasi-divine powers of the monarch.[2] The artistic production at the court gave the ultimate producer behind them, the monarch, divine and wondrous potency to conjure up new versions of reality. The masques at times explicitly confirmed this godlike status, *News from the New World*, for instance, informing James I that the dazzling light pervading the hall was a result 'of the pietie, wisdome, Majesty reflected by you ... from the divine light, to which onely you are lesse' (522: 306–8).

The audience at court was confronted with a spectacle including sumptuous costumes, elaborate scenery and special effects such as characters descending from the clouds, apparently miraculous lighting effects and accompanying music. This evidence of divine powers of creation appears to have provoked boundless amazement and wonder. The Venetian ambassador, commenting on *The Masque of Beauty*, said that 'the abundance of beauty of the lights [was] immense', and Antonio Correr, also of the Venetian delegation, recorded his impressions of *Oberon, The Fairy Prince* in 1611 thus: 'the rock opened discovering a great throne with countless lights and colours all shifting, a lovely thing to see.'[3] The spectators' wonder is sometimes pointed up explicitly by the masque text, as in *The Golden Age*: 'Lowd musique. | PALLAS *in her chariot descending.* | *To a softer musique.* | Looke, looke! Reioyce, and wonder!' (421: 1). Pallas's command makes explicit the sense of awe conjured up by the aura of divinity made tangible in the here-and-now. The same anticipation and verbal pointing up of audience reaction can be found in *The Vision of Delight*, where Peace is obliged to wake an audience 'turne[d] dumbe', their blood 'fixe[d] ... as if you Statues stood' (467: 128, 135). The audience's admiration at this element of divine creation supports the notion that the masque aimed to achieve far more than mere spectacle. It was an exercise in the creation of a new universe, an attempt to redefine, in concrete spatial terms, the nature of the monarch's realm.

The masque was thus an eminently spatial mode of comment upon a kingdom said to constitute the monarch's 'other body'. This chapter aims to explore the manner in which that spatialized representation of royal rule functioned, but also in which it increasingly failed to control the real state of affairs in the kingdom.

The geography of order

The audience at Jones's and Jonson's first documented masque, *The Masque of Blackness*, saw an opening scene which portrayed 'a *Landtschap*, consisting of small woods, and here and there a void place fill'd with huntings' (169–70: 24–5). The masque was a way of performing concepts of order and disorder, and the visual topic employed to do this issued a clear message about the spaces of order and disorder under the monarch's jurisdiction. The portrayal of a hunting scene evidently pandered to James's favourite pastime – one which generally took precedence over affairs of state, to such an extent that the king spent as little time as possible in London, preferring his houses at Newmarket and Royston and the opportunities for hunting afforded by the surrounding countryside. In the initial stage curtain painting, a hunt shows nature ceding to the presence of human culture; hunting emblematizes the monarch's mastery of the environment under royal power. Hunting for James was very literally a function of royal control: on the days when he returned successfully from a hunt, the king was jolly and happy to devote himself to perusal of state papers, but when the quarry had escaped him, he would return home morose and lock himself away in his chamber in a black depression. Hunting, then, could be seen as a manifestation of James's egotism and conviction that the world, whether natural or human, was made to obey his will. The numerous plaques erected in the forest around Royston marking the places where the otherwise pacific monarch had slain a deer or a stag were a further expression of this royal will to spatial mastery.

The entire structure of the masque revolved around the notion of establishment of order in spaces of natural disorder. *The Masque of Queens*, which followed on the heels of the preceding *Masques of Blackness and Beauty*, commences with a malevolent geography of disorder, disharmony and death, occupied by crooning witches:

> 1. CHARME [sings]:
> *Dame, Dame*, the watch is set:
> Quickly come, we all are met.
> From the lakes, and from the fennes,
> From the rockes, and from the dennes,
> From the woods, and from the caues,
> From the Church-yrds, from the graues,
> From the dungeon, from the tree,
> That they die on, here are wee.
>
> (284: 53–60)

The rhyming couplets (reportedly James's favourite verse form) constantly reinforce the impression of inverted nature and the association of the hags with that malignant natural environment. This is the landscape which is posed against the ordered landscape of imposed royal control, epitomized for instance in the hunting scene of the previous masque. Of course, the imposition of such aestheticized order entailed a degree of poetic licence which carefully elided less attractive aspects of royal practice. These representations of nature under the beneficent control of the king ignored the mundane, decidedly un-ideal results of James's passion for hunting – namely, the fact that the king's hunting parties caused considerable damage to the rural landscape, destroying crops and impoverishing the local area upon which the royal retinue was parasitic.[4]

The clearest manifestation of James's will to spatial mastery was his aspiration to reunite Scotland and England as Great Britain. In the early years of his reign, James was pleased to call himself Emperor of Great Britain, abandoning this practice, however, as it became increasingly clear that his ambitions for union would not be successful. The project was blocked by Parliament, and was not realized until a century later.[5] The putative achievement of union was, however, a prominent feature of inaugural encomiums and entertainments upon James's accession,[6] and was celebrated early on in the *Masque of Blackness*, in the form of a newly resurrected 'Britania': 'With that great name BRITANIA, this blest Isle | Hath wonne her ancient dignitie, and stile, | *A world, diuided from the world*' (177: 246–8). In this flattering praise of the king's aspirations, Britania was seen as bringing together the constituent parts of the British Isles in a harmonious whole. Other plays of the period also echoed this notion, *Cymbeline*, for instance, declaring that the ancient kingdom of 'Britain's a world | By itself' (3.1.12–13). The union of the three countries made it a discrete territory, compact, complete, possessing clearly delineated borders which, with the advent of the peace that James made with Spain in 1604, after decades of war, were no longer threatened by invasion. But the fact that James's hoped-for union of England and Scotland would not be fully ratified until a century after his accession to the throne underlines the fact, once again, that the spatial mastery which he assumed to be one of his attributes was largely a fiction.

It is perhaps for this reason that the masques constantly insist upon reasserting spaces of conquest, repeatedly *producing* the mastery which James wished to believe was already a *fait accompli*. The masques, particularly during the early years of James's reign, were clearly divided into two sections, first, an antimasque, in which elements of disorder were paraded, only to be swept from the scene in the second component, that of the subsequent main masque. The structure of the masque is thus one of a simple binary opposition, antimasque/masque, reducing the world to clear couplings of moral values and their negation. Whether belonging to the disorderly antimasque or the orderly masque, the values represented there were clearly identifiable in their moral allegiance: Iron-age presents itself in *The Golden Age Restor'd*, calling forth its accomplice 'Euills': Avarice, Fraud, Slander, Ambition, Pride, Scorn, Force, Rapine, Treachery, Folly and Ignorance respectively (422: 30–45); in *The Masque of Beautie*, the elements of beauty are paraded in the same way: Splendor, Serenitas, Germinatio, Laetitia, Temperies, Venustas, Dignitas, Perfectio, Harmonia (186–9). Such easily identifiable moral values made the masque an agonistic form which displayed the triumph of good over evil, of order over chaos, implicitly pointing to the monarch as the ultimate agent of cosmic coherence. In *The Golden Age Restor'd*, Pallas quells the mutineers of the iron age without even needing to do battle with them: 'Hide me, soft cloud, from their prophaner eyes, | Till insolent rebellion take the field, | And as their spirits, with their counsels, rise, | I frustrate all, with shewing but my shield' (422: 25–9). The binary structure of the masque is inevitably conflictual in character, with one-half of the opposition eliminating or eliding the other half.

The temporal structure of the masque is also a spatial structure. This is so in two main ways. First of all, the temporal structure is clearly a hierarchy, with the lower orders of Evil being conquered by the higher orders of Good. Having called up the forces of malevolence, Iron-age then proclaims:

> We may triumph together,
> Vpon this enemie so great,
> Whom, if our forces can defeat,
> And but this once bring *vnder*,
> Wee are the *masters of the skyes*,
> *Where all the wealth, height, power, lyes*,
> The scepter, and the thunder.
>
> (422: 47–53; my emphasis)

The vertical indices of hierarchy are clearly visible and work to reinforce the pervasive early modern notions of social hierarchy of which the monarchy embodied the pinnacle. Of course, the attempt at rebellion, that is, to overturn the natural hierarchy of Good over Evil, to bring disorder into the established (vertical) order of things, is unsuccessful. This vertical hierarchy and its reiterated assertion is evident in countless masques.

Secondly, the agonistic structure operates on a horizontal axis as well. The negative values performed in the antimasque are swept from the stage in the main masque section. The masque offers an idealized view of the Jacobean kingdom in which territorial control of a fictional microcosm of the kingdom is played out. The figures of Evil take the stage only in order to be all the more effectively eradicated, their place being taken over by the metaphorical figures of Good. The masque represents a bloodless war for control of a fictional but tangible space, leading to an absolute victory. The geography of order is clearly reinforced, not only by the spatial configurations of the antimasque/masque dichotomy, but also by the rigid vertical and horizontal hierarchies implied in the structural oppositions of the masque.

The monarch as centre of the masque

Crucial to the masque and generator of the hierarchized spatial structures enumerated above, is an instance qualitatively separate from its stage-based universe: that of the monarch himself. The court masque was essentially a centripetal system with the King as its centre. This centrism was a tangible figure of the political system of absolutist monarchy concentrated at court.[7] Thus John Hampden said of the monarch: 'He is the first mover among these orbs of ours, and he is the circle of this circumference, and he is the centre of us all, wherein we all as the loins should meet. He is the soul of this body, whose proper act is to command.'[8]

In the *Masque of Blackness*, this centrism is confirmed by the journey to Britain undertaken by the drama's Ethiopian princesses. Discovering that their unparalleled black beauty has been challenged by the ladies of a land lauded by the poets, they are 'now blacke, with blacke despaire' (174: 164). In a vision, however, they are told to seek this land upon which the sun never sets, and whose name ends with 'Tania' – Britannia. Their search is rewarded by their arrival in the realm of Albion, literally sailing into James's court on a large cockle-shell. Thus England is confirmed as the luminary centre of the world: the direction of flow of action is exclusively towards Albion. In this drama, there is no trace of the centrifugal drive to exploration and conquest typical of the Renaissance; rather, the world's movement is one of centripetal attention to this imagined centre of the universe.

Similar vectors of centripetal discovery were at work in *Oberon*, where the outward force of James's fame results in the centripetal force of the masquers' journey towards the seat of the monarch's rule, culminating in their arrival on the masque stage. In *Oberon*, James is explicitly named as the gravitational centre of the masque universe:

> Melt earth to sea, sea flow to ayre,
>   And ayre flie into fire,
> Whilst we, in tunes, to ARTHVRS chayre
>   Beare OBERONS desire;
>   Then which there nothing can be higher,
> Save *IAMES*, to whom it flyes:
> But he the wonder is of tongues, of eares, of eyes

Who hath not heard, who hath not seene,
Who hath not sung his name?
The soule, that hath not, hath not beene;
But is the very same
With buryed sloth, and knowes not fame,
Which doth him best comprise:
For he the wonder is of tongues, of eares, of eyes.

(351: 300–13)

The centripetal movement underpinning the masque – from an outer world towards the monarch as centre of the masque universe – remained even when, later on in James's reign, the structural dichotomy of the masque became more complicated. Thus in the masque of 1624, *Neptune's Triumph*, the centripetal operation remained. In this drama, it was Prince Charles's and Buckingham's return from a futile mission to Spain in 1624 to gain the Infanta as future queen, which was to be celebrated: 'By this time, the Island [upon which the masquers are seated] hath ioynd it selfe with the shore: And *Proteus, Portunus and Saron*, come forth, and goe vp singing to the State, while the masquers take time to Land' (693: 361–5). The masque glosses over the reasons for the *departure*, as the unsuccessful mission represented both a humiliating failure of James's policy, and one which in any case was deeply unpopular with the English people: Parliament even went as far as to formulate a petition requesting that Charles be married to a Protestant princess. Rather, it is Charles's *return* to England, and the attractive force of the crown as centre of the kingdom, which is stressed by the drama. The masque performs the movement from periphery to centre, manifestly propelled by the gravitational force of the monarch's central position in the hall in the seat of state, for clear political reasons.

To complement these centripetal structures, the court masque made use of important images of solar eminence. In the *Masque of Blackness*, Jonson selected from a wide range of names for the sun, alternating his terminology to construct a sequence (or dramatic syntax) which becomes a solar history inevitably leading towards the motivating force of the dramatic universe of the court, James himself.[9] The '*Sunne*' initially grants his favours upon the Ethiopian ladies, guaranteeing the permanence and quality of their hue. This status goes unchallenged in a primeval phase of history, the audience is informed, the Ethiopians being the first people created on earth (Jonson includes a classical reference in the margin of his text to substantiate his claim) (173: 138ff). Subsequently, it is Phaeton's movement around the globe which displaces the unique status of the Ethiopian ladies, to their great dismay (174: 155ff). Finally, this progression of solar bodies culminates in 'Sol', who presides, apparently, over Great Britain:

> *... where bright* Sol, *that heat*
> *Their blouds, doth neuer rise, or set,*
> *...*
> *To comfort of a greater* Light
> *Who formes all beauty, with his sight.*
>
> (175: 190–5)

This then becomes the goal of the Ethiopians' travels towards Albion. Further information is given subsequently, when we learn that Albion is 'Rul'd by a Svnne, that to this height do grace it, | Whose beams shine day, and night, and are of force | To blanch an Æthiope, and reuiue a Cor's' (177: 253–5). Thus the permanence of the Ethiopian colour is questioned by the displacement of the primeval sun for this most recent sun, that of Albion.

The play upon the sun, connected with allusions to the erudite light of the King's learning (Britannia is 'Rul'd by a Svnne' whose 'light scientiall is, and (past mere nature) | Can salue the rude defects of euery creature' [177: 253, 256]) becomes itself a flattering meditation upon the royal person, easily able to recognize himself in the range of symbolic interpretations which he was wont to weave around his own person. When, for example, on his procession south from Scotland upon his accession to the English throne, James was surprised by a sudden rainstorm in Berwick, he redeemed the situation with an impromptu interpretation of the event, endowing the elements with symbolic attributes: the rainstorm was a good omen, the sun before the rain represented his happy departure, the downpour the grief of Scotland, and the succeeding fair weather the joy of England at his approach.[10]

To allude to James as the sun was to make him the prime motor and cause of perhaps what was the most striking aspects of the court masques in the eyes of contemporary spectators: the astounding display of lights engineered by Inigo Jones through his use of massed candles and coloured liquids. The comments made by members of the Venetian embassy quoted at the beginning of this chapter are typical of spectators' wonder at the masque's deployment of light. The conflict of light and darkness was a standard trope, for instance, in the *Masque of Beauty*:

> When *Loue*, at first, did mooue
> From out of *Chaos*, brightned

So was the world, and lightned,
As now! *Eccho*. As now! *Ecch*. As now!
Yeeld, *Night*, then, to the light,
As *Blacknesse* hath to *Beautie*;
Which is but the same duety.
It was for *Beauty*, that the World was made,
And where she raignes, *Loues* lights admit no shade.
Ecch. Loues lights admit no shade.
Eccho. Admit no shade.

(190: 281–92)

Thus the conflicts of the masque were played out, symbolically, in the very tangible terms of light and darkness, while the darkness of the evening hall and the array of light provided the immediate material signifiers for the moral logic of the masque.[11] The temporal 'now' in this song was also a concrete allusion to the spatial 'here' of the court performance, 'brightned' and 'lightned' to a dazzling degree.

In the text of the *Masque of Beauty*, the reader is told that 'the *Throne* whereon they [the Masquers] sat, seem'd to be a Mine of light, stroake from their iewels, and their garments' (189: 253–4). The stage throne, with its transformed Ethiopian ladies, now successfully blanched, alludes clearly to the throne opposite it in the middle of the performance hall, the seat of state where James and his retinue sat watching the masque. The royal throne in the hall was implicitly the seat of illumination in the intellectual sense of the word, for James was renowned for his erudition and learning, for his 'light scientiall' (177: 256). But light is also used in the concrete visual sense. In *Love's Triumph* the hall is '*by the splendor of your rayes made bright*' (737: 72), and in *Love Restored* the performance hall is lit up by 'the vertue of this Maiestie, who proiecteth so powerfull beames of light' (382: 194–5). In a real sense, the King was the source of the light in the masque, as he was the motivating force behind the masque production, its very condition of possibility; the masques were executed by royal command (frequently at the bidding of Queen Anne). Thus when in the masques the King was deemed to be the source of light and harmony, this was not meant as an idle metaphor. Rather, reinforced by the often 'stunning' or 'blinding' effects of light, these claims alluded to the important role of light in Renaissance cosmologies. Neither corporeal nor immaterial, light served as an intermediary between the corporeal concrete world of nature and the incorporeal world of spirits, attributing to the monarch a position between the realms of heaven and earth.[12]

However, the fictional, diegetic movement from an outside world towards the court as centre of the masque universe, and the implicit construction of James as solar source of the 'derived' lighting effects of the masque were complemented by a far more concrete form of royal centripetal representation in the masque, namely, that of the transgression of the stage space and the approach towards the King's seat of state. In the *Masque of Beauty*, there is clearly a spatial progression, from the outward realms of darkness, towards the central source of light, the monarch. This progression is inaugurated by the movement from a stage curtain representing a scene of night towards a brightly lit scenery piece representing the masquers on an island: '*Here, a curtaine was drawne (in which the* Night *was painted,) and the* Scene *discouer'd, which … I deuised, should be a <n> Island floting on a calme water. In the middest thereof was a seat of state, call'd the* throne of beautie, *erected: diuided into eight squares and distinguish'd by so many* Ionick *pilasters. In these* Squares *the sixteene* Masquers *were plac'd by couples*' (186: 161–9). The sombre curtain, an allusion to the *Masque of Blackness* which provides the prior action of the story, is peeled away to reveal the scene of the Masquers re-beautified. With each successive stage in the dramatic progression, the stage–audience separation is abolished a degree further, thereby intensifying the proximity of the transcendent order thus revealed – culminating in the masquers' descent from the stage to mingle with the other members of the court.

Transgression of the masque stage-space

In this moment of climax, at which the masquers left the stage to engage in dances with selected members of the court audience, the sense of theatre was abolished, the identity of fictive and real worlds was affirmed, and the masquers moved from the realm of neoplatonic ideas into the social reality of the court.[13] What is striking about the symbolic operation of the meeting of fiction and reality is that it was achieved by spatial means. The masquers left one space and entered another.

The masquers were inserted into the fiction, embellished by the wondrous effects of the dramatic mythology, and then 'revealed' in their true identity (though this was probably known all along by the audience). The overall mechanism worked to place members of the court within a heightened and flawless fictional microcosm, and then to allow this fiction to flow back into the larger context of the court. The King was alluded to diegetically or by elements within the masque, such as the island, the display of light or so on, but remained strictly outside the masque-world; he formed the pole of attraction which drew the masquers out of the masque-world back into the world of the court. And at the end of the performance, selected members of the masquing team would complete the centripetal movement towards the King, physically pointing up the union of the idealized masque world and its principal mediator in the world of the court. Orazio Busino, chaplain to the Venetian Embassy, reported in 1618 that at the end of *Pleasure Reconciled to Virtue*, 'When the performance of these twelve accomplished knights was completed, after they had overcome the sloth and drunkenness of Bacchus with their prowess, the Prince went in triumph to kiss his royal father's hands, by whom he was embraced and warmly kissed';[14] and Daniels' *Tethys' Festival* records the closure of the masque with the sudden appearance of '*the Queen's majesty in a most pleasant and artificial grove, which was the third scene, and from thence [the masquers] march up to the King, conducted by the Duke of York and noblemen, in a very stately manner.*'[15]

The centripetal vector of movement towards the King thereby achieved the definitive bridging of the gap between the fiction of the masque world and the court reality. Jones's architectural stage-scenes can thus be understood as passages through which the masquers passed on their progress towards the monarch; Jones's continuing work on the perfection of illusions of depth would appear to confirm this preoccupation with an axial perspective representation of distance from and proximity to the monarch.[16] Whilst the masquers cross the boundary from fiction back into court reality, the King is both implicated in but outside the masque world, its very condition of possibility as figured within the masque, but also its semi-divine correspondent here on earth.

The masquers' traversal of the threshold to the dancing floor culminated in their inviting their ladies to join them in an *extended* masque world, one made up of pattern and harmony. As the dances come to an end, a surprised Prometheus fears that the dancers intend to return to their masque world, but the chorus assures him that 'Sure each hath left his heart | In pawne to come againe, or els he durst not start' (417: 256–7). Nature, moreover, bids the masquers stay on the dancing floor, to refine their pleasures with a kiss, and the Chorus adds: 'No cause of tarrying shun, | They are not worth his light, goe backward from the Sun' (417: 266–7). Abruptly the axis of attraction dancing-floor/masque-world has been reversed into an axis dancing-floor/sun (that is, the King). In this way, the centre–periphery hierarchy according to which the masque world is initially privileged over the here-and-now of the court, is exchanged for a new centre–periphery hierarchy. Now, however, the same attractive power of Ideal values is anchored in the royal box, before which the masquers and their partners are urged to tarry. The last couplet harnesses the primacy of the Ideal world of the masque to create its equivalent in the Sun-King as embodiment of Platonic ideals and knowledge: those who 'goe backward from the Sun' 'are not worth his light' (417: 267), for now the solar-centric monarch makes his court take priority over the fictional space of the masque-world previously created on stage.

The preoccupation with such Platonic knowledge shows that the transgression of the masque's stage-space had an educative value. *Pleasure Reconciled to Virtue* gives, in one of the songs, a clear exposition of the function of the dances which sealed the fusion of masque and court spaces. The dances were to provide a visual expression of seamless harmony of intellect and bodily accomplishment which offers a concrete embodiment of pleasure and virtue, beauty and discipline:

> *Then, as all actions of mankind*
> *Are but a Laborinth, or maze,*
> *so let your Daunces be entwin'd*
> *yet not perplex men, vnto gaze.*
> *But measur'd, and so numerous too,*
> *as men may read each act you doo.*
> *And when they see ye Graces meet,*
> *admire ye wisdom of yor feet.*
> *For Dauncing is an exercise*
> *not only shews ye mouers wit,*
> *but maketh ye beholder wise,*
> *as he hath power to rise to it.*
>
> (488–9: 261–72)

The dance is a visual, spatial embodiment of transparent grace and complexity, a pattern which educates the viewer, and persuades him to elevate himself to the same moral standard. Dancing is a sort of spatial rhetoric which exerts a beneficent influence upon the spectator. The dance, accompanied by a song text which elucidates it, can be seen as a microcosm of the operation of the masque as a whole. The visual element is complemented by the verbal text, thus embodying the reconciliation of various domains of aesthetic activity and their didactic presentation to a receptive audience who is to be transformed by the educational experience. The dance is seen as an artistic performance which says something about the performer (*not only shews ye mouers wit*) but which also includes the spectator in its powerful effect (*maketh ye beholder wise,* | *as he hath power to rise to it*). The dance was the point at which the actor/spectator division was consciously and deliberately abolished, so as to enable the transmission of divine-royal knowledge to the privileged group of spectators.

For this reason it is significant that the masquers, though clad in sumptuous finery, were not disguised to the point of being unrecognizable to the audience; their identity and position in the social hierarchy remained visible through the costumes and the symbolic roles[17] – what Campion in *The Lord Hay's Masque* termed 'their feigned persons'.[18] Of the masquers in *The Masque of Beauty*, the text explicitly mentions that the steps to the throne are 'couered with a multitude of *Cupids* (chosen out of the best and most ingenuous youth of the *Kingdome*, noble, and others) that were the *Torch-bearers*' (188: 232–3). Effective disguise was evidently in no wise an aim of the masque text, nor of the masque performance itself. The function of costume was not to make the masquers' true identity unrecognizable, but rather, to supplement it with a new dimension.

The metaphorical process which transformed Prince Henry, say, into Oberon, necessarily had to be susceptible of lateral displacement, otherwise the transfer of the masquers into the world of the court would not have been possible, and would not be perceived as the tangible transport of court personalities back into the nether-world of the court, bringing aspects of the ideal world with them. Thus the metaphorical operation achieved on the illusionist masque stage had to be supplemented by a metonymic movement which brought the masquer back into the here-and-now of performance, allowing the courtier's true identity and place within the court hierarchy to remain visible. A metaphor which completely obliterated its vehicle would lose the effect of the combination of the two elements: in the metaphor, tenor and vehicle must always remain to some extent distinct, so that neither the contrast between them nor the process of superposition is lost. It is for this reason that Limon's suggestive contention that the court is drawn into the masque fiction, such that its members play themselves, the masque audience thus being transformed into stage character impersonating court hierarchy, is unhelpful: for it tends to reduce the masque to a single metaphorical action, whereas the metonymic operation was crucial to the success of the symbolic transformation undertaken by the masque.[19] The masque functioned around a pre-programmed and largely transparent dialectic of disguise and revelation, a dialectic, moreover, which was thoroughly spatialized, so that metaphor was always already in the process of slipping over into metonymy. The anchoring of the fictional world of the masque in the concrete context of the court also occurred through the operation of deixis. Deixis anchors the fictional world of the drama in the here-and-now of the theatrical performance, and was of course an inherent part of the court masque as of any other theatrical performance. 'CHROMIS, MNASYL, None appeare? | See you not, who riseth here?' demands the first Satyr, in the very first lines of *Oberon* (341: 1–2), centring the incipient action of the masque in the *here* of the moon's rising and his own witness of that event, a double dramatic entry which crystallizes the masque universe in a place awaiting the arrival of further characters.

But there is also a second order of deixis at work in the court masque which anchored the fictional universe not only in the immediate place of performance in the broader sense, but in the more specific context of performance which was the Jacobean court. Thus the Silvane addresses the fairies and elves:

> Then let your nimble feet
> Tread subtle circles, that may always meet
> In *point* to him [James]; and figures, to expresse
> The grace of him, and his great empresse [Anne].
> That All, that shall to night behold the rites,
> Perform'd by princely OBERON, and these knights,
> May, without stop, *point out* the proper hayre
> Design'd so long to ARTHVRS crownes, and chayre.
>
> (353: 361–8; my emphasis)

It is significant that here the indexical function of deixis, *verbal pointing* which operates to link dramatic action and the place of performance, is foregrounded.[20] The spectators are assisted in the task of situating the fiction in the context of performance by the verbal 'pointing-out' at work in the characters' dialogues. Thus the deixis of the court drama explicitly anchored the ideal deities of the masque world (Arthur, his queen, and Oberon) in the here-and-now of the social topography of the court. Eternal, ideal identities are thus implanted in the temporal, specific place of the court, making the idealistic fiction tangible by attaching it to personages in the court. This form of deixis radicalizes and extends the functioning of dramatic deixis as it is usually understood, so that it takes on the supplementary referential valences sketched out in the previous chapter, thus pointing to the context of performance.

This radicalization and extension of deixis takes place in two ways. First, the fictional character is inserted into an 'I' or a 'here', into a concrete bodily identity or place, without, however, that real identity being erased by the fiction. On the contrary, in the court drama reference to the place of performance is progressively intensified. It is important that the audience do not forget that Oberon is Henry, that this is Whitehall, and that the political context of performance – the *hic et nunc* of the drama – is the Stuart dynasty, for the whole purpose of the masque is to invest these royal personages with idealized value.

This masque deixis radicalizes and exceeds the customary functioning of theatrical deixis in a second way. To anchor the attributes of Oberon in the person of Prince Henry is to remain, spatially speaking, within the space of the stage performance; whereas to point to James in his seat of state and to plant the character of Arthur in his person is to transgress the limits of the performance space altogether, and to anchor a fictional identity in the identity of the monarch, who never numbers among the masquers. This form of monarch-oriented deixis constitutes a radical transgression of the performance space, drawing the fiction over into the real context of performance. The dancing which occurred when the masquers descended from the stage and danced with other courtiers, sometimes taking off their masks and merging with the audience, was also part of the deictic operation, embedding the fictional world within the court in its entirety.[21]

This idealization of the court carried out by the masque-deixis seems however to have become increasingly problematic as the Jacobean reign advanced, and as the conflicts within the court, and between monarch and parliament, became increasingly visible. The early masques began in an antimasque other-world, culminating in idealized Whitehall. In this later phase, the masque commenced in a burlesque antimasque court-world and progressed towards an idealized pastoral masque-world. Orgel suggests that the shift of the position of the pastoral from the antimasque to the main masque, after 1616, may be explained by the need to find a fictional site more easily idealizable than the increasingly resistant here-and-now reality of the court. The pastoral culmination of the later masques served to cover over conflicts in the monarch's entourage with a pastoral setting expressing only the most benign aspects of absolute rule.[22]

Evidently the 'syntax' of the masque structure was highly problematic. A further aporia was the referential reach of the fictional masque universe. Where were the limits of the possible worlds to which it made reference? To what extent did the masque refer to the world outside of the court, that is, to the real kingdom of James I? There was a clear transition from Elizabeth's public processions and open-air entertainments in which she voluntarily assumed the leading role, to James's much more exclusive indoor court masques, with a concomitant removal of the landscape to the banqueting-hall, and the loss of much of the tangible symbolism of the natural environment which had allowed Elizabeth to present herself as being actively involved in the creation of her realm.[23] The antimasque does include rare hints of the outside world, Mercurie in *Mercurie Vindicated* claiming to 'haue ouer-heard one o' the *Artists* say, Out o'the corruption of a Lawyer was the best generation of a Broker in suits' (414: 170–1). Such sneering references served principally, however, to keep the outside world at bay.

In general, however, the relationship between court and kingdom as it was presented in the masque was one in which the monarch was placed within a one-way vector. James conceived himself as a beacon for his people, but he himself did not look at them; he received their adulation, but did not respond, as in his frigid and reluctant participation in his own triumphant procession through the ceremonial arches erected in London for his accession. James had written for his son in *Basilikon Doron*, 'If then ye would enioy a happy raigne, | Observe the Statutes of your Heuenly King';[24] much the same upward gaze towards a Divine King, without the hint of a corresponding downward acknowledgement, was expected of the people of the realm. The court masque translated this attitude into images of divine grace bestowed from above upon the monarch and transferred in turn to the masquer-courtiers mixing among the aristocratic and diplomatic audience. The masque constituted a closed-circuit universe to a great extent excluding the world outside of the banqueting hall.

The contamination of the masque world

However, the court drama increasingly blurred the ostensibly hermetic divisions between inverted antimasque-world and idealized masque-world. As James's reign went on, the dramas tended to betray the intimate links between, rather than the implacable opposition of antimasque and masque. At the end of the antimasque of the *Masque of Queens*, the text records a typical transition – if it can be rightly called thus – from anti-masque to masque:

In the heate of they^r *Daunce*, on the sodayne, was heard a sound of loud Musique, as if many Instruments had giuen one blast. W^{t}h w^{c}h, not only the *Hagges* themselues, but they^r *Hell*, into w^{c}h they ranne, quite vanishd; and the whole face of the *Scene* alterd; scarse suffring the memory of any such thing: But, in the place of it appear'd a glorious and magnificent Building, figuring the *House of Fame*, in the vpper part of w^{c}h were discouerd the twelue *Masquers* sitting vpon a Throne triumphall, erected in forme of a *Pyramide*, and circled w^{t}h all store of light. (301–2: 354–63)

There is a radical caesura ('quite vanishd … scarse suffring the memory of any such thing') between antimasque and masque, between hags and masquers. Orgel suggests that there could be no gradual progression from masque to antimasque, for the dramatic structure necessary to achieve such a progression would imply interaction and conflict between the two sites and moral states of disorder and order, of evil and good, of darkness and light. There could be no meeting, no dialogue between the two halves of the masque structure, and it was for this reason that the transformation had to be so abrupt and apparently unmotivated.[25]

The antimasque was both banished from the world of the masque, yet paradoxically, necessary for its existence. In the *Masque of Queens*, the one exception to this erasure of the antimasque from the stage is the later display of the bound hags before the queens' chariots (314: 715, 719). Subsequently, *Perseus'* or *Heroique Virtue's* speech (302: 367ff) claims this victory can never be reversed. Yet it is reiterated here as a means of demonstrating the power of *Virtue*, as if that superiority would become insubstantial without an opponent enabling its continual restatement. Similarly, attributes attached to the devilish dance of the hags recur in other parts of the masque: for example, 'a *magicall Daunce*, full of præposterous change', is an index of the destructive power of the unnatural hags and of their attempts to overturn the natural order and the eternal Ideals which it reflects (301: 345), whereas elsewhere the word 'change' is used with a strongly positive value, connoting complexity and skill on the part of the dancers, as in the *Masque of Beauty*, where the text records a 'most curious *Daunce*, full of excellent deuice, and change' (191: 320–1). This dramatic interdependence of ostensibly diametrically opposed terms figuring in the antimasque and masque alike has a curious technical counterpart. The sudden transformation of the antimasque world of disorder into the masque world of harmony and perfection was often effected by the use of the 'machina versatilis', a rotating two-sided scenery-flat which allowed a rapid exchange of one perspective scene for another.[26] (On occasions, as in *Tethys' Festival*, Jones also used three-sided, triangular *periaktoi* which offered the possibility of two scene-changes within the course of the performance.[27]) Thus the perspective scenery for the opposed masque segments were simply the recto and verso sides of a single scene mechanism, and thus inextricably linked to each other. Jones had two repertories of stage pictures: on the one hand, images of nature untamed, tempests, stormy seas, flaming hell scenes, wild forests; on the other hand, images of earthly and cosmic harmony, elegant piazzas and palaces in the classical style, the safety of a port, the beauty of a garden.[28] Once these polarized repertories are seen as two sides of the same 'machina versatilis', however, the element of opposition must be strongly relativized.

Similarly, at the level of the dramatic action, the court masque was characterized more and more by the reappearance of elements of the antimasque in the midst of the masque. At the very end of *Neptune's Triumph for the Return of Albion*, the cook reappears on stage announcing, 'I have another seruice for you, Brother *Poet*, a dish of pickled Saylors, fine salt Sea-boyes, shall relish like *Achoues*, or *Caueare*, to draw downe a cup of *nectar*, in the skirts of a night.' The sailors and the poet put in a brief word before the '*Antimasque* of Saylors' begins (699: 517–31). Here, antimasque and masque alternate; the antimasque of sailors is intended to display James's naval might ('See yond', his fleete, ready to goe, or come, | Or fetch the riches of the *Ocean* home' [698: 510–1]), but does this in the register of the burlesque antimasque rather than that of the elevating and decorous masque. The spaces of antimasque and masque, of comic foil and encomium appear to have become quite interchangeable by this stage of the development of the court drama.

At the same time as the erosion of the barriers between antimasque and masque, the erosion of the barriers between masque world and the reality outside is also visible. The first stage in this erosion is that of the emergence of the court as the focus of the antimasque rather than some fictional pastoral setting. In *Neptune's Triumph*, the cook concocts an antimasque made up of court intrigues, catering to an audience, he says, 'Such as doe relish nothing, but *di stato*' (689: 245). Epitomizing such *di stato* titbits, the masque plot, the tale of Charles and Buckingham's pointless journey to Spain in the hope of gaining the Infanta's hand, and their return to England, recounted in mythical guise by the poet to the cook, is effectively absorbed into the antimasque section (686–7: 130–74). Ironically, it was typical staple of such court gossip, the conflict between the quarrelsome Spanish and French ambassadors, which prevented the mask being staged. Ultimately, there can be no banishing of the antimasque world from the world of the masque, as the world of the court furnishes the place of performance of the masque. The primacy of the real context – the Banqueting Hall itself – overruns the fictional place of the drama. The antimasque did not merely allude to real conditions at the court; it was, physically, situated there. This gives credence to the cook's bombastic rejoinder to the offended poet: 'Sir, this is my roome, and region too, the banquetting house. And in matter of feast, and solemnitie, nothing is to be presented here, but with my acquaintance, and allowance to it' (682: 24–7). Increasingly, the antimasque was not a mere subsidiary foil to the idealism of the masque; rather, the masque was parasitic and dependent upon the antimasque, the former having its very condition of possibility in the latter.

This later mode of portrayal of the court, although customarily kept within the bounds of the antimasque, had more to do with the grotesque 'realism' of Jonson's city comedies than with the idealism of the earlier masque. Mercury in *Mercurie Vindicated by the Alchemists at Court* says: 'It is through mee, they ha' got this corner o' the Court to coozen in, where they sharke for a hungry diet below staires, and cheat vpon your vnder-Officers, promising mountaines for their meat, and all vpon *Mercuries* security' (411: 68–72). This racy speech is a manifestation of the conflicts at court which the masque surreptitiously articulates only to erase them with the pastoral. Likewise, where earlier masques could relegate change and instability to a world of disordered nature, *Mercurie Vindicated* has Vulcan pleading: 'Precious golden *Mercury*, be fixt; be not so volatile' (410: 25–6). Volatility and impermanence have entered the court. Inadvertently, references to such volatility, for example to the 'change' marking court dances, gave expression to the fact that court identity constantly needed to be reaffirmed; the power politics of court society involved constant wrangling for preferment, and success as a royal favourite was by no means permanent.[29]

Instability was rife in the life of the court. In *Cymbeline*, Shakespeare recounts Posthumus's promising but short-lived debut as a member of the king's bedchamber in the opening scene. The dramatist goes on to couch roller-coaster careers at court in clearly spatial terms: 'the art o'th' court, | As hard to leave as keep, whose top to climb | Is certain falling, or so slipp'ry that | The fear's as bad as falling' (3.3.45–8). By 1610, the date about which this play was probably first performed, the court had evidently already gained a public reputation for the mercurial fate of its aspirant members – which did not prevent Shakespeare borrowing from the masque the strange mythical interlude in which Jupiter descends and declares that Posthumus will, after an initially ill-fated career at a fictional court, gain Innogen's hand (5.5.187–207) – a resolution of that lord's misfortunes which is redolent of the fairy-tale conclusions of the Jacobean court performances.

In a more satirical vein, *Mercurie Vindicated* covertly alluded to the sales of honours and titles. If below stairs various forms of disreputable alchemy were being practised, above stairs was characterized by more refined forms of alchemy: 'Marry aboue here, Perpetuity of beauty, (doe you heare, Ladies) health, Riches, Honours, a matter of Immortality is nothing' (411–2: 92–4). From 1611, when the order of baronets was invented simply for the purpose of selling these titles – such was the desperation of the impecunious monarch – the market for aristocratic titles burgeoned, until the demand was saturated, with a consequent devaluation of the rank in question. A baronetcy was originally on sale for £1,095, but by 1622 the price had dropped to £220. The sale of honours is presented in a ridiculous manner in *Mercurie Vindicated*, so that the accusation is not directly aimed at actual practices; and it is James himself who is instituted as arbitrator in clearing up this malpractice; none the less, the more serious practices mentioned alongside beauty and health were practices of favouritism encouraged by James himself.[30]

Other aspects of the antimasque would have been all too readily identifiable by spectators as facets of court life. In the antimasque of *The Fortunate Isles*, Jonson had a gullible student Mere-Fool taken in by the alluring mythology of the Rosicrucians. James was vigorously opposed to the Rosicrucians in the 1620s for their apocalyptic, mystical thought, and their links with radical Protestantism.[31] Yet what the melancholy student Mere-Fool is offered, the award of offices at the Court of Ovtis, is redolent of the corruption and trafficking of offices at the Jacobean court:

> The Farme of the great Customes,
> Through all the Ports of the Aires Intelligences;
> The Constable of the Castle *Rosy-Crosse*:
> Which you must be; and Keeper of the Keyes
> Of the whole *Kaball*, with the Seales; you shall be
> Principall Secretarie to the Starres.
>
> (712: 131–6)

Despite Jonson's having couched these guarded criticisms of court practices in the veil of a religious sect James detested, some allusions within the antimasque of the Court of Rosy-Cross may have come dangerously close to that of James. Whence the proleptic apology: 'Great King, | Your pardon, if desire to please haue trespass'd' (722: 435–6).

Thus, by a stroke of irony, reversing the order of the masque (beginning with a scurrilous antimasque court and proceeding to a purified mythical pastoral setting) meant that the entertainers presented the court to itself in all its worldliness. The seedy court of the antimasque increasingly contaminated the pastoral idyll of the masque, so that the foregrounding of the court's corruption was never entirely out of sight. The earlier masque deixis which situated the fiction of the idealized masque world in the here-and-now of the court was gradually replaced by a rather less comfortable form of dramatic deixis which ran very close to the wind, in political terms, and demanded that the concluding masque be couched in safely pastoral language.

Inevitably, the emphasis upon the court as a place of worldly transactions and political scheming pushed the dramatic image of government back into the wider world, abolishing the hermetic separation from the realm manifest in the earlier court masques. There is little evidence that the masque was genuinely concerned with the realities of the kingdom. The masque appeared to insulate the monarch from his people, and was seen by contemporaries such as Arthur Wilson, writing retrospectively in 1653, to 'wrap up' the King's spirit 'and keep it from descending towards earthly things', rather than making 'the beholders wise'.[32] If the court masque was at times concerned with political events, it was principally with a view to keeping at bay unpleasant political realities such as unrest and incipient popular political participation – and not in order to provide political answers to the problems concerning the mass of the people in Jacobean England.

The most we see of the real kingdom is usually through the filter of the antimasque. In *For the Honour of Wales* three Welshmen (as in *Cymbeline*, it is Wales which is presented as the real counterpoise to the ideal world of the court), Griffith, Jenkin and Evan, stand before the mountain Craig-Eriri with the intention of presenting themselves at court, and reel off a punning speech crammed with Welsh place-names, from Abergavenny and Aberconway, through Caerleon and Cardiff, to Llanmouthwye (503: 172–83). This antimasque scene creates a colourful verbal canvas in which the linguistic and geographical margins of the kingdom resonate at the centre of the realm. Significantly, the Welsh interlude replaced the mythical Hercules-antimasque of *Pleasure reconcil'd to Vertue* performed earlier the same year, offering instead of an overly ribald classical context, a less offensive glimpse of Britain's exotic margins.[33]

In *Newes from the New World*, in a rare exception to the intention of political isolation at work in that masque, the abolition of the court/kingdom distinction is dramatized with particular force in the opening of the drama, where for the first time, we hear of the 'common people' and 'their pleasure in beleeving of lies are made for them, as you have in *Paules* that make'hem for your selves' (515: 52–5).[34] The common folk and the aristocratic patrons of Paul's Walk are brought together in their common activity of gossip-mongering and information-gathering (albeit with a view to discrediting their subversive interest in current political affairs). Moreover, what links these two segments of the English population is not only a shared thirst for news, but a shared network of news transmission. The masque thus foregrounds, perhaps unintentionally, the operations of information circuits, which effectively connected the various parts of the country, the capital and the provinces, with increasingly intensive relays of communication. In the opening scenes of *Newes from the New World*, a factor newly arrived at court, in conversation with a printer and a chronologer, describes his business:

> Gentlemen, I am neither Printer, nor Chronologer, but one that otherwise takes pleasure i'my Pen: A Factor of newes for all the Shieres of *England*; I doe write my thousand letters a weeke ordinary, sometim<e> twelve hundred, and maintaine the businesse at some charge, both to hold up my reputation with mine owne ministers in Towne, and my friends of correspondence in the Countrey; I have friends of all rancks, and of all Religions, for which I keep an answering Catalogue of dispatch; wherein I have my Puritan newes, my Protestant newes, and my Pontificiall newes. (514: 33–43)

Here an England traversed by the peregrinations of political information intrudes into the masque's solipsistic politics of representation.

This is astonishing, in the rarefied and idealized version of the court presented in the masques performed until this date. All the distinctions upon which the society of the day was based, and which culminated in the sense of superiority dramatized in the court's sealed-off distance from the realities of everyday life in the kingdom, and even more so in the monarch's distance both from his people and the parliament, are blurred, though not abolished, in the factor's speech: 'Towne' and 'Countrey' (and implicitly, as the place of the conversation is the Court, that spatial instance of power as well); all social ranks (as evident in the meeting of the common people and gentry at Paul's Walk noted above); and opposed religious persuasions. News was a business, and mercantile interests during the Renaissance had always been prone to leap over political and religious divisions in order to maintain trade links; such forces drove the ubiquitous distribution of exotic goods and innovative knowledge across the Renaissance world.[35] This economically driven transgression of boundaries and flattening of hierarchies (political power, social rank, religious merit) was, however, radically foreign to the world of the masque, and it is a sign of profound disturbance that such transgression could penetrate even into the antimasque representation of the corrupt court. This process of economic expansion is a spatial process: 'And I hope', says the printer, 'to erect a Staple for newes ere long, whether all shall be brought, and thence againe vented under the name of Staple-newes; ... Newes, that when a man sends them downe to the Shieres where they are said to be done, were never there to be found' (514–15: 45–51). This dynamism diegetically penetrates into the provinces; performatively, it has already invaded the sealed world of the court masque.

As the Jacobean period went on, court drama was increasingly pulled in two directions: on the one hand, towards the perfection of reified myths which constructed the monarch as the embodiment of classical virtues, and on the other hand, towards a complicated engagement with versions of a tarnished reality which the masque could none the less not afford to admit openly. The masque was thus torn between representations of two varieties of social space: on the one hand, perfect but reified spaces of celestial order and harmony, and on the other hand, unruly spaces of human activity whose nether-world dynamism was driven by forces radically foreign to the heavenly ideals underlying the geometrical perfection of visual classicism. The ideals of political harmony and stability were increasingly fraught in James's realm as his reign went on; it is the turbulent spaces beyond the court as they were represented in the Jacobean theatre which constitute the subject of the remaining chapters of this study. In particular the King's financial problems occasioned the increasingly acute political conflicts of the first half of the seventeenth century. Typically, the exorbitant cost of the Whitehall masques were a visible target for critics of the Jacobean court. Criticism concerning financial recklessness arose out of varying opinions regarding the appropriate manner of ruling a kingdom. But such criticism was also symptomatic of the massive significance of money in increasingly undermining traditional, hierarchical notions of society. It was the relentless advance of an emerging capitalism which was primarily responsible for radically transforming the early modern period's spatial representations of its world.

3
The Dumb God: Money as an Engine for Mobility

Exchange on the space of the stage

The Jacobean court masque strove to create a fictional universe of royal mastery far from the realities of early modern England. But questions of money tended to break relentlessly into the charmed world of the masque – whether in the form of allusions to court corruption, or in disparaging comments about the commercial world without. But what does money have to do with space, and with stage-space? The grand old man of spatial theory, Henri Lefebvre, asked this in his classic study on the 'production' of space: if the basic social form at the heart of Marx's *Capital* is exchange, how can this central economic concept be employed to elaborate an analysis of matters such as space and of the production of space?[1]

One answer would seem to be that any exchange, involving the movement of the entities exchanged between at least two if not more partners, entails in some form or another a spatial structure based upon reciprocal abundance and lack in opposed places. As Edward Misselden said in his 1622 treatise on *Free Trade*,

> it hath pleased God to inuite as it were, one Countrey to traffique with another, by the variety of things which the one hath, and the other hath not: that so that which is wanting to the *one*, might be supplied by the *other*, that all might have sufficient.
>
> Which thing the very windes and seas proclaime, in giuing passage to all nations: the windes blowing sometimes towards one Country, sometimes towards another, that so by this diuine iustice, euery one might be supplyed in things necessary for life and maintenance.[2]

Exchange only arises with the necessity of obtaining an entity which one lacks at the price of another, and thus implies communication between different regions, across varying distances.[3] Not only the products moving between distinct places, but the places of production themselves are subject to the rules of rarity, value and exchange.

In sharp contrast to the reified and idealized spaces presented in the court drama, the Jacobeans lived in a society in which the constitutive spaces of everyday life were permeated by the influence of economic transformation. In the early modern period, physical space became increasingly commodified: more and more previously communally used land became privately owned; the development of cartography arose out of the increasing tendency to delimit, measure and value land in terms of market worth; and merchants' homes came to be seen as an extension of the commercial shop space; when Coke coined the phrase 'the house of an Englishman is to him as his castle', it was in legal defence of the privacy of the domestic realm, which was increasingly the object of state surveillance in the interests of market regulation, as more and more English artisans' houses also became their workshops during the sixteenth and seventeenth centuries.[4] To the extent that exchange and commodification are spatial operations, they lent themselves to representation upon the stage, as shown above, a primarily spatial and visual form of representation. This was all the more so that the novel space of the early modern playhouse was itself the result of a drive to commodify the theatre product: the playhouses arose out of an attempt to exploit more effectively the paying-power of spectators by enclosing the audience space.[5]

This affinity between the stage and representations of exchange was even more pronounced in the Jacobean theatre for the simple reason that it was a theatre which depended utterly upon the expansion of the money economy. That the playhouses sprang up in London was partly a function of the rapidly growing size of the city's population which made a professional theatre financially viable. In particular the influx of a large and wealthy aristocratic population to the nation's capital fostered various forms of conspicuous consumption, of which the thriving London theatre was a prominent manifestation. The dramatists themselves were part of this radical upsurge of production and consumption, generally lower- or middle-class men who through university or, like Shakespeare, grammar school education, rose to positions of prominence – Shakespeare becoming successful enough, significantly, to buy his father a coat of arms.[6] The dramatists represented a vanguard of literary artists able to break free for the first time from noble patronage and sell their wares on the open market, financing their theatrical enterprises by joint-stock ventures, even though a semblance of aristocratic protection was maintained. The age saw large numbers of professional writers without patronage producing a substantial body of secular, urban literature (ballads, plays, pamphlets and satires) published in the wake of the failure of traditional moral ideologies, and linked to the flourishing publishing trade and the new dynamic theatre.[7]

In this context the theatre was itself a consumer product, an integral part of an emerging capitalist economy. Keynes is reputed to have said that England obtained Shakespeare when it could afford him – presumably meaning that Shakespeare could develop only in a commercial theatre, and that a commercial theatre could flourish only when there was sufficient surplus wealth to pay for it.[8] One Jacobean commentator observed of theatregoers: 'Yea many of them in their hearts [are] willing to consume many Patrimonies, yearely spending many pounds on these vaine representations.'[9] Jonson described the theatre as a 'commodity' (*The Alchemist*, 'To the Reader'), while Robert Wilson's *The Three Ladies of London* declared: 'Then young and old come and behold our wares and buy them all. | Then if our wares shall seem to you well woven, good and fine, | We hope we shall your custom have another time.'[10] Typically, the theatre itself was envisaged as a market-place by Dekker in *The Gull's Horn-Book*: 'The theater is your Poets Royal Exchange, vpon which their Muses, that are now turned to Merchants, meeting, barter away that light commodity of words for a lighter ware then words: *Plaudites*.'[11]

In this chapter it is argued that the theatre explicitly referred to its own place within the money economy, and was receptive to and articulated the strong sense of change brought about by the transformations of that economy. It is generally accepted that the emergence of the capitalist economy was the principal motor for the cultural and social upheavals of the Renaissance, which in turn unleashed momentous transformations of social and political space;[12] the theatre played an important social role, alongside complaint literature, for instance, in articulating the extent, pace and qualitative feel of such transformations through its plot and performance innovations. To what extent the theatre was able to offer solutions to the strong sense of insecurity provoked by those disturbing transformations – the stage being an important element in that generalized spatial restructuring of early modern English society and thus not removed from the issues it was addressing – is a difficult question to answer, as the theatre's stance on the very transformations which brought it into being was necessarily a highly ambivalent one. This chapter begins by examining two spatial aspects of the money economy: on the one hand, money and spatial mobility, and on the other, space, cost and acceleration. Subsequently, it will scrutinize the imbrication of the stage itself in the very spatialized economic processes which it could not help but portray. Finally, it will be shown that the theatre enacted its own implication within economic processes by dramatizing the difficulty of keeping everyday life separated from the influence of the money economy.

Money and spatial mobility

In some early modern writings, the merchant's eagle-eye for opportunities for trade becomes an active geographical force. John Wheeler's 1601 *Treatise of commerce* displays a generative textuality propelled by the endeavours of the Merchant Venturers, doggedly accumulating place-names and creating a texture of Northern European towns: the enumeration of the geography of Flanders passes through Bridges (Bruges), Middelbourgh, Antwerp, Bergen op Zoom, moving up into North Germany, and subsequently reverts to a further enumeration of 'the partes, and places which they trade unto, … the Townes, and Portes lying between the rivers of *Somme* in *France*, and *Scawe* in the Germane sea.'[13] Behind the immense mobility of the merchant's panoramic gaze is the far-reaching dynamism of trade itself. Wheeler claims that 'in a woord, all the world choppeth and chaungeth, runneth and raveth after Martes, Markettes, and Marchandising, and passe into Trafficque … in all times, and in all places.'[14] The terrific alliterative drive enacts the increasing span of economic activity: the triad moves from a pluralization of sites of commerce ('Martes, Markettes') to the final dissipation of place into process ('Marchandising'), culminating logically with the unlimited 'in all times, and in all places'. This dynamic progression thus dramatizes the gradual erosion of the bounded market-place during the early modern period described by Agnew, and the increasing intrusion of the market into everyday life. Whereas commerce was originally contained and regulated in the market-place, the particular place was subordinated more and more to the 'placeless' process which ranged itself around the place.[15] By virtue of its ubiquity, the money-based exchange economy increasingly left its imprint upon all aspects of social interaction.

At a period in which theoretical writing on the money economy was in its infancy, only developing significantly in England towards the end of the Jacobean era,[16] the theatre was one artistic medium which attempted to explain, albeit in narrative rather than analytical form, the all-pervasive influence of the market. This explanatory function was important for early modern people who experienced the transformation of markets *in medias res*, in a situation where the functioning of the new economic mechanisms became increasingly intangible and invisible for members of society.[17] Agnew has argued that the Renaissance theatre did not merely reflect changes in commercial capitalism, but rather, both modelled and materialized these relations.[18] Unpacking his statement, one might add: modelled, to the extent that it implicitly claimed to offer insights into the functioning of the economy which could otherwise only be experienced passively and with a sense of perplexity; materialized, to the extent that the theatre was constituted, borne along by and thus intimately involved with the very changes it pretended to explain.

It is no surprise, then, to find this ubiquity of the market everywhere alluded to in Jacobean drama. The apparently limitless extension of exchange mechanisms is shown in miniature in *The Merchant of Venice* through the play's tentacular chains of lending and borrowing. Bassanio would like to borrow from Antonio, but as Antonio's wealth is already fully invested in his maritime projects, he allows his credit to be used as security on a loan which Antonio receives from Shylock, who in turn is himself unable to raise the sum of 3,000 ducats, and thus avails himself of Tubal's assistance (Act 1, Scenes 1 and 3). A related 'placelessness' of the market, in the sense of the transgression of the boundaries of the market-place or market-hall, can be seen in Trinculo's eagerness to turn his capture of Caliban to profit, even when stranded on a desert island.[19] Likewise, in Jonson's 1620 masque *Newes from the New World*, a herald accuses a printer of being 'some dull tradesman … that thinke there's nothing good any where; but what's to be sold' (514: 12–14). The ubiquity of the market is bewilderingly forceful when an euphoric Sir Mammon thinks of seizing not only lucrative metals, but also of the regions bearing those metals – and then proposes their conversion into other locations which similarly stand metonymically for wealth: 'Yes, and I'll purchase Devonshire and Cornwall, | And make them perfect Indies!' (*The Alchemist* 2.1.35–6). The very fabric of the land is metaphorically loosened by the power of acquisitive mercantilism, a sentiment not unfamiliar, albeit in less exotic form than that proposed by the delirious Sir Mammon, to those dispossessed of their land by the expansive accumulation of property pursued by large land-owners. Under the pressure of the 'everywhere' of commercial interest, specific places and the social loyalties they embodied became 'nowheres'. Thus Middleton's ploughman in *Father Hubburd's Tales* complains: 'Now was our young master with one penful of ink doing a far greater exploit than all his forefathers; for what they were a-purchasing all their lifetime, he was now passing away in the fourth part of a minute; and that which many thousand drops of his grandfather's brows did painfully strive for, one drop now of a scrivener's inkhorn did easily pass over; a dash of a pen stood for a thousand acres: ... it seemed he made no more account of acres than of acorns.'[20] Similarly, Massinger has the avaricious Luke in *The City Madam* exclaim, 'Here lay | A manor bound fast in a skin of parchment, | The wax continuing hard, the acres melting' (3.3.35–7). Economically driven mutability made land a fluid commodity.

The logic of exchange is thus clearly a spatial logic, and a dynamic one. It is not by chance that money is referred to by the term 'liquid', with its capacity to move from one place to another in ways that goods can not. Money made economic activity more flexible, efficient, and faster, by standing in for a part of the traditional exchange of kind, thus inserting additional links into the process of exchange and extending its expanse.[21] Money takes the place of something else, replaces the real spaces taken up by unwieldy objects of barter, thus conveying spatial flexibility upon the moneyed subject, whose coins represent the compact potential for the purchase of something elsewhere. Just as it stores values as the basis for exchange, money also stores space.[22]

By replacing one commodity within the act of exchange by a piece of metal, it converts not only the commodity which it buys, but also the commodity which it replaces (the syntagmatic and paradigmatic axes of the exchange respectively), into something quite different, thus inaugurating a powerful process of transformation. Edward Misselden, in his 1623 treatise entitled *The Circle of Commerce*, defined exchange as the '*Permutation* of any one thing for another: whether it be, *With mony* or *Without Mony*. *With Mony*, when either Merchandize is exchanged *For mony*, or *Mony for mony*. The former of these is called *Buying and Selling*, for mony is now become the price of all things, which from the beginning was not so. ... And so by degrees all things came to be valued with mony, and mony the value of all things.'[23] As early as the mid-sixteenth century, J. Price in *A discussion on the coinage* (1553) declared that 'money is the common measure of all things that are vendible.'[24] Money's voracious potential to reduce everything to its own common denominator had deep spatial implications. The exchange process was potentially unlimited, opening onto an infinite world of objects, as money could figure as an exchange-equivalent for almost everything. Such liquidity became a commonplace on the stage. The character Rock, in Webster's *A Cure for a Cuckold*, neatly exemplifies this notion in announcing: 'Ha, ready money is the prize I look for, | It walks without suspition any where, | When Chains and Jewels may be stayed and call'd | Before the Constable' (2.2.86–9). 'Keep nothing that is transitory about you', Face orders the submissive Dapper in *The Alchemist*, and proceeds to strip the unfortunate victim of all his loose coinage, thus performing the volatility of money in its infinite transmutability into other commodities (3.5.30). Soldiers, according to Flamineo in Webster's *The White Devil*, earn 'a poor handful, | Which in thy palm thou bear'st, as men hold water; | Seeking to grip it fast, the frail reward | Steals through thy fingers' – this fluidity is so all pervasive that he can claim, along with his companions to have 'poured ourselves | Into great fights', human labour itself becoming an ethereal, volatile quality not unlike money (3.1.44–50).

Money is frequently attributed an almost kinetic energy to produce spatial translations. 'These Moors are changeable in their wills', Iago advises Roderigo in *Othello*: '– fill thy purse with money', thus translating the malleability of his victim's will into the fluidity of gold, and in turn into his own intended social mobility; for Iago's avowed goal is 'To get his [Othello's] place' (*Othello*, 1.3.346–7, 385). In *Volpone*, gold is apostrophied as 'thou son of Sol | (But brighter than thy father)' (1.1.10–11). Hence, money possesses the power to invert habitually stable hierarchies of value:

> Dear Saint,
> Riches, the dumb god that giv'st all men tongues,
> Thou canst do nought, and yet mak'st men do all things;
> ...even hell, with thee to boot,
> Is made worth heaven!
>
> (1.1.21–5)

Money achieves the transformation of heaven into hell, the utter inversion of the cosmic hierarchy of the Christian universe. Here the ordered and value-laden arrangement of space is inverted by a force which renders value arbitrary. Economic value is the prime mover which drags all other forms of value in its wake.

Money's ability to stand in for other commodities, replacing one half of a commodity–commodity exchange with a purely symbolic value, resulted in a sense of the evaporation of the materiality of goods. This notion of the ephemeral quality of the monetary part of the exchange extended even further when both elements of the exchange were purely symbolic. Already by the mid-sixteenth century there was a thriving market in the exchange of notes of credit, the so-called 'bills of exchange', with fairs at Besançon from 1536, and from 1579 at Piacenza, devoted almost entirely to the trading of credit notes among the representatives of the main trading companies and banks.[25] The market for currency exchange was also developing rapidly, as Thomas Mun remarked with some concern in 1621:

And for the exchanges of money, vsed betwixt Nations, although the true vse thereof, is a very lawdable and necessarie practise, for the accomodating of Merchants affaires, and furnishing of Trauellers in their occasions, without the transporting of Coyne from one State to another, wiuth danger and losse, both to the publique and private wealth; yet is the abuse thereof verie preiudiciall vnto this Kingdome in particuler; whilest in the interim the benefit doth arise vnto other Countries, who diligently obseruing the Prizes whereby the monies be exchanged, may take advantage ... For in respect the prizes of the Exchanges, doe rise and fall according to the plentie or scarsitie of money, which is to be taken vp or deliuered our, the exchange is thereby become rather a Trade for some great moneyed men, then a furtherance and accomodation of reall Trade to Merchants, as it ought to be in the true vse thereof.[26]

Here, money's power to reproduce itself at will is seen to be a logical but perverse outgrowth of its capacity to transform other products into its own likeness. This was ground for considerable worry in the Renaissance, for through its novel and disturbing power to replicate itself, money was considered to usurp the naturally created order. Usury was one prominent focus of concern about the unnatural characteristics of money, with Bacon summarizing a common attitude: 'it is against nature for money to beget money.'[27] The acquisitive desire for gold was thought to be unnatural and a transgression of the natural state of things.[28] The actors were not immune from this execration of usury as usurping natural processes of production, as their relatively profitable profession was deemed to be based upon 'play' rather than upon an honourable form of work, thus constituting a 'lazy' trade like usury, to cite another early modern commonplace of money-lending.[29]

The functioning of the money economy showed that anything could be converted into a monetary value, thereby losing its inherent value as a distinct and unique product. Exchange appeared to become less and less a material process. Value increasingly came to be seen as being measured not by inherent worth, but by the arbitrarily fixed exchange-value, governed by the laws of rarity and supply/demand. Significantly, in 1574 the French economist Jean Bodin had proposed a theory of the relative worth of goods, rejecting concepts of a just price based on the notion of an intrinsic worth in favour of the view that prices represented the relationship between money available and goods available.[30] Writers such as Gerard de Malynes were violently opposed to the increasing influence of these ideas in England at the beginning of the seventeenth century.[31] Yet as late as the mid-1620s, Malynes and Misselden conducted a debate over the nature of money, in which Malynes claimed that the weight and purity of coin determined values, so that prices should be dictated by intrinsic money value and set by royal authority: 'This is to be done onley by his Maiesties Proclamation, according to the aforesaid Statues and Proclamation of exchanges, prohibiting that after 3 moneths and ensuing the same, no man shall make any exchanges by Bills or otherwise, for moneys to be paid in forreine parts, or to be rechanged towards this Realme vnder the true *Par* or *value* for *value* of our moneys ... which shall be declared upon a *paire of Tables* vpon the *Royall Exchange in London.*'[32] Against this centralized and static notion of the value of money within the kingdom and beyond its borders, Misselden claimed that exchange was based upon commerce in money, in goods, or in both, values being fluid and anchored in local practices: 'it is the plenty or Scarcitie of Commodities, their vse or *Non-vse*, that maketh them rise or fall in price.'[33] This liberation of market-value from intrinsic value is illustrated, well in advance of such theoretical debates, in *Troilus and Cressida*:

> *Troilus*: What's aught but as 'tis valued?
> *Hector*: But value dwells not in particular will.
>   It holds his estimate and dignity
>   As well wherein 'tis precious of itself
>   As in the prizer.
>
>   (2.2.51–5)

Troilus represents the more innovative standpoint, Hector that of the traditional conception of intrinsic worth. In the experience of importing goods from overseas, the notion of intrinsic worth also came under pressure. Exotic goods that the explorers and traders brought back to their homeland from overseas gained value precisely by virtue of their distant origin – their rarity, and not an intrinsic utility, made them valuable. The Indian shells, the costumes fit to 'provoke the Persian', the perfumes of 'gums of Paradise, and Eastern air' with which Sir Mammon plans to deck his imagined harem (*The Alchemist* 2.2.72, 91, 94), or the exotic birds that Volpone offers Celia as enticements towards a liaison with him (parrots, nightingales, peacocks, 'estriches', phoenix – *Volpone* 3.7.202–4) are indices of wealth because obtained far away – and within the context of the play, entirely illusory and insubstantial. Here, free-floating value is entirely separated from use-value and coupled to the new mobility of the expanding early modern markets.

This extraordinary reach and corrosive potency of the market meant that its effects pervaded the subtlest interstices of social relations. Social place, so intimately connected with geographical location in early modern England, could equally rapidly become volatile under the influence of money. In *The Surueyor's Dialogue*, John Norden had a farmer protest, 'You prye into mens tytles and estates, vnder the name (forssooth) of Surueyors, whereby you bring men and matter into question often times, that would (as long as they haue) lye without question. And oftentimes you are cause that...customes are altred, broken or sometimes perverted or taken away by your meanes.'[34] Norden clearly identified (ironically, within a text which was instrumental in that process) the disturbances of old patterns of social relationships embodied in the land, relationships abruptly become prey to the 'place'-destroying measurement, valuation and commodification of land. Changes in the structure of the agricultural economy forced poorer farmers from the land, which in turn often passed into the hands of City merchants working to accumulate landed property. William Harrison noted in his *Description of England* (1577) that merchants 'often change estate with gentlemen, as gentlemen do with them, by a mutual conversion of the one into the other.'[35] 'Mutual conversion', with its overtones of fiduciary exchange, indicates the spatial transformation of social identity under the corrosive influence of economic forces. Likewise, a poem by Robert Copland revealed disquiet at the fact that

> Marchant men trauell the countree,
> Ploughmen dwell in the citie,
> Which will destroy us all shortlie,
> As will be seen in hast.[36]

Copland's concern arises out of the apparent ease with which such mercantile mobility can occur, thus disturbing notions of the 'right' place of various social identities. Such conversion of rural identity for an urban, or indeed a court identity, is dramatized in Tourner's *Revenger's Tragedy*, in a scene where Vindice espouses the conversion of ostensibly useless virginity into social capital, employing the metaphors of rural dispossession to give weight to his arguments. The supposedly unproductive wealth of the pure and virginal countryside ('green fore-parts', 'fair trees') are reworked, by an aggressive and violent process of 'cutting' to become

'Fair meadows', dispossessed and enclosed. The fixity of contours of country society, conceived as a bastion of traditional community ethics, is destabilized by images of social mobility: 'farmers' sons agreed...To wash their hands and come up gentlemen', thus abandoning their link to the socially and economically nurturing soil; and 'Tailors ride down' to 'measure'em [the property deserted by farmers moving up or down the social ladder and away from their land] by the yard', thereby symbolizing the commodification of landed property. In this process of dispossession and transfer, 'All thrives but Chastity', who, in old-fashioned prudishness, refuses to surrender her hidden wealth, thus impeding economic growth and damaging not only her own prospects in abstaining from participation in the market, but also 'The commonwealth', which otherwise 'has flourished ever since' (2.1.217–26).

A frequent trope of attacks on the conversion of land into liquid wealth was that of the exchange-of-land-for-clothes. In 1620 John Williams preached a 'Sermon on Apparel' in which he thundered against gentlemen who sold up their estates in order to purchase the fine clothing necessary to make an impression and gain favour at court. In the passage just quoted from *The Revenger's Tragedy*, 'Fair trees...Are cut to maintain head-tires' (2.1.224–5). And in *Every Man out of his Humour*, Ben Jonson ironically advised a city gallant newly arrived from the land: 'at your first appearance, t'were good you turned foure or fiue hundred acres of your best land into two or three trunks of apparel (you may doe it without going to a coniuror)' (1.2.40–3). The conversion of landed estates into elegant finery symbolizes the conversion of a set of social obligations and relationships constructed around the mutually binding ethical values of the land-owning classes and their local commoners, into mere appearance and self-serving ambition. The values of 'stewardship' and social responsibility are cashed in for values of ephemeral self-interest.[37]

The putative communitarian social values embodied in the fabric of a rural community whose focus was the land-owning gentry estate were also under attack from another quarter. As James I became more and more pressed for money, he not only created, but also began to sell aristocratic titles, traditionally connected to a place and a set of responsibilities for a local community. In turn, he discovered that the right to nominate persons for the lucrative award of knighthoods could also be put to good profit and be sold to his courtiers. James buried his former indignation at the sale of knighthoods and began to distribute the right of nomination among his courtiers. From them these rights passed, like stocks and shares, into general currency among London financial speculators, so that in 1606 Lionel Cranfield could buy the

making of six knights from his friend Arthur Ingram for £373. 1s. 8d.[38]
A market which dematerialized the status-symbols of aristocratic land-ownership and place-bound feudal rights and duties produced some odd paradoxes: there were, for instance, practical difficulties in finding enough places to which to attach the titles. One sceptical buyer who had acquired an Irish earldom discovered such a scarcity of places not already occupied by an earl that when the authorities at last found him a vacant town he felt it necessary to send a servant to check that it actu-ally existed.[39] When a Scottish gentleman in Jonson's *Eastward Ho!* declares 'I ken the man weel, hee's one of my thirty pound knights' (4.1.178), there is a double reference, on the one hand, to the devalua-tion of honours and titles, their dislocation from traditional landed identity, and on the other, to the prevalence of favours handed out to James's Scottish compatriots at court, to the fury and resentment of the native English courtiers who felt that their privileged domain was being usurped by foreigners.

In the face of this undermining of the value of social place, other spa-tial parameters gained in acceptance as markers of stable value, the best known being oppositions such as city/country or court/country.[40] The country stood for a scale of values ostensibly out of reach of mercenary acquisitiveness. When Lord Owemuch alias Follywit pretends to be robbed during his stay at Sir Bounteous Progress's country house, the offended guest aggrievedly demands, 'Is this the courtesy o'th' country, Sir Bounteous?' (*A Mad World* 2.6.35–6). Lord Owemuch's question both reposes on the idea of the country as the place of still intact values of hospitality, while, by the same token, through the mercenary and cyn-ical exploitation of disguise, enacting the dynamic solvent power of the market which such notions were supposed to thwart. Thus the theatre was a powerful indicator of the disturbing spatial changes wrought in society by the ubiquity of the money economy.

Space, cost and acceleration

While the Jacobean drama often bemoaned the spatial mobility, dis-continuity and transformation of the new money-dominated market, it also was able to portray with great acuity such profit-driven dynamism. In *The Merchant of Venice*, Bassanio opens his petition to Antonio for financial assistance with an anecdote of his youthful pastime of shoot-ing practice: if one arrow went astray, he would shoot another after it, and finding the second arrow, recuperate the first as well (1.1.140–52). His simile is intended to justify his ostentatious investments in raising his status in the eyes of Portia and gaining her heart; Bassanio thus aims to motivate Antonio to fund a further campaign for her conquest. What the simile also reveals, however, is the clear understanding of financial investment not just as a temporal action, but as a spatial undertaking as well: money is invested elsewhere, and then recuperated; it is brought back home, and returned to the obliging backer of the operation. The investment of capital in a potentially profitable enterprise is figured in terms of the distance involved in financial outlay – such distance is thematized from the opening lines of the play onwards with Antonio's ruminations about his commercial and maritime projects, his goods and ships. For Portia's hopeful suitors, she represents an undertaking where the investment of capital is spatialized in the long journeys embarked upon: 'Nor is the wide world ignorant of her worth, | For the four winds blow in from every coast | Renownèd suitors' (1.1.167–9). Bassanio claims that this investment is justified, for he believes that the initial outlay has already been rewarded by the first portents of a later 'return' upon his investments: 'Sometimes from her eyes | I did receive fair speechless messages' (1.1.163–4). Thus the tropes of romantic pursuit and erotic attraction are overlaid with those of financial investment and international trade. Bassanio's romantic undertaking and his considerable investments do indeed bring him handsome returns, underlining the emergent moral imperative of financial mobility which underlies the drama.

The risk inherent in investment means that space can figure not only as a crucial aspect of the commodity to be acquired, but also as a liability to be minimized. In a drama dominated by the fluidity of processes of exchange, immobility, when seen from the perspective of commercial activity, is thus often regarded as a negative factor. In *Michaelmas Term*, Shortyard pretends to object to Quomodo paying off his debts to him in kind – in the form of £200 worth of cloth. Shortyard claims that this 'commodity' is not liquid enough, not easily enough convertible: 'The mealy moth consume it! Would he ha' me turn peddler now? What should I do with cloth?' His scornful 'peddler' stands for a wearisome and plodding form of geographical and commercial mobility implicitly overhauled by more lucrative modes of profit generation. To which Quomodo asserts the mobility (both geographically and in the substance and value) of this scorned wealth: 'There's no merchant in town but will be greedy upon't and pay down money upo'th'nail; they'll dispatch it over to Middleburgh presently and raise double commodity by exchange' (2.3.176–86). None the less, it transpires that this mobility is indeed fallacious: 'The passage to Middleborrow is stopped', meaning that Easy and

Shortyard can no longer dispose of their cloth, thus triggering the next stage of the feathering of Easy (2.3.354) – the debt for the cumbersome and immobilized goods will be transferred onto his person.

Immobility is coded negatively because space becomes assimilated to cost, and to leave space intact is thus to allow costs of production to remain high. Distance is expensive; speed reduces expense.[41] Harvey notes that 'The medieval merchant discovered the fundamental concept of "the price of time" only in the course of exploring space. Because trade and exchange entail spatial movement, it was the time taken up by this spatial movement which taught the merchant to attach prices, and hence the money form itself, to working time.'[42] During the Renaissance, production processes tended, with the development of more sophisticated technology, to become more complex, entailing longer distances between extraction of raw materials, production of goods and eventual sale. The more instantly an exchange could be executed, the more profitable it would become; delays in execution led to soaring costs. In recognition of the pecuniary imperative of spatial-temporal efficiency, the theatre offers examples of frantic profit-driven characters, for example the avaricious, unscrupulous and immensely successful lawyer Harry Dampit in *A Trick to Catch the Old One*: 'Report it, Harry Dampit, a trampler of time: say, he would be up in a morning, and be here with his serge gown, dashed up to the hams in a cause; have his feet stink about Westminster Hall, and come home again; see the galleons, the galleasses, the great armadas of the law; then there be hoys and petty vessels, oars and scullers of the time. … Then I would be here, I would trample up and down like a mule; now to the judges … then to the Hall again, then to the chamber again –' (1.4.40–53). His 'trampling of time' is a strikingly corporeal embodiment of the capitalist drive to compress the time invested in overcoming distance. Dampit is not an attractive character, but his dynamism remains none the less immensely compelling, and exerts a perverse fascination which exactly reflects the theatre's own ambivalence regarding the market in which it thrived and which it also execrated.

Both Quomodo and Dampit are characters condemned by the dramas in which they appear. Yet their accelerated commodification of space is one in which the dramas themselves partake. Evidence of this acceleration can be found not just in individual characters but also in the very plot construction of the plays themselves. Here the spatial dynamism of a Harry Dampit becomes one element of the broader narrative dynamic in which all the characters are caught up, determining the bewildering complexity of their movements on and off stage. *A Trick to Catch the Old*

One displays striking examples of this spatio-temporal acceleration when Witgood and his colleagues are informed, 'One Master Hoard with a guard of gentlemen carried her [the Widow] out at back door a pretty while since, sir' (3.3.79–80); this action, however, has occurred precisely 15 lines previously. Time is contracted at the moment of the seizure of the Courtesan by Hoard's vanguard. This telescoping of time constitutes a bewildering acceleration of the action which Witgood rightly names 'madness' (3.3.85). But Witgood's professions of bewilderment sound hollow, for these rapid spatial shifts are in large part orchestrated by himself with a view to bringing his still sequestered wealth back into his own pocket – and that of the audience into the actors' coffers.

The drama's portrayal of the acceleration of exchange renders the stage ambiguous in a further respect. The dream of eliminating costly steps in the long process of production motivates the enthusiasm for alchemy in Jonson's *The Alchemist*. Alchemy functions in this play as a metaphor for processes of transformation of values which are not bound by the normal limitations of time, distance and work; that is, changes and exchanges of values which apparently defy the resistance customarily posed by legitimate processes of production. The play is about liberation from constraint. *Volpone* also dramatizes a similar attempt to reduce overheads and (spatial) investment, with the protagonist declaring: 'Why, this is better than rob churches, yet, | Or fat, by eating once a month a man' (1.5.91–2). Both church desecration and 'biting' usury (monthly 'eating' of a man) are double movements, involving an outward investment or spatial expedition in order to bring back wealth, albeit with already minimal effort. Volpone's scheme depends upon persuading a series of fawning suitors to shower him with gifts in the hope of recouping a massive inheritance upon his ostensibly imminent death. It eliminates a prior outward-bound investment, bringing in inward-bound wealth simply with the help of a purely virtual outward movement in the future, the inheritance upon which his suitors pin their hopes. Similarly, Sir Epicure Mammon's jubilation at the anticipated attainment of the alchemical short-cut to wealth is based upon a significant analogy between the world of riches and the riches of the New World, where adventurers were drawn by the prospect of huge wealth to be plundered:

> Come on, sir. Now you set your foot on shore
> In *Novo Orbe*; here's the rich Peru
> And there within, sir, are the golden mines,
> Great Solomon's Ophir! He was sailing to 't

Three years, but we have reached it in ten months.
This is the day wherein, to all my friends
I will pronounce the happy word, 'Be rich!'
This day you shall be *spectatissimi*.

(2.1.1–8)

The attraction of overseas voyages to the colonies, as with privateering expeditions, was, paradoxically, that the profits to be made there potentially far outstripped the investment in terms of time and distance covered. Greenblatt comments that the exchange of trifles for native goods of great value was driven by the dream of a quick profit; the Europeans saw these exchanges as transactions in which full signs were exchanged for empty signs.[43]

It is difficult to tell, however, at exactly which point these examples of short-cut investment fall over into what Todorov has called the 'refusal of exchange', where legitimate exchange is reduced to the transgression of exchange.[44] It is the blurred line between increasingly accelerated exchange, which overcomes but also places a value upon distance, and the eradication of exchange, which constitutes one facet of the ambivalence associated with economic exchange as it is portrayed upon the Jacobean stage. For in its images of spurious alchemy and factitious New Worlds, the stage points eloquently towards its own activity. It was, in the last analysis, the stage's particular mode of functioning within the money economy – exchanging fictions for money, admitting paying spectators to a world of illusions – which endowed it with such a degree of ambiguity regarding the processes upon which it depended for its livelihood.

The theatre and the transformative power of money

What is the place of the stage within the processes it portrays? Rather than sagaciously *describing* a process it scrutinizes from an objective distance, the drama *performs*, synecdochically, a process of which it is a part. Exchange and fluidity themselves supplanted the inherent worth of goods or moral positions as an object of meditation, as these stable values were undermined by the increasingly blurred moral categories of fluctuating values of exchange – and this was nowhere more true than in the theatre. It would hardly be exaggerated to say that spectators paid to come and see economic fluidity enacted on the stage.

In an important theory of deixis in dramatic discourse, Elam has underlined the functioning of speech in the theatre as an assertion of the spatio-temporal coordinates (the here-and-now) of the speaker's utterance by means of deictic elements such as demonstrative pronouns and spatial and temporal adverbs. Each theatrical speech-act is a means of defining the speaker's identity as a position taken up within the dramatic world, as in the case of Antony's paradigmatic 'Here is my space' (*Antony and Cleopatra* 1.1.36). Dramatic dialogue is thus an interaction of speaker-positions, and dramatic action accordingly constituted out of switches of 'deictic orientation': 'each time the speaker changes indexical direction, addresses a new "you", indicates a different object, enters into a new relationship with his situation or his fellows, a new semiotic unit is set up.'[45] Dramatic dialogue constitutes what one might term a 'positional economy': dramatic positions, codified in dialogue and made concrete on the stage, are also an integral part of the thrust and parry of economic competition and rapidly fluctuating value. Words are counters of commerce no less potent than money, no less ethereal but equally able to corrode the stolid permanence of their environment by virtue of their multivalency and their openness to dangerous inflation or deflation, or appropriation. A major part of the attraction of the Jacobean theatre was its ostensive performance of the positional economy. The theatre functioned as an accurate spatial and verbal gauge of the mercurial instability of contemporaries' changing financial fortunes.

The intimate relationship between the dramatic positional economy and the money economy is nicely illustrated by an example from Middleton's *A Chaste Maid in Cheapside*. Yellowhammer, upon forestalling the marriage between his much-valued daughter Moll and Touchwood junior, seizes the wedding ring just as it is about to be used to seal the conjugal union which would have snatched his daughter out of his power:

> *Yellowhammer*: I dreamt of anger still, here take your ring sir;
>   Ha this? Life 'tis the same: abominable!
>   Did I not sell this ring?
> *Touchwood Junior*: I think you did, you received money for it.
> *Yellowhammer*: Heart, hark you knight,
>   Here's no inconscionable villainy –
>   Set me aworke to make the wedding ring,
>   And come with an intent to steal my daughter;
>   Did ever runaway match it?
>
> (3.1.35–43)

Money puts exchanges to work provoking circulations which are 'runaways', whose consequences cannot be controlled by those who initiate them. As a popular ballad had it, '*Money is my Master*: | Yet once it was a servant unto mee.'[46] For the ring whose sale profited Yellowhammer's goldsmith's business almost deprives him of his daughter. She, ironically, was intended by him as bait to snare the aristocrat Sir Walter Whorehound and his large estates so as to further enhance the goldsmith's fortune.

Exchange is a process which respects no hierarchies of value except the value of profit. Thus Yellowhammer, whose attitude to his daughter Moll is one of profit (towards the end of the play, the girl's mother, addressing her husband, refers to the daughter as 'your jewel', and her brother Tim compares dying Moll's change in complexion to 'Gold into white money' – 4.2.64; 5.2.20), discovers that his own authoritarian paternalism enters into contradiction with the very same commercial ethos which governs his goldsmith's trade: the free flow of goods turns against his attempt to impose market logic upon his own family. The open market of the larger world unexpectedly invades the 'closed' family domain, which Yellowhammer nevertheless expects to be able to manipulate according to the selfsame principles of the open market. There is a self-defeating attempt to maintain at the same time porous *and* sealed boundaries between the two domains (and the sorts of market forces which rule there).

Significantly, it is the ring, passed previously from goldsmith to buyer (Moll's suitor) and then back to the goldsmith, which is the vehicle of this paradoxical situation. The ring symbolizes the closure and unity of a new family unit, but at the same time the openness of this ostensibly regulated market; it also symbolizes the purity of love whilst embodying the most materially tangible form of wealth and economic value, gold; a ring is habitually a gift motivated by love, but is also the result of a commercial exchange, as Touchwood's dry commentary makes quite clear: 'I think you did, you received money for it.' The ring, as a highly mobile object of value, embodies the fluidity of the new markets. Its circular form symbolizes the unlimited processes of circulation of commodities, and the capacity of market exchanges to transgress the very boundaries individuals set up to protect themselves against the all-too-ubiquitous effects of their own transactions. It is the return of the ring to its original producer at a moment in which his fortune is under threat from several directions which renders tangible the impossibility of mastering the fluidity set in motion by the money economy.

Much of the comedy of the plays is produced by extraordinarily convoluted sequences of successive acts of appropriation, expropriation and re-appropriation. Follywit in *A Mad World* confidently announces, referring to his grandfather who has locked up the grandson's inheritance until after his death, 'I'll pay him again, when he dies' (2.2.37) – Follywit's intention being to 'borrow' beforehand the riches that he is supposed to obtain only after Sir Bounteous's death. Thus he aims to reverse the strategy reserved for himself, and turn it against the older man. Inauspiciously, an overly self-righteous Follywit declares: 'craft recoils in the end like an overcharged musket and maims the very hand that puts fire to't' (3.3.10–11); this is said in justification of his theft of Sir Bounteous's riches, claiming that his grandfather had earned his wealth by similar robbery; such robbery is simply turned against him by his nephew. But the very spatial form of Follywit's statement, that is, its reversibility, is proved true by 'backfiring' upon its enunciator himself. The ethics of money exchange allows no limits to such reversals, such that Follywit – this, of course, is the deeper significance of that character's name – will fall victim to the same process later in the play. It is Follywit's 'in the end' which reveals his inadequate understanding of the processes at work here. There is no 'end' inherent in the amoral pragmatism of the workings of exchange. Once convertibility is set up as a working principle, no value can assert itself as non-convertible, with the result that everything can be drawn into the transmutation of valuation and exchange.

The point at which Follywit decides to abandon his cunning is the point at which he himself becomes victim of another's cunning, in his trust of the alluring Courtesan (Act 4, Scene 5). There is a curious tension in the moment of his passion for the Courtesan: on the one hand the traditional moral values driving the play's condemnation of greed and dissembling is confirmed by Follywit's reversion to moral rectitude; on the other hand, the fact that he immediately falls foul of the combined plotting of the Courtesan and her mother merely confirms the ubiquitous operating of cunning and greed in the play. The subversive counter-moral issued by the parable of conversion is that only the utterly unscrupulous trickster wins at the end of the day. This self-contradicting ethic is repeated, in an intensified form, in the final scene of the play. Follywit and the Courtesan discover each other's true identity (Act 5, Scene 2). Both realize they have been deceived by the other. Frank Gullman, who believed herself finally an 'honest' woman by her pending marriage to Follywit (4.5.137), sees that she is married to a thief (5.2.242), and Follywit in turn discovers that the 'gentlewoman and ... virgin' he has wedded is in fact the common prostitute whom his grandfather has already bedded (5.2.259–69). The respective plotting by the two wits effectively cancels out the other's efforts – although the

Courtesan has the small comfort of being 'beforehand' in her trumping of Follywit (5.2.243).

Sir Bounteous Progress may intone, in the closing lines of the play, 'Who lives by cunning, mark it, his fate's cast; | When he has gulled all, then is himself the last' (5.2.282–3). None the less, it is somewhat disturbing that the final effective principle capable of reversing venal cunning is not the force of good, but an equal and opposite force of venality. Greed appears to have become counter-productive within the dramatic economy of the play – but only by virtue of its universal status. This can perhaps be qualified to some extent by Hoard's statement: 'Who seem most crafty prove oft times most fools' (*A Trick to Catch the Old One*, 5.2.195). The very principle of exchangeability implies that the manipulator of exchanges is himself not immune from the process which he (only ever temporarily) employs. For the process is seen to be larger than the individuals who mistakenly believe they alone wield it. The only limits to the process of reversibility are to be found in the limitations of its users, as Hoard makes clear. Granted, greed and its concomitant cunning, generator of infinite reversals, do appear to possess some self-imposed braking mechanisms: 'Always when we strive to be most politic, we prove most coxcombs; *non plus ultra*' Middleton tells us (4.3.36–7). Yet if it is greed and politics alone which create limits to their limitless operations, this in effect merely confirms greed and politics' absolute domination of the world of action and ethics. Manley comments on this unsettling perspective: 'Based on the farcical logic of exploitation – on the always reversible mechanism of position lost and gained – the plays produce what is at once an exhilarating release from the illusion and fantasies that drive the city's predatory frenzy and an equally dizzying recognition that frenzy is a universal condition.'[47]

Significantly for an art-form generated by the interaction of words and space, the imbrication of words and the money economy became increasingly prominent in Renaissance culture. The exchange of discourse and exchange of wealth blend into each other in Jesuit texts on gold cited by Greenblatt, which then modulate liquidly into discourse on preaching, apparently displaying the convertibility of gold and the Word of God.[48] In Venice, money emerged in a real sense as a means of communication: rather than exchanging real liquid money, the Venetian giro-bank used a rapid and efficient, but presumably unstable, *verbal* exchange of purely theoretical credit and debt values between users' accounts.[49] With the equivalence of words and money, the value of words becomes unsteady. Jonson's description of 'Riches' as 'the dumb god that giv'st all men tongues' (*Volpone* 1.1.22) alludes to the manner by which money, itself being 'dumb', comes to be inscribed by all manner of connotations; in its difference to that which it represents, it can be attributed widely varying meanings and values, just as it is the difference between signifier and signified which makes linguistic meaning possible but also founds its polysemic potential.[50] Money functions by not being that which it represents, a differential status which allows it to stand in for anything.

In a similar manner, words assume an astonishing range of meanings susceptible of almost limitless expansion, to a threatening degree. When Justice Overdo attempts to police irregularities of commercial conduct at Bartholomew Fair disguised as a madman, he is confronted with his own name repeatedly invoked like an incantation by the insane Trouble-All; apparently cut free of his own bodily presence, Overdo's name takes on a metaphysical value: 'I mark no name but Adam Overdo', claims Trouble-All, 'that is the name of names; he is the only sufficient magistrate; and that name I reverence; show it me' (*Bartholomew Fair* 4.6.143–5). Thus the value of words, like money, is never entirely within the control of the user. Words, within the context of the drama, can easily be seized by others and turned against their users, thereby transforming characters' positions within the deictic 'economy' of the play. Ironically, Overdo finds himself accused of theft in terms he himself uses, in his customary judicial role, to prosecute others for their price abuses: 'Mine own words turned upon me like swords' (3.5.213). The language of the Jacobean drama, as a mode of designating valued objects, and itself a currency of constantly changing value, appears to be irrevocably contaminated by instability of value – an instability which is essential to the vitality of the drama. Thus Lamprey assures the Widow alias the Courtesan, on behalf of Hoard: 'He can join land to land, and will possess you | Of what you desire' (*A Trick to Catch the Old One* 3.1.200–1). The commercial transaction is overlayed with sexual connotations, which in turn are endowed with the reversibility of linguistic and commercial exchanges. For to possess is both verb of taking ('He ... will possess you ... ') and of giving ('He ... will possess you | Of what you desire'). Even the semi-sexual offer of 'join[ing] land to land' is ambiguous: whose land will be augmented, and whose land will become a mere supplement to the principal possession? One is tempted to ask who is screwing who, the answer being, of course, in Jacobean comedy, everyone.

Theatre criticism has made much of 'verbal scenery', and the power of words to create place and its atmosphere on the stage, as it were, out of 'nothing'. This 'nothing', while offering the possibility of wish-fulfilment on the stage, also contains the converse potential for deflation. In *Michaelmas Term* Quomodo has the naive country gentleman Richard Easy run up debts he is unable to pay off, thus permitting Quomodo to seize Easy's estates placed as security upon the gentleman's credit. Upon gaining the country estate by these less than legal means, Quomodo celebrates his success with an imaginary dialogue: ' – Whither is the worshipful Master Quomodo and his fair bedfellow rid forth? – To his land in Essex! – Whence comes those goodly load of logs? – From his land in Essex! – Where grows this pleasant fruit? says one citizen's wife in the Row. – At Master Quomodo's orchard in Essex. – Oh, oh, does it so? I thank you for that good news i'faith' (3.4.13–18). This is a rehearsal of Quomodo's newly attained public status as a land-owner, his own words mimicking, or rather invoking, others' words as he would like to hear them – words which advertise his worth and circulate just as money circulates, to the credit of the rich merchant. But this sudden exchange of land against debt, celebrated as *fait accompli* by Quomodo in an extravaganza of deictic self-assertion, is, on the stage, nothing but words, and as such can be equally easily reversed. Very rapidly, Quomodo's proleptic verbal possessions are proved to be no more than vain blustering. Ironically, it is he himself who inadvertently puts his signature to a statement relinquishing all claims to the very lands which he believed now to be his (5.1.105–8). Place created by words can be equally rapidly dematerialized by words as they function within the tight confines of a money economy.

The power of language to work such reversals of position is also seen in action in Portia's performance as the lawyer Balthasar at Shylock's hearing in *The Merchant of Venice*. Portia's defence of Antonio is a brilliant rhetorical exercise which depends upon measuring the precise values of words. Shylock demands justice, in absolute terms, and Portia replies, 'be assured | Thou shalt have justice more than thou desir'st' (4.1.313–14). Once justice is quantified by Shylock's absolute demand for a pound of flesh, which would signify absolute economic triumph over the man who has constantly undermined the usury market in Venice with his infuriating no-interest loans (1.3.41–3), the process of quantification can no longer be contained, and returns against its instigator. Shylock's attempts to fall back upon mere threefold recuperation of his bond fail: 'He hath refused it in the open court. | He shall have merely justice and his bond' (4.1.335–6) – here the 'merely' signifies that what was a supreme value (total financial annihilation of his opponent), has suddenly shrunk, leaving him bankrupt. The very justice which Shylock invokes, and moreover, the intransigence with which he demands it be meted out against Antonio, is subsequently turned against him with the same severity, effectively depriving him of far more than he ever stood to gain.

But this artful reversal of the terms of Shylock's contract of bond achieved by Portia is also a performance in the literal sense of the word which demonstrates that the power of the Jacobean stage to invert verbs and values depends upon its status as fiction. Portia's juggling of verbal value is underwritten by her discourse, for she is not the lawyer she claims to be. Her own discourse is as real *and* unreal as the terms she judiciously weighs up. The deictic position she takes up between the warring parties, but also between their conflicting readings of the wording of bond contract, is no more than a position established merely by the verbal, performative assertion of an identity. Portia's rhetorical stance on the stage is called into existence by her own words: she 'poses' in the sense of 'positing' a newly created position, a situation not yet extant. When Portia says to Shylock, 'thou hast incurred | The danger formerly by me rehearsed' (4.1.358–9), she is ironically referring to the double factitiousness of her own role as male lawyer – a theatrical performance so masterfully brought off that all those present are fooled by appearances. The verb 'rehearse' underlines the fact that the court scene is a drama, at multiple levels: first, before the assembled parties, who enjoy her sparring with Shylock and applaud her expertise at the end; secondly in that she plays a fiction which she is not; and thirdly in that this performance is itself played before the audience of the theatre. The play can allow the 'rehearsal' of alternative scenarios, and the exchange of one (mortal, tragic) for the other (romantic, comic), because it constitutes a fictional world in which chains of events are not bound into irreversible causal sequences.

The play can be seen as a global act of deixis, in which the theatrical event says 'Let hypothetical world, b, c or d exist in real time a_1 and real performance space a_2.' The creation of a fictional world, precisely, is a modelling function, at one remove from the constraints of reality, making possible a degree of flexibility in modes of experience of that world. In a similar manner, money is an abstract 'model' which stands in for an equivalent commodity, from which it is necessarily spatially distanced, thus bringing flexibility into the exchange process, allowing exchange where an equivalent commodity in kind is not immediately available. The theatre exchanges fiction for money, thus condensing two forms of abstracted value, and thereby completing its own implication in the slippery dynamism of economic exchange. Both the theatrical and the money economy are positional, generating exceedingly plastic, indeed unstable modes of participation in social life. Such an equation between the theatrical and the money economies opened up vertiginous vistas guaranteed to destabilize the Jacobean sense of social reality.

One secondary level of deixis accompanying the primary level of deictic dialogue also evinces this commercially-driven mutability: namely, the extraordinary rapidity with which some dramatists carry out scene changes, to the horror of later classically-oriented theatre theorists. The secondary deictic act of asserting 'This is a house/street/palace' is constantly being modified. Rapid and confusing transactions with money transformed everything around into abstract qualities, in an ever-accelerating process of mutation, one which easily escaped from the control of those who initiated it, as William Scott observed in his advice for merchants: 'Velocity doth intangle it selfe: whence it comes to passe, that haste is slowe, an over ardent way in dealing is never without many indiscreet actions and wrongs: Even in play, he that is carried with an eanest thirst of gaming, troubleth himselfe: and the more he troubleth himselfe, the more he loseth.'[51] Such 'velocity' was performed literally in the 'places' portrayed on the stage. The rapidity of scene changes was yet another function of dramatic positional economy at work under the aegis of the ubiquitous and ineluctable convertibility unleashed by the money economy.

Perhaps this is why the theatre, while clearly being motivated by the transformative power of the money economy, from its rapid dialogues through to the constant surprises of its plot structures, also – paradoxically – displayed considerable concern over the accelerated mutability of all things under the pressure of ubiquitous market forces. There was great concern at the collapse of notions of a moral economy of production in the face of the insidious effects of money.[52] Conservative thinking saw the dangerous inversion of the traditional hierarchy of commodity exchange and forms of community as a perversion of the natural order. 'Intrinsic', non-convertible social values supposed to be served by commodity exchange appeared to be assimilated and subordinated to the law of the market. Thus Timon execrates money for its power to corrode moral values and community cohesion:

> Thus much of this will make
> Black white, foul fair, wrong right,
> Base noble, old young, coward valiant.
> …
> This yellow slave
> Will knit and break religions, bless th'accursed,
> Make the hoar leprosy adored, place thieves,

> And give them title, knee, and approbation
> With senators on the bench.
>
> (*Timon of Athens* 4.3.28–38)

From this and similar polemics it is clear that the money economy aroused considerable anxiety among Jacobean commentators by virtue of its capacity to dissolve former stable structures of values, whether economic, social or moral.

The theatre participated volubly in such tirades against the convertibility of time-honoured communitarian moral values into monetary values. But in dramatizing the exchange of organic contexts of life for qualities that seemed, by comparison, relatively immaterial, the theatre highlighted the very process which had permitted its own emergence. Whence the irony of uttering a discourse of moral reprobation in a theatre which was itself a product of the selfsame economic transformations condemned by its actors. More productively, what may appear to be hypocrisy on the part of the fledging theatre enterprise can be also seen as an ambivalent position which allowed a kind of stereoscopic or schizophrenic view of the economic world, both from within and without, a double vision which we have already designated as characteristic of the Jacobean theatre. The theatre thundered against the perversions of the market economy, yet could not extract itself from that economy. In what follows, it will be suggested that the theatre itself dramatized the impossibility, within the emerging money economy, of setting up sheltered spaces out of reach of the power of money, thus performing an active engagement with its own context of emergence.

Spatial-financial ambivalence in the plays

One function of the Jacobean theatre was to make tangible by the act of performance the processes of transformation set in motion by the money economy, processes which spectators could otherwise only experience in inarticulable ways; Agnew comments that the 'theater bestowed an intelligible albeit Protean human shape on the very *form*lessness that money values were introducing into exchange; for such an achievement, spectators were alternately grateful and horrified.'[53] Not only spectators but also dramatists appear to have been torn between fascination and revulsion, between approbation and moral disapproval at the processes which they depicted. Like their audiences, playwrights were involved in a transitional period of history, and were informed by conflicting notions of the process in which they were caught up. As we have seen, some contemporary attitudes resisted and denied the new social trends rather than actively engaging with them. It has been remarked that theories of society are only effective if they are as mobile and dynamic as the forces which they strive to explain and control. Whence the obvious weakness of early modern appeals to traditional morality in the face of insurgent economic forces.[54] In this respect, the Jacobean playwrights appear to have been more versatile. The playwrights were informed by still operative 'residual' social theories which tended to look back to an earlier age of putative organic social organization and stability of values; conversely, however, they were simultaneously enabled and empowered by novel and exciting forces which contradicted all notions of stability and intrinsic value or worth. It is therefore no surprise to find that the plays, albeit with different accents and varied weighting, generally display a profound ambivalence toward the economic processes in which they were embedded.

Typical of this trend is an episode in *The Travels of the Three English Brothers* in which the renowned comedian Will Kemp tells an expatriate English aristocrat in Venice about the latest theatrical events on the London stages, particularly relishing a recent play called *England's Joy* (9.68–71); the play, with its doubtless ironical title, never existed, but the author Richard Venner was able to hoax the audience with plot descriptions at a non-performance in March 1602, taking the door-money and disappearing.[55] The pact made with the paying audience entails that even if the things presented on the stage are illusions, fakes, lies, at least the performance paid for is real; this is the exchange which is transgressed in *England's Joy*, and it is here that the division between an acceptable fiction and an unacceptable fiction lies. The fact that Will Kemp finds this such a witty event, and that the audience to whom the anecdote was told (which may well have included earlier spectators duped by the trickster playwright) are also apparently expected to find it amusing, reveals a curious tension within the theatre's relationship to its own fictionality – a relationship at once clearly disapproving yet at the same time secretly delighted. For a play both is and is not what it claims to be, and an audience which pays to go to the theatre must always reckon on being short-changed in some way or another, as Jonson warned the reader in *The Alchemist*: 'beware at what hands thou receiv'st thy commodity; for thou wert never more fair in the way to be coz'ned than in this age in poetry, especially in plays' ('To the Reader'). Likewise, when the poet John Hall noted that the 'Man in business is but a Theatricall person, and in a manner but personates himself',[56] it would be equally possible to reverse the formulation, deeming the actor to be a businessman conducting his affairs in equally devious and deceitful ways.

The same tension is addressed in Jonson's *Bartholomew Fair*, in which the transgressive exchange is explicitly foregrounded on the stage. The fairs of the Liberties – Bartholomew Fair was held in August in the liberty of Smithfield – were places beyond the normal jurisdiction of commercial control, outside the reaches of the regulation of the clearly defined civic market-place or market hall; tolls and prohibitions against foreigners and 'usury' were suspended, slack book-keeping was common; the boundaries of the fair were much more porous than that of the city market, offering openings to middlemen, peddlers, unlicensed and rural artificers.[57] It is precisely such unlicensed activity that Judge Overdo endeavours to apprehend, disguising himself as a madman in order to better discover commercial malpractice. However, the counterfeit madman, by the very discretion of his presence, effectively contributes to the theft of his own brother-in-law's wallet by a pickpocket (Act 2, Scene 6). By perverting his own intrinsic social identity, albeit in service of his juridical function, the judge, rather than preventing the smaller infringements of legal exchange, produces the ultimate form of transgression of exchange, theft. The very attempt to enforce regulation upon this wild market outside of the city limits is carried out with means which contradict the associated concepts of the just price, the correspondence of intrinsic worth and market worth, and the link between inner value and outer signs: namely, disguise and dissimulation. Even more contradictory is the fact that whilst the play's Induction insists upon the audience keeping to the terms of the contract they have implicitly made with the playwright by paying their money, the story itself dramatizes the essentially unregulated and perverse economy of play-acting, going as far as to situate that action in the same marginal and economically ungovernable Liberties in which the theatre (the Hope) stood.

Whilst the framing Induction assumes that the prices exactly determine the degree of criticism allotted to respective audience members, the content of the drama tells us that the 'value' of an actor is constantly fluctuating, always less than what it claims to be, and thus inherently at odds with a regulated market whose prices are fixed and 'just'. How did the theatre deal with this tension within its self-reflexive allusions to its own functioning? Three examples, Shakespeare's *Merchant of Venice* and Middleton's *The Changeling*, followed by *A Mad World, My Masters*, can provide an answer to this question.

The double geography of *The Merchant of Venice*, divided between Venice and Belmont, organizes the universe of the play according to two opposed principles, pragmatic mercantilism on the one hand and pure romance on the other. Venice was constituted and defined in contemporary opinion as a place of commerce: for Jacobeans, the city was a source of wonder for the 'vnmeasurable quantity of all sorts of marchandise to be brought out of all realmes and countries into this Citie, and hence againe to be conueyed into so many straunge and far distant nations, both by land and sea ... as though the Citie of *Venice* onley were a common and generall market to the whole world.'[58] It is precisely this generalized market principle which is excluded from Belmont. Portia's mode of carrying out her father's instructions regarding her marriage is designed to protect the realm of love from the economic factors which frequently governed marriage negotiations among the nobility. When Portia refers to her 'worthless self' (2.9.17) she epitomizes this attempt to extract love from the process of exchange. The caskets are so arranged as to present the suitors with a choice between riches and herself. In order to sever the connection between love and financial gain, Portia's portrait is placed in the casket carrying the signs of a worthless metal. 'I am locked in one of them [the caskets]. | If you do love me, you will find me out' says Portia to Bassanio (3.2.40–1). In other words, true love endows a knowledge which is not tempted by outward riches (gold and silver), and which discovers the veritable correspondence between outward and inward values by ignoring variable mercantile rates. Love disdains outward, socially determined signs of value, and remains aloof from the commodity market, where values are set collectively by supply and demand. Thus Bassanio, who knows to choose in accordance with Portia's wishes, condemns silver as 'thou pale and common drudge | 'Tween man and man' (3.2.103–4); it is a prostituted metal, given value by collective desire rather than by inherent worth. In contrast, the lead casket asks the suitor to make a sacrifice, to 'give and hazard all he hath', to discard financial interest in favour of disinterested love.

Against this assertion of the separateness of the domains of love and mercantile interest, the play persists, however, in emphasizing the contamination of the domain of romance by that of mercantilism. When Shylock discovers the flight of his daughter Jessica with her booty, it is difficult to tell what causes him most pain, the loss of his daughter or the loss of his ducats (2.8.15–17); the boundaries between the two seem to blur and human relations are apparently assimilated to monetary relations. There is nothing particularly surprising about this, as Shylock embodies the economic domain of Venice. Contamination by mercantile values of the domain of love is more shocking, however, in Belmont. In the prelude to Bassanio's choice of the caskets, he meditates: 'So may the outward shows be least themselves. | The world is still deceived with ornament' (3.2.73–4). The dictates of the market meant that tradesmen could not be trusted to operate honestly within a consensual 'moral economy', producing an avalanche of seventeenth-century treaties on reading inward intentions through outward physical signs.[59] The only way to escape from the market manipulation of appearance, Bassanio suggests, is to reverse the deceptive relations of inner and outer. Choosing that which promises least worth proves one's immunity to the ubiquitous greed of a society increasingly governed by mercantile values. But does Bassanio's simple reversal of outer appearance of worth truly constitute an escape from the mercantilization of personal relations? Is not Bassanio simply calculating the risks of representation of value? Similarly, Portia's lead casket asks the suitor to invest everything, to 'give and hazard all he hath'. This demand for sacrifice can also be understood, however, as a demand for risk, with a view to gaining a massive return on an investment. Here, it is less a question of mercantile as opposed to romantic, than of the degree of risk the entrepreneur is prepared to incur in his investment.

Moreover, for one who disdains the realm of economic values, Portia expresses her selfhood in relation to Bassanio in terms surprisingly coloured by economic thought, even if it is ostensibly to outgo quantifiability:

> ... for you
> I would be trebled twenty times myself,
> A thousand times more fair, ten thousand times more rich,
> That only to stand high in your account,
> I might in virtues, beauties, livings, friends,
> Exceed account. But the full sum of me
> I sum of something which, to term in gross,
> Is an unlessoned girl ...
>
> (3.2.152–9)

It is clearly altruistic love which motivates this speech, yet it is an altruism so permeated by economic values that the gift of selfhood is thought in terms of banking and brokering. Again, when Portia declares: 'Myself and what is mine to you and yours | Is now converted' (3.2.167), the lover's compact could be seen here as a form of alchemy, by which riches are generated apparently out of nothing. But in fact, Bassanio has invested considerable resources in the undertaking (his arrival at Portia's residence is heralded by 'gifts of rich value' financed presumably by Shylock's loan and Antonio's good name – 2.9.90), which are now recuperated in the form of the wealth secured through the financial contract of marriage.

An even more disturbing contamination of the disinterested personal domain by the values of mercantilism can be detected in the person of Antonio. Obliged by the failure of his commercial enterprises to forfeit his pound of flesh as agreed, Antonio clears all debts between himself and Bassanio, in the tradition of friendship and altruism for which he is reputed – yet strangely, he obliges Bassanio to come to witness his death: 'all debts are cleared between you and I if I might but see you at my death. Notwithstanding, use your pleasure. If your love do not persuade you to come, let not my letter' (3.2.316–19). This may appear to be a simple desire for companionship at the moment of doom, but the clearance of debts is not as generous as it would seem: it is conditional upon a proof of love, such that the gift given is reclaimed in the form of a sign of love. Antonio's letter of ostensibly altruistic cancellation of debt is in fact a covert instrument of emotional manipulation which forces a response from the receiver. Moreover, the loan and security offered by Antonio is redeemed only in the form of Bassanio's 'freely' accepted obligation to be a witness to the spectacle of Antonio's martyrdom: 'Pray God Bassanio come | To see me pay his debt, and then I care not', says Antonio (3.3.35–6). That is, Bassanio is to consent to the spectacle of his own infinite indebtedness to Antonio, for no repayment on his part could possibly match Antonio's ultimate sacrifice performed – in all senses of the word – for his friend's happiness. The play refers on other occasions to 'sad ostents' and to 'ostents of love' (2.2.188; 2.8.44); what Antonio intends to perform is a kind of theatrical 'ostention' of sacrificial love which combines both of these prior meanings, thus dragging friendship back into the commercial arena by placing it under the sign of a debt so great as to be unpayable.

Antonio, whose altruistic act of offering himself as security upon the loan which has made it possible for Bassanio to gain Portia's love, initially thinks himself able to outbid her love by his sacrificial death:

> Tell her the process of Antonio's end.
> Say how I loved you. Speak me fair in death,
> And when the tale is told, bid her judge
> Whether Bassanio had not once a love.
>
> (4.1.271–4)

The prospect of his own potential death allows him to contemplate the attainment of a personal moral value which would outstrip the love of any wife of Bassanio, a judgement with which Portia is proleptically invited to concur. Ironically, it is Portia, in the guise of the young doctor of law Balthasar, who deprives Antonio of this *coup d'éclat* by saving him at the last moment from Shylock's knife. When, after the court case, Portia, still disguised as the lawyer, asks Bassanio for his ring in payment for her services, Bassanio explains his reluctance to part with the ring as it was given him by his wife (Portia). Antonio, however, overrides such paltry-minded excuses, commanding his friend, 'My Lord Bassanio, let him have the ring. | Let his deservings and my love withal | Be valued 'gainst your wife's commandëment' (4.1.446–8). It is not clear to whom the possessive '*my* love' refers: does it indicate 'my love for you', or possibly 'your love for me'? In fact, these two vectors of love are one and the same, for together they add up to Antonio's possession-oriented love for himself. His narcissistic preoccupation with his own status as untrumped lover is at the centre of a predatory economy of self-regard which is determined to marginalize and eliminate potential competitors: 'Let ... my love ... | Be valued 'gainst your wife's commandëment.'

Especially dangerous to his monopoly of the market of love are women who threaten to outdo his efforts on behalf of his male friends, thus usurping the exclusive relations of debt which he fosters. There is a tense moment during the court scene, when both Portia and Nerissa comment adversely, in a double aside, upon their husbands' avowal of a greater readiness for sacrifice on behalf of Antonio than to themselves, whom the men believe absent in Belmont (4.1.285–6, 290–1). Antonio's urging Bassanio to give up Portia's ring is thus an attempt to recuperate his threatened position as market-leader on the stock market of love. Whence the pertinence of Portia's question: 'Which is the merchant here, and which the Jew?' (4.1.171). Despite the struggle between them, it would appear that there is much that binds Antonio and Shylock. One almost has the impression that Antonio is as reluctant to give up his fate as Shylock is to relinquish his pound of flesh; the two are joined in a relationship where both stand to gain from the other: Shylock his ultimate revenge, Antonio the ultimate confirmation of his narcissistic self-image.

Thus it is clear that the two principal binary oppositions structuring the play according to the division interest/disinterest or mercantilism/love, namely, the distinctions between Venice and Belmont, and between Jew and Christian, are quite flimsy. The geographical distance between the two cities in no way extracts Belmont from the world of commerce. At the same time, Shylock's justification of his revenge

(3.1.54–68) blurs the boundaries between himself and Antonio, between Jew and Christian, such that we have to ask whether the priority of human relations over monetary relations, espoused by Antonio early on in the play, is really in his monopoly. But an even more primordial commonality links these apparently opposed protagonists. Antonio places a pound of his own body as security upon Shylock's loan to Bassanio (Act 1, Scene 3), which in turn is to help him gain Portia's love – in other words, her body. Thus Bassanio's investment in the undertaking links the two domains; the successful conjugal union of Bassanio and Portia's bodies is mirrored in the sadistic linking of Antonio's body and Shylock. Indeed, immediately after the happy union of Bassanio and Portia, followed neatly by Graziano and Nerissa, Lorenzo arrives with Jessica to bring news of Antonio's imminent fate (3.2.230ff). Selfhood in its physical, passionate form (whether that of love or hatred), expressed in images of the most atavistic relationship to otherness, eating, connects characters to one another.[60] It is no coincidence, then, that Shylock, echoing a typical trope of 'biting' usury, sneers 'They flatter me, | But yet I'll go in hate, to feed upon | The prodigal Christian' (2.5.13–15), playing upon the resonances of usury as a form of cannibalism and as a parasitic feeding upon fellow human beings, embodied in the pound of flesh. Bassanio admits, implicitly, to being equally involved in this parasitic and inhuman business, when, later in the play, he confesses to Portia that he has 'Engaged my friend to his mere enemy, | To feed my means' (3.2.260–1).

In the last analysis, mercantile egotism and exploitation links all the characters in the play (even Jessica, upon eloping with Lorenzo disguised as a page, says 'I am glad 'tis night, you do not look on me, | For I am much ashamed of my exchange' – 2.6.34–5) with a web of bodily corrosion and parasitic interdependence. All the characters, despite the play's claim to erect a trade-free zone where people act for purely altruistic motives, are driven by mercantile self-interest in some form or another. In Shakespeare's drama, the 'placeless' market has penetrated into the most hidden recesses of human relations, contradicting the play's apparent resolution of the central dilemma by the concluding distribution of Shylock's wealth to the other characters and the Venetians' 'mercy' towards the stranger in their midst.

The second example, Middleton's significantly titled *The Changeling*, similarly refuses to accept exchange as a working principle for social relations. The burden of the play is to issue a protest about treating individuals as interchangeable minions, albeit within an aristocratic context rather than the emergent commercial world discussed in the preceding sections. This portrayal of 'exchange' in an elevated sector of society which typically liked to see itself as far removed from the encroachments of the money economy (though this was far from the case) provides a useful contrast to Middleton's presentation of exchangeability in his comedies. The servant De Flores is persuaded to perform the murder of Alonso for which his lady Beatrice does not want to be held responsible. He, however, refuses to disappear as rapidly and conveniently as Beatrice hopes, demanding her virginity as payment for his act. This forfeit Beatrice pays off by sleeping with De Flores on the night of her wedding with Alsemero. In turn, Beatrice has her chamber-maid Diaphanta bedded by her husband Alsemero in place of herself. Once Diaphanta has performed the service of losing her virginity on behalf of Beatrice, the lady plans to take the place of the chamber-maid: 'About midnight | You must not fail to steal forth gently, | That I may use the place', commands her mistress (4.1.124–6). Diaphanta does indeed perform the bride's duty with Alsemero while Beatrice copulates with De Flores. Diaphanta, however, like De Flores, cannot be so easily marginalized once she has served her purpose. She refuses to leave the bedroom, where she is obviously relishing the love-making with Alsemero, thereby potentially scuppering the smooth completion of the earlier contract. Her resistance to objectification moves De Flores and Beatrice to create the conflagration in which Diaphanta is burnt to death, as the guilty Beatrice subsequently confesses: 'Alsemero, I am a stranger to your bed, | Your bed was cozened on the nuptial night, | For which your false bride died' (5.3.159–61). Fulfilment of one contract designed to off-load Beatrice's guilt onto a minion entails a subsequent transfer of responsibility onto another minion, likewise to be discarded after conclusion of the transfer. In other words, for Beatrice, identity, when it is a matter of unpleasant tasks, is exchangeable. Middleton thus insists on clearly identifying personalized guilt on the part of the powerful, and upon the intact agency and worthy identity of members of the subordinate classes such as De Flores and Diaphanta.

Only when responsible assumption of identity can be no longer deferred (Act 5, Scene 3) does Beatrice die, having been wounded by the uncompliant De Flores – who in turn publicly commits suicide, thus declaring his guilt and taking upon himself the consequences of that guilt. His integrity demands a public declaration of place: 'Yes, and the while I coupled with your mate | At barley-brake; now we are left in hell' (5.3.162–3). The allusion to the game of barley-brake, in which a couple in the middle of a hall ('in hell') tried to catch others running through the central space, is illuminating; by a process of exchange, the central couple strives to have others take their place 'in hell'. De Flores, rather than passing the buck, accepts the position which is rightfully his.[61] The moral integrity of the commoners – their refusal to change places with others in order to evade responsibility – is thus held up against the doubtful conduct of the nobility whose members readily treat their 'inferiors' as exchangeable pawns in the machinations of power.

But Middleton's moral outrage against exchangeability and the consequent mutability of moral values as evinced in *The Changeling* is belied by the ambivalent stance he takes in the comedies. Once processes of exchange are removed from the context of aristocratic arrogance and placed within London citizen society, exchange is presented in an altogether more positive light. The principal pleasure afforded by these city comedies lies in that those characters who create barriers against dispossession are tricked into their own dispossession at the hands of the wits. Sir Bounteous entertains those who rob him, and subsequently adds insult to his own injury by innocently giving Follywit/Sir Owemuch additional gifts to compensate what has ostensibly been stolen from his guest; Harebrain, arrogantly confident that his wife will not escape from his possessive grasp, urges her to 'take my man', thinking thereby to gain proof of her fidelity (3.1.99), an offer which she overtly refuses, while covertly complying, thus indeed dispossessing him of his most treasured possession. Behind the putative condemnation of socially unpleasant characteristics, it is the trope of market-driven chiasmus which structures these plays. In simultaneously rehearsing the mobility of contemporary life and controlling it, Middleton and other playwrights exploited the audience's enjoyment of such mobility, but fulfilled, in the last analysis, the moral function that Heywood was to claim for the theatre a decade later. Thus the playwright himself profited from a duplicity of functions similar to that performed by his characters. Whereas *The Changeling* criticized the nobility for shifting onto others the social functions which it behoves them to assume, Middleton's comedies depend upon the very same mechanism, namely characters' assumption of multiple, apparently mutually exclusive social roles in the interests of economic gain. This mechanism intensifies social role rather than displacing it as in *The Changeling*, but the basic principle, that of the malleability of moral values and identities, remains the same. The difference between condemnation and approbation is clear: where transferability is a residual aspect of a receding feudal form of society it is caustically attacked on the stage; when transferability is a function of the theatre's mode of existence in the capitalist economy, however, it is presented to the audience in a fundamentally positive light, despite all disclaimers to the contrary.

The city comedy is thus patently ambivalent in its stance regarding the primacy of the market law of the ubiquitous mutability of values. At the close of a drama such as *A Mad World, My Masters*, everything has reverted to a normal state of affairs and the moral order has been restored: the gallant has been caught in his own trap, the righteous are rewarded for their morally upright stature. Yet mobility has been performed, enacted, made visible, even if it is not ratified by the stamp of permanence. The pleasure of the audience lies not only in the rescue of the righteous from their predicaments; it also arises from vicarious identification with the joyful cunning of the villains. The dramatist thus profited simultaneously from the audience's sense of moral rectitude, and from its enjoyment of moral transgression – a transgression founded on mobility and exchange. The plays' resolution of economic fluidity in no way blunted the economic efficacy of their previous narratives of transgression. Such strategies made of the dramatists defenders of the traditional order, moral conservatives, purveyors of narratives lagging behind the real direction of increasingly accelerated economic rationality, *and at the same time*, quite conscious profiteers from the portrayal of the mobility resulting from accelerating economic processes. Thus Lawrence Manley correctly underlines the high degree of self-awareness on the part of the theatre regarding its ambiguous position within the exchangeability of the money economy: 'Like the verse satirists, the city comedians discovered in urban life a degree of arbitrariness, interchange, and mobility that undermined the possibility of identifying moral integrity with any portion of the existing social body. Yet unlike the satirists and the scourging presenters of the comical satires that descended from them, the city comedians learned better, through the theater marketplace, than to insist upon investing themselves with an "essential difference".'[62]

If, as was seen in the preceding chapter, the court masque became increasingly porous to the world outside the court, the other London theatres were from the outset entangled in the new realities of the capitalist money economy from which they emerged. Their ambivalence was thus structural to their existence in a way in which the masque's increasing ambivalence was not. The following two chapters will examine two further symptoms of the transformations wrought by the money economy, social and demographic mobility, and will reveal in the Jacobean drama the same ambivalent combination of jubilant portrayal of this constitutive mutability alongside anxious attempts to control the very dynamism which created the drama.

4
Mean Persons and Counterfeit Port: Social Mobility

Social mobility in the Renaissance

The economic changes produced by developing capitalism triggered an unprecedented upheaval in social structures. The powerful new agency of the new economy invested individuals and social groups previously subordinated in late medieval society with new forms of social independence and power. The incipient dynamics of capitalism dissolved hitherto stable relationships between individual and family, community, and social estate. The growth of population faster than food supplies or employment opportunities, and the spread of the money economy ushered in a society dominated by competition. For many, their place in society, both geographically and ideologically, was no longer secure or could no longer be taken for granted.[1]

The questioning of rigid social hierarchies in early seventeenth-century English society forms the subject of this chapter. In a society where values became increasingly mutable under the influence of a money-based economy, and where intellectual questioning of assumed hierarchies was also gaining momentum, it is no surprise to find an increased interrogation of rigid and authoritarian social structures, and more importantly, evidence of real social mobility. A 1600 pamphlet by Nicholas Breton, *Pasquil's Madcap*, contained the significant couplet: 'Coin alters natures in a thousand kinds, | And makes a beggar think himself a king.'[2] The causal link between the transformations of value, both economic and social, wrought by the capitalist economy, and an ensuing manifestation of new social mobility, was plain to the writer. This is a period in which a transformation, to quote Christopher Hill, of English society from 'a deference society dominated by an aristocracy of the armigerous, ... to something beginning to look more like ... a society of relative equality, of social mobility, of promotion by merit', was in progress.[3] Hill's qualifications are significant, for the precise degree of mobility, the number of persons actually affected by this new mobilization of social groups, and the resistance to and temporal parameters of that mobility are the subject of considerable debate.

What can be ascertained beyond all doubt from the textual evidence of contemporary commentators is their clear sense of social transformation and of the impact of social mobility in their writing. Rather than resolving questions of the degree of social mobility, questions which lie outside the domain of theatre history, this chapter merely aims to chart the ways in which this indubitable sense of social mobility among contemporaries, whatever its real dimensions may have been, was registered on the Jacobean stage. If the theatre was indeed intimately implicated in the social transformations of the sixteenth and seventeenth centuries, reflecting those changes in its own spatial form, then it can be assumed that social mobility in particular left a considerable imprint on the dramas of the era. In this chapter, the performance of social mobility in the Jacobean drama will be examined in three sections dealing with three units of social identity in descending scale of magnitude: changes in relationships of land ownership; changes within the identity of the aristocratic family; and lastly, at the point where the theatre self-reflexively foregrounded its own mode of functioning, changes in the sartorial marking of individuals' social rank.

Mobility of land

The most visible expression of social mobility during the period examined was mobility of land. Land transfers have been estimated as being 250 per cent higher at their peak level about 1610 than in the 1560s. There were attempts to freeze the mobility of land all through the sixteenth century, and by the 1620s the rate of land transfers had begun to drop; generally, social mobility of this variety, that is, entry into the landowning gentry from classes below, had been reined in by 1700.[4] The significance of land was double. It was the most stable form of wealth in the often unstable nascent capitalist economy; it was regarded as a securer investment than, for instance, sales of offices at Court, or the grant of monopolies.[5] And possession of land was the qualifying factor which determined membership of the nobility. Changes in the possession of land were thus a clear index of mobility in the most sought after (because least mercurial) form of wealth. Further, they were a clear index of movement up and down the social hierarchy, a movement which simultaneously confirmed the existence of hierarchy, but even more pronouncedly cast into question its validity.

The emergence of new professions growing out of the new economic order, causing increased blurring of the boundaries between citizens and gentry, was one symptom of the larger transformations making for a sense of social confusion in early modern England. Previously clear artic-ulations of social hierarchy, such as the concept of the three estates (knights/clergy/commons) constructed around two binary distinctions (master/servant, earthly/spiritual), were no longer adequate to deal with a new order which included emergent social groupings based in the pro-fessions, such merchants, yeomen or lawyers and doctors, all of these rapidly acceding to land ownership. These four professions increasingly had to be taken into account as they disturbed the former hierarchies based upon distinction between ownership of property and lack of own-ership.[6] Novel six-part schemes attempted to accommodate new distinc-tions within society. Such innovative schemes functioned as a means of containment, helping to map the process of social change both taxo-nomically and topographically. Likewise, the new ternary model of court/city/country replaced the vertical hierarchy of the three estates with a horizontal and less immediately visible model of social competition. The entry of geography into social models figures an attempt to make tangi-ble a sense of change in social structures, to ground it in something other than social privilege, and at the same time, betrays a certain flattening of a formerly immanent sense of rank. The loosening of the connections between inherited land and inherited social hierarchy focused the con-temporary gaze upon land as the contested object of social transforma-tions. Manley comments: 'Based on geographical rather than social "place", this new ternary model assumed – indeed required – mobility in order to function.'[7] The mobility within such new six-part or ternary schemes of social distinction was clearly a reactive mobility, a struggle to take account of a phenomenon already in operation. Such schemes were symptomatic of a movement so forceful as to impose itself upon observers and render urgent the business of finding explanatory narratives to deal with bewilderingly novel experiences of social life.

An important rider to commentary on social mobility in early modern England must be added. In a population of which 90 per cent belonged to the lower classes, many forms of social mobility would have gone unrecognized because they occurred among the anonymous and, for contemporary commentators, largely undifferentiated mass of the poor. The actual degree of real mobility accounted for among the 10 per cent of members of society at the privileged top end of the social spectrum may have been, in consequence, comparatively minimal. None the less, this did not prevent contemporaries from experiencing it as unprecedented and threatening.[8] As David Morse comments, 'crises are rarely as obvious as they might seem ... what makes for crisis is the widespread conviction that there is one, the sense that people have at particular historical moments that everything is at stake.'[9] This broader *quantitative*-framework is important in discussions of social mobility during the Jacobean period. It does not, however, change the *qualitative* force of the radical and all-pervasive effects of the freedom to buy and sell land which prevailed in England between 1530 and 1660.

Jacobean drama frequently comments upon social mobility as a matter of changing property relationships. As a shift of spatial coordinates the transfer of land or the attempt to have land change hands is an ideal trigger for narrative action, following Lotman's theory of *sujet*-laden narrative structure: only transgression of a hitherto stable situation merits narration. The transfer of property thus often serves as the focus of the action of Jacobean drama, generating passions which are central to the suspense of the plot's events. In Middleton's *No Help, No Wit Like a Woman's*, a triangular love relationship is described, both in form and content, as a spatial affair. Mistress Low-Water is courted by the sleazy Sir Gilbert, who hopes to persuade her to accept his advances by promising financial security – security he in turn thinks to gain from a prospective marriage with the widow Lady Goldenfleece. Mistress Low-Water indignantly ruminates:

> What a strange path he takes to my affection,
> And thinks't the near'st way – t'will never be –
> Goes through mine enemy's ground to come to me.
>
> (1.2.100–3)

The dynamism of cross-country mobility describes not only the characters' tactics within amorous manoeuvres, but also the real economic conditions which govern their aspirations within the triangular relationship. Mistress Low-Water's assessment of the situation is accurate in more ways than one. Lady Goldenfleece is her 'enemy' precisely because of 'ground', as it was Low-Water family lands which were originally lost to the now widowed Lady Goldenfleece, and which make her 'desirable' to both Sir Gilbert *and* Mistress Low-Water. Subsequently, Sir Gilbert will be neutralized as a median instance, and Mistress Low-Water will set about the conquest of her lands in a more direct manner, by becoming herself a suitor (appropriately disguised as an attractive young man) for the hand of Lady Goldenfleece.

Contemporaries imposed a fiendish intentionality upon this transformation of property-owning relationships by identifying noble and ignoble actors in the drama of dispossession. Quomodo of *Michaelmas Term* dispossesses gentry land-owners purely out of a sense of vindictive pleasure, planning 'to cleave the heir in twain, | I mean his title, to murder his estate, | Stifle his right in some detested prison' (1.1.104–5). Such stereotyping posed the naive country gentleman (in this case Easy) against the unscrupulous city merchant determined to wrest land from its rightful owners. The establishment of clear binary oppositions between rural virtue and an acquisitive, amoral city ethic, however, actually obscured the complex economic links between the two.[10]

Raymond Williams notes the ideological character of the common topos posing rural gentry goodness against city merchant cynicism, 'for what is never enquired into is the real past and present of that "settled" and "lawful" country order from which they come. ... There is then, no simple contrast between wicked town and innocent country, for what happens in the town is generated by the needs of the dominant rural class.'[11] Primogeniture, which excluded younger sons from inheritance of family property, meant that the aristocracy often had links to the professions: a typical example would be the late Stuart landowner Sir George Sandes, whose younger brothers studied medicine at Leiden, took up soldiering in the Low Countries, or were apprenticed to merchants and a London woollen draper respectively. Many prominent merchants and professional men had close family links to the landed gentry: many merchants were the younger sons of the gentry; a large number of adolescent sons of the gentry received their inheritances in the form of the considerable fees necessary for their apprenticeships in the metropolis. From the over 8,000 apprentices bound to the members of 15 London companies during the period 1570–1646, for instance, a not negligible 12.6 per cent were the sons of knights, esquires and gentlemen. Furthermore, in the most prestigious trade and retail companies, gentry apprenticeships made up between a quarter and a third of new entrants.[12] In turn, city merchants, aspiring to the landed status of the gentry, would often buy back into country lands once their wealth permitted. Indicative of such changes was the tightrope act undertaken by Edward Bolton in *The Cities Advocate* of 1629: he was careful to defend traditional 'degree' and indicate respect for the natural superiority of the gentry over the merchants; at the same time, he provided legitimacy to gentry who went into City commerce and apprenticed their sons, and to merchants who aspired to gentry status: 'as an Apprentise being a Gentleman-borne remains a Gentleman, which addition of splendour, and title, as God blesseth his labours, so a worthy Citizen is capable of honour and Armes, notwithstanding his Apprentiship.'[13]

The dramas did display some degree of awareness of the intertwining of economic interests between merchants and gentry, but the expression given to those market-driven connections is not always particularly illuminating. Quomodo, for instance, states: 'They're busy 'bout our wives, we 'bout their lands' (1.1.109). Such jocular gestures towards complex interconnections hide rather than reveal the primarily economic complicity between the established land-owning class and the newly prominent class of merchants who possessed capital but not the social status of the landowner. Elsewhere, however, the satirical tone conceals a more realistic appraisal of the mutually intertwined interest of merchants and gentry, such as the moment when Middleton's wealthy goldsmith Yellowhammer (in *A Chaste Maid in Cheapside*) declares:

> Sir Walter's come.
> He was met at Holborn bridge, and in his company
> A proper fair young gentlewoman, which I guess
> By her red hair, and other rank descriptions,
> To be his landed niece brought out of Wales,
> Which Tim our son (the Cambridge boy) must marry.
> Tis a match of Sir Walter's own making
> To bind us to him, and our heirs forever.
>
> (1.1.33–40)

The reciprocal binding between the two social groups – the merchants hope to accede thus to land, the gentleman hopes to marry his family back into commercial wealth – is clearly, if cynically, expressed in Yellowhammer's comments. The bridging function links London commercial wealth and rural landed wealth across the natural civic boundary of the river. A similarly perceptive glimpse of the real interactions between merchant and gentry is given in *The Revenger's Tragedy*, in a passage in which 'farmers' sons' 'come up gentlemen' and 'Tailors ride down' (2.1.219–23), figuring in anthropomorphic form the flow of merchant capital into, for instance, nascent industrial projects such as mining, in which the gentry as land-owners were also heavily involved; or the upward social mobility of yeoman land-owners who were able to consolidate their properties, thus improving their social status, in the context of the favourable conditions created by fixed-rate, long-term land leases at times of rising prices of agricultural products. The victims of this sort of transfer were the tenant farmers forced off the land by the enclosures entailed by industrial projects, or gentry land-owners who obtained sinking returns (in real terms) from the long leases they had signed with tenants.

One other group profited enormously from the unprecedented mobility of land: the lawyers. The lucrative activity of litigation over land transfers of wealth, a huge upsurge of legal business, propelled the social ascent of many lawyers. The drama frequently targeted the legal profession, describing its activities in spatial terms. The Induction to *Michaelmas Term* has the typified character Michaelmas Term gloating:

> my hand's free,
> From wronger and wrongèd I have fee,
> And what by sweat from the rough earth they draw
> Is to enrich this silver harvest, Law;
> And so through wealthy variance and fat brawl
> The barn is made but steward to the hall
>
> (9–14)

Once again the transfer of wealth from country to city, from nature to non-nature, from manual work to specious verbiage is figured in spatial or, more precisely, in metonymic architectural terms. Behind the legal appropriation of land is a mode of devious legal practice which anticipates upon the gains to be had from astute mooting. It is perhaps not insignificant that Jonson's tirades against lawyers in *Volpone* are couched in spatial images: describing their capacity 'with most quick agility, [to] turn, | And re-turn; makes knots, and undo them; | Give forkèd counsel' (1.3.56–8); and their ability to 'gull the court' and 'quite divert the torrent | Upon the innocent' (5.2.16–17). The transfers of property mentioned by Michaelmas Term are a second-order phenomenon, a spin-off from a prior process of social change upon which the lawyers are parasitic.

The drama was quick to point out the losers in the social changes brought about by mobility of land. One group who suffered from such changes were those affected by rural unemployment, migration and vagrancy in the wake of enclosures; stage representations of this phenomenon will be examined in more detail in the following chapter, in connection with patterns of demographic geography. A second group who suffered from changes in land-ownership relations were the gentry family whose profligacy or financial mismanagement caused them to lose their property. Here the drama frequently translated downward social mobility into a spatial movement. The scholar Beveril in *No Help,*

No Wit Like a Woman's returns home to find his sister and her husband dispossessed:

> *Beveril*: My sister fled!
> *Sandfield*: Both fled; that's the news now. Want must obey;
>   Oppressions came so thick, they could not stay.
>   (2.2.177–9)

The Revenger's Tragedy contains a similarly pithy formulation of the loss of landed property squandered by parents' financial mismanagement:

> I have seen patrimonies washed apieces,
> Fruit-fields turned into bastards,
> And in world of acres,
> Not so much dust due to the heir 'twas left to
> As would well gravel a petition.
>   (1.3.51–5)

Here property inheritances are eroded in a highly appropriate concretization of the abstract concept of financial ruin. Such losses were often attributed to the insidious influence of the patterns of conspicuous consumption set by the Jacobean court, thus establishing another convenient binary opposition which countered a wasteful and ostentatious court culture with a spendthrift rural life-style; there were indeed some Puritan land-owners who confirmed these sorts of moral topographies in increasing their fortunes by dint of sober living and careful and considered husbandry of their land.

Fragmentation of kinship structures

At the heart of the social mobility embodied in the mobility of land was a corresponding erosion of the family as the social face of the landed property in which it was anchored. In a famous quip in *Cymbeline*, Posthumus lets loose a tirade against women's promiscuity couched in terms which speak loudly of a particular early modern vision of family existence:

> We are bastards all,
> And that most venerable man which I
> Did call my father was I know not where
> When I was stamped. Some coiner with his tools
> Made me a counterfeit.
>   (2.5.2–6)

The notion of the dynastic family as a financial entity, to whose survival the clear establishment of paternity in service of the maintenance of an inheritance lineage down through time was crucial, is enunciated here in the compact conceit of the sexual act as the minting of money. Preserving the integrity of wealth is a matter of preserving the integrity of family boundaries. Erosion of those family contours reduces family wealth, in turn lessening the social value of a name. When *The Revenger's Tragedy* envisions 'Fruit-fields turned into bastards', in the passage just quoted, the destruction of landed wealth is seen simultaneously as the break-down of a system of lineage: 'Not so much dust *due to the heir 'twas left to* | As would well gravel a petition' (1.3.51–5; my emphasis).

The upheavals of economic change, of the growth and shrinkage of fortunes, had direct consequences in the concrete spatiality of land possession, but also in the contours of social identity which were grounded – often literally, in the association of name and place – in landed possession. Witgood's uncle, for instance, in *A Trick to Catch the Old One*, having mortgaged his nephew's lands, conveniently forgets the name of Witgood Hall, effectively alienating the family name from the place name (2.1.93). The rise of cartography signalled a property-driven interest in lands as an empirical entity rather than as the embodiment of dynastic family identity. New maps of the land evinced a shift in ideas about the key aspects of social power – the dynastic royal family as a central cartographic signifier was gradually supplanted by the immediate and visible transparency of the land itself. This change entailed a shift from the vertical figures of dynastic continuity to horizontal figures of the land as expanse;[14] a similar lateral displacement of the vertical process of 'stamping' is at work in Posthumus's diatribe against adultery.

The changes visible in shifts of land ownership can be seen as interlocking with the transition from the early modern dynastic family as a socio-spatial entity and a prominent image of social cohesion, towards more individualistic social groupings evincing new spatial structures. This crisis in the family is evident in Shakespeare's drama from *Coriolanus* onwards: if the family survives in *Coriolanus*, saving Rome, by the time of *King Lear* the disintegration of the family is the trigger of social disruption, disappearing altogether in *Timon of Athens*.[15] Clearly the family was a powerful focus of social malaise growing out of spatial change, a malaise which was expressed in spatial form on the stage. Even if the aristocratic family was not absolutely representative of the customary nuclear family configuration in early modern England, as noted above, disturbances portrayed within fictional stage images of the family none the less effectively crystallized unease over social relationships.

The transformation of the large aristocratic family was articulated in Elizabethan and Jacobean laments upon the death of traditional hospitality. The tradition of hospitality made the house a metonymy of the web of social relationships constituting its environment, so that, in the words of Bachelard, the house figures as a 'cell' and as 'world'.[16] The houses of the French aristocracy of the *ancien régime* made visible in their construction the network of social relations whose centre they formed, as Norbert Elias has shown. Similarly, the great hall at Penshurst, the home of the Sidney family, for instance, functioned as the exemplary place of aristocratic hospitality, a hospitality symbolic of responsibility and order, justifying power and authority, and thus embodying in a physical place a universe of hierarchized feudal social relations.[17] It was this central web of relationships which was felt to be fraying in the Jacobean period. Lupton lamented the demise of the personified character 'Hospitality': 'This true noble hearted fellow is to be dignified and honor'd, whersoeuer he keepes house: It's thought that pride, puritans, coaches and couetousnesse haue caused him to leaue our Land. ... he kept the olde fashion, good, commendable, plaine: the poore about him wore him vpon their backes; ... but now hee's dead, to the grief of all *England*.'[18]

A proclamation issued by Elizabeth in 1597 explicitly attributed 'the decay and lack of hospitality' amongst the gentry to 'the immeasurable charges and expenses which they are put to in superfluous apparelling of their wives, children, and families.'[19] A similar explanation of changes in traditions of hospitality is given by the ploughman in Middleton's *Father Hubburd's Tales*, who declares that 'the world was turned upside down since the decease of my old landlord, all hospitality and good housekeeping kicked out of doors, all thriftiness and good husbandry tossed into the air, ploughs turned into trunks, and corn into apparel.'[20] These laments make an explicit causal connection between aristocratic wastage and the death of rural hospitality. The connection is structured, paradoxically, by a shift from one place of aristocratic potlatch to another. The hospitality potlatch is seen here as being part of the cycle of fertility symbolized by the plough, whereas the second form is reduced to mere sterile (merely visual) exchange value.[21] The metaphors used depend upon the more intimate spatial dimensions of the household world, in which contrary to the custom of receiving guests, anthropomorphized hospitality is itself ejected from its own metonymy, the domain of the house. The dynamic proxemics of ejection turn the symbolic value of the great house against its own traditional social function.

In the plays, this transformation of aristocratic hospitality is a recurring motif. In the wedding celebrations in *No Help, No Wit Like a Woman's*, the rebuffed Sir Gilbert, playing the role of 'Fire', laments:

> I was once a name of comfort, warmed great houses
> When charity was landlord; I have given welcome
> To forty russet yeomen at a time
> In a fair Christmas-hall. How I am changed!

$$(4.3.60–4)$$

Sir Gilbert complains that the fire of charity has given way to the fire of lust, with the result that Mistress Low-Water (in disguise) has been preferred by Lady Goldenfleece to the likes of Sir Gilbert himself. His complaint thus needs to be taken with a pinch of salt in its immediate dramatic situation. None the less, such laments were heard often enough in other contexts to have a degree of resonance for the audience. Moreover, although the play does not respect Sir Gilbert as the author of tradionalist sentiments, it honours them elsewhere: by virtue of her cunning trickery, Mistress Low-Water manages to restore her family's lands to their original owners. Her faked marriage to the widow lady Goldenfleece is annulled on the wedding night, but not without her brother Beveril succeeding her as husband for the disappointed widow. Thus the identity of 'name' of place and family as representative of a traditional ethic of social hierarchy and responsibility is finally restored.

Some critics have asked whether the ethic of ostentatious hospitality did in fact exist. It may have been regarded as a rather risky mode of investment, with Robert Sidney, for example, impoverishing himself through his hospitality at Penshurst.[22] It is also possible that lamentations of the decline of hospitality may frequently have referred to the draconian reductions to the number of servants employed in aristocratic households between 1590 and 1620, from an average of a hundred or so to three or four dozen.[23] More significant than the historical accuracy of these putative trends, however, is the Jacobeans' acute sense of shift in social practices. Contemporaries experienced the transformations as quite momentous enough to merit being articulated in such laments. What is sensed and expressed in such imagery is the massive impact of economic changes upon time-honoured social relations.

These messages of lament register the rapid assimilation of the old feudal order, embodied in a highly visible form of architectural construction, to an increasingly privatized capitalist mode of production.

The Jacobean period saw the progressive demise of buildings of civic, and thus collective, significance: monuments figuring community coherence were outstripped by a spurt of private building, from the mansions of merchants and lawyers to the hovels of the urban poor.[24] The rise of map-making and county atlas compilation was an index of the increasing documentation of private property. Chorographies functioned more and more as catalogues where the gentry could find their manors, monuments and pedigrees described. Such texts progressed from an earlier association with royal chronicles to the topographical recording of real-estate and family history.[25]

The shifting consciousness, from being part of an extensive and hierarchical social fabric, towards notions of privatized ownership, can be sensed in the destruction of the syntactic fabric of place in Witgood's renunciation of ownership of 'manors, manor-houses, parks, groves, meadow-grounds, arable lands, barns, stacks, dove-holes and coney-burrows' in *A Trick to Catch the Old One* (4.4.230–2). Here the land exists as a list of reified and fetishized commodities reduced to verbal signifiers apparently torn out of the syntax of human relationships. Without the bonding of densely woven social relationships, the drama offers a bleak vision of social interaction entirely based upon the cynical exploitation of distance and isolation. Easy, the country gentleman come to London in Middleton's *Michaelmas Term*, is advised by Shortyard to win and hold the friendship of his newly-found city friends by promising to pay for the following evening's entertainment: 'Thus make you men at parting dutiful | And rest beholding to you; 'tis the sleight | To be remembered when you're *out of sight*' (2.1.172–5; my emphasis). In this world far from the virtues of the rural society of Essex, it is only by virtue of debt and proleptic, interested generosity that social distance can be overcome. The new social order functions around mobility and the production of distance as a social reality. It is driven by profit, and only profit can bridge the gaps which profit has created. The ultimate expression of this disintegration of rural networks of social cohesion is Easy's subsequent pathetic lament upon being deserted by Master Blastfield: 'Methinks I have no being without his company' (3.2.6). Economic constraints were thus felt to pose distance, isolation, and the disintegration of social unity against earlier relationships of mutually reinforcing hierarchical duties and responsibilities, particularly in the spatialized aristocratic family. The putative collapse of the family unit is exemplified in the inversion of family piety evident at the opening of *A Mad World, My Masters*. There, the loyal lineage of grandfather–father–son is disturbed by the rapacious greed of the younger for the wealth of the elder.

This perversion of filial piety is a mark of the disturbance of extended aristocratic family structures, of which the country house was the concrete embodiment. Jacobean theatre frequently employs the manor house as the embodiment of social disorder and disintegration. The house signifies inward strife and self-destruction. In *The Revenger's Tragedy*, the house is a closed and secretive construction, rather than a site of openness and feudal responsibility: 'But I had so much wit to keep my thoughts | Up in their built houses' says Hippolito (1.1.70–1). In Webster's *The White Devil*, Cornelia bewails the metaphorical collapse of the house riven by its own internal tensions and perverted sexual lust:

> My fears are fall'n upon me: oh my heart!
> My son the pander! Now I find our house
> Sinking to ruin. Eathquakes leave behind,
> Where they have tyranniz'd, iron, lead, or stone,
> But – woe to ruin – violent lust leaves none.
>
> (1.2.221–4)

Here the house is both the social network and the concrete and thus financial construct which shelters that social network. Rather than that social unity offering support and ethical parameters for the actions of its members and the wider sectors of society subordinated to it, the family is seen to function as a restrictive space depriving its members of liberty. Thus Vermandero in *The Changeling* gloats over the effect of his daughter Beatrice's marriage on her groom Piracquo: 'He shall be bound to me | As fast as this tie can hold him' (1.1.224–5).

That such immutable and rigid structures could be described critically is an index of the extent to which they were being eroded by a new set of social forces in the Jacobean era. Castiza says, 'The world's so changed, one shape into another | It's a wise child that knows its mother' (2.1.163–4). The changes that she evokes are not just interpersonal and familial (here she speaks of the loss of her natural mother for an unnatural one who plays bawd and hires her out to Lussurio in return for financial reward). Rather, the figure used is that of transformation of shapes, appositely describing the later Tudor and early Stuart sense of the changeableness of the world. Castiza's turn of phrase exemplifies the sense of potential convertibility of any entity into something else, a figure of the exchange process where the corrosive influence of money could convert all entities into other quite insubstantial and unrecognizable forms. It is that process of exchange ('The world's so changed') which appears to encroach upon the social spaces of the collective kinship identity, producing other, still more unstable spaces of newly emergent social identities.

The problem of the fundamental interrogation of the dynastic family and, at the same time, the exploration of possibilities of social existence beyond the available sites of family identity, is what is at stake in Shakespeare's *Romeo and Juliet*. The play foregrounds the agency of clan identity from the very outset, with Gregory saying: 'The quarrel is between our masters and us their men' (1.1.18–19). The clan conflict which the play describes does not arise out of individual aspirations or aggression. Rather, it is in the conflict between collective groups that individuals find their place. Once again, the family as extended social unit constituted of responsibilities and obligations – even when this social form may have had a merely mythological or symbolic existence – is regarded in a critical light symptomatic of the demise of particular notions of collective and individual identity.

Romeo is an important exception here. It is significant that he is absent from the inaugural brawl between supporters of the Capulet and Montague houses. Rather, as his father puts it, Romeo 'is to himself – I will not say how true | But to himself so secret and so close' – the repetition and qualification is a significant index of a sense of shifting modes of selfhood which the father has difficulty in articulating (1.1.145–6). Such a condition of separateness, a result of his brooding on his disappointed love for Rosaline, is not without its dangers: 'Tut, I have lost myself. I am not here' (1.1.194), says the lovelorn young man. In stark contrast to this, his friends say to him later on in the play, 'Now thou art sociable, now thou art Romeo' (2.3.82), which is surely more than simply a comment upon his personal qualities, or a description of his recovery from a moment of lover's blues. Rather, it can be understood as a statement about the reassuring re-establishment of a familiar mode of identity in a social system under pressure from new forces.

It is questionable whether, in the terms of this play produced on the eve of the Jacobean era, a place outside of the family entity, a social existence as a free-standing individual, is really sustainable. Certainly others' perception tends to bring Romeo as self-conscious outsider back into line. When he gatecrashes the Capulet feast, he is identified in purely spatial terms: on the one hand, by his slot in a collective entity, and on the other, as being out of place in the opposed entity: 'Uncle, this is a Montague, our foe, | A villain that is *hither come* in spite' (1.5.60–1; my emphasis). Romeo's transgression, despite his own sentiment of not belonging to either of these collective domains, is clearly a spatial transgression, and is perceived as such by his peers. Ironically, Romeo's presence at the Capulet celebration in fact merely confirms the spatial mode of which it is a function, that of the aristocratic clan structure investing individuals with a collective identity originating outside of themselves.

More radically disturbing, however, is Romeo's decision to repeat this movement of transgression, not in confirmation of that collective mode of spatiality, but in setting that identity to one side. 'Can I go forward when my heart is here?', he asks, 'Turn back, dull earth, and find thy centre out' (2.1.1–2). 'My heart' directly contradicts 'here', for 'here' is Capulet territory, an anathema to his Montague identity, but it is perhaps this 'my' which enables this very contradiction. The possessive pronoun signals the emergence of an individual consciousness through the experience of romantic self-preoccupation. His action of vaulting the wall is a spatial means of combating a spatial mode of identity. Indeed, the leap over the wall of the Capulet estate tends to deny the existence of that collective identity altogether, positing the irrelevance of collective spaces in the face of individual desire. This is certainly the drift of Juliet's discourse: 'Deny thy father and refuse thy name | ... And I'll no longer be a Capulet', she suggests (2.1.76–7). She explains to Romeo that ''Tis but thy name that is my enemy, | Thou art thyself, though not a Montague' (2.1.80–1). This is, strictly speaking, a *non sequitur* according to the ethos of the spatial collective, where name, and thus identity, is conferred by a place within the household. Identity without a name, that is, without a place, is thus a logical impossibility. In opposition to this model, Juliet would like to install a non-spatial mode of identity, in which things could be cut loose from their place within a semantic space – a rose, for instance – and retain their meaning by virtue of their own essential properties: 'That which we call a rose | By any other word would smell as sweet' (2.1.85–6); or in terms of human identity, 'Thou art thyself.' This new self is entirely self-referential, just as the lovelorn subjectivity is eminently concerned with its own feelings. Indeed, Juliet suggests Romeo ought to 'swear by thy gracious self' (2.1.155), taking himself as the verbal reference point of truth, rather than some other linguistic entity which might draw his identity back into the collective structures of place, name, household or family.

Just as Romeo's absence at the beginning of the play gave concrete illustration to his mother's description of him being 'not at this fray' (1.1.114), likewise Romeo's behaviour is spatially revealing when he intervenes in a row between the Montague, Mercutio, and his Capulet challenger, Tybalt. The stage directions tell us, '*Romeo beats down their points and rushes between them*' (s.d. 3.1.88). Romeo, having secretly married

Juliet, now belongs to both houses – or rather, this being, spatially speaking, as feasible as being in two places at once (given that the marriage has not been ratified, let alone orchestrated, by the collectivity), he falls between the two spatial blocs. Such a position between the two entities cannot, however, be sustained for more than an instant. An unusually detailed stage direction inform us that: 'Tybalt under Romeo's arm *thrusts Mercutio in*' (my emphasis), with the result that Romeo is dragged back into clan strife, killing Tybalt moments later in revenge for the murder which happened *under the aegis of*, or in defiance of (it is difficult to say which) individualized non-alignment with collective identities. The stage direction makes tangible in bodily proxemic form the difficulties of extracting individual subjectivity from the corporeally performed entanglements of collective social identity and the socio-spatial deadlock of feud traditions. Romeo's former exteriority, now re-assimilated to the structures of clan identity, is taken up, curiously, by the mortally wounded Mercutio crying 'A plague o' both your houses' (3.1.99).

Within the drama's social logic, the space of individualism, falling as it does into the interstices between the networks of the aristocratic households, cannot as yet hold its own. As a non-place, it does not yet offer the subject a sustainable and visible position of social identity. None the less, it possesses, within the materiality of stage performance, a clear spatial language derived from and in opposition to that of the tentacular structures of the feudal family, even if that emergent spatial language is rapidly dissolved back into the still dominant parameters of kinship. The isolation of a self which defines itself exclusively in reference to itself, constituting a space which is as yet unsustainable, culminates in Romeo's 'I have lost myself' and his subsequent graveside 'I come hither armed against myself' (1.1.194; 5.3.65).

Juliet's response to this new extra-familial space of individual identity is the ambivalence expressed in her words, 'My only love sprung from my only hate' (1.5.137). Her utterance indicates her simultaneous identification with two quite opposed modes of social existence, paradoxically linked in a spatial movement which at once binds and separates, the trajectory of 'sprung from' – at once a genealogical term of lineage, and a verb indicating irrevocable distance (as Juliet herself will later use the expression: 'O bid me leap, rather than marry Paris' – 4.1.77). The ambiguity of her situation perhaps contributes to her failure, in the last analysis, to transcend her identity as a member of the Capulet house; she falls back into an appearance of maidenly obedience towards her father, albeit for tactical reasons; more significantly, she dies, finally, in her own family's tomb. The 'vault' (4.3.32) which she (rightly) fears, is none other than an avatar of the collective house-hold, where successive generations are enshrined together. Or perhaps this is simply symptomatic of the misogynist bias of the play, which rat-ifies the imprisonment of the woman in the collective ethos while con-ceding to the male an emergent form of social mobility. Both Paris as the potential aristocratic husband, and Romeo as the maverick individ-ual, finally succeed in penetrating the house of Capulet, although their presence cancels each other out in the process.

Similarly ambivalent is Friar Laurence, whose theory of humours is based on a series of correspondences between the human body and the cosmos.

> Two such opposèd kings encamp them still
> In man as well as herbs – grace and rude will;
> And where the worser is predominant,
> Full soon the canker death eats up that plant.
>
> (2.2.27–30)

His vision is an organic one where plants, man and human society form a continuum of interrelated and balanced forces. Within this concep-tion of correspondences, the body itself is a house whose 'eyes' windows fall | Like death when he shuts up the day of life' (4.1.100–1), corre-sponding to and linked synecdochically with the household to which it belongs, and the broader body and house of society. The play demon-strates the tragic results, for the civic body, of the unbalancing of such forces, and suggests that the disequilibrium must be purged out of the system (at the cost of several members of the body politic) in order to re-establish the natural harmony of the constitutive elements. This explains Friar Laurence's paradoxical acceptance of the young lovers' marriage: for the priest, it forms part of the collective mentality, where marriage functions not as the fulfilment of individual aspirations, but as a means to consolidate the interests of two collective entities: 'For this alliance may so happy prove | To turn your households' rancour to pure love' (2.2.91–2). The old priest is prepared to countenance the risky undertaking if it serves the common-weal: his attitude positions him halfway between old and new; indeed he ventures into the uncertain territory of individual aspiration precisely in order to defend an old order of collective existence, not unlike the late sixteenth-century writ-ers of complaint literature who, paradoxically, confirmed the arrival of the new individualistic order of competitive market capitalism to the extent that they attacked it on the basis of an older collective ethic.[26]

Within the world of the play, one instance is clearly not ambivalent, namely, that of the Prince and the citizens' watch. The Prince embodies a form of superior collective cohesion, exemplifying an organic identity ('My blood for your rude brawls doth lie a-bleeding' – 3.1.188) and a revenge ethic ('Mercy but murders, pardoning those that kill' – 3.1.196). None the less, the Prince and the citizens exemplify a new force behind the emergence of a nascent individual subjectivity, that of the centralized and absolute state accumulating adequate power to quell the strife of its quarrelling nobles. The destructive potential of aristocratic internecine conflict had been, in England, long since reined in, but *Romeo and Juliet* alludes, in an as yet inarticulate fashion – having no other language to speak, regarding the Prince, than the language of collective identity – to an association between state power and emerging economic forces which were already causing the erosion of collective forms of social connection, not only among the nobility, but at all the levels of society. It is the aristocratic or clan family, not so much in its real as in its social symbolic capacity, which became the focus, in Shakespeare's drama, for signs of the impending demise of collective structures of identity. At this stage, however, the notion of an organic social body still held good – according to an ideal vision of society in which 'each part is fixt in's proper place | And not chaost together.'27

By the time of *The Changeling*, this coherent structure was crumbling; strife between aristocratic families and the defence of collective structures by the tactics of revenge, are implicitly combated by the drama itself declaring the revenge ethic a pathological perversion of social identity. Granted, Tomazo's mental peace can only be restored, after the murder of his brother, by the execution of the murderers, that is, by the restoration of equilibrium. At Act 5, Scene 2, it appears that the two absentees from Vermandero's castle, Antonio and Franciscus, are likely to be accused of Alonzo's murder, thus perpetuating the chain of futile deaths rather than restoring any form of stability by means of retribution. But in the Epilogue, Alsemero says:

> All we can do to comfort one another,
> To stay a brother's sorrow for a brother,
> To dry a child from the kind father's eyes,
> Is to no purpose, it rather multiplies:
> – Your only smiles have power to cause re-live
> The dead again, or in their rooms to give
> Brother a new brother, father a child:
> If these appear, all griefs are reconciled.
>   *Exeunt omnes.*

The 'multiplication' to which Alsemero refers, caused by attempting to salve these psychic wounds within the dramatic universe by means of repeated retribution, would signify the continuation, in the same vein, of the tragic structure of the dramatic action. Rather, the fictional world of the tragedy is to be terminated by the approving smiles of the appreciative audience, which allows the actors to withdraw (literally) into 'their rooms' where their dramatic identities can be abandoned, and the gruesome events of the play erased. The spatial abolition of the closure of the stage universe, opening it up, in one direction, to the audience space, and in the other, to off-stage 'rooms', cancels the tragic character of the dramatic world. Middleton seems to be suggesting that the recreation of equilibrium by revenge is not a feasible solution, this being a mere perpetuation of a negative world order, functioning along the lines of exchangeability, of an-eye-for-an-eye. In place of this stultifying world of repetition, the drama enacts the capacity to transfer between alternative worlds, such that a critical view of society and of other possibilities of collective reconciliation is gained. Flexibility in the social role of individuals allows old social structures (inflexibility, imprisonment, collective family identity) to be abandoned. Such flexibility is indicated spatially and tangibly. It is the possibility of quitting the concretely portrayed (stage) space of collective family identity for the off-stage space of exchangeable social identity (in the form of putting off costumes), which in Middleton's play, in stark contrast to Shakespeare's earlier drama, allows social cohesion to be secured and defended. In the putting-on and putting-off of costumes, self-reflexively foregrounded by Middleton's actors' departing words, this drama points to a third domain of social mobility ostentatiously thematized on the Jacobean stage, that of costuming as a marker of social belonging.

Costume and social mobility

Land, as the very basis of social prestige, was shifting, and the house, as metonymy of the family as curator of landed wealth and social responsibility, was also an unstable figure. The position of members of all social sectors was increasingly mobile, though to what extent is difficult to say. Evidence that this mobility was a cause of concern can be found, however, in the considerable efforts made by the authorities to curb slippage in social hierarchy. A further significant example of 'negative' indexes of social mobility is to be found in attempts to control apparel as a marker of social status, to keep people 'in their place' by fixing the correspondences between social rank and its outward sartorial signs.

Sumptuary legislation was passed in 1533, and Elizabeth issued 10 proclamations during her reign enforcing this legislation, presumably some indication of the ineffectual character of such endeavours to restrict social mobility. The legislation was eventually repealed in 1603, though only because Parliament rejected new bills that would have given the crown sole power to regulate dress. New sumptuary legislation was passed in 1621, and Charles forbade the selling and wearing of imitation jewellery in 1636. Such forms of social regimentation broke down altogether after 1640.[28] Vestimentary markers of social status, by definition, were notoriously fluid, and such fluidity was a cause for concern. Philip Stubbes wrote in his *Anatomie of Abuses*:

> But nowhere is there such a confuse mingle mangle of apparell in Ailgna, and such preposterous excesse thereof, as everyone is permitted to flaunt it out, in what apparell he lusteth hymself, or can get by any kinde of meanes. So that it is very harde to know, who is noble, who is worshipfull, who is a gentleman who is not: for you that have those, which are neither of the nobilitie, gentilitie, nor yeomanrie, no, nor yet of any magistrate or officer in the common wealth, go daiely in Silkes, Velvettes, Satens, Damskes, Taffaties, and such like: notwithstanding, that they be bothe base by birth, meane by estate, and servile by callyinge. And this I compte a greate confusion, and a generall disorder in a christian common wealth.[29]

Echoes of the same disquiet are to be found in the Jacobean theatre. When Coriolanus, clad in 'mean apparel', arrives at the house of his long-time enemy Aufidius in Antium, he is abused by the porter and serving-men, until his arch-foe recognizes and welcomes the intruder. The serving-men then persuade themselves that their judgement was not as poor as their mistake would imply: 'By my hand, I had thought to have strucken him with a cudgel, and yet my mind gave me his clothes made a false report of him. ... Nay, I knew by his face that there was something in him. He had, sir, a kind of face, methought – I cannot tell how to term it' (*Coriolanus* 4.5.150–8). Appearance is retrospectively perceived as a mere sheen, easily penetrated, in defence of the ostensible evidence of the signs of social rank – but when it comes to giving the elusive signs of noble birth real descriptive content, the serving-men are at a loss to define them.

More than mere lip-service is being paid here to the signifiers of social hierarchy, but at the same time, signifiers and signified appear to be utterly uncoupled, outer appearance no longer grounded in inherent social identity. In Middleton's *A Trick to Catch the Old One*, Lucre complains: 'There's more true honesty in such a country serving-man than in a hundred of our cloak companions: I may well call 'em companions, for since blue coats have been turned into cloaks, we can scarce know the man from the master' (2.1.139–42). Lucre's own sense of social hierarchies has not been eroded by the loss of clear sartorial distinctions; none the less, perception of those distinctions has become difficult. Two movements are at work here: one is the continued existence of clearly marked social rank, as a valid concept and a notion of essential value, the other is the erosion of hierarchies as a structure constituted of visible but all too easily removed – and thus merely exterior, conventional – signs. The fact that a blue coat, the standard uniform of a serving man, can be so easily abandoned, implicitly casts into question the innate validity of class hierarchies. The country/city opposition serves then as a second-order bulwark against this sense of change: good old country values continue to be embodied in the trustworthy serving-man, despite the erosion of visually buttressed hierarchies by social mobility and the concomitant sense of mutability. A retreat to a topography of rural values secures a topology of social degree and a topology of hierarchized costume. Such a reactive strategy is necessary because the schemes of costume are no longer capable of reflecting a reality now too complex to be contained by the traditional contours of social organization.

But if the stage enacted disturbing scenarios of social mobility in the stories it told, a far more fundamental threat was in the very fabric of theatre: namely, the assumption of roles and the concomitant wearing of costumes visibly carried out upon the stage. In the body of the actor, the possibility of social movement and mutability was paraded before the spectators. Thomas Harman's *Caveat for Common Cursitors* in its 1566 edition stated that 'as the comedians were to act, so the actions of their lives were chameleon-like, that they were uncertain, variable.'[30] J. Cocke fulminated that the player's 'chiefe essence is, *A daily Counterfeit*: He hath been familiar so longe with out-sides, that he professe himself...to be an apparent Gentleman. But his thinne felt, and his silk Stockings, or his foule Linnen, and faire Doublet, doe (in him) bodily reveal the Broker: So beeing not sutable, hee proves a Motley: His mind observing the same fashion of his body: both consist of parcells and remnants: ... [he] is himself the Taylor to take measure of his souls liking.'[31] Cocke's accusations hover between affirmation of an intact sumptuary regulation, by virtue of which the player's inadequate attire betrays his usurpation of gentle status, and perplexed admission of the disarray of such fixed rules of social rank. For the player appears to be quite capable himself of determining who he is and where he belongs in society, thus becoming a social 'Rogue errant', in the author's words.[32] The heterogeneity of the actor's outward trappings are deemed to be symptoms of the worrying disunity of a society in which individuals can migrate at will from their God-given places. The same unsettling link between the mutability of costume on the stage and social identity is present in John Earle's characterization of the stage gallant as 'one that was born and shapt for his cloathes; ... his business is in the street: the Stage, the Court ... He is a kind of walking Mercer's Shop, and shewes you one stuffe to day and another to morrow.'[33] Costume is the very contradiction of stability, both spatial and social. This notion becomes sharpened even more when Earle describes the player: 'He do's not only personate on the Stage, but sometimes in the Street, for he is mask'd still in the habit of a gentleman.'[34] The travesty of aristocratic identity becomes all the more threatening once it is transferred from the stage to the street, embodying mobility both vertical, by virtue of his 'gentleman's habit', and horizontal, by the act of leaving the fictional domain of the theatre. The players' costumes, often aristocrats' cast-offs sold to the actors by servants who had received them as presents, were thus an index of the mutability of their social place and identity. As Stephen Gosson said in his *Plays Confuted in Five Acts*, 'for a meane person to take upon him the title of a Prince with counterfeit port, and traine, is by outwarde signes to shewe them selves otherwise then they are, and so with in the compasse of a lye.'[35] The 'otherwise' signals a shift from the norm, from the received standard; deviation leads towards the realm of social 'untruth' or perversion of social morality by virtue of the confusion of the signs of social rank. The actor's mobility of appearance functions as a figure of social mobility. It is the players' costumes which form the focus of the supercilious speech made in the university play *The Return from Parnassus*, where the student actors reveal their disdain for, but also their envy of, their professional counterparts:

> Vile world, that lifts them up to high degree,
> And treads us down in groveling misery,
> England affords those glorious vagabonds,
> That carried erst their fardels on their backs,
> Coursers to ride on through the gazing streets,
> Sooping it in their glaring satin suits,
> And pages to attend to their masterships.[36]

The links between the mobility of the touring actors and upward social mobility (symbolized here by the spatial inversion of the burden-carrying actors subsequently themselves being carried on horseback) are made visible by the 'glaring satin suits', in which the costumed duplicity of the actor is embodied. The ostentatious sartorial finery is matched by an equally ostentatious display of servantry and landed estates.

The concern behind these attacks on the players is doubtless that the business of acting undermines the correct functioning of social meanings crucial to the good order of society.[37] Acting undermines the transparency of social status, a transparency expressed by Middleton's Weatherwise in *No Help, No Wit Like a Woman's*, who maintains his faith in the old order of things, where appearances faithfully transmit essences: 'By my faith, one may pick a gentleman out of his calves, and a scholar out on's cheeks; one may see by his looks what's in him' (3.1.168–70). It is precisely this reliable visibility of social status which is undermined by the deceitful character of the stage.

Every reference to costume on the stage thus functions self-reflexively to designate the theatre's own basis in vestimentary transformability and mobility. Host in *A Trick to Catch the Old One*, jesting with Witgood, says to his friend: 'Wilt thou command me now? I am thy spirit; conjure me into any shape' (1.2.21–2). Here the mutability of spirits is implicitly compared to the mutability of actors and their capacity to transform themselves into new 'shapes'. Helgill in *Michaelmas Term*, seeing the Country Wench dressed in her new finery, exclaims: 'You talk of alteration, here's the thing itself' (3.1.1). The young woman (played by a boy dressed up in a women's clothes, and now donning a second set of female attire), embodies alteration itself, by virtue of the transformative power of costume; by a curious alienation of the 'thing itself', of essence, into the essence of mutability, costume becomes an index of non-essence, of social arbitrariness.

We obtain a glimpse of the wider implications of the theatre's destabilization of the codes of vestimentary appearance when Enobarbus in *Antony and Cleopatra* muses upon defeated Antony's increasing alienation from reality, evinced in his challenging Caesar, who has just won the day militarily, to a duel. It is most unlikely, scoffs Enobarbus, that Caesar will allow himself to 'be staged to th' show | Against a sworder', that is, a gladiator (*OED*, 'sworder', 1a) (3.13.29–30). Both the slave's challenge to an emperor, and the reduction of royalty to a spectacle for popular entertainment, exemplify the social topsy-turvy associated with the theatre. It is this explicitly meta-theatrical train of thought which flows immediately into Enobarbus's subsequent disgusted observation to the effect that: 'men's judgements are | A parcel of their fortunes, and things outward | Do draw the inward quality after them | To suffer all alike' (3.13.30–3). Antony's judgement has been shattered by the 'outward' context of his misfortunes, with the result that he is no longer capable of coherent 'inward' cognition. Contingent exterior circumstance sways the normally fixed character of truth and intellection, in turn upsetting the clarity of social hierarchy. The theatrical metaphor of the stage is then spatialized through the interaction of inward and outward, and made dynamic by the force of 'draw...after them'. Here the link with theatre and with its corrosion of incontrovertible social signification becomes clear: rather than outward signs conveying given, fixed social values, it is the outward appearance which creates a dynamism radically opposed to traditional stability, 'drawing' ostensibly essential qualities such as rank, breeding or nobility in its wake, rendering them malleable, mutable and fluid. In Enobarbus's admittedly scornful formulation, the accidentals of peripheral circumstances affect inward perception; this is an spatially extended version of the concomitant problem of outward signs and their inner meaning. In the latter problem, the uniforms of social caste, rather than marking out and thus anchoring distinctions, make them mobile and thus contingent. In Enobarbus's formulation, the appraisal of the contours of reality and consequent political actions taken are sucked into the contingent fictions of theatre, a situation which radicalizes the mere instability of sartorial status-marking. In both scenarios, judgement is *deluded* by outward appearance, instead of being *informed* by the signs of time-honoured social categories; in Enobarbus's imagery, however, the mere 'appearances' of theatrical fiction dare to upstage hard political realities and hierarchies and displace their priority.

Costume thus functioned to question social hierarchies, as the cast-off costume continued to signify a social status, but also the mobility and thus emptiness, of that selfsame sign of status. Not only were the signs of status made mobile in the mutability of the actors on the Jacobean stage, this mutability was also extended to become a form of social critique. *The White Devil* frequently uses costume to wield withering criticism against the powerful. Brachiano says of Isabella's brother Francisco: 'all his reverend wit | Lies in his wardrobe; he's a discreet fellow | When he's made up in his robes of state' (2.1.189–91); and Flamineo says of Camillo:

> This fellow by his apparell
> Some men would judge a politician,
> But call his wit in question, you shall find it
> Merely an ass in's foot-cloth.
>
> (1.2.49–52)

Fransisco, in turn, significantly disguised as the Moor, reduces costume to mere markers of arbitrary place without any real qualitative difference: 'What difference is between the duke and I? No more than between two bricks, all made of one clay: only't may be one is placed on the top of a turret, the other in the bottom of a well, by mere chance. If I were placed as high as the duke, I should stick as fast, make as fair a show, and bear out weather equally' (5.1.105–11). The costume renders the signs of difference and rank indifferent; the spatialized discourse functions as a covert attack on traditional privileges, even if the 'Moor' defuses this dangerously democratic sentiment into a discourse about spurious racial differences. The theatrical metaphor, when taken to its logical performative extreme, reduces all social ranks to a common denominator, mercilessly levelling all hierarchies.

Even more disturbing was the real (as opposed to merely symbolic) power of the acting profession, by virtue of costume, not just to disturb the signs of status, or to criticize the factitiousness of apparent social worth, but to usurp social place by assuming the very signs of status which costume tended to undermine. The most extreme form of such usurpation was the actors' imitation and expropriation of royal spectacle. A clear index of the genuine political danger constituted by the visibility of the stage, and its capacity to destabilize the signs of royalty, is the fact that such subversive potential was alluded to by none other than the monarch himself. James I remarked upon, and carefully limited, this political threat in his *Basilikon Doron* when he declared: 'It is a true olde saying, That a King is as one set on a skaffold, whoese smallest actions & gestures al the people gazingly do behold: and therefore although a King be never so precise in the dischargeing of his office, the people who seeth but the outwarde parte, will ever judge of the substance by the circumstances, & and according to the outwarde appearance (if his behaviour be light or dissolute) will conceive preoccupied conceits of the Kings inwarde intention.'[38] He was echoing a similar statement made in 1586 by Elizabeth.[39]

The essential assumption in James's vision of royal spectacle is that appearances have priority over essences, and so that the royal person must take care that only the truth of his good government is conveyed, rather than incidental impressions such as light or dissolute behaviour. Already here, James concedes that appearances may not always faithfully translate essences, though this is seen as a mere irrational anomaly in the system of royal spectacle. However, just as James's statement was appropriated by the actors themselves for their own purposes (as in Heywood's *Apologie for Actors*, which stated that: 'we [actors] are men that stand in the broad eye of the world, so should our manners, gestures and behaviours, favour of such government and modesty, to deserve the good thoughts and reports of all men'[40]), so the functioning of appearances on stage was also perverted in the common theatres. Significant in James's formulation is his belief that appearances cut loose of the true essence of the monarch's necessarily benevolent rule could give rise to 'prejudged conceits [which] will (in the meane time) breed Contempt, the Mother of Rebellion and disorder.'[41] The scission of the tightly controlled link between outward appearance and inward reality allows a democracy of thought among the spectators which is deemed to carry the danger of social unrest.

Thus Cornelia in *The White Devil* says: 'The lives of princes should like dials move, | Whose regular example is so strong, | They make the times by them go right or wrong' (1.2.294–6). The rulers are reminded of their exemplary role for the nation, like a sundial which regulates the day's work. This injunction delivered to the court and its famed decadence is uttered by the actors playing rulers on the stage, and thus assuming the exemplary role of the monarch and of royal spectacle. There is a veiled threat in the person of an actor imitating the Lady, and taking over the moral voice of social authority. The process of moral appropriation evident in the chain of citations, leading from Elizabeth's comments on the monarch's place upon the stage, via James's repetition of the conceit, to popular appropriations of the simile, is replicated in the appropriation of the trope of the monarch's solar centrality, subsequently seized and travestied upon the stage in the sundial metaphor. This exemplifies what Manley has called the 'desacralizing spread of theatrical consciousness',[42] by virtue of which the humble aspire to moral heights normally reserved for the powerful, mimicking their betters in a dangerously disrespectful seizure of certain prerogatives of rule. Triggering this usurpation of ordained hierarchies was the usurpation inherent in the act of donning a costume and thereby a social role and identity.

Combating social mobility

The dramas frequently demonstrate their awareness of the inherent social instability in theatrical factitiousness, and in particular in costume as a mode of disguise. Once a disguise is assumed, no social relationship is stable and trustworthy until that disguise is definitively laid down. Significantly, the Jacobean theatre was obsessed with the *removal* of costume.

It is illuminating to examine the relationship maintained between Jonson's characters Mosca and his master Volpone in the ubiquitous atmosphere of cunning, deceit and deception of *Volpone*, and the role played in this context by the renunciation of disguise. It is tempting to see the working relationship between the two villains as the one site in the play where cynicism does not reign, just as it is tempting to see a similarly untarnished rough fellowship and mutual trust between Follywit and his henchmen in *A Mad World, My Masters*. But when, in Act 3 Scene 5 of *Volpone*, the relationship between the two tricksters becomes a theatrical one, as Mosca performs and Volpone enjoys the discomfort of the suitors told one after another of their loss, the apparent innocence of their friendship is revealed for what it is. The spectators are alerted to the fact that even among the orchestrators of this performance 'hoax', portraying Volpone's death and financial succession, the theatrical relationship, which the play shows from the outset to be inherently exploitative, is operating. It will dominate the closing action of the play. In the final scenes, the actor (Mosca) succeeds in gulling the spectator (his master Volpone). The spectator-master only recovers the upper hand by revealing himself in turn to another set of spectators, the court of law, for what he is, an actor in disguise. Upon renouncing his false identity, Volpone can reassume his authority as a noble, an authority which allows him to restore the stability of truth in his own defence, be it at the cost of losing his ill-gotten gains. With the laying down of the master's disguise, and the reassertion of degree, hierarchy and aristocratic status, normal social conduct is restored, and the stage effectively closes down its power to destabilize social relations through the epistemological confusion of stage costume. The drama itself appears to be reluctant to give more than brief rein to the epistemological chaos which it is capable of letting loose: as Manley has commented, 'this exhilarating release from the confines of...social categories was also a terrifying exposure to the mobility of social life, of the mere positionality of differences which organize a world in transition.'[43] There were good reasons for the dramatists to rein in the disorder conjured up by their dramas.

The spectre of social disorder haunted the Jacobean imagination. The era saw massive inflation as food production lagged behind expanding population levels; at the same time, wages remained unchanged, such that the real earning power and economic conditions of the bulk of the English population deteriorated radically in the period. Wages in the building industry, for example, had dropped, in the years before the Civil War, to less than half of what they had been in 1510; the surplus of labour permitted employers to keep wages artificially low. Arthur Standish could write in 1611 that food had become 'more deere in price within these last six yeares than in twentie yeares before: and if the dearth of victuals shall happen to increase but a few yeares to come ... the poore man by his labours shall not get wherewith to relieve himselfe and his family.' Those higher up the hierarchy of social privilege were more than aware of the threat to social order posed by poverty. Town authorities were constantly concerned about social distress as a potential cause of political disorder, and land-owners deeply feared insurrection driven by rural poverty. There were outbreaks of agrarian revolt in 1597, 1607 and 1628–31. Rural revolt was endemic in one part of England or another in the 1630s, though this picture needs to accommodate the fact that disorder was often limited and localized, with some consistently poor areas never experiencing disorder. None the less, the threat was perceived as being a potent one, Simonds d'Ewes speaking of 'the hoped-for rebellion' in 1622, and Sir Robert Cotton warning of revolt by 'the loose and needy multitude' in 1628. They were only several voices among many.[44] It is no coincidence, therefore, that *Coriolanus* opens with a corn riot, reflecting a common preoccupation of the times.

Social mobility further up the social ladder, as representatives of the middle classes broke into the gentry, or as merchants accumulated commercially-based forms of social power which made them competitors with the nobility, also generated fear and aggression on the part of a ruling class which perceived its privileges as being under threat. The sale of titles, for example, was hailed as dangerously undermining social hierarchy, one contemporary commentator claiming that 'the ordinary purchasing of Armnes and Honours for Money [is] very preiudiciall to true Nobilitie and politique gouernment', and another, that 'It introduceth a strange confusion, mingling the meaner with the more pure and refined metal.'[45] More generally, James I could execrate in *Basilikon Doron* that 'Paritie, the mother of confusion & enemie to Unitie'.[46] Evident in these evaluations of the threat of social mobility at both ends of the social ladder is the clear element of reaction which characterized much response to increased fluidity in social relations in Jacobean England; certainly the fear aroused by the anarchic events of the Civil War meant that by 1700 social mobility had been reined in considerably.[47] Such reaction against social mobility was also evident on the stage.

As we have seen, the Jacobean drama constantly emphasizes the difficulty of clearly demarcating social rank, in showing distinctions between people who are not citizens and who think like them, in distinguishing between court and gentlemen, in differentiating lower classes and rogues.[48] Much of the action on the Jacobean stage could be seen to perform a disturbing fluidity of social status, a fluidity out of which the professional theatre itself as an economically viable under-taking of course emerged. From this standpoint, mobility and trans-gression would be the only really meaningful categories with which to analyse the social commentary of Jacobean drama. Yet at the same time, the category of transgression only exists through a dialectical relation-ship with the category of order, and it would appear likely that the same coexistence of transgression and reaction can be found to be performed on the stage.

The forceful expressions of reaction to social mobility alluded to above were often couched in clearly spatial language: 'Noble-men weare pullde doune, which is the foundation off monarkeye – monarkeye soone affter fell.'[49] It is no surprise then, that such reactions had their concomitant in strategies of containment performed – with spatial means – on the stage. The spatiality of the stage as an instrument in service of social order is directly addressed in Shakespeare's *Tempest*, in which control of social mobility is effected via the dramatization of the wedding masque in Act 4. From the very first scene, where the storm threatens social hierarchies, the play deals with the threat of sedition. The storm signals the possibility of the world being turned upside-down, and of the socially inferior boatswain ordering his aristocratic passengers, in a movement of symbolic social inversion, 'Keep below' (1.1.10); such sedition will be punished after the storm has abated, threatens Gonzalo (1.1.27–32). Elsewhere, however, the ineffectual and inebriated uprising on the part of Stephano, Trinculo and Caliban is ridiculed within the play. Sedition is contained by belittling it, or by restricting it to the ranks of the nobility, making it an affair of internal strife between competing dukes. All these examples of sedition, how-ever, are further contained by their projection into a faraway place, that of Prospero's magical island, an other place where the temporary inver-sions of hierarchies inherent in the storm serve the larger restoration of 'legitimacy' as Prospero understands it, in a universe orchestrated by his powers to control representation and perception.

A similar restoration of socio-spatial order occurs in Act 5 of Jonson's *Alchemist*, in which the return of the master Lovewit signals the closure of the performance space of the tricksters' appropriated house, and the imminent closure of the performance space of the play itself. Spatial identity reverts to its proper shape as the house is reappropriated by the owner, obliging Face in turn to reassume his true identity as Jeremy the servant – and thence his true place in the social hierarchy. But at the same time, this reversion to an earlier social order and corresponding identity also serves as an alibi for the villains, Jeremy brazenly asserting that no one has visited the plague-stricken house, where he has of course been present for the duration. The subversive force of this counter-appropriation of the reversion to the space of order, however, affords the villains no positive gains, so that this final twist in the plot does not unduly disturb the restoration of property and propriety.

In Act 5 of Middleton's *No Help, No Wit Like a Woman's* the pace of the action accelerates in proportion to the imminent resolution of the relationships between the characters. The complexity of the dizzying exchanges of the final moments of the play appears to be directly correlated to the degree of order such exchanges are designed to restore. Mistress Low-Water is replaced by Beveril as Lady Goldenfleece's husband. Simultaneously, the arranged marriage between Philip and Jane, and Sandfield and Grace respectively, orchestrated by Sir Oliver Twilight, is averted at the last moment, upon the abrupt discovery of the crossed identity of the two young ladies in question (they were mistakenly swapped in early childhood upon recuperation from the wet-nurse). Thus Philip is able to legitimize his marriage to Grace, temporarily thought to be his own sister, and Sandfield can marry his beloved Jane. The series of abrupt exchanges does not prevent the conclusion of the play being characterized by a satisfying sense of resolution: 'This is Grace, | This is Jane; now each has her right name and place' (5.1.462–3). Indeed, it is the force of acceleration which, paradoxically, is recuperated to cement the restoration of social stability.

Most interestingly, as suggested above, *Romeo and Juliet* attempts to deal with a still partially monolithic system of collective family allegiance perceived as being dangerous for the state and for social order, leading as it does to social conflict. Against this collective familial ethic the individual and its desires are posed. New individual aspirations and questioning of collective existence fail, in the tragic ending of *Romeo and Juliet*, but not without offering a resolution of civil strife, and more significantly, with the maintenance of individual transgression of collective structures. Juliet may be restored to her rightful familial place along with other members of the Capulet clan in the family monument, but significantly, Romeo is also entombed there. Death effectively neutralizes his movement of transgression into the 'enemy camp', but also embalms it – a fitting image for the contradictory moment of tension between the still extant old order and the emergent yet none the less threatening new organization of personal space established in opposition to public space. Thus both individual social mobility and the excesses of collectivized clan identity are simultaneously contained, in a paradoxical spatial configuration which announces its intermediate situation in a transitional moment. It is likely that it is the threshold position of *Romeo and Juliet*, situated as it is at the beginning of our period, which accounts for the paradoxical status of the play's socio-spatial functioning. The other plays mentioned were produced somewhat later, when this inertia had given way to irreversible change. Whence their reinforcement of the dynamism of social mobility – and, simultaneously, their anxious attempts to reassert the stability of social space as portrayed in the space of the stage.

5
Masterless Men and Shifting Knavery: Demographic Mobility

Demographic mobility in early modern England

The Renaissance was an age of centrifugal energies – social and geographical structures were opening up and releasing people, driven by the force of competitive individualism, towards new horizons. This increasingly accelerated and expansive geographical impulse will be addressed in this book under several categories: that of mobility within England, in this chapter, and that of mobility beyond English shores in the following chapter. As the exemplary focus of geographic mobility in the Jacobean era, London figures as the place at which geographical mobility within England and beyond the borders of the realm fused in an extraordinary meeting of internal and external travel. And it was in the London theatres that the most intense representations of mobility, both internal and external, were portrayed and, to the great concern of contemporaries, embodied.

Some forms of mobility were the result of increasingly energetic commercial activity which generated new routes of communication within Britain. The intense regionalism of Britain in the sixteenth century is evinced by Bishop John Bale's concern, in 1544, that the northerners would not understand his language.[1] Jacobean drama is replete with allusions to other 'dark corners of the land' such as Wales in *No Help, No Wit Like a Woman's*, of which a desperate Savourwit says 'there's the best hills | To hide a poor knave in' (4.1.250–1), or colonized Ireland, where 'the wild Irish' play football with their foes' heads (*The White Devil* 4.1.136); a perplexing reference to 'th'wild of Kent' presumably refers to the Weald, but the linguistic confusion is significant (*Michaelmas Term* 2.3.296). Against this isolation of the various regions of Britain, trade was an important factor in opening up inner-British routes of communication.

The spread of internal trade was evinced in a major increase in the numbers of chapmen and other itinerant retailers tracing their trade routes across the counties. Grain peddlers and cattle drovers from Wales and the western counties opened up routes towards London; by 1600 there was a well-established driving-trail into Kent from the Marches. As trade routes connected various regions, the inns which marked stops along the way became new focal points for economic and social structures, serving obviously as hotel, coach and wagon park, posting house, but also as warehouse, bank, exchange, scrivener's office, auction-room, exhibitions, information bureau.[2]

Under the Stuarts, postal routes were increasingly established, radiating out from London, though it was not until the reign of William and Mary that postal communication no longer travelled exclusively via the capital. Parallel to the postal routes however, other forms of communication, particularly the transmission of reports of current events, were contributing to the geographical coherence of the land. News contributed to an increasingly coherent sense of the interaction between the local and national dimensions of the country. The City served as a place where news was gathered and synthesized as a narrative of events integrating information about the capital, to be retransmitted subsequently to the counties. Such modes of communication became even more intense during the Civil War.[3] The distribution of news, complete with details of the particular shires in contact with London (Sussex, Derbyshire) is ridiculed as a crass mercantile undertaking in the opening scenes of Jonson's masque *Newes from the New World* (1620) (515: 48–9), but the very possibility of mentioning such transformations of modes of information transmission indicates how important such developments were becoming.

Geographical mobility and changing economic structures also resulted in transformations of the visual representation of the land. Surveying and mapping were a function of centralized government's policy to efficiently monitor and tax the regions it administered, but equally of the increasing wealth of private individuals and their will to assert local independence in the face of government control.[4] To that extent mapping simultaneously represented an increasing knowledge about and thus accessibility of the regions of England, and conversely, a mode of regional self-knowledge signifying increasing resistance to absolute monarchical rule.

All these factors of rapid change meant that there was considerable mobility within the English population, some communities experiencing an extraordinary rate of turnover. At Honiger in Suffolk, only 2 of

the 63 family names registered for the period 1600–34 were still in the register for 1700–23; in a single decade between 1618 and 1628, just over half the population of Cogenhoe in Northamptonshire departed and was replaced. It would seem that a high degree of mobility among the middle and labouring classes, quite part from the impoverished population of chronic vagrants, was quite normal. Samples from sources for the late Elizabethan and early Stuart periods suggests that around 80 per cent of the population moved at least once in their lifetime, while scattered autobiographical material suggests that more frequent moves were by no means an exception. Many adolescent servants left their homes in their teens to work elsewhere on annual contracts, eventually finding permanent employment and settling with their families until their children in turn moved on. Other forms of mobility were provoked by seasonal labour such as harvesting. Surprisingly, established families and some tenant farmers were also relatively mobile. Such mobility among the population was varied, depending upon push-and-pull factors of economic depression and opportunity respectively, as well as regional differences.[5]

Mobility within England was also partly the result of 'internal colonization', as the increasing demand for food drove farmers to push back the frontiers of Cumberland, Westmoreland and south-west England, in the search for new areas of arable land; there was an extensive movement away from more established 'fielden' villages to the forest areas, creating a new pattern of scattered hamlets consisting of a single class of rural cottagers, with the manor house often far away. There was also considerable mobility caused by the expanding population of late sixteenth- and early seventeenth-century England, as people moved to the more sparsely populated areas such as the Cambridgeshire Fens, which could support a larger population on an abundance of common lands and with prolific possibilities for fishing and fowling; likewise the weaving districts of Norfolk, Suffolk and Essex saw a large growth in population as the weaving industry could absorb new employees.[6]

Such rural mobility, however, was not only caused by population growth and the demand for increasing agricultural production, but also by eviction and rural proletarization arising from the rapid advance of the wool industry and coal mining.[7] Enclosure of land formerly worked by small farmers was a major and much condemned cause of rural mobility in the Renaissance. Philip Stubbes complained that

Landlordes make Marchandize of their poore Tenants, racking their rentes, and settyng them so straight upon the tenter hookes, as no man can live on them. Besides that, as though this pillage and pollage were not rapacious enough, they take in, and inclose Commons, Moores, Heathes, and other common pastures where out the poore commonaltie were wont to have all their forrage and feedyng for their Cattell, and (which is more) Corne for themselves to live upon: all which are now in moste places taken from them, by these greedie Puttockes, to the great impoverishing and utter beggarying of many whole Townes and parishes.[8]

Lupton wrote of the enclosing Landlord:

the Parish hee eyther winnes by Composition, or famishes by length of time, or batters down by force of his lawlesse Engines: Most of the Inhabitants are miserably pillaged and vndone, he loues to see the bounds of his boundlesse desires; ... Enclosures make fat Beasts, & leane poore people; ... Husbandmen hee loues not, for he maintaines a few shepheards with their Currs.[9]

The large body of complaint literature, of which Stubbes's and Lupton's texts are fine examples, reflected a genuine crisis in English society, where the erosion of traditional rights by new rapacious landlords created widespread rural dispossession.

In this period of transition from late feudal economic structures, the separation of small farmers from their land increasingly delivered them up to the vagaries of rural wage labour, vulnerable to fluctuations of the market. The steady reduction of copyhold land-tenure contracts (which entailed nominal services as payment for land tenure) and gradual replacement by leasehold (which implied defined rights over land for a stated time in return for rent) was a major factor in the dispossession of small tenants. Between the early sixteenth century and late seventeenth century, there was a reduction in the proportion of tenants on copyhold land from two-thirds to a third. The period saw the progressive if not complete elimination of smaller tenants, and a corresponding move towards the future tripartite division of rural economy: landlord, prosperous tenant farmer and agricultural labourer. In the Jacobean era, enclosure, which was by then not a new phenomenon, continued unabated, receiving legislative support from the Commons, which generally represented the interests of well-to-do gentry. In contrast, the Crown had been largely opposed to enclosure with its depopulating effects – in part as it reduced the availability of a conscriptable population for armies, in part because the provision of a minimum of common arable land prevented popular revolt and encouraged population stability, and additionally, as enclosure represented the increasing transfer of wealth from taxable common land to privatė possessors. 1597 saw the last acts against depopulation, 1608 the first limited pro-enclosure act, and 1621 the first general enclosure act, despite opposition by some MPs who feared agrarian disturbances; there were frequent anti-enclosure riots and risings in Gloucestershire, Worcestershire, Shropshire and Wiltshire during this period. After 1640, no government tried to stop enclosures, nor to raise income by fining enclosers. Even more extensive in some areas than the dramatic dispossession visible in enclosure, was the slower process of 'engrossing', whereby larger yeomen would gradually consolidate their lands; as smaller husbandmen, hampered by higher rents and lower margins of profit than their wealthy neighbours, were eventually forced to sell up and move on.[10]

Not surprisingly, this topical issue was also the subject of Jacobean drama. Disruption of rural land-ownership structures makes up one of the plot strands in the anonymous play *Arden of Faversham*. In the opening scene we are informed that Arden has received all the lands of the Abbey of Faversham from the Lord Duke of Somerset by letters patent sealed and signed with the royal hand (1.3–7). But this gift of land encroaches upon traditional land rights. A smallholder named Greene complains to Arden's wife:

> Your husband doth me wrong
> To wring me from the little land I have.
> My living is my life; only that
> Resteth remainder of my portion.
> Desire of wealth is endless in his mind
> And he is greedy-gaping still for gain.
> … I had rather die than lose my land.
>
> (1.470–5, 518)

Another character likewise embodies the dislocation of traditional property relations and the subsequent poverty for those at the bottom end of the social ladder. The sailor Dick Reede implores the hard-hearted Arden:

> My coming to you was about the plot of ground
> Which wrongfully you detain from me.
> Although the rent of it be very small,
> Yet it will help my wife and children,

Which here I leave in Faversham, God knows,
Needy and bare. For Christ's sake, let them have it.

(13.12–17)

The plot of the play principally turns around Arden's murder at the hands of his unfaithful wife and her lover, and their rightful discovery and punishment under a Christian scheme of godly conduct. But Arden has so many enemies in the play also because he infringes traditional structures of rural subsistence, and thereby dislocates social relationships of mutual support and assistance.

It was when rural dispossession triggered waves of migration, however, that it became more threatening, and offered the most potential for dramatization, both on the stage and elsewhere. Coupled with the economic depression of the second decade of James's reign, eviction, poverty, death and disease among rural peasantry were the major factors contributing to demographic mobility in the period. Such mobility was of course not restricted exclusively to the rural poor: an older pattern of vocational or professional mobility was maintained, as country people came to the cities to take up apprentices, for instance. However, traditional 'betterment' migration was supplemented by a surge of uncontrolled 'subsistence' migration during the period 1580 to 1640. It was this new and disturbing form of migration, characterized by wandering hordes of 'masterless men', which was of particular concern to the authorities. A growing population, land dispossession and endemic poverty levels (estimated at between 20 and 30 per cent of the population for our period) produced a steadily growing vagrancy problem, probably rising slightly faster than population growth. Savage penalties were imposed upon vagabonds: homeless people flocked to London, where whipping posts were set up every hundred yards to punish 'sturdy beggars'. A 1563 Act obliged labourers to buy a ticket of release in order to transfer to a new employer, and stipulated that a labourer moving to another job and accepting wages higher than the legal maximum fixed by JPs could be punished by a crippling fine and imprisonment.[11]

Clearly the authorities were eager though increasingly impotent to control the population wandering the roads, a population which the establishment feared as a fluid and unpredictable catalyst for social unrest and saw as a direct threat to property. Contemporaries saw a correlated threat of geographical mobility and the destruction of social hierarchy: 'Rooted to the land by an agricultural economy, the idea of social order is inseparable from topography: the stability of vertical social ranks depends upon the spatial fixity of subjects in the landscape.'[12] 'Masterless men' were seen as having left the hierarchy of social subordination which founded traditional conceptions of organic society, and consequently lost their place in the tissue of mutual and interrelated connectedness which was thought to constitute that society. Related expressions of the fear of geographical mobility can be found in many contemporary references to 'masterless men', for instance in *King Lear*, where Edgar disguises himself as a fraudulent wandering madman, Tom O'Bedlam (Folio 2.2.168–84). Edgar's disguise and adoption of the mobile identity of the vagrant is one index of the broader spatial dislocation of the realm incurred as a result of Lear's division of his kingdom.

One play goes so far as to attribute cosmic significance to the vagrancy problem. In Middleton's *No Help, No Wit Like a Woman's*, the amateur astrologer Weatherwise retains his faith in the predictions of the almanacs, but warns against their waning significance in the organic order of the universe and of the social consequences of the loss of that order: 'Well, take your courses gentlemen, without 'em, and see what will come on't; you may wander like masterless men; there's ne'er a planet will care a half-penny for you' (3.1.128–30). His admonition to those of his friends who set no store by almanacs raises the perspective of a universe in which over-arching structures of coherence and organization no longer hold good, one similar to contemporary society, manifestly inadequate to hold in check menacing numbers of free-floating individuals. Interestingly, however, the vagabond situation of masterless men is represented here as a passive state which may befall the subject caught in a larger process of social disintegration, rather than as evidence of an active and malevolent influence working against the forces of social cohesion. Middleton's identification of the causal relationship between changes in social structures and the mobility thus unleashed was a more accurate description of the state of affairs than the customary one-sided branding of the masterless men as a mobile and undisciplined force of social subversion; the masterless men are presented here as victims of the progressive collapse of social structures. It is none the less significant that the vagrants are placed within the somewhat fanciful framework of the astrologer's almanac, suggesting a nostalgic harking-back to an older vision of cosmic and social interrelatedness which the realities plainly belied – although it is equally important that Weatherwise is a figure of ridicule in this play, even if his statements would have had a familiar ring for the audience.

Such ambivalence is entirely absent in Beaumont and Fletcher's *Beggars Bush*, where the masterless men sing of an alternative commonwealth under the leadership of their 'upright-man', crowned as a travesty-king: 'In the world look out and see, | Where so happy a prince as he? | Where the nation live so free, | And so merry as do we?' The song emphasizes the band's freedom from constraint, underlining the fact that liberty from institutional determination is first and foremost a spatial liberty: 'Be it peace or be it war, | Here at liberty we are, | And enjoy our ease and rest: | To the field we are not prest; | Nor are called into the town | To be troubled with the gown' (Act 2, Scene 1; p. 31). Despite the positive note struck by the play, the disturbance of hierarchical notions of the state and social institutions caused by geographical mobility is clearly articulated.

The movement of vagrants which so concerned contemporary commentators converged to a large extent upon London, such that the rapidly growing city became the focus of geographical mobility within Britain. This fluidity is reflected in the liquid metaphors of a Sandwich tradesman's 1604 complaint, metaphors which successively flow into a single overwhelming and uncontrolled urban mass: 'all our creeks seek to one river, all our rivers run to one port, all our ports join to one town, all our towns make but one city, and all our cities and suburbs but one vast and unwieldy and disorderly Babel of buildings which the world calls London.'[13] It has been estimated that an average of 7,000 immigrants were entering London a year between 1605 and 1660, and though many of these may have left again, the figure may have been as much as 50 per cent higher. London increased six-fold to 350,000 between 1550 and 1650, and experienced a 70 per cent increase in population between 1500 and 1600. Even the high urban death-rates did not slow the capital's exponential growth: in 1603 and in 1625, when the city lost 15 per cent of population through plague, the losses were made up within two years. London's growth from 60,000 in 1500 to more than 500,000 by 1700 made it an urban phenomenon rivalled only by the rise of Amsterdam. Mobility of population was most intensely evident in London, with a high proportion of its population having lived there for less than a generation, or living there for only part of the year. There were numerous attempts to stem the growth of London and thus to control the mobility of its population. From the 1580s through to the end of her reign, Elizabeth militated against the growth of London by passing acts and issuing proclamations against further building in the city. Between 1614 and 1627 there were nine royal proclamations against seasonal visitors in winter and spring in an attempt to alleviate overcrowding in the capital. James alone passed eight proclamations dealing with the subject of new buildings.[14]

The city provided a favourite refuge for the criminal poor. Vagrancy arrests rose twelve-fold from 1560 to 1625, a period in which the metropolitan population quadrupled. In particular the suburbs were a haven for vagrants, with London sheltering as many as 30,000 'masterless men' in 1602. As is well known, the Liberties, where the public theatres were largely situated, lay outside the jurisdiction of the City authorities. Middlesex, to which the Liberties belonged, suffered from a comparative lack of policing as compared to the City, a frequent cause of concern to the City government; but at the same time Middlesex represented a burden of law and order for which the City fathers were reluctant to assume responsibility. As the suburbs grew, control and policing from the old city grew increasingly problematic; the government of outer London steadily disintegrated, as the suburbs became vulnerable to political unrest and agitation.[15]

London correspondingly figured on the stage as a focus for geographical movement and dynamic activity in direct opposition to the forces of law and order. Emblematically, *The Alchemist* opens with the departure of the Master from his house in plague-stricken London. This scenario figures the fragility of social control in the face of geographical movement within the city: the masterless house becomes the site of the criminal activities of the masterless men. Significantly, the villain Face is a 'translated suburb-captain' (1.1.19), a figure from the underworld of the periphery of the city, disguised ('translated') and thus possessing a disturbingly mobile identity, but also geographically mobile within the precincts of London (whence the secondary resonance of 'translated').

In *A Trick to Catch the Old One*, the city house also becomes a site of instability, of dynamism and productivity escaping from the control of authority. Lucre proposes to his nephew the 'uncle's house' as the place to 'strike the stroke', that is, to make a marriage-bargain which Lucre hopes will in turn prove profitable for him (2.1.317). The bawdy secondary meanings of an uncle's house, a place of prostitution, and of striking the stroke, which hardly needs explanation in that context, multiply the semantic possibilities of the situation – but in a manner contrary to the profit multiplication for which Lucre hopes. For an uncle's house is exemplary of the city as a place of scurrilous (sexual) transactions under the aegis of respectable commerce. Witgood appears to be making a transaction which will profit his uncle, as the marriage of the nephew with a rich widow is sure to produce a favourable financial spin-off for the immediate family, a spin-off not dissimilar to the vicarious pleasure the uncle gains at the thought of the sexual activities of the pair in an upper room of his house. But Uncle Lucre is gulled in his own house, which he puts at Witgood's disposal for the nephew not to seal a lucrative contract with a wealthy widow, but with a mere courtesan. At the same time, Lucre's (second) wife is plotting for her son (from a previous marriage) to court the widow, thus safeguarding her and her son's interests over against those of Lucre's nephew Witgood. Not only the courtesan is assimilated to the semantic register of the scurrilous meaning of the 'uncle's house'; Lucre's wife also acts in a manner less than faithful to her husband. Whereas, in this play, the country house is subject to the binary logic of possessed–dispossessed (it will be recalled that the uncle mortgages Witgood Hall, thus effectively dispossessing the nephew of his property), the city house is a multiple and contradictory place, the site of complex struggles for power and possession. This multiplication of the significance of an apparently single place, in this case the uncle's house, is a figure of the multiplicity taken on by London as a focus of disturbing geographical immigration with consequent implications for social instability.

These dramas use London dwellings as a focus for social mobility and social fluidity. In this way, the dramatists played upon contemporary imaginations of various houses of disrepute. The brothel as a place for illegitimate rendezvous figured along with taverns and tippling-houses or alehouses as gathering places for the migrant underworld population of the cities. Alehouses were favoured by itinerant Puritan preachers and lecturers – or later in the period, the Levellers with their doctrine of social mobility – as meeting places, making inns and taverns 'a form of refuge and amenity for an alternative culture'[16] – a culture largely propelled by the unrest generated by demographic mobility, and in turn activating new forces of social mobility. Where the patrons of the alehouses saw them as foci of local community (with Arthur Dent claiming: 'If neighbours meete now and then at the alehouse … meaning no hurt: I take it to be good fellowship, and a good means to increase a love among neighbours; and not so hainous a thing as you make it'[17]), the authorities saw them as a potential source of social unrest, and made concerted and repeated efforts to clamp down on the burgeoning numbers of unlicensed inns with their local, and more concerningly, their migrant clientele. It would appear that the law-makers were less concerned about moral collapse through alcohol, than about the influence of travellers and people cut loose of the ordered hierarchies of traditional society.[18]

In the light of this contemporary urban imagery, it is highly significant that the band of tramps in Beaumont and Fletcher's *Beggars Bush* set to work with their cozening in a tavern on the outskirts of Bruges (Act 3, Scene 1). Bruster has commented upon the manner in which London tended to slide back into the foreign settings of many Jacobean dramas;[19] here, a Liberties alehouse is visible through the flimsy alibi of the Flanders setting. The thinly veiled allusion to the vagrants' London tavern could equally lead one to invert Bruster's formulation: under the pressure of menacing numbers of vagrant wanders and mobile criminals, the London of the Jacobean stage becomes itself a place of foreigners, a haven for 'strangers', and thereby a confusing myriad of places rendered 'alien' to its inhabitants.

Mobility and the stage

It is in the context of rural vagrancy and of the constantly shifting population of London that we need to examine the theatre as a phenomenon tied up in demographic mobility. Significantly, the shift of the landed rich and the dispossessed rural poor to the city furnished part of the substantial urban population necessary to constitute the critical mass of the regular paying audience, thus making the public theatres a viable commercial undertaking.[20] More pointedly, though, actors were regarded during the Elizabethan/Jacobean period as a type of vagrant. The actors' troupes were released from the customary punishments reserved for vagrants only by their affiliation with an aristocratic, or, after James's accession, royal patron. Belonging to a Lord enabled the players, strictly speaking included among the illegal vagrants under English law, to obtain a licence to play around the country. The 1604 legislation governing their mobility makes this clear: 'All Fencers Bearwardes common Players of Enterludes, and minstrels wandringe abroad, (other then Players of Enterludes belonging to any Baron of this Realme, or any other honourable Personage of greater Degree, to be authorized to play under the Hande or Seale of Armes of such Baron or Personage) shalbe taken adjudged as Rogues Vagabondes and Sturdie Beggers, and shall suffer such Paine and Punishment as is in the said Acte in that behalfe appointed.'[21] Such licensing mechanisms kept the actor in his place, as it were: 'The wandering actor is allowable, in other words, as long as he carries with him written evidence that he is still located within the topography of subordination, despite his geographical dislocation.'[22] Thus, for instance, Sir Bounteous in *A Mad World, My Masters* enquires of the players: 'And whose men are you, I pray?' (5.1.43). The question of social affiliation is simultaneously a question of social location, which in turn is a question of spatial fixity or mobility. Through their hierarchical social affiliation, the players were extracted from the mass of wandering vagrants cut loose from kinship networks and hierarchies, and reinserted within a master–servant relationship. 'Belonging', in the phrasing of the 1604 legislation, is thus at once social and spatial, a matter of taking one's place within a socio-spatial order – 'order' possessing a thoroughly coercive signification, as vagrants could be viciously whipped and interned as punishment for their mobility.

Conversely, however, far from taking the players off the list of vagrants, the licensing mechanisms also reinforced their identity as masterless wanderers. The players are included among the list of other categorized mobile members of society – but in brackets, as an anomaly – which allows them legal mobility, but does not exempt them from being classed as a variety of vagrant. Stubbes posed the rhetorical question: 'Are [the players] not taken by the Lawes of the Realme for roagues and vacabounds: (I speake of such as trauailethe Coutreis, with plaies & Enterludes, making an occupation of it) & and ought so to be punished if they had their deserts.'[23] I.G., following Stubbes, gave an answer: 'by the lawes of this Realm of England [the actors] were mustred in the Catalogue of the seuerall kindes of Rogues and Vagabonds, and ought so to be punished, wheresoeuer they be taken, if they had their deserts. ... And what difference is there between the one sort & the other, but euen none at all?'[24] Interestingly, the identification of the actors with the masterless men was one that the dramas themselves on occasions underwrote, as when Follywit's band of rogues disguised as touring actors describe thus the action of their play: 'We sing of wand'ring Knights, what them betide | Who nor in one place nor one shape abide' (*A Mad World, My Masters* 5.2.18–19) – thereby offering a description, self-evident for many contemporaries, of their own masterless mobility.

The association of the players' troupes with vagrancy clearly depended upon a number of factors. Four principal aspects of the contemporary image of masterless men furnished the pretext for the criminalization and prosecution of vagrants: namely, the notion that they were poor, able-bodied (and thus capable of working), mobile and disorderly. These four characteristics, which all added up to make masterless men a putative threat to the status quo in state and society,[25] were also thought by contemporaries to describe accurately the identity of the roving players. Even an avowedly enthusiastic play-goer such as Donald Lupton appears to have subscribed to all aspects of the actor-vagrant stereotype when he said, 'Sometimes they flye into the Countrey; but tis a common suspicion, that they are either poore, or want cloaths, or a new Play: ... they are many times lowzy, and yet shift so often.'[26]

Vagrancy has provided Renaissance scholars with a fertile metaphor in recent years. Taylor's study *Vagrant Writing: Social and Semiotic Disorders in the English Renaissance* uses the actors' vagrancy and their threat to social disorder as the starting-point for a reading of unsettled modes of signification in the seventeenth century: 'As the antitheatrical discourses suggest in their dual attack against the actor's vagrancy and against the vagrancy of theatrical mimesis, within the terms of the Commonwealth imaginary it is not possible to disentangle the semiotic force of social disorder from the social force of a disorderly semiotics.'[27] Despite this gesture towards the links between stage meanings and social disorder, however, the emphasis is predominantly upon the conflicts between 'lawful' and 'vagrant semiosis' rather than upon the semiotics of vagrancy. Vagrancy functions here as a metaphor for subversion rather than as a concrete social phenomenon in its own right. In this respect, Taylor's analysis tends to lag behind the real context – a context spatially problematic and contested – in which theatricality was produced.

The significance of discourses of vagrancy was in fact much more pragmatic and real. The threatening connotations of vagrancy and their symbolic force for contemporaries allowed the charge of vagrancy to be transferred to other groups whose effect on society was perceived as dangerous: in our case, the actors and their drama. Examination of the plays shows that the meanings attached to the actors' troupes and their purported status as vagrants had a very concrete force. The association of acting and vagrancy was one which did not merely create an ideal 'vagrant semiosis', though the stage, as indicated above, did contribute to a corrosive loosening of signifier–signified links, particularly in the realm of visual symbolism. More potently, the association of acting and vagrancy called up visible and tangible possibilities of the social disorder which so concerned the authorities. The habitually enumerated aspects of the phenomenon of vagrancy (able-bodied unemployment, mobility and social disorderliness) were concretely displayed in the person of the early modern actor. In what follows, I shall suggest that it was precisely the spatial character of the stage which made drama a dangerous art-form: various aspects of the vagrancy of acting were performed in the space of the stage.

Theatre, like vagrancy, symbolized an attack on the value of work as indicator of a place, both social and geographical, within an ordered society. By an act of 1610 any able-bodied man or woman who merely threatened to leave his or her work and run away from the home parish could be sent to the house of correction or treated as a vagabond.[28] To avoid work was to undercut the given moral order of things, in which work was a duty of the subordinated members of the social body, an immediate derivative of their place in society. John Northbrooke declaimed that 'amongst all the whole rablement, common players in interludes are to be taken for roges, and punishment is appointed for them to bee burnte through the eare with a hot yron of an ynche compasse; and for the second fault, to be hanged as a felon, &c. The reason is, for that their trade is such an ydle loytering life, a practice to all mischiefe, as you hearde before.'[29] The player's occupation had no place in the traditional form of social organization, so that he had no productive, industrious place within an organic scheme of the commonweal.[30]

Furthermore, playing and vagrancy both infringed not only the moral but the economic order as well. Itinerant begging was state controlled and liable to punishment when practised without a licence precisely because it was seen to undermine the legitimate functioning of the economy; begging was often more lucrative than sporadic and poorly-paid waged employment in early modern England.[31] Unsurprisingly, theatre was also described as akin to begging: 'for goe they [the players] neuer for braue, yet are they counted and taken but for beggers. And is it not true, liue they not uppon begging of euery one that comes.'[32] The stage tended to de-realize the customary relationships to wealth, in particular severing the link between work and material gain, thus evoking the dangerous image of a paradise on earth where there would be no need to work for one's livelihood. The university play *The Return from Parnassus* accused the common actors of being social parasites: 'With mouthing words that better wits have framed, | They purchase lands, and now esquires are named.'[33] Playing as a perversion of work was discussed above in the chapter on the fluidity of values under the money economy, but can also be linked to the factitiousness of acting and the consequent mobility of a social identity untrammelled by the yoke of physical labour. Volpone with his 'gown | …furs, and night-caps', and his 'feigned cough' and other fictitious complaints, is a player who generates wealth by his acting, thereby drawing others to invest in his performance (1.2.84–5, 124). Likewise, Dol Common's invocation to Subtle in *The Alchemist* to 'labour kindly in the common work' refers to their common project of hoaxing the eager believers in the wealth to be gained from alchemy (1.1.156). Once again, the performance constitutes a counterfeit form of work where nothing tangible meriting payment is produced.

In general, then, there was a contemporary association between the stage and idleness: I.G. wrote in his broadside against Heywood that spectators 'yearely [spend] many pounds on these vaine representations. By which meanes, the actors of them find such sweete gaines to maintaine their idle life, that they give their whole industrie to various and mimicall inuentions.'[34] The contrast of 'sweete gaines' arising perversely from an 'idle life', the shocking clash of 'industrie' with 'mimicall inuentions' was what was so scandalous for contemporaries: the theatre travestied the relationship between just labour and deserved reward. Mullaney notes that the drama 'earned its living by a theatrical sleight of hand, translating work into play.'[35] The most extreme extension of the hollowness of the theatrical performance as an essentially false means of earning a livelihood is the amusing example of the hoax play mentioned above, *England's Joy*. Similarly, the players' companies were regarded by the authorities as a travesty of the traditional professional associations, the guilds, and of their power to determine qualifications and employment and thus the market.[36] Interestingly, though the actors' companies were not guilds, some of the actors did retain their membership in other guilds, their boy-players being apprenticed in the respective guild. The actor-apprentices were thus, in the eyes of the city fathers, taken away from a legitimate craft or trade, making the acting companies, Orgel suggests, a form of unlicensed guild or 'antiguild'.[37] The theatres thus came to be seen as a perverse influence which habitually distracted apprentices, whether as players or as spectators, from their otherwise gainful occupations, as a 1597 petition shows, claiming that the plays 'maintain idlenes in such persons as have no vocation & draw apprentices and other servantes from their ordinary workes.'[38] Clearly the stage represented an alternative space within the commonwealth where wealth could be gained without legitimate work, by selling factitious narratives, thus liberating the actors from the customary hierarchical structures and coercive stability which governed normal relations of labour.

The plays frequently refer to their own mode of production in coded terms which make the actors the counterparts of the masterless men with their wily schemes to hoodwink unwary local people. In the final scene of Middleton's *A Mad World, My Masters*, Follywit and his companions attempt to carry through their scheme to cozen Sir Bounteous Progress at his country property in the guise of a group of travelling players. In *No Wit Like a Woman's*, Savourwit crows: 'Our knavery is for all the world like a shifting bankrupt; it breaks in one place and sets up in another; he tries all trades from a goldsmith to a tobacco seller; we try all shifts from an outlaw to a flatterer; he cozens the husband and compounds with the widow; we cozen my master and compound with my mistress; only here I turn o'th'right hand from him; he is known to live like a rascal, when I am thought to live like a gentleman' (2.2.186–92). Not only the roving good-for-nothing Savourwit and his accomplices, but the players' troupe as well are avatars of the dangerously cunning, masterless men who shift from one place to another in search of their prey; what the vagrancy literature narrated in colourful detail, the actors performed, before a consenting audience, on the stage. There is no significant difference in the presentation and dramatic function of Middleton's resourceful and knavish wits with their assumed roles, and Beaumont and Fletcher's itinerant beggars in *Beggars Bush*, who pick the pockets of their tavern audience while performing magic tricks and feats of juggling (Act 3, Scene 1). The scheming of the wits and the scheming of the masterless men both amount to making a living from 'dissembling', duplicity and disguise, a constant theme of the vagrancy literature.[39] Philip Stubbes accused the actor of playing 'the parte of a dissemblyng Hipocrite: And to be breefe, who can call him a straight dealyng man, who plaith a Cozeners tricke.'[40] J. Cocke, in a passage quoted above, noted that 'The statute hath done wisely to acknowledge him [the Player] a Rogue errant, for his chiefe essence is, *A daily Counterfeit*: He hath been familiar so longe with out-sides, that he professe himself (being unknowne) to be an apparent Gentleman';[41] Cocke's fantasy is that of the vagrant arriving in a place where he is not known, using his anonymity to cozen the locals with a disguise that would otherwise be seen through immediately; this is a common scenario in the vagrancy literature, and a scenario no less common in Jacobean comedy.

Such dissembling and the skilled employment of disguise mobilizes an attack on property, as evinced in the example of the Courtesan in *A Trick to Catch the Old One*. There the Courtesan plans to play the rich widow from the country, in order to con Witgood's uncle, saying: 'I will so artfully disguise my wants, | And set so good a courage on my state, | That I will be believed' (1.1.74–6). As demonstrated in an earlier chapter, the identity of the aristocrat was bound up with place: 'state' condenses 'estate' in the literally physical, topographical sense, embodying the financial value of such landed property and the class rank associated with property; the state of the nobility was grounded, precisely, in their estates. But in the courtesan's case, this condensation of rank and spatial stability is spurious. She is landless and mobile, about to leave Leicester for London, following a typical itinerary of immigrants or vagrants towards the capital, to deceive her lover Witgood's uncle into ceding a share of the nephew's patrimony. She is not anchored in a rural place, and to some extent, could possibly be seen as a forerunner of the emergent 'pseudo-gentry', whose aristocratic status was based upon commercial wealth rather than the possession of landed estates, and who gradually gained in prominence and numbers from about 1600.[42] However, in stark contrast to the 'pseudo-gentry', her wealth consists of mere artifice, 'disguise' which conceals 'wants', bringing her closer to the wandering poor. Her mobility, driven by poverty, mimes that of the large proportion of the English population which flowed to London in search of employment, more or less legal, in the wake of the transformation of relations of rural land possession, enclosure, and the resulting changes of labour relations. Here, the artifice of the stage facilitates the artifice of land-ownership; thus the space of the stage self-reflexively alludes to its deceitful capacity to create fictional places, thereby in turn disturbing the sacrosanct qualifications for elevated social rank. The places created upon the stage and occupied (be it merely metonymically, by virtue of noble attire, as in this case) by costumed actors, have the power to erode the material reality of actual geographical places upon which power and privilege grounded their authority.

Thus, the factitiousness of the drama is an inherently mobile spatial phenomenon. To the extent that the drama creates a multiplicity of fictional places in the real space of the stage, dramatic art thus involves being in several places at once without leaving the singular space of the stage. The basis of drama is thus mobility through fiction. Iago, for instance, brazenly asks:

> And what's he then that says I play the villain?
> ...
>
> How am I then a villain,
> To counsel Cassio to this parallel course
> Directly to his good? Divinity of hell:
> When devils will the blackest sins put on,
> They do suggest at first with heavenly shows,
> As I do now.
>
> (*Othello* 2.2.327, 339–44)

Out of Iago's strategy two positions arise, one of which is honest counsel, the other treacherous 'villainy'. Paradoxically, it is impossible to separate these two contradictory and yet (in pragmatic terms) identical positions, just as truth and falsehood are confused in the act of 'play', and hell and heaven blended in 'shows'.

The spatial character of this aspect of the drama is more clearly manifest when Follywit in *A Mad World, My Masters*, staying at his uncle Sir Bounteous's country house, ruminates upon the best way of orchestrating the theft of his uncle's riches: 'We now arrive at the most ticklish point, to rob and take our ease, to be thieves and lie by't' (2.4.87–8). The pun on 'lie' is an obvious allusion to the verbal factitiousness of theatrical double-dealing, but there is also inherent spatial meaning of simultaneously prowling about the darkened house and of having the *alibi* – the term itself is significant in this context – of lying slumbering in bed. How to be in two places at once is Follywit's dilemma. Follywit and his companions, having stolen Sir Bounteous's treasure, revert to their roles as visiting noble and retinue, and are bound in their beds by the 'villains' as proof of their innocence as co-victims; and to that end, one actor needs to retain his freedom, so as to do the binding and to unbind them later on. 'Pox on't, I'll have the footman 'scape', decides Follywit (2.4.79). This one free, mobile element (significantly, a 'man on foot') guarantees the apparent immobility and real mobility of identity of the others. The 'vagrant' footman bridges the gap between the apparently incompatible roles of victim and executor of the theft and the distinct spaces allotted to those roles, between real space (that of mobility and theft) and the other, fictional space of the *alibi*: the immobility of being bound in one's bed.

But beyond the structural prominence of mobility in Jacobean drama, the real threat of the theatre came from the fact that this multiplication of places was performed in a public location, that is, was made *spatially tangible* in a place where large numbers of people gathered to meet. The notion of the shared identity of actors and vagabonds in the minds of contemporaries is confirmed by the increasing refusal by City authorities to allow touring players' companies to play at all at times of economic crisis. The possibility that mobile populations not subject to the control of traditional social hierarchy might form the nucleus of rapidly spreading popular rebellion was always an object of middle- and upper-class apprehension. The fear of unrest which might possibly by sparked off by touring companies was such that in the worst famine years, plays by touring companies were banned altogether, for instance in Canterbury, where the City authorities feared riots. Any crowd that was not gathered for church attendance, a royal procession or civil pageant, or an execution, was perceived by the authorities as a potential source of rioting; this perception obviously applied to the theatres. Some documents of state control of theatre displayed less concern about the content of dramas than the place where they were enacted: what was permissible in the private house of a nobleman, played occasionally before friends and guests, was potentially threatening when transferred to a public place of regular performance.[43] Thus, for instance, Elizabeth expressed concern in 1601 about the staging of *Richard II* shortly before the Essex uprising, complaining that 'this tragedy was plaied 40^{tie} times in open streets and houses'.[44]

Moreover, the polemical literature for and against the theatre constantly stressed the power of the theatre as an educative or mis-educative institution. As Bacon stated in his charges pronounced at the trial of the Earl of Essex, Sir Gilly Merick 'procured to be played before them [a group of incipient conspirators] the play of deposing king Richard the second...which he [Merick] thought soon after his lordship [Essex] should bring from the stage to the state.'[45] The virtual homonym *stage/state* stresses the easy passage of images of authority or of its subversion from the one to the other, but simultaneously contains an implicit condemnation of anyone daring to take the factitious simulations of the one for the real power of the other. The fear of public gatherings of such masterless multitudes was driven by the fear of 'imitation' facilitating the spread of vice, just as human intercourse in the cramped theatres facilitated the spread of disease; in 1591 Robert Greene intoned against the masterless men, claiming that 'These cony-catchers...putrify with their infections this flourishing estate of England.'[46] Similarly, there is a curious ambiguity in the petition of 1597 cited above which claimed that the theatres were 'the ordinarye places for maisterles men to come together & to *recreate* themselves' – connoting both anti-social leisure and dangerous multiplication.[47]

The Induction of Jonson's *Bartholomew Fair*, a play whose setting was one of the notorious meeting places for rogues and vagabonds, anxiously admonished the members of the audience to 'severally covenant and agree, to *remain in the places* their money or their friends have put them in, with patience, for the space of two hours and an half or somewhat more', and demanded that they 'be *fixed and settled* in [their] censure' (70–2, 91; my emphasis). What is expressed here, in oblique terms, is the concern that the coalesced 'mobility' of the underclasses, gathered together in the theatre, might work as a catalyst mobilizing popular protest and unrest. The threat posed by performances of seditious mobility can be illustrated by a further episode from *A Mad World, My Masters*. Before the final resolution of the play's plot, the actors of the play-in-the-play only narrowly escape unmasking at the hands of the local constable who catches them riding away after the theft has been carried out. They successfully discredit his claims to authority by drafting him into the fictional world of the play, thus disqualifying his protests against their manhandling of him. When his true status as a representative of the law is subsequently re-established, Sir Bounteous Progress asks in astonishment, 'Why, art not thou the constable i'th'comedy?', thus dramatizing the destabilizing effect of the contamination of reality by the vertiginous force of acting (5.2.157–8). External reality, in this case the constable's arrest of Maworm and Hoboy for the theft of Sir Bounteous's riches, is assimilated to the fictional world of the play-within-the-play so as to de-realize the arrest, and to discredit the constable's claims to judicial authority. Certainly Sir Bounteous perceives it so: 'This is some new player now; they put all their fools to the constable's part still' (5.2.81–2); and subsequently, his puzzled question repeats the same notion: 'Why, art thou not the constable i'th'comedy?' Here precisely, the blurring of boundaries between fictional world of the stage, and the real world off-stage is performed by the theatre itself. The outraged constable reasserts the divisions between fiction and reality: 'I'th'comedy? Why, I am the constable i'th'commonwealth, sir' (5.2.159–60). But the alliteration of *comedy* and *commonwealth* (like that of *stage* and *state* cited above) merely demonstrates how fraught this distinction is. The immense political resonance of such confusion is evinced in Jean Wilson's comment that, 'By the time Charles was executed the fusion of representation of reality, and familiarity with theatrical convention, was such that the mode of the King's death could be used to undermine his kingship – a king on a stage connected to a place of theatrical entertainment is not a true king, but only an actor playing a king.'[48]

The designation of the actors as 'unstable fellows' in *A Mad World* (5.2.88) is telling in so far as it describes their own capacity to destabilize reality, to make it 'uncertain' (an earlier epithet in the same play used to describe the actors). But 'unstable' also describes their vagrant status as prowling rogues, and by extension, their capacity to upset the categories upon which social order, in very pragmatic and mundane ways, closely depends. The constable's attempt to 'arrest' the actors by pinning down their identity is barely effective against their 'instability'. This capacity to destabilize social barriers depends less upon a confusion of semiotic operations by which social order is legitimized (as in Taylor's argument for 'vagrant semiosis'), than upon the spatial operation of the blurring of boundaries between real and fictional spaces. Follywit's skilful assimilation of the constable to the dramatic fiction is a self-reflexive allusion to the play's own space. The overlapping of *comedy* and *commonwealth*, of *stage* and *state*, exemplifies the tendency discussed above for audience/actor boundaries to become porous in the Jacobean theatre, and for the real space of performance to be assimilated to the fictional space of the drama for long enough for the meanings created in the fiction to be transferred to the real context of performance.

This capacity on the part of drama to invade reality or to assimilate it for short periods of time depends upon the performance aspect of the theatre – the fact that both fictional space and performance space, fictional time and performance time, are congruent. It is the perform-ance aspect of theatrical fiction which gives its incantatory power, in other words, its power to provoke 'imitation' and 'contagion' as the Jacobean critics of the theatre were wont to fear. Such performance made this evocative power tangible in a way which the more ideal oper-ations of textualized semiotic vagrancy (ideal because they are not car-ried out through the same intensely concrete spatialization) could not. The theatre does indeed put into motion a semiotic vagrancy of the type analysed by Taylor, in so far as it creates fictional worlds opening up other signifying systems than those of the real occupied by the specta-tor. But this creation of fiction remains purely virtual until the textual fiction (be it embodied in actors' cue scripts or a subsequent printed ver-sion of the drama) is concretized in the mobile space of the stage. Semiotic mutability presupposes the spatial fluidity of the stage space to make that mutability of signification tangible and public. It is in this sense that the Jacobean theatre is a vagrant theatre, and one whose mobility, both semiotic and concretely spatial, was accurately identified by the authorities as a gathering place for 'ill disposed persons in great multitudes ... causinge tumulte and outrages.'[49]

This potential for disorder is confirmed once again by the dramatists' own eagerness to curb the unsettling force of the mobility of social iden-tity performed in their plays. This desire to damp the mobility – demo-graphic, social, semiotic – associated with the players is evident for instance in Middleton's *A Mad World, My Masters*. It is said of the 'uncertain players', that 'now up, now down, they know not when to play, where to play, nor what to play; not when to play for fearful fools, where to play for Puritan fools, nor what to play for critical fools' (5.1.28–31). In this way their vagrancy is limited, their 'uncertainty' or instability brought under control by being converted from a potent force of disturbance into the simple pragmatic difficulty of knowing which type of drama to play in which theatre-location to which sort of audience. In this way, the flexibility of the travelling players is cast back upon the audience; the players are not held to be responsible for the unsettled nature of their profession. Similarly, it is highly significant that Follywit, that most appealing master of cunning, and one likely to gain the adhesion of the audience, is restored to 'his own shape' at the end of the play, and pledges himself to 'my hereafter stableness of life' (s.d. 5.2.186; 5.2.254).

Once again, the ambivalence evident in Jacobean drama and remarked upon in the preceding chapters is manifest. The plays are the product of the mobility of the actor, both in the internal necessity of costume change and the occupation of multiple roles by a limited number of actors, and by the necessity of playing at many different venues (the King's Men's movement between the Globe, Blackfriars and the Court, not to mention regular performances outside of London, is exemplary of this mobility). Jacobean drama was not shy of alluding to these material factors in its production, and constantly incorporated such topoi into the action of the plays. Yet at the same time, the dramatists were wary of foregrounding mobility too much, presumably for fear of provoking the disorder contemporaries saw as a danger directly associated with demographic mobility, and thereby endangering their own economic livelihood. The plays thus include brakes to the very mobility of which they were a product and to which they themselves frequently referred.

A similar ambivalence will also be evident in the form of mobility examined in the following chapter, external to Britain. A broader form of mobility is portrayed in the Jacobean travel dramas, dramas which extended the mobility of the English population at home beyond the bounds of the kingdom. The travel drama thereby possessed an analogous capacity to disturb contemporaries' sense of the nature and cohesion of their social surroundings and the political order under which they lived.

6
Travelling Thoughts: Travel on the Stage

Travel and the stage

In his polemic against Venice as contemporary kitsch, Régis Debray remarks that the lagoon which separates the city from the 'profane world', and which until recently it was necessary to cross by boat in order to reach the city, functions as a 'semiotic caesura' making it possible for Venice to play the role of city as 'representation' or 'spectacle'.[1] For early modern travellers, the sea voyage constituted a similar semiotic and epistemological rupture. The ocean-crossing to the Americas was the most extreme example of this rupture, being variously understood as a terrifying ordeal or a rite of passage, severing the traveller from previous ways of understanding the world.[2] A striking concomitant of this notion of the sea journey as semiotic caesura can also be found in the position of some of the theatres on the far side of the Thames in early modern London.

To attend theatres such as the Globe or the Rose, better-off theatre-goers would hire a boat to cross the river, an aspect of theatre-going sufficiently novel to be remarked by the Swiss visitor Thomas Platter: 'On September 21st after lunch, about 2 o'clock, I and my party crossed the water, and there in the house with the thatched roof witnessed a performance of the tragedy of the first Emperor Julius Caesar.'[3] The traffic between the City and the Bankside created such profitable business for the watermen that they saw their profession threatened at times of plague or when moves were made to close the theatres, as in 1591–2 or 1614.[4] Such closures meant the loss of custom from the 'three or four thousand people, that were vsed to spend their monies by water', claimed John Taylor the 'Water Poet'; in 1615 he estimated that there were 40,000 watermen working on the Thames between Windsor Bridge and Gravesend, profiting from the large traffic in waterborne passengers, 'the cause of the greater halfe of which multitude, hath beene the Players playing on the Bank-side, for I haue knowne three Companies besides the Bear-bayting, at once there; to wit, the Globe, the Rose, and the Swan.'[5]

Not surprisingly, the watermen figure in plays such as Middleton's *Chaste Maid in Cheapside* as important accomplices in Moll's flight from her father's tyranny, or in the puppet-play-in-the-play in *Bartholomew Fair*, where the sculler Cole ferries Hero and Leander back and forth across the Hellespont-Thames between Puddle Wharf, the Bankside and Trig Stairs (5.4.105ff). In Jonson's *Eastward Ho!*, the Thames also becomes a transgressive site of travel, albeit one travestied by bathetic deflation, when Sir Petronel Flash, hoping to have reached the coast of France, discovers to his chagrin that he has been washed up on the 'cost of Doggs' – 'Y'are ith' *Ile a Doggs*', a putative Frenchman informs him (4.1.173). Even when subject to comic reversal, the Thames, described in 1632 as 'highway to the Sea, the bringer in of wealth and strangers',[6] signifies the inauguration of travel. The act of crossing the river, thematized in the plays themselves, was a significant marker of the partial transgressiveness of the theatrical experience. This 'foreignness' did not represent a *real* disjunction from the fabric of London city life, as will be evident from examples of travel plays given later on in this chapter; but this would not necessarily have lessened the exotic character of a visit to the theatre on the other side of the natural barrier of the Thames. Thus the very experience of theatre-going would, in many cases, have implied an element of transgression and border-crossing – a form of travel.

The Renaissance has been epitomized as 'a time of creative energy, enthusiasm, expanding horizons, collaborative enterprises, bravura entrepreneurialism and intellectual excitement.'[7] Such excitement at the prospect of exploring new vistas and transgressing existing boundaries, of pushing towards hitherto unattainable horizons, is expressed in Witgood's expression in Middleton's *A Trick to Catch the Old One*, 'I reach at farther happiness…Oh, for more scope!' (3.1.117, 240). Indeed, in some of Middleton's plays, it is the impossibility of translating such energy into real action which is shown to breed social disorder. In *The Changeling*, it is Alsemero's cancelled voyage which functions as a clear augury of the looming tragedy, as Jasperino, astonished at Alsemero's voluntary renunciation of his freedom to travel, correctly senses: 'I never knew | Your inclinations to travels at a pause | With any cause to hinder it, till now' (1.1.26–8). Here, travel signifies freedom, not merely spatial but also intellectual and social, and the rest of the play demonstrates the catastrophic results of the social immobility and constraint of the aristocratic family caught within the strait-jacket of a revenge ethic.

In the context of this vitiated urge to travel, it is interesting to consider Platter's observations of the theatre-goers of London: 'With such pastimes and other occasional activities the English wile away the time, learning in the comedies what is happening in other lands, ... because many Englishmen do not care to travel but are content to experience foreign things at home.'[8] Platter's impression of English insularity may have been more or less accurate,[9] but it is certain that the theatre was more than simply an ersatz for travels not willingly undertaken by the stay-at-home inhabitants of the blessed isle. The plays did not replace experiences of travel, and most certainly did not aspire to do so. Nor, in most cases, did they relay particularly precise or detailed information about travel.

Far more, they were informed and generated by the general atmosphere of excitement at the expansion of horizons, as the quotations from Middleton show, and by debates regarding English participation in overseas expansion. As Loomba observes of Richard Brome's *The Antipodes*, the protagonist's pathological obsession with travel 'dramatises the hold of the enormous range of travel literature during the early years of colonial expansion upon the public imagination.'[10] The appropriately-named Peregrine studs his conversation with such figures as Prester John and the Great Khan, known from the narratives of Sir John Mandeville and Marco Polo. 'In tender years', Peregrine 'always loved to read | Reports of travels and voyages', and such books would 'convey his fancy round the world' (1.1.188–92; 1.3.25; 1.131–2, 137). A contemporary equivalent of Peregrine can be found in Richard Hakluyt, whose 1589 dedication of his *Principall Navigations, Voyages, Traffiques and Discoveries of the English Nation*, describes his youthful passion for travel narratives: 'According to which my resolution, when, not long after, I was removed to Christ-church in Oxford, ... I fell to my intended course, and by degrees read over whatsoever printed or written discoveries and voyages I found extant either in the Greeke, Latine, Italian, Spanish, Portugall, French or English languages.'[11] The encyclopaedic *Principall Navigations* in turn made such accounts available to the broader public in England, fuelling public interest in travel.

But Platter's somewhat dismissive description of the English theatre-goers can be read as more than a negative assessment (the theatre figuring as a poor compensation for the real travels that Platter himself has dared to undertake). On the contrary, it can be understood in a thoroughly positive sense: theatre is a way of creating, within the settled stability of the source culture, similar modes of perception to those gained in travel. In Platter's words, it is a way of 'experiencing foreign things at home'. When the Swiss traveller's statement is viewed from this angle, the theatre can be seen not as competing with travel, inadequately attempting to supplant it, but rather as complementing it, producing similar epistemological effects to those engendered by the real experience of voyages.

In Middleton's *No Help, No Wit like a Woman's*, we hear of a 'brave travelling scholar entertained into the house o'purpose, one that has been all the world over and some part of Jerusalem.' We are informed that 'he talks as he goes and writes as he runs; besides, you know 'tis death to a traveller to stand long in one place' (3.1.136–8, 152–4). The mobility that this enquiring spirit appears obliged to maintain upon returning to his native land, perhaps for fear of losing the intellectual flexibility arising out of long contact with the puzzling vagaries of foreign peoples and alien modes of thought, is dispersed through the whole of the action of Middleton's play, which effectively makes the source culture the object of a critical gaze. The transgressive experience of travel, and the concomitant cultural defamiliarization arising out of it can be found in the dramas at quite unexpected places. In *Troilus and Cressida*, Calchas (Cressida's father) declares, upon defecting to the Greeks:

> I have abandoned Troy, left my profession,
> Incurred a traitor's name, exposed myself
> From certain and possessed conveniences
> To doubtful fortunes, sequest'ring from me all
> That time, acquaintance, custom, and condition
> Made tame and most familiar to my nature,
> And here to do you service am become
> As new into the world, strange, unacquainted.
>
> (3.3.5–12)

The experience of entering 'as new into the world, strange, unacquainted' was one that the theatre-goers could obtain even within their own city. When Sebastian and Antonio in *Twelfth Night* are washed up on the foreign shores of Illyria, Sebastian, who already knows this part of the world, organizes accommodation for his master 'In the south suburbs at the Elephant' (3.3.39), tangentially alluding to a tavern on the Bankside in Southwark;[12] London is thus transformed into a far-away, exotic location in foreign 'parts, which to a stranger, | Unguided and unfriended, often prove | Rough and unhospitable' (3.3.9–11). Thus when Jonson broke with the tradition of situating the action of dramas in foreign lands, announcing in the *Alchemist*, 'Our scene is London' (Prologue, 5), he effectively rendered London not more familiar, but rather foreign to the spectators' gaze. *Bartholomew Fair* confirms this trend in declaring, 'When't comes to the Fair once, you were e'en as good go to Virginia, for anything there is of Smithfield' (Induction, 9–10).

Why is the travel play particularly apt to perform the spatial and epistemological rupture embodied in the voyage? One answer to this question can be found in the spatial principles underlying literary art. Lotman suggests that the inherent spatial structures of literary topoi or commonplaces express other non-spatial relations of the text. It is here that the particular modelling function of artistic or literary space is to be found. The most basic 'commonplace' or topos of literary creation is one linked intimately to the very construction of narrative, namely to the act of narration itself (what the Russian Formalists called the *sujet* as opposed to the *fabula*, or more recent narratologists *narrative discourse* as opposed to *story*). The *sujet*-value of a narrated event is dependent upon the amount of information an event carries, how worth mentioning it is, how improbable its occurrence is. Upon this basis, it would be possible to construct a typology of *sujet*-less and *sujet*-laden texts. The *sujet*-less text confirms the unquestionable, solid character of schemas of order in the world – mostly encoded in the form of binary oppositions. The *sujet*-laden text tends to disturb such spatial oppositions, by having constitutive dividing lines crossed by an agent in the text. Crossing such dividing lines is inherently improbable, and thus 'makes a good story'. It is precisely the transgression of some sort of a semantic boundary, disturbing the habitually binary divisions of 'us' and 'them', 'here' and 'there', which provides the information-laden events making up the *sujet*-chain. A spatial movement of transgression thus triggers the temporal movement of a succession of acts of narration. Therefore the character of an event is always dependent upon the spatial-classificatory structure out of which it arises – and which it transgresses. The *sujet* is always, to a greater or lesser extent, in conflict with the spatial structure of the text's vision of the universe – for otherwise there would be no story to tell.[13]

Thus the tension between the power of traditional hierarchies and sacrosanct frontiers, on the one hand, and the pressure to move beyond such established and restraining categories, on the other, often forms the essential motive of a play's dramatic action. In Middleton's *No Help, No Wit like a Woman's*, for instance, two journeys determine the action of the play: a first, during which a mother and daughter are captured by pirates, and a second, in which the son, Philip, travels to Antwerp: 'I saw a face at Antwerp that quite drew me | From conscience and obedience; in that fray | I lost my heart; I must needs lose my way' (2.2.130–2). These two journeys together form the mainspring of the dramatic action, which is driven by the pressure of the a series of opposed values: here/there, possession/loss, family cohesion/family fragmentation. The action is propelled by the transgression of the family boundaries, with all the concomitant complications introduced by that act of departure. If the act of transgression of a semantic boundary as generator or narrative is the essential spatial characteristic of literary activity, as Lotman maintains, then the travel drama would appear to be a quintessential form of literary production, all the more so that the spatial transgression is actively and dynamically performed on the stage, and not merely recounted in diegetic form. The travel drama can be said to be the art-form *par excellence* which, tangibly and visually, performs the topos of transgression.

In the plays analysed in this chapter, transgression can be seen at work in the form of departure, in the loss of cultural familiarity, in the confrontation with alterity, and – possibly but not necessarily – in the transformation of the traveller through that confrontation with cultural otherness. The process of transgression may culminate in the traveller introducing the acquired foreignness into the place originally left behind. In the examples given below, the transgression of boundaries is sometimes neutralized within the plays' limits, in which case transgression acts as a foil for the confirmation of cultural value. Conversely, transgression may be allowed to unfold its consequences for the source culture. However, as soon as the thorny issue of *how* the stage achieves these effects of transgression and the recognition of transgression in the minds of the audience is addressed, it becomes clear that aptness of the stage to represent the act of travel is highly questionable. Paradoxically, it is precisely out of that doubtful capability that the stage makes visible the tactics by which it could most powerfully function as a spatial art-form to disturb its viewers.

Limitations and potential of the stage in travel drama

When the early modern players in England moved from the market-place or the street to the established theatre buildings in order to maximize their takings by making theatre an exclusive experience, access to which was conditional upon payment, they did not merely give up the fabric of real life in which their drama had formerly been embedded. Their move also exacerbated the technical problems of representing travel, with its immense distances, within the constrictions of the theatre building. As Peter Holland observes, 'Placing a voyage on stage is, of course, a direct route to dramaturgical difficulty. The readiest way of demonstrating the limitations of the stage is to move spaces.'[14] And indeed, the travel plays were all too aware of the limitations of their own spatial resources in portraying movement across large geographical expanses. *Henry V*, which opens by addressing the question of how to represent static expanses on the stage ('Can this cockpit hold | The vasty fields of France?' – Prologue, 11–12) also confronts the even thornier problem of dynamic expanse. The Prologue to Act 3 opens with the brave declaration: 'Thus with imagined wing our swift scene flies | In motion of no less celerity | Than that of thought' (3.0.1–3). It requests the audience to imagine Dover pier, the channel waves, and then the approach to Harfleur, not only visually, but so as to become implicated in the mobility of the military expedition: 'Follow, follow! | Grapple your minds to sternage of this navy, | And leave your England' (3.0.17–19). What is quite extraordinary is the boldness with which Shakespeare attacks the problem of representing travel over large distances, drawing the audience into the dilemma and making them the guarantor of its resolution.

Other plays dealing specifically with travel, such as Day, Rowley and Wilkins' *The Travels of the Three English Brothers*, confess themselves quite overwhelmed by the task at hand:

> Should our tedious muse
> Pace the particulars of our travellers,
> Five days would break the limits of our scenes
> But to express the shadows. Therefore we
> …
> Present you with the fairest of our feast,
> Clothing our truth within an argument
> Fitting the stage and your attention.
> (Prologue, 16–23)

Not only the countless details of the journey but also its geographical dimensions are reduced to a size 'fitting' the stage and the audience's perceptive capacities. Despite this exercise in spatial reduction, at the end of the play the playwrights still appear to doubt the success of their undertaking, questioning the accuracy of such a simplification of the details of the narrative of overseas travel – about which, they fear, members of the audience may be better informed than themselves:

> If we should prosecute beyond our knowledge,
> Some that fill up this round circumference,
> And happily better know their states than we,
> Might justly call the authors travellers,
> [*=liars, like the authors of many overly fanciful travel narratives*]
> And give the actors too the soldier's spite.
>
> (Epilogue, 24–8)

Significantly, it is the dimensions of the theatre which are taken to limit the theatre's capacity to represent the truth, such that the authors' ventures beyond that constraint cannot be regarded as fully trustworthy. Similarly, Heywood's *Fair Maid of the West* also declares its utter incapacity to do justice to the geographical space which links the quite disparate localities of its action, Cornwall and North Africa: 'Our Stage so lamely can express a Sea, | That we are forst by *Chorus* to discourse | What should have beene in action. Now imagine…' (319).[15] Here the drama explicitly admits its technical inadequacy, and equally explicitly, proposes a solution, in a remarkably candid meta-theatrical discourse on space. The playwright resorts, as so often, to verbal scene-painting in order to create the illusion of what is simply not to be achieved on stage by mimetic, iconic means. As so often, the audience is called upon to use its imagination in support of this illusion.

But these admissions of the weakness of the theatre's capacities to represent the dynamism of travel can be deceptive, for the theatre possesses a range of other resources which allow it to portray the results of travel in ways that make for a challenging and disturbing dramatic form. *The Sea Voyage*, for instance, makes considerable use of the gallery above: 'Yes, 'tis a ship! I see it now, a tall ship' cries the marooned Sebastian from above the stage (1.2.1). In this way, the raised stage becomes a schematic physical icon of the island upon which the action takes place, surrounded by a sea of spectators; the view from the 'hill' above offers the possibility of breaking out of the closure of the theatre building by simulating a vista available to those on the heights but not to the audience at the same level as the island. But later, Aminta cries from above that while the newly arrived crew and adventurers are busy squabbling over the booty found on the island, the previous two castaways have boarded the newcomers' ship and have made their bid for freedom (1.3.210ff). Thus the place above remains locked within the imprisoning bounds of the island, in accordance with its position inside the circle of the theatre. The above is the place from which the ship is observed arriving and departing, thus representing the possibility of sight beyond the boundaries of the island, but not of genuine escape. Ascent into the gallery is a vertical movement which cannot be converted into a horizontal freedom.

Subsequently, however, the above proves to possess greater transgressive capacities than originally evident. Initially, the above is confirmed as a frustrating index of visual experience without a kinetic concomitant:

> *Albert*: ... When we gain the top of this near rising hill
> We shall know further. *Exeunt and enter above.*
> ...
> The air clears too, and now we may discern
> Another island, and questionless
> The seat of fortunate men. O that we could
> Arrive there.
> *Aminta*: No Albert, 'tis not to be hoped.
> This envious torrent's cruelly interposed.
> We have no vessel that may transport us,
> Nor hath nature given us wings to fly.

$$(2.1.63–72)$$

But in fact, this view from above, despite the initial appearance of an insuperable distance, is an anticipation of Albert's arrival on the neighbouring island of the Amazons, and of the subsequent evacuation of the party to that island – albeit as prisoners of the merciless women. The last appearance above is that of Sebastian and Nicusa (the original two castaways), who have been set back upon the island by a vengeful Raymond in Act 4, Scene 1, wrathful at not having found there his sister (Aminta) and Albert (her ravisher) after Sebastian's confident report of their presence. At Act 5, Scene 2, Sebastian and Nicusa sight, once again, a ship coming towards the island, this time carrying Crocale, who will in turn bring them back to the island of the Amazons to be reunited with their wives. This final sighting does indeed signal definitive rescue – and thus a genuine and completed horizontal movement – but also the dissolution of the whole journey in the castaways' return to Europe. In the last analysis, the above is crucial in opening up the closure of the stage to the wide horizons of the ocean, but also, in deferred form, it is the instrument of the dissolution and termination of the journey-narrative.

At the very moment in which the above ceases to embody the con-sciousness of insuperable isolation, it dissolves the illusion of travel, bringing the travellers back to their native land and collapsing the drama of voyage back into the here and now.

Horizontal as well as vertical stage-structures, such as the double stage-doors, were also available to the dramatists to convey the geographical dimension of the drama. In Heywood's *Fair Maid*, two opposed poles of action are immediately presented as dynamic nodes in the dramatic structure of the play, possessing the power to 'draw' the main actors. Gold constitutes the one attractive force in the play: 'They are all on fire | To purchase from the Spaniard', explains Carroll in the opening lines of the play: 'If their Carracks | Come deeply laden, we shall *tugge* with them | For golden spoil' (263). The other attractive force is Bess Bridges, the maid of the play's title, at the Castle tavern, 'a Girle worth gold', as the subtitle tells us: 'The Castle needs no bush, | Her beauty *draws* to them more gallant Customers | Then all the signes ith' towne else.' The first Captain explains that Bess is 'a most *attractive* Adamant', and Carroll admits that this 'Adamant | Shall for this time *draw* me to, wee'll dine there' (264; my emphasis). Two forms of desir-able mineral draw the men of the play, thus mobilizing the otherwise static space of the stage, and setting it within a dynamic tension with its double exterior. The interior–exterior dynamic was possibly figured iconically in the opening of the two stage doors which quite concretely open onto the spaces of contiguity flanking the stage. Later on, the same binary structure will be employed in reversed form, as the hero Spencer lies dying (or so it initially seems) on the Barbary coast. Goodlack asks, 'Sir how cheare you?' and Spencer replies:

> Like one thats bound upon a new adventure
> To th' other world: yet thus much worthy friend
> Let me intreat you, since I understand
> The Fleet is bound for England, take your occasion
> To ship your selfe, and when you come to Foy,
> Kindly commend me to my dearest *Besse* …
>
> (283)

Here, the centre has been shifted to North Africa, but the double direc-tion holds good: death (as the risk entailed by travel and adventure) in one direction, and England and Bess in the other. The possibility of departure through the two stage doors continues to concretize the dou-ble vector structuring the play's dynamism.

The use of the above or the two stage doors, nevertheless, does not solve the essential problem created by the challenge of enacting a journey on stage. The theatre can portray a place, a point in space; it can also portray limited segments of motion, motions that can be accommodated within the admittedly generous boundaries of the open stage. It is more difficult, however, to portray motion between points in space wide apart, in other words, distance. This must generally be conveyed verbally (or diegetically, to use Issacharoff's terminology[16]). Does the theatre merely function thereby as a mimed supplement to narrative, rather flatly trying to compensate for the written travel account's inevitable elimination of tangible geographical space? One compromise solution employed in *The Travels of the Three English Brothers* combines diegetic resources with performative means in reduced format in the form of a commented dumb show. In this way the play offers a 'scale model' of the journey as a preliminary conceptual framework into which the scenes of 'foreign parts' can subsequently be inserted:

> First see a father parting with his sons;
> Then, in a moment, on the full sails of thought
> We will divide them many hundred leagues.
> Our scene lies speechless, active but yet dumb,
> Till your expressing thoughts give it a tongue.
>
> (Prologue, 27–31)

The spatial dimensions of the stage must be amplified by the verbal commentary, in order to make the stage space signify something which it manifestly is not. The dumb show provides the general fabric in which the incongruity of scale is of little importance because this form of mime clearly declares its differentiation from the rest of the drama. This general framework facilitates the spectator's imaginative reconstruction of the various geographical places with the help of the schematic model which links them in a coherent whole.

Disguise, so important in Renaissance theatre in general, is also crucial to the spatial operation of travel drama. The use of disguise was of course a means of allowing persons to travel where not otherwise possible (for example, Charles's and Buckingham's incognito journey through France to woo the Infanta). It allows characters in the plays to penetrate foreign territory. But it can also function to render those characters foreign to each other. In earlier chapters, it was claimed that disguise, particularly as embodied in the players themselves, was understood as a perverse and subversive displacement of identity in the social-place-obsessed Renaissance. Here, disguise equally functions as a mode of shifting identity, not just from one subject-position to a fictional other, but in real terms of presence and absence. In *The Fair Maid*, Spencer and Bess, searching for each other in the Mediterranean (Bess deliberately, in the hope of recovering the body of her ostensibly deceased lover; Spencer indirectly, thinking to return to London via Barbary with an English merchant, though this plan is interrupted by capture at the hands of the Spanish) do indeed encounter each other upon the stage, when Bess and her crew in turn capture the Spanish occupiers of Fiall (318–19). Bess is disguised as a sea captain, so that Spencer, released along with the other English prisoners, does not recognize her – unsurprisingly so, as he believes her to be at home in Foway patiently awaiting his return from the wars. Bess, in turn, having just been informed that Spencer, apparently buried in Fiall, has subsequently been disinterred and cremated and his ashes scattered to the winds (314–15) is equally convinced of his ineluctable absence, and is thus incapable of recognizing her lover. Thus disguise functions to shift the characters' identity out of a space which they none the less physically occupy, just as the performed journey shifts persons from one fictional geographical context to another, whilst maintaining their presence *here* on the stage.

Indeed, the spatialized dialectic of presence and absence is the key to the semiotic functioning of the travel stage. The larger journey performed on the stage in turn displaces characters into a fictional 'there' which is in reality *here*, and suspends or erases the cultural rules of the physical 'here' by placing the characters in an effective 'there'. On the travel stage, the opposed values of 'presence' and 'absence' are mapped onto 'here' and 'there'. This dialectic of presence and absence lies at the heart of the travel play, which despite constantly decrying its own insufficiency to portray the large canvases its stories demand, whirls the spectators backwards and forth between England and Morocco, sometimes alternating between locations every couple of minutes. These transitions must be facilitated on occasions by a discursive gear-change to compensate for the giddying rapidity of the spatial shifts. When this does not occur, misunderstanding rapidly arises, as in the scene in which Spencer almost loses his life intervening in a duel in Fiall, where the action is not clearly localized until Spencer announces: 'I kill'd a man in Plimouth, and by you | Am slaine in Fiall' (282). The physical presence of the stage and the real absence of the foreign place portrayed, the real presence of the actors and the factitiousness of the characters performed and disguises assumed, are specific to the travel drama. But they are also part and parcel of the interaction, essential to theatre, of the concrete here-and-now of performance and the 'elsewhere' of the drama, the reality of *sujet* (theatrical *narrative discourse*) and the fictiveness of *fabula* (dramatic *story*) – in short, the real presence of an unreal and thus absent universe of invention.

More easily surmountable on the stage than the irreducible problem of physical distance, is the portrayal of *cultural* distance, or the overcoming of that distance, in the form of an encounter of two individuals on the stage. The theatre can also exploit the performance itself, as the encounter of spectacle and spectators, to confront the audience with a foreign place. Thus the stage itself cannot encompass large expanses with any degree of credible realism; but it can *superimpose* contrasting places, simultaneously or in succession; this spatial contrast can in turn be duplicated along the actor–spectator axis, so that the global theatre experience becomes in itself a confrontation of the familiar and foreign. This is implied by the closing lines of the prologue of *The Travels of the Three English Brothers*, part emotional-moral manipulation, and part anxiously beseeching request:

> If foreign strangers to him [the traveller-protagonist] be so kind,
> We hope his native country we shall find
> More courteous. To your just censures then
> We offer up their travels and our pen.
>
> (Prologue, 43–6)

In the relationship of foreigners to the traveller hero, the audience is presented with a challenging isomorphism of its own relationship to their compatriot on the stage.

This meeting of mutually counterpoised worlds is implied in *Antony and Cleopatra* when Maecenas expresses his astonishment that Antony so openly displays his union with Cleopatra: 'This in the public eye?', he asks, to which Caesar replies, 'I'th' common showplace' (3.6.11–12). The 'showplace' is in Egypt, that 'other place' for the Roman speaker. Conversely, at the very end of the play, Cleopatra, still in Egypt yet threatened with deportation to Rome, imagines herself being mocked on the Roman stage (5.2.210ff). This chiastic structure is of great significance, for it implies that the relationship between 'here' and 'there', structured so that 'theatre' is always in the *other* place, is reversed in the real time and place of performance. In the Globe, the 'other place' of the 'foreign' theatre is inserted into the here and now of the spectacle being watched by the London audience; the theatre-goers are thus confronted with a union of native and foreign 'in the public eye', 'I'th' common showplace'.

Similarly, in *The Travels*, Sir Anthony, meeting the renowned comedian Will Kemp in Venice, is keen to know what new plays have been running at the London theatres. Will Kemp, true to form, gives only jesting answers, recounting 'the old play of Adam and Eve acted in bare action under the fig tree' and the recent hoax play called *England's Joy* (9.61–71). News of plays travels widely, like other news, such that the audience sees themselves reported as far abroad as Venice. The actor–audience relationship reported by Kemp in a foreign place is transported not only in diegetic form, but is also performed, Kemp's bawdy providing Sir Anthony with familiar popular theatrical entertainment: 'Jesting Will', laughs the expatriate nobleman (9.64). Thus the audience itself is placed in this European configuration not only as observers of a European panorama, but also as 'participants' in that mobility to the extent that their role can be reported as far away as (fictional) Venice, and that a stage-figure in a foreign capital can take up by proxy their position as spectator of Will Kemp's well-known antics.

The theatre creates a relationship to foreign places which can best be summed up by Antony's parting words to Cleopatra, upon his departure for Rome: 'Our separation so abides and flies | That thou residing here goes yet with me, | And I hence fleeting, here remain with thee' (1.3.103–5). Here and there, self and other, native and foreign can no longer be clearly separated when the stage begins to blur such boundaries. The travel play enacts the encounter with foreignness: the foreign is brought home; at the same time, the familiar is made foreign. The stage is simultaneously in and out, here and there, part of London but also an 'other' (fictional) place, oscillating between importing the foreign into the native country, and casting the native culture into a foreign environment. This explains the abrupt switches of stage-place, by virtue of which two locations, in *Antony and Cleopatra* Rome and Egypt, are forced into proximity with one another. Thus the audience is also constantly changing the point of view from which it observes the drama: now it is looking at Rome from Egypt, now it regards Egypt from the standpoint of Rome. The onstage–offstage relationship is constantly reversible, as the nature of the here/there relations switch, and centre and periphery are exchanged the one for the other.

Travel in a time of transition

So often, what cannot be portrayed visually in the travel drama must be imagined by the audience, or sketched out in reduced or emblematic form within the restricted dimensions of the stage. The epilogue of *Travels of the Three English Brothers* embodies both principles: 'But would your apprehensions help poor art | Into three parts dividing this our stage, | ... Think this England, this Spain, this Persia' (8–11). Later stages would overcome such problems of spatial representation by supplementing the stage space with a perspective mode of scenery capable of depicting vast expanses and depth of field.

These later theatrical techniques, in use only after the Restoration, made manifest a congruence between the techniques of perspective representation and the early modern drive towards exploration. When facing a perspective image of a landscape, the viewer's visual axis can be thought of as the radius of an imaginary disc-like visual plane whose edge corresponds to the central horizontal axis of the scenery viewed or the painting gazed at. This visual plane 'must be thought of as extending infinitely in all directions so that it forms a vast 360-degree circle about the viewer. As the viewer looks straight ahead, the furthest "edge" of this plane forms the horizon.'[17] The space thus concretized in the perspective representation of a landscape corresponds to the concept of infinite space increasingly being debated at this period, as well as to the Renaissance mobilization of Euclidean planar, straight-line space, which made possible the notion of 'homogenous', undifferentiated 'absolute' space offering no resistance to perception. These developments were crucial concomitants of the rise of what Spengler called 'Faustian space', a space of unlimited conquest and aggressive exploration.[18]

But this perspective scenery, the visual sign of a new experience of geographical space, was not part of the theatrical experience of the public stages in the early seventeenth century. The perspective stage as it was deployed in the Jacobean masque, where the masquers descended from the stage into the hall, was only used in conjunction with traditional 'pre-proscenium' stage spaces. The later stagecraft alluded to the subjective configuration subsequently made possible by new experiences of travel. A plastic form expressing such novelties was, however, not yet available to the audiences during the Jacobean period. The dissonance between the ambitions of the travel drama and the representational capacities of the Jacobean stage can be seen as a symptom of the transitional character of developments of English trade and exploration at this period. Several important aspects of this transitional formation can be identified.

First of all, English overseas trade developed only slowly, which meant that there was a gap between calls for expansion and a more aggressive trade policy, and the real state of English overseas commerce. The period from the early seventeenth century through to the civil war marked a shift from the prominence of the Merchant Adventurers'

Company, trading semi-finished woollen cloths principally with the Low Countries and Germany, with exports still at a peak around 1614, to the increasing dominance of the Levant and East India Companies in trade and in London politics by 1640. In 1550 English commerce had been essentially concentrated in the North Sea and the Atlantic coast of Europe. Some advances were made after 1600 towards the Americas and the Far East, but even in 1640 woollen cloth exported to Europe still amounted to 80 per cent of all English exports, though this also included expansion into the southern European market, itself in turn an early sign of the long-term reorientation of British trade towards more distant markets around the globe.[19] In the years 1602–4, various initiatives had been launched to give new impetus to English presence overseas. The East India Company was founded in order to preclude the total exclusion of the English from that market by the Dutch competitors, and in 1604 the Wiapoco colony in Guiana was set up. In 1607 the Virginia Company was established, with two colonies being planted in north and south Virginia respectively. A decade later in the 1620s, the colonies in Guiana, in the Caribbean and in Virginia were still in existence, but only just. Jacobean promoters of American colonies found it very hard to overcome public resistance: Jamestown nearly collapsed, being saved only by repeated appeals to national sentiment. Substantial migration to Massachusetts only began in the late 1620s and the 1630s. And the colony in Nova Scotia, established in 1629, was almost immediately sold to the French.

Thus the progress of English overseas trade and colonization in the 1610s and 1620s was sluggish; there was strong Portuguese and Spanish resistance; the Dutch possessed far superior resources which were freed up after the suspension of hostilities between Holland and Spain in 1609, hampering English efforts in the Far East until much later in the century; and the economic recession of the Thirty Years' War from the 1620s put a damper on English advances in all trading regions. Moreover, English merchants had difficulties in mounting the large amounts of capital necessary for the successful pursuit of such international undertakings; the country lacked banks, and the city of London had only a few large merchants and many small entrepreneurs who were shy of high-risk undertakings. English overseas trade was already far more sophisticated in the 1630s than in 1600, but the changes which would make London an international entrepôt were only to come about after 1660; effectively, new expansion really only occurred with the Restoration.

Furthermore, royal disinterest put a brake on the rise of trade. Admittedly, Elizabeth's political interests did not for the most part seriously conflict with expansionist plans, though had they interfered with her political interests in Europe, she would have blocked the activities of a Drake or a Ralegh. Expansionist movement could thus be strengthened and identified with patriotism as it did not conflict with the political mood of Elizabeth's late reign. James's reign did see a more effective establishment of colonies, but his policy, like that of Elizabeth, continued to give overseas expansion a low priority (indeed, his intervention could have disastrous results for overseas trade and for the English economy as a whole, as was the case with his patronage of the Cockayne project in 1614 to the disadvantage of the Merchant Adventurers, which subsequently caused a trade war with the Dutch). At no point during James's reign was there ever a focused policy for colonial development; any substantial projects were launched by joint-stock companies with only nominal support from the government. In general, as Tawney and Appelby have pointed out, Stuart governments were more concerned with maintenance of order and stability than with economic progress, and fostering overseas trade was consequently of no great interest to them.[20]

Moreover, whereas the gentry had been heavily involved in plunder voyages, which admitted of an easy transfer of the ethos of land warfare to sea warfare, it was none the less the merchants who had supplied most of the capital; and though the aristocracy had been involved in internal trade, its members initially lent little in the way of financial support to overseas trade. All in all, colonization and overseas expansion were widely discussed during the Jacobean period, but little practised until after 1630.[21]

Secondly, the political climate from 1604 was generally at odds with expansionist policies. In the Spanish wars upon which Elizabeth had embarked there was a clear identification with notions of English Protestant patriotism and the privateering war against the Spanish focused on the Atlantic. Richard Hakluyt's *Principall Navigations*, in their 1589 and 1598–1600 editions, and Samuel Purchas's *Purchas His Pilgrimes* of 1625, represented a concerted endeavour to construct an English tradition of maritime enterprise and patriotism which would spur the nation on to future prowess overseas. And indeed, it was a continuing identification of the expansion movement with English nationalism which kept the movement for colonization going through the trials and tribulations of the Jacobean years.[22] But such aspirations largely conflicted with the policy of peace-making espoused by James, who was consistently careful not to offend Spain, only supporting expansion in areas claimed but manifestly not possessed by Spain, such as North America and the East Indies.

Conflicts between the nationalist Protestant party at court and the King were latent from the outset, becoming increasingly crystallized in the person of James's very popular son Prince Henry until his death in 1612. Henry was a close friend of Ralegh, a proponent of aggressive expansion in the New World; he was investing in the Virginia Company in 1609, even sending out a colonizing party which founded a colony called Henrico; in 1612 the East India Company came under his protection and in that year a voyage in search of a North-West Passage was also made under his patronage. Henry associated himself with the spirit of the high Elizabethan age, in stark contrast to the subdued national policy promoted by his father.[23]

A decade later it was Prince Charles and Buckingham (the latter spurring on the Prince after their fruitless journey together to Madrid to woo the Spanish Infanta, an undertaking which may have been a covert bid for increased autonomy with regard to James[24]), who pushed for English intervention in the Continental war on the Protestant side. Their belligerence was in direct opposition to James, who was loath to aggravate Spain, and would later attempt to adjudicate between the warring parties in his cherished role as peace-maker. Samuel Purchas, addressing Prince Charles in the dedication of the massive *Purchas His Pilgrimes*, alluded quite clearly to this continuity of a militant Protestant tradition of English enterprise overseas, while tactfully accommodating James's patently unsuccessful attempts to mediate in the European crisis:

> in a World of acclamations to your ioyfull designes, a world of Pilgrimes seemed sutable; ... the English Martialist everywhere following armes, whiles his Countrey is blessed at home with BEATI PACIFICI; the Merchant coasting more Shores and Islands for commerce, then his Progenitors haue heard off, or himselfe can number; the Mariner making other Seas a Ferry, and the widest Ocean a Strait, to his discouering attempts; wherein we ioy to see Youre Highnesse to succeed Your Heroicke Brother, in making the furthest Indies by a *New Passage* neerer to *Great Britaine*.[25]

Such rifts in opinion about foreign policy may also have resonated, for instance, in Massinger's *The Maid of Honour* (1620). The author pointedly had a Sicilian make a rousing speech about the necessity of a strong navy. A reference to England's past naval supremacy under Elizabeth drove the point home.[26]

Thirdly, the Jacobean experience of travel was one in a process of slow but unfinished development, marked by travellers' ongoing sense of vulnerability and inadequate knowledge. There is a significant semantic slippage in the early modern spelling of 'travel' as 'travail', as in Sir Thomas Palmer's *Essay of the meanes how to make our Trauailes, into forraine Countries, the more profitable and honourable*.[27] Symptomatic of such insecurities was the book of advice to travellers translated by Sir John Stradling, one of many published during the Renaissance. It was offered to the young Earl of Bedford before departure upon 'these your dangerful voyages', designed to equip the young traveller 'with the meanes how to vse and demeane yourself towardes [foreign peoples] for your owne safetie and defence.'[28] *The Merchant of Venice* has Solanio imagining himself anxiously 'Peering in maps for ports and piers and roads' in anticipation of the perils of sea travel (1.1.19), and Peregrine, in Jonson's *Volpone*, avails himself of Sir Politic Wouldbe's knowledge, which, 'if your bounty equal it, | May do me great assistance in instruction | For my behaviour, and my bearing, which | Is yet so rude and raw' – to which Sir Politic, astounded, asks, 'Why, came you forth | Empty of rules for travel?' (2.1.108–12). The period was marked by several quite distinct geographical experiences which co-existed in a tension between tradition and rupture, between extant knowledge and exploration. On the one hand, there was the long-established trade with the Mediterranean and the Near and Middle East, the 'Moorish' or Turkish world, where relations between travellers and the native population were based on an even balance of commercial forces, in which negotiation was paramount; on the other hand, there was the radically new experience of the New World, with a predominantly aggressive mode of colonization.[29] The travel dramas dealt predominantly with the older Mediterranean arena, with the exception of a few plays such as *The Tempest*, whose locational allusions appear to place it in an indeterminate space combining aspects of the Mediterranean and the Atlantic or Caribbean.

This tension between older and newer arenas of expansion coincided with a tension between traditional and more innovative schools of geography at a time marked by the gradual arrival in England of the increasingly scientific and empirically founded 'new geography'. Hakluyt, in the 1589 dedication of his *Principall Navigations*, described being instructed by his cousin, in 'the division of the earth into three parts after the olde account, and then according to the latter, & better distribution, into more: he pointed with his wand to all the knowen Seas, Gulfs, Bayes, Straights, Capes, Rivers, Empires, Kingdomes, Dukedomes, and Territories of ech part.'[30] Hakluyt's description of this inaugural experience relies upon the paradigmatic opposition of traditional and innovative geographical knowledge. In 1605 Richard Verstegan still felt obliged to apologize for putting forward a novel geographical theory based upon empirical observation rather than the ancient authorities.[31] But new geographical knowledge was on the rise; 20 years later, Purchas proudly claimed in his *Pilgrimes* 'out of a Chaos of confused intelligences [to have] framed this Historicall World, by a new way of eye-evidence.'[32] Maria's malicious description of Malvolio in *Twelfth Night* – 'He does smile his face into more lines than is in the new map with the augmentation of the Indies' (3.2.74–5) – has been read as a reference to Edward Wright's *Hydrographiae Descriptio* of 1599; equally, it has been taken as alluding to the enhanced accuracy of the maps included in the second edition of Hakluyt's *Principall Navigations*, which 'carefully avoided the more imaginative sort of speculations and effectively announced the arrival of scientific geography in England.'[33]

Similarly, new methods of navigation were being introduced little by little among merchant mariners, starting with the ground-breaking publication in English of the standard navigation manual of the day, Martín Cortes's *The arte of Nauigation*, translated by Eden at the behest of the Muscovy Company in 1561 and reprinted with corrections and amendments in 1571. As Andrews notes, 'Coasting, with its reliance on accumulated knowledge of the lie and appearance of the coast, of tides and of the sea-floor, and on dead-reckoning by compass, sand-glass, log-line and traverse board, remained the essential basic skill for all masters. Only slowly and in response to the necessities of ocean sailing did English masters adopt charts and elementary methods of celestial navigation to supplement their traditional technique.'[34] Such navigation techniques were modes of representing knowledge which could not be encompassed within the immediate gaze of a viewer and which necessarily went beyond the perceptual limitations of a navigator in the here-and-now. But it would still be some time before these advanced navigation calculations became part of the standard training and skills of English mariners. The Jacobean age was in this respect a period of transition between traditional and innovative methods of navigation. Significantly, a similar tension has been detected in the Jacobean drama. It appears to draw upon both the 'poetic geography' of the ancients, and the new, empirically based geography with its increased attention to concrete detail and ethnographic knowledge. The dramas are the site of a tension between these two ways of representing cultural and geographical otherness.[35]

Thus there was a disparity between, on the one hand, Jacobean discourses of travel, which, by the mid-century, had taken up a prominent place in the public imagination to such an extent that they could be parodied, for instance, in Jonson's *Eastward Ho!* or Brome's *The Antipodes*; and, on the other hand, the sober realities of what was actually possible to do in terms of overseas expansion in Jacobean England, given the constraints imposed by royal foreign policy, the financial mechanisms and institutions available to London merchants, the superior mercantile power of competitors such as the Dutch, or the skills available to mariners. It would be absurd to attempt to establish a rigid causal link between the slow progress of English overseas interests, and the similar gap in the aspirations of the travel drama and the material resources at the disposal of the theatre. None the less, this disparity reflects to some degree a similar contradiction between material possibilities and discursive aspirations at the level of real commercial practice. And it is surely significant that when, after the Restoration, English overseas trade did burgeon at an explosive rate, a new form of theatre better equipped to portray expanses of space in a pictorial, naturalistic mode was also coming to the fore.

It is unsurprising, then, that the travel drama of the Jacobean period was not so much concerned with portraying an overseas world as yet little appropriated for English commercial power, as with using travel as a foil for reflections of the English nation itself. Typical of this specular (and clearly didactic) function of the drama is Greene and Lodge's Nineva play, unsubtly entitled *A Looking-Glass for London and England*. The play ends with Jonas turning towards the London audience ('You Ilanders') and admonishing them with the words, 'O London, mayden of the mistresse Ile, ... I set a looking Glasse before thine eyes' (2604, 2612, 2624). The travel drama, in keeping with the manifest contradiction between ambitions and means in the material production of performance, and not unlike other forms of travel literature as recent research has shown, often had little to say about the other place, but was far more a way of reflecting the here-and-now.[36] 'What is discovered at the end of the voyage,' suggests Richard Marienstras, 'is not really other worlds: rather, different moments of our own.'[37] In what follows, it will be suggested that the spatial strategies utilized in the travel drama primarily served either to confirm English images of national selfhood, or to question them. In the spatial configurations of the travel drama, otherness was either there to reinforce selfhood, or to infiltrate and corrupt it, and in the last analysis, to cast it into question. As Greimas has suggested, spatial language can be seen in the first instance as a language by which a given society signifies itself *to* itself. To this end, the society has recourse to strategies of exclusion, defining itself spatially in opposition to what it is not. This fundamental disjunction affording possibilities of negative self-definition subsequently permits internal articulations which offer richer modes of signification.[38] In choosing this approach to the travel drama, the 'question of the indigenous other' examined in exemplary manner by Todorov, and embodied in particular in recent analyses of *The Tempest*, is not so much elided as refocused and reoriented.[39] For Shakespeare's interest in the indigenous people of the New World as it was expressed in *The Tempest* is to a large extent untypical of the travel drama. Rather, it was the opportunity of regarding *self as other* which constituted the predominant epistemological burden of stage representations of travel.

Narcissism and images of national identity

The stage's capacity to make the 'here' into a 'there' and to make the familiar foreign offers intriguing possibilities of seeing oneself from outside. The portrayal of foreign places on the stage arguably had more to do with gazing at the English nation than at the exotic countries the stage-travellers passed through on their theatrical peregrinations. Many travel narratives displayed the same bias. Thus, in the year of the defeat of the Armada, the English translator of Albrecht Meier's guide for travellers dedicated his work to Sir Francis Drake. He placed his translation within the context of 'the occurrents of this yeare, not so myraculous to the Astronomer, as parturient to al men of spirit, wherein for military & marine matters, as expeditions, plantings, discoueries, & voyages of the largest compasse, there is growne so vniuersall a consent and disposition in this triumphant kingdome, that all Christianitie stands now at the gaze, attending from vs some notable effect & consequence.'[40] In this text, travel means performing upon the world stage as a representative of the elect English nation; the gaze of the reader is directed at the English traveller and not at the foreign land through which he travels.

Likewise, the preface to Robert Harcourt's *Relation of a Voyage to Guiana* (1613) portrays the South American colony as an arena for the assertion of national identity, in which the natives are regarded principally as a foil for the patriotic cause. Harcourt is concerned to ensure that 'our Nation (being in valour inferiour to none other vnder Heauen) bee moued and stirred vp to the vndertaking of this noble action of *Guiana* ... as great effects may be wrovght ... as euer was obtained by the Spanish Nation.' In this project motivated predominantly by the international standing of the nation in competition with the traditional archenemy Spain, the natives figure as important accomplices: 'Moreover, one singular aduantage wee haue before them to further, and aduance our enterprise, by the peculiar loue and affection of the people in those parts, towards our Nation before all others.'[41]

By extension, the lack of interest in the reality of the foreign place portrayed upon the stage is not only evidence of ethnocentricity, but also the result of the structural character of the representation of the other at the centre of national selfhood. For the performance of cultural alterity on the English stage necessarily functions as a refractor of images of national identity; the representation of an other place cannot but sharpen the contours of the site of performance, focused more intensely by its contact with a cultural opposite. Such refraction can however lead in two contrary directions: on the one hand towards narcissism and the confirmation of positive images of the native land, as is already manifest in the texts cited above; or on the other hand toward a critical view of national characteristics.

Narcissistic images of national selfhood on the stage catered to the tastes of a militantly patriotic audience. The absence of such images could sometimes lead to the failure of a play, as may have been the case with the initially hostile reception of Beaumont and Fletcher's *Knight of the Burning Pestle*. Thus the fictional experience of leaving behind England enables Sir Anthony Sherley in *The Travels of the Three English Brothers* to see his native land in clearer focus, its outlines sharpened by the pretence of distance:

> My country's far remote,
> An island, but a handful to the world;
> Yet fruitful as the meads of paradise
> Defenced with streams such as from Eden run;
> Each port and entrance kept with such a guard
> As those you last heard speak. There lives a princess
> Royal as yourself, whose subject I am
> As these are to you.
>
> (1.131–8)

In this proud encomium, the autarchic completeness of the island is emphasized by the fact that the waters all around function as a moat which make of it a paradise, and that possible openings in the country's boundaries ('Defenced with streams ... Each port and entrance kept with such a guard') are carefully policed. The island status, with its strictly demarcated boundaries, allows England to define itself clearly in a way which was not possible for other European countries at a period in history when inland frontiers were frequently still fluid or only vaguely defined.[42] Moreover, the coast of England allowed a clear (negative) definition of self through the potential threat of neighbouring enemies. The mention of Elizabeth in this description of England was not fortuitous, for images of the state as *hortus conclusus*, an enclosed garden walled off from enemies, resonated with images of Elizabeth as the virgin Queen. In the famous Ditchley portrait clearly evoked in the play's association of the closure of the island with its virgin monarch, Elizabeth I is portrayed standing upon a map of England. Discrete island nation and unsullied virgin queen exist in a relationship of reciprocal and mutually reinforcing symbolism. It is equally significant that the Ditchley portrait was one of a group of portraits of Elizabeth marked by a style which dominated the years following the Armada, the crucial event of maritime warfare forming England's collective perception of itself at the end of the sixteenth century and at the beginning of the seventeenth. This attainment of the capacity of self-definition through bellicose opposition was also the result of concern about the vulnerability of the British coastline, its 'feminine' porosity, which in turn drove advances in map-making, making possible the emergence of a global visual image of the country.[43]

Thus the audience of *The Travels of the Three English Brothers* had the thrill of viewing their own country from afar, of being able to identify with their country as a completed, flawless entity – as a world within a world, as James was pleased to say. It is precisely the distance created in the process of self-reflection which makes wholeness possible, smoothing over the fault lines of internal heterogeneity which were so obvious in everyday experience. There were relatively frequent outbreaks of violence against foreigners. Elizabeth ordered the expulsion of all 'blackamoors' from the realm in 1601, and the English parliament refused English nationality to Scots following James V's accession to the throne as James I.[44] And Jonson, Shakespeare and Middleton ridiculed the Welsh with stereotypes which remain readily recognizable today. (It is interesting that the New Globe Theatre, as a prominent and tangible icon of English cultural identity in a contemporary era of increasingly diffuse and disoriented notions of national identity, chose for its 1997 opening season *Henry V*, featuring the definition of Englishness externally against the French, and internally against the Welsh, the Scots and the Irish.)

Such reinforcement of national identity was frequently evinced in the dramas. Part of the mythology constructed by the *Fair Maid of the West* is the image of social cohesion engendered by the expedition to the Mediterranean under Bess's command: Goodlacke and Roughman, both Bess's suitors in most dishonourable ways (Roughman attempts to gain her love by force, and Goodlacke, thinking his friend and her beloved Spencer is dead, sues for Bess's favours in the hope of obtaining his ostensibly deceased friend's wealth), are reconciled to each other and brought under her authority (310–11). Bess's name indicates that she embodies nostalgia for English solidarity under Elizabeth in the days of the Spanish war, where the English nation was virtually identified with the small fleet that defended the Channel in 1588.[45]

Similarly, *The Travels of the Three English Brothers* constructs a religious topography of the known world in which Christian England is set at the centre, embodied in the valorous and enterprising Sherley brothers (and, surprisingly, given the militant Protestant context in which the play was produced, including the Pope [Scene 5]), and poses Jewry, the evil infidel Turks and, to a lesser extent Persia, against the Christians. At this period the Persians enjoyed a reputation as Pagans less culturally distant and less politically or militarily hostile than the Turks, and could even be envisaged as military allies against the infidel Muslims. In the play, the Turks figure to a considerable extent as an anachronistic displaced version of the Catholic powers in Europe. Significantly, the apocalyptic religious language used to speak of the Turks in the opening pages of Richard Knolles' *Generall Historie of the Turkes* (1610) does not differ a great deal from that used to describe the Catholic Antichrist by other polemicists.[46]

These narcissistic pictures of English identity generated by the presence of Englishmen and -women abroad nourished and were borne by a popular groundswell of support for the anti-Spanish sentiment which long years of war had entrenched in a broad segment of the population, but whose political foundation was removed by James's peace with Spain in 1604, to the intense displeasure of many. In 1606 Shakespeare had serving-men in *Coriolanus* welcome the resumption of hostilities with Rome: 'Why, then we shall have a stirring world again. This peace is nothing but to rust iron, increase tailors, and breed ballad-makers. ... Peace is a very apoplexy, lethargy, mulled, deaf, sleepy, insensible' (4.5.223–9). Despite the peace, the essential attitudes of anti-papism and anti-Spanish sentiment remained firmly established, so that James's plans to marry Charles to the Infanta, the execution of Ralegh, and James's determination not to be drawn into the Continental conflicts on the side of his son-in-law Frederick were interpreted as popery in the royal person. In this context, the patriotic drama catered to a receptive audience.

Images of national identity: challenges

However, the frequently contestatory political resonance of travel plays points to the fact that narratives of a journey overseas did not necessarily confirm images of national identity, for such images took various forms according to the political aspirations of conflicting factions. Indeed, the drama as a performance of confrontation with alterity inherently contains in itself an element of disturbing alienation. *The Travels of the Three English Brothers*, despite its patriotic ideology, contains a significant vignette of this threatening confrontation with destabilizing images of selfhood filtered through alterity. Towards the beginning of the play, as part of the diplomatic overtures, the Persian monarch and the English visitors present their respective cultures by means of dumb shows. Both the Sophy and the Sherley brothers mime their respective modes of waging war: the Persians kill the vanquished enemy soldiers, the Christians show clemency and merely take prisoners (1.41ff). What is performed in this play-within-the-play is the confrontation, via theatre, with foreigners in their archaic role as threatening enemy. In a dense multiplication of the self-referential levels of theatricality (the Persians and the English watch each others' shows, with the audience constituting a third instance of spectatorship) the play presents a *mise en abyme* of its own threatening creation of spectacles of foreignness. Within the play's fictional world, the Sophy clearly regards such performance of foreign (English) ways as dangerous, saying 'Our self will sit | And so justly censure of your state in field' (1.71–2), although his judgement is presented as fair; Sherley likewise projects onto the Sophy the role of a controlling instance wary of the infiltration of the home society by foreign bodies, when the English visitor requests that the Sophy 'license' his 'small retinue' to 'shadow forth my country's hardiment' (1.61–4). The terms used clearly link the presentation of foreignness with state censorship of drama. Thus the play creates an isomorphic relationship between inter-cultural and intra-cultural manifestations of otherness. Cultural alterity (whether 'inter' or 'intra') is dangerous enough to be sanctioned by the language of control.

In some cases, the plays employ narratives of travel to raise problematic aspects of English society, only to resolve them by the same narrative, thereby neutralizing the very element of critique triggered by the transgressive departure. Here the travel drama would appear to fulfil a function of venting social tensions, somewhat akin to that of carnival in Bakhtin's classic analysis.[47] In *The Fair Maid of the West*, Heywood raises the questions of love between the aristocratic Spencer and the barmaid Bess Bridges (Spencer's friend Goodlacke warns him: 'Come, I must tell you, you forget your selfe, | One of your birth and breeding, thus to dote | Upon a Tanner's daughter'; Spencer reacts sharply: 'Prethee speake no more, | Thou telst me that which I would faine forget, | Or wish I had not knowne' – 265). A second problem raised by the play is the complicated web of mercantile interests and aristocratic honour which drives Spencer's participation in a privateering expedition against Spanish colonies on the Barbary coast. Spencer denies being motivated by profit, pleading honour as his motivation instead (265), yet on several occasions, duels prove the gentleman's undoing (269–70; 281–3). Duelling, as the most extreme manifestation of aristocratic honour, was a problem which James tried to address in legislating against such socially endorsed violence, though the force of upper-class consensus militated against his efforts.

The unresolvable problems of Bess's low birth and Spencer's responsibility for the death of his duelling partner drive him abroad. The dilemma of a cross-class marriage is resolved by Bess's voyage to Barbary in search of Spencer. In the first place, early modern travel tended to raze class differences, levelling hierarchies and making formerly transgressive liaisons possible.[48] Furthermore, once out of the country, Bess's value is enhanced by her being elevated, upon her encounter with the Moorish prince, to the object of his desire, and by her being compared to the good Queen Elizabeth. The problem of a conflict between pillage and honour in the other direction is resolved by the encounter with Bess in the very regions where both gold and honour have been sought. Bess is a 'Girle worth gold' precisely by virtue of her honour, thus reconciling in herself both the nobility aspired to by Spencer and the financial values he is careful to deny. The play thus rehearses, and then resolves, contradictions within aristocratic society, by placing them on a vertical plane of desire for travel and desire for companionship with a loved person. The contradictions between love and money, and honour and money, which initially appear to exacerbate the distance – geographical, relational and ethical – caused by travel are, in the last analysis, overcome by travel, so that the two lovers are reunited on the Barbary coast, simultaneously permitting the eradication of the problematic aspects of social descent. As the opposed poles of foreign voyages and sexual desire are reconciled by the meeting in North Africa, so the vertical contradictions arising from class differences are smoothed over by Bess's transformation into an exotic princess.

The Sea Voyage, in a manner not dissimilar to that of *The Fair Maid of the West*, launches a critique of contemporary society through its portrayal of the pitfalls and benefits of overseas travel, only to diffuse the selfsame critique with a return to England. The play creates two narratives located in quite distinct spaces: a first narrative consisting of a shipwreck followed by internecine strife among the castaways on a desert island, and a second narrative which sketches an island paradise occupied by a group of European women turned Amazons. Both these narrative spaces function as a critique of the society which the European travellers have left behind them. The third part of the play brings about the contact of these two domains so as to compensate the lacks of the respective foreign spaces, thereby cancelling out the implicit criticisms of society at home, to which the characters can then duly return.

In the opening scene of the play, which quite consciously emulates that of *The Tempest*, a group of seafarers are shipwrecked upon a barren island. 'We were bound', they say, 'For happy places and most fertile islands | Where we had most constant promises of all things' (3.82–4). Such promises were frequent during the Jacobean period; William Morrell's not untypical description of New England evokes

> Westwards a thousand leagues a spatious land
> ...Of fruitfull mold, and no less fruitless maine
> Inrich with springs and prey high-land and plaine.
> The light well tempered, humid ayre, whose breath
> Fils full all concaues betwixt heaven and earth
> So that the Region of the ayre is blest
> With what Earths mortals wish to be possest.[49]

Instead of such a paradise, the seafarers find themselves upon a barren island which negates such tropes of bountiful nature:

> Here's nothing but rock and barrenness,
> Hunger and cold to eat. Here's no vineyards
> To cheer the heart of man, no crystal rivers
> After his labour to refresh his body
> If he be feeble. Nothing to restore him
>
> (1.2.23–8)

The list of negative topoi continues:

> Nor meat nor quiet;
> No summer here to promise anything,
> Nor autumn to make full the reaper's hands.
> The earth, obdurate to the tears of heaven,
> Lets shoot nothing but poisoned weeds.
> No rivers, no pleasant groves; no beasts.

Rather, the island harbours 'Serpents and ugly things, the shames of nature, | Roots of malignant tastes, foul standing waters' (1.3.133–43). One by one, all the images of natural fertility which the New World is said to put at the disposal of the colonizer almost without labour are negated. Here a counter-narrative of the New World emerges as in Harcourt's *Relation of a Voyage to Guiana*, which early on describes an island containing 'no inhabitants, no fresh-water, neither fruitfull tree, plant, herbe, grasse, nor any thing growing that was good, only an abundance of vnwholsome Sea-foule.'[50]

However, this negation of traditional topoi of fertility – almost in the literal sense of sterile 'commonplaces' – is attributed not simply to the environment itself, but to strife between the seafarers. Barely arrived on the desert island in the opening scenes, the prospect of treasure virtually provokes a mutiny on the spot, confirming the warning issued by the established castaway Sebastian, whose exile on the island arose out of earlier disputes amongst gold-greedy travellers (1.3.178–86). The failure of colonial travel dreams is shown to be the work of the colonizers themselves; the voyagers cause each others' destruction, their mismanagement causing them to be stranded upon the inhospitable island. The anti-utopia of the first narrative place in the play represents a critique of the social tensions brought with them by the settlers, tensions which, for example, hampered the development of the 1607 settlement in Jamestown.[51]

The second narrative place is a neighbouring island upon which, unbeknown to Sebastian, his wife and other female members of the original party of colonizers to which he belonged, have created a life. This is the 'blest place' (2.2.196) where the Amazons live by hunting, as bounteous as the other island is cursed. The women's society builds upon an extant Amazon society already established on the island when they arrived after the loss of their menfolk at the hands of pirates, apparently several decades earlier. Crucial to the decision to establish a feminine commonwealth was the rejection of the cruel and violent masculinity which, the older Amazons believe, brought about the death of their beloved husbands. In Rosellia's defence of what has been attained through the Amazon existence, namely freedom, now in danger of being lost with the arrival of male intruders, a second critique of society at home is formulated:

> The sovereignty
> Proud and imperious men usurp upon us
> We confer on ourselves, and love those fetters
> We fasten to our freedoms. Have we, Clarinda,
> Since thy father's wrack, sought liberty
> To lose it uncompelled?
>
> (2.2.189–94)

The absence of men has left these women free to live their own lives, without the burden of a masculine culture of violence, a discourse which doubtless drew upon the lively debates on the virtues and vices of femininity and masculinity carried on throughout the first half of the seventeenth century.[52] However, it is the murmurings of dissent on the part of several women which imply that this material paradise is held, within the play's ideological system, to be no less sterile than the island where the other castaways are incarcerated with their treasure of gold. These opposed spaces are clearly gendered: on the one hand, the barren island, occupied exclusively by men (apart from Aminta, who later represents, for the desperately hungry adventurers, the only edible flesh at hand), constitutes a society sterile because of the self-destructive greed of its inhabitants; on the other hand, the luxurious Amazonian paradise is a feminized space which is equally doomed to sterility through the absence of men to fructify it.

The Sea Voyage thus separates travel narrative into two flawed parts: first, the brutal realities of power and greed generated precisely by the discovery of fantastic riches, but without the redeeming rewards of a fertile colonized space; and secondly, a utopian, paradisical existence predicated upon the rejection of masculist violence, but condemned to sexual monotony and eventual extinction. Both narratives contain, however, an element of topical social critique which will be speedily erased once the two spaces are reunited, creating a harmonious microsociety which can return to the place whence it came.

Thus the third movement of the play works to reunify the two spaces hitherto rigidly separated. Albert, having swum across the straits which separate the two islands, begs the Amazons to rescue at least his lover Aminta from the hell he has left behind him. Rosellia cedes to the murmurings of her discontented Amazon troop, allowing limited contact and temporary sexual traffic with the island of men according to a topos already set by Mandeville's account of Amazon society (2.2.235–45).[53] The dramatic action increasingly welds together the two spaces, while revealing the common history which binds these ostensibly discrete locations. By the end of the play, the fragmentary preceding narratives have been brought together, along with their respective protagonists, reuniting the older husbands and wives (Rosellia and Sebastian) and the younger characters through two fortuitous romantic unions (Raymond and Clarinda, and Aminta and Albert). The closing pairing-off of these couples achieves the reconciliation of the separate masculine and feminine spaces, and the reconciliation of topoi of wealth (the treasure island) and of feminine paradisical fertility (the Amazon island).

Thus all the social contradictions thrown up by the voyage are resolved, allowing the journey in turn to be dissolved:

> When awhile
> We have here refreshed ourselves, we'll return
> To our several homes; and well that voyage ends
> That makes of deadly enemies, faithful friends.
>
> (5.4.110–13)

Thus mutually contradictory conceptions of 'abroad' (from 'industrious...
plantations in the happy islands' [5.2.87–8], easy wealth, and piracy, through to marooned desolation), are finally resolved in a congregation of the various characters which is also a reconciliation of their disparate notions of the voyage and the spaces which embody those various 'narratives' of travel, thus 'mak[ing] of deadly enemies, faithful friends'. With the eradication of the contradictions at the heart of these disparate notions of travel, the social critique briefly articulated is likewise retracted. In this drama, the reconciliation of the various versions of the voyage involves the cancelling out of the voyage and its potential for disruption of notions of society at home, in a movement not dissimilar to Bacon's admonitions that the traveller returning home after a journey 'doth not change his country manners for those of foreign parts.'[54] The voyage should not disturb the sense of native identity, nor hinder the erstwhile traveller's reintegration in his native land. This form of voyaging is carefully controlled so as not to sow dissonance in the sense of national identity.

The displacement of identity: *Antony and Cleopatra*

Not all travel drama, however, launches a critique of society at home only to withdraw, recuperate or neutralize it so as to conclude the play's action harmoniously. In contrast to the examples of recuperated challenges to English identities enumerated above, *Antony and Cleopatra* uses the spatial displacement of the travel drama to destabilize the identity of the protagonists and thus to question the workings of ethnocentrism and territorial political power.

Cleopatra, in keeping with the custom of using a synecdoche to link territory and sovereign, is repeatedly addressed as 'Egypt' by her lover Antony, thus combining and intensifying what Balandier has called the two principal forms of dangerous 'otherness': woman as the 'Other' at home, and the native as the 'Other' abroad.[55] On the one hand, this gendering of the foreign land can be regarded as an example of the spatial representation of gender in the drama.[56] On the other hand, it can be seen as an example of the reverse operation: the sexualization of the foreign, exemplifying what Jeanne Addison Roberts has termed the 'female wild'.[57] Here, the spatial movement, driven by an attraction or even magnetism towards the unknown, is figured in terms of sexuality. This is not mere erotic caprice on the part of the playwright, but fulfils an important cultural function: namely, to make explicable at a visceral level, for an audience of early modern spectators for whom the foreign signified the barbarous, the monstrous, the absence of human nature, an otherwise incomprehensible attraction to the foreign. In a context in which cultural relativism was a rare attitude, and where for most contemporaries there was only one 'Nature' dictating the terms in which Europe and the New World were seen,[58] the eroticization of the foreign makes tangible the notion that the foreign can be a source of fascination. Foreignness is constructed according to a series of gender tropes which make the desiring journey into the unknown palpable and sensual. Thus the explicitly eroticized pull of the exotic is given literal expression by Antony:

> Egypt, thou knew'st too well
> My heart was to thy rudder tied by th' strings,
> And thou shouldst tow me after. O'er my spirit
> Thy full supremacy thou knew'st, and that
> Thy beck might from the bidding of the gods
> Command me.
>
> (3.11.56–60)

Cleopatra's seductive power rests upon her mobility and her *distance* beyond the simple categories of presence or absence.[59] It is the *distance* of the foreign which makes it so fascinating, it is the unattainability of the other which constitutes its seductiveness. If Egypt is attractive by virtue of being gendered, then Cleopatra's seductive power, embodied in her distance, can also be read in inverse form as the seductive power of the foreign land stemming from its location just beyond the horizon of the known world.

The Queen can never be described directly in the dramatic dialogue because she is played by a boy (a real description of Cleopatra would only have induced comic deflation). Likewise, Egypt can never be concretized in the theatre because the drama is performed at the Globe in Southwark, London. But it is precisely the elision of direct representation of the foreign which makes it seductive, for this elision conveys the strong sense of the elusiveness of the foreign land, its tendency to slip constantly out of the grasp of verbal representation. This can perhaps explain a scene which otherwise appears merely comic, when a drunken Lepidus questions an equally inebriated Antony on the characteristics of Egyptian fauna:

> *Lepidus*: What manner o' thing is your crocodile?
> *Antony*: It is shaped, sir, like itself, and is as broad as it hath breadth.
>   It is just so high as it is, and moves with its own organs. It
>   lives by that which nourisheth it, and the elements once out
>   of it, it transmigrates.
> *Lepidus*: What colour is it of?
> *Antony*: Of its own colour, too.
> *Lepidus*: 'Tis a strange serpent.
> *Antony*: 'Tis so, and the tears of it are wet.
>
> (2.7.40–8)

Lepidus would have obtained more illuminating information about the crocodile had he, for instance, delved into George Sandys' account of the creature in a narrative of travel to Egypt, arranged under virtually identical categories to those of Lepidus's enquiries.[60] However, the fact that Antony's replies are tautologies one and all suggests that any statement about the foreign is merely a function of the questioning culture, so that the object of discourse constantly escapes from any attempt to capture it by description; in other words, all that can be said about the foreign is, precisely, that it is foreign. The foreign land remains out of reach of expository discourse, at one remove from the language of the visitor, and thus constantly tantalizing, beckoning.

In *Antony and Cleopatra* Egypt embodies what Schülting has called 'spatialized femininity' or a 'feminized space' which resists physical traversal and textual description, a feminized *Terra Incognita* which threatens to upset or annihilate the European text.[61] The danger detailed by Schülting is evident in the play, for the warning issued to Lepidus directly following this buffoonery is more than an allusion to the fact that he is no longer steady on his feet, and not equal to a philosophical discourse of the type embarked upon: 'These quicksands, Lepidus, | Keep off them, for you sink' (2.7.58–9). More important is the oblique reference to the notion that such descriptions of the foreign, by saying nothing, can entice the observer to pursue a constantly receding goal. If the crocodile symbolizes the feminized foreign (Antony calls Cleopatra 'my serpent of old Nile' – 1.5.25), then it also points to the danger of this sexualized domain of alterity, whose pursuit potentially precludes return. As Loomba comments, 'If the African or American woman stands in for Woman as Nature, ripe for ravishing, her Eastern counterpart becomes the embodiment of Women as Artifice – ever ready to ensnare.'[62] Feminized Egypt, it would seem, is situated at the point where Africa merges with the Orient.

The reference to quicksand is thus equally apposite to Antony. He has been captivated by an attraction for the foreign which ultimately brings about his downfall. This fascination leads him away from the constitutive values of social stability, delivering him up to loss of his true patrician identity and thereby of his social role. From the very moment of Antony's arrival in Egypt, his situation is defined in terms of a radical change of location, no longer the stable position of the Roman military master, but the unstable and fluid site of a man captivated by a constantly receding source of attraction. We are told that

> Upon her landing Antony sent to her [Cleopatra],
> Invited her to supper. She replied
> It should be better he became her guest
> Which she entreated. Our courteous Antony,
> Whom ne'er the word of 'No' woman heard speak,
> Being barbered ten times o'er, goes to the feast,
> And for his ordinary pays his heart
> For what his eyes eat only.
>
> (2.2.226–33)

The moment of disembarkation, rather than representing a movement of invasion or conquest, is marked by a reversal of roles. Antony, ostensibly the imperial Roman conqueror, is placed in a passive position, and is conquered by Cleopatra. Rather than his landing constituting a moment of possession, it marks his ceding to the seductive power of the foreign, always at one remove, visible but elusive. This sudden entry into a space which he no longer controls or possesses robs Antony of his acquisitive, dominating masculinity.

When Cleopatra flees from the midst of the sea battle, Antony flees after her, merely repeating a movement of unmasculine pursuit which has marked his actions from the inaugural banquet onwards: 'I never saw an action of such shame. | Experience, manhood, honour, n'er before | Did violate so itself' (3.10.21–3). Antony's movement is 'feminine' and inverts manhood in patently spatial terms. The clearest evidence of

Antony's abandonment of masculinity for a position of 'feminine' lack is his abandonment of the male-based Roman dynasty for Cleopatra's sake. His attachment to Egypt signifies femininity in so far as it represents a spatial, geographical betrayal of masculine values; whereas the attachment to his wife Octavia was clearly – and quite legitimately within such structures – a form of adherence to masculine Rome, the woman functioning, in her capacity as a reconciling union between Antony and Caesar, merely as a link between men.

After the triumvirate has collapsed, and Antony and Caesar find themselves at war, the sea battle against Caesar is to be waged at Pharsalia, where Pompey had also been beaten. This would appear to be tactically unwise, as Enobarbus points out, for in this way, Antony gives up his sure footing on land, 'quite forgo[ing] | The way which promises assurance, and | Giv[ing] up yourself merely to chance and hazard | From firm security' (3.7.45–8). A humble soldier drives the point home:

> O noble Emperor, do not fight by sea.
> Trust not to rotten planks. ...
> > > Let th'Egyptians
> And the Phoenicians go a-ducking; we
> Have used to conquer standing on the earth,
> And fighting foot to foot.
>
> > > > > (3.7.61–6)

Antony's fateful decision to fight at sea possesses a certain logic within the spatial symbolism of the play; for in choosing the uncertain element of water, he merely confirms the fluid and unstable position he has taken up in opting for the ever-increasing attraction of the (gendered) foreign, thus '[kissing] away | Kingdoms and provinces' (3.10.7–8). In leaving Italy for Egypt, Antony has travelled into the realm of uncertainty beyond the solid contours of the Roman homelands: the foreign element effectively begins where Italian earth stops. The final outcome of Antony's journey into the nebulous, gendered space of the exotic land is a complete loss of his footing:

> Hark, the land bids me tread no more upon't,
> It is ashamed to bear me. Friends, come hither.
> I am so lated in the world that I
> Have lost my way for ever.
>
> > > > > (3.11.1–4)

Antony's 'losing his way' summarizes the entire course of his action in the play, his quitting the Roman patrician community for the assumption of a spatial deviance which can never be reversed, as the object of its quest can never be attained.

In a culture which defined identity in clearly spatial ways, Antony's defection to Egypt has radical consequences for his identity, in others' eyes and in his own. In abandoning his allegiance to Caesar and to the Empire, there is a clear sense of Antony no longer being himself: Philo disapprovingly says, in language which seems for us quite self-contradictory, accustomed as we are to notions of internalized and fixed personal identity: 'Sir, sometimes when *he is not Antony* | He comes too short of that great property | Which still should go with Antony' (1.1.59–61; my emphasis). 'Is' and its negation should be understood in terms of place and of behaviour which places an individual in relationship to the collectivity by virtue of which identity is attributed. In the act of taking off his armour in the final scenes, Antony symbolically puts off the contours of socially recognized identity of the warrior and statesman, becoming a nobody. Whence his humiliated and self-abnegating request, made via his ambassador to Caesar, 'To let him breathe between the heavens and earth, | A private man in Athens' (3.12.14–15). A private man has no identity. Being excluded from public function, he is of no significance. To leave the public place for the foreign is to become an individual: but as Belsey remarks, Antony's declaration 'I am | Antony yet' (3.13.92–3) is an index of his increasing isolation, the catastrophic result of defection and failure, rather than his attainment of modern individual identity.[63]

This way of seeing his defection, however, assumes a one-way gaze upon the exotic world of Africa. Whereas Cleopatra counts herself among a Mediterranean community of 'us that trade in love' (2.5.2), in keeping with the commercial exchanges and reciprocal trade partnerships which characterized the European contacts with the Mediterranean and the Near East, the Roman approach to Egypt is imperialist and militaristic, as was the European conquest of the New World in the Americas – a relationship which admitted of no dialogue with the cultural 'Other'.[64] At the end of the play, Thidias, the ambassador sent by Caesar to Cleopatra, says to her: 'But it would warm his spirits | To hear from me that you had left Antony, | And put your self under his shroud, | The universal landlord' (3.13.70–2). In this universal command of space wielded by Roman imperialism, whoever does not submit to that hegemony is placeless. This concurs with Ovid's boastful claim that the boundaries of Rome were the boundaries of the world, taken up in Shakespeare's *Cymbeline* when the protagonist refers to 'Caesar's ambition | Which swelled so much that it did almost stretch | The sides o'th' world' (3.1.48–50).[65] By annihilating places outside its hegemony, Rome denies the possibility of genuine social life beyond its own borders. Rome contributes to destroy any semblance of community that Antony might have enjoyed with Cleopatra, and Egypt is thus assimilated into the control of Rome; it is no longer 'beyond the pale' a place outside of civilized community, but rather, is devoured by civilization, such that Antony possesses no space whatsoever.

This approach to Egypt is necessarily predicated upon a mutually exclusive relationship between community and the foreign. According to this logic, 'us' constitutes a community of belonging in a manner which is clearly tautological, a fact that has logical consequences for anything outside of that closed and self-constituting group. In contrast, 'them' can only ever be the absence of community.[66] This point of view assumes the non-reversibility of the gaze upon the foreign; for it, looking back from a 'there' towards a 'here' is literally unthinkable, a non-existent category in this particular structure of thought. To leave behind the community of 'here' is, by definition, to leave behind community *per se*, to be nowhere and to fall into isolation. This is the scheme of things to which the play appears to subscribe. Entering a foreign world implied, for early modern ethnocentrism, the potential loss of one's civilized nature; in Renaissance England, Ireland, for instance, was perceived as a dangerous colonial space in which the colonizers were likely to lose their identity and become degenerate.[67] Antony's capitulation to the forces which work to isolate him appears to underline his own acceptance of the notion that existence outside the boundaries of civilization signifies non-existence *tout court*.

However, there are signs that the theatre may also simultaneously offer some resistance to this idea of the foreign as a mere place of dissolution of identity. Certainly the optimistic lover does not view Egypt in that way in the opening lines of the play:

> Let Rome in Tiber melt, and the wide arch
> Of the ranged empire fall. Here is my space.
> Kingdoms are clay. Our dungy earth alike
> Feeds beast as man. The nobleness of life
> Is to do thus; when such a mutual pair
> And such a twain can do't – in which I bind
> On pain of punishment the world to weet [know] –
> We stand up peerless.
>
>   (1.1.35–42)

This is a courageous declaration of indifference to the symbols of imperial ethnocentrism, and a levelling of the hierarchies of centre and periphery which sees Rome and Egypt as essentially no different in their constitution out of common earth which feeds the inhabitants of Egypt and Rome alike. Against Roman nobility, Antony sets the lover's couple, which 'stands up peerless'; against the urban monuments of empire, he sets mother earth. At the beginning of the drama, Antony opposes to the 'arch | Of the ranged empire' a form of the 'melting' which will later define his own insubstantiality, when that over-arching imperium deprives him of his authority and place. *Antony and Cleopatra* thus articulates, in its opening scenes, a possibility of other spaces which render the absolute claims of empire utterly relative and local. 'Here is my space' announces Antony, though the play will little by little dispute his claim, until he and Cleopatra, through their double suicide, eventually give up the space they occupied, albeit eluding by such a draconian strategy assimilation into the Roman celebrations of military triumph.

Thus the play gives a brief alternative glimpse of radical assimilation to a foreign culture, a phenomenon which appears to have posed a real threat for contemporaries. In 1518 a law was passed in Lisbon condemning to death 'lançados', Portuguese who had 'gone native', although there is no evidence that this legislation was ever enforced. Death sentences were also proclaimed for the servants who absconded from the English settlements in Virginia, preferring the life among the Native Americans to service to their masters. Spenser, in his *View of the Present State of Ireland*, articulated a fear of English defections to the barbaric Irish culture, seduced by the perverse power of Irish women into betraying their mother tongue. Of the large number of English seafarers coming to Barbary (on the north African coast, where Algiers, Tunis and Salle were Turkish regencies ruled by Viceroys sent from Constantinople) a considerable number converted to Islam; narratives of travel to Barbary were replete with instances of conversion, forced or voluntary. The exact extent of these conversions is not known, but certainly it was enough to seriously disturb contemporaries who perceived the numbers as enormous. When a barber-surgeon named William Davies visited Tunis in 1614, he claimed that it contained more converts than Turks.[68] The issue was topical enough to be treated in a 1612 play by Robert Daborne entitled *A Christian turn'd Turk*. The English pirate Ward is persuaded to convert to Islam by the seductions of a Turkish woman, who subsequently brings about his death, thus demonstrating the dreadful consequences of apostasy. Clearly the appropriation of another cultural or religious space than that of one's origin was perceived as highly threatening to the integrity of the source culture. And this seems to have been all the more so when the renegade performed his defection upon the autochtone stage, in dumb-show rituals which cannot but have advertised the theatricality they shared with the performance itself (F2v–F3r).[69]

This analysis has remained until now within the boundaries of *Antony and Cleopatra's* fictional (dramatic) narrative. Once, however, the analysis is broadened to include the moment of performance, the truly subversive character of the play becomes evident. If one imagines the deictic statement *par excellence*, 'Here is my space', being enunciated upon the stage of the public theatres, it is possible to see an isomorphic relationship between the place of Egypt within the context of Roman imperial expanse, and the position of travel drama in the geographical space of London's theatre landscape. This isomorphism allows us to place Enobarbus's famous account of Cleopatra within the immediate context of its theatrical enunciation:

> From the barge
> A strange invisible perfume hits the sense
> Of the adjacent wharfs. The city cast
> Her people out upon her, and Antony,
> Enthroned i'th' market-place, did sit alone,
> Whistling to th'air, which but for vacancy
> Had gone to gaze on Cleopatra too,
> And made a gap in nature.
>
> (2.2.218–24)

The magnificent spectacle of Cleopatra draws the people out of the centre of the city, leaving the erstwhile representative of imperial power, the visiting member of the triumvirate, quite alone on the market-place. But this example of desertion of the centre for the greater fascination of the ostensibly peripheral, but in actual fact magnetically attractive, spectacle of monarchy is one that Antony himself will subsequently emulate. The centrifugal pull to the periphery experienced in Antony's inaugural visit encapsulates his own subsequent relationship to the centre of imperial power.

More significantly, however, this diegetic account of the people leaving the city to gaze on a spectacle of foreignness, leaving a vacuum in the city centre, such that the spectacle of exoticism effectively undermines centralist power, also describes the attractive force of the public theatres in the Liberties. Part of the city fathers' resentment of the public theatres arose from the fact that the new commercial theatres were felt to have usurped the former prominence of civic pageantry and the traditional processions. The new theatres, with their performances of exotic locations, intriguing plots and colourful costume, effectively cast the pomp and ceremony and displays of civic authority into the shadow, causing a centrifugal pull towards the new places of entertainment outside the city walls. They also constituted a peripheral and less controllable site of consumption away from the centralized 'marketplace'. The theatres' relationship to power was not exclusively one of centre–periphery – some actors' companies were sponsored by nobles, and later by the monarch, and some dramatists, such as Middleton, wrote both for the public stage and the civic pageants; but such partial and occasional convergence of the interests of the theatres and civic power by no means excluded considerable tension between the two institutions.

Early on in the action, as Antony has learnt of the newly looming political crisis in the Roman state, and has resolved to tear himself away from Egypt in order to fulfil his civic duty, he employs a consciously theatrical metaphor which foregrounds the material performance context. Antony has just heard the news of the death of his wife Fulvia: 'She's good being gone; | The hand could pluck her back that shoved her on. | I must from this enchanting queen break off' (1.2.119–21). Fulvia's absence from the 'stage' of life makes her abruptly more attractive to her hitherto indifferent husband, and it is her sudden 'exit' which motivates him to leave Egypt for Rome. The image of entries and exits is thus coupled with travel, thereby pointing up the fact that the return to the centre of empire is, in dramaturgical terms, nothing more than an exit offstage from 'Egypt' and a re-entry onstage at 'Rome'. Just as the two dramatic places are separated only by the crossing of the threshold of the tiring house, so the action of 'breaking off', of leaving behind the exotic feminizing space of idleness which 'hatches' evil, for the masculine space of real actions of civic signification, is reduced by the stage to a mere question of perspective. Thus *Antony and Cleopatra* precludes any process of 'splitting' of self and cultural 'Other' into stereotypical images, for the two are constantly brought together on the same stage. Here the Shakespearean drama achieves what Greenblatt has identified at work in the travel narratives of Herodotus and Mandeville: the discovery and articulation of hidden links between radically opposed modes of being and hence some form of acceptance of the 'Other', a mode of self-identification with alterity which is also self-estrangement.[70] The inadequacy of the stage to really represent large expanses is at the same time its capacity to create a synecdoche of place with a remarkable economy of means, consequently being able to combine or contrast such geographical synecdoches at will according to the trope of metonymy which underlies synecdoche, thus allowing the most surprising superimpositions of apparently radically opposed cultures. Thus, without any apparent sense of unease, Cleopatra in Egypt can leave the stage, to be replaced, almost immediately, by Pompey in Rome (Act 2, Scenes 5 and 6). The stage thus declares, ostensively, the intimate entwining of self and 'Other'. This ostensive blurring of boundaries is simply the extension of a process already at work in individuals: Cleopatra remarks of Antony: 'He was disposed to mirth, but on the sudden | A Roman thought hath struck him' (1.2.76–7). By having Antony able to occupy both Egypt and Rome – the same actor standing on the same stage increases the ambivalence which infiltrates this form of cultural identity fundamentally understood in terms of spatial positioning – and able in both places to be pulled back towards the other, the stage demonstrates that cultural identity can be radically confused, made multiple, by the encounter with the 'Other'.

Moreover, the experience of watching such drama may have been similarly unsettling, for the position of the spectator, in an era before perspective scenery, was no more distanced from the action of the open stage than the locations concretized on the stage itself were discretely separated from each other.[71] The implication of the audience in the performance, an imbrication of 'here' (yard and galleries) and 'there' (stage), replicates the interlocking of 'here' and 'there', of 'us' and 'them', which is acted out upon the stage. The audience could not have been immune to the elimination of the 'here'/'there' distance on the stage, because the very spatial configuration of the Jacobean theatre precluded such distance; the drama operated with the 'contagious' force of foreignness brought near.

Antony and Cleopatra thus disputes the absolute claims of any imperial power or ethnocentric speaker to represent the only possible viewpoint from which to regard the world, insisting rather upon the co-existence and reciprocal questioning of multiple viewpoints. Caesar, upon learning of Antony's suicide, laments that the world was simply too small for both of them, that the two men were of too great a stature to 'stall together | In the whole world' (5.1.26–40). This is deceptively ingenuous, however, for Antony is absent in Egypt for the greater part of the play, and it is for this that he is resented. Antony, in leaving behind the Roman world, questions its absolute validity, and poses an inadmissible alternative to its ethos of dynastic communal obligation. The very fabric of the play opens up new vistas and shows how this can become a subversive act.

Travel as transgression and transposition in *The Tempest*

In *The Tempest*, the questioning of absolute power is levelled in an even more direct manner at instances of royal power in England. The storm and shipwreck as inaugural catastrophe burst open the current state of affairs and open up new possibilities on two levels: on the one hand, possibilities of dramatic action triggered by the transgression which drives dramatic plot; on the other hand, possibilities of political renewal. Both narrative and political novelty are spatially propelled in the first scene of *The Tempest*.

Thus this play opens with a similar questioning of an absolute political order to the one activated in *Antony and Cleopatra*: as in *Antony and Cleopatra*, place has to do with power, and with the narratives and performances in which power is legitimized or contested; the disruption of place performed in the first scene of the play is also a disruption of ways of representing power, both in verbal and performative form. Whence the significance of the boatswain's cry amidst the storm: 'What cares these roarers for the name of king?' (1.1.15–16). Here the sacrosanct name of the monarch, against which slander could incur the gravest punishments, is disempowered. The seventeenth-century implications of such an utterance were massive. A royal proclamation of 1601 offered £100 to anyone providing information about those who slandered the royal person, and a lawyer's clerk was hanged for that offence the very same year. A man was racked twice in 1626 for writing a private letter which contained 'words and insinuations against His Majesty'.[72] The storm thus creates a 'world turned upside down', in which the boatswain can temporarily reverse social hierarchies, ordering his aristocratic superiors, 'Keep below' (1.1.10). The same spatial contestation of power is evinced by the argument between Antonio and Sebastian as the ship goes down: 'Let's all sink wi'th' King' – 'Let's take leave of him' (1.1.60), where loyalty to the monarch is debated in spatial terms. However, it will transpire in the course of the play that such spatial transgression can equally serve to justify the absolutist status quo, by virtue of the terrible example of social unrest; the nascent rebellion on the island furnishes Prospero with an opportunity to demonstrate his benevolent autocracy, and thus to re-establish his previously usurped rule in Milan.

The spatial disruption marked by the storm is preceded by a prior spatio-political rupture, that of the voyage to Tunis in order to wed the king of Naples' daughter, Claribel; the shipwreck which deposits the party on Prospero's island occurs on the return trip. This double rupture has profound consequences, because it opens up a potential political vacuum in the state of Naples, with the king isolated on the island, his son Ferdinand apparently drowned, and Claribel far away in Tunis. Sebastian is interested in obtaining his brother Alonso's throne of Naples, and Antonio is equally interested in Alonso's fall, as this would release him from the relationship of dependence which was the price to be paid for the latter's military support for the earlier coup against Prospero. Thus the island opens up a space in which the power relationship may be reconfigured in new ways equally advantageous to Sebastian and Antonio. But this rupture also undoes the new usurping order established much earlier after Prospero's banishment, thus eventually making it possible for him to redeem what he lost so long ago, by restoring Ferdinand to a grateful Alonso and coupling him with his own daughter at one fell swoop. The play assembles all the parties from the former disruption, but under the sign of a new rupture facilitating a novel reconfiguration of the power relations between them. The shipwreck is thus a moment of spatial dispersion, an explosion which breaks apart the existing power relations, making possible the creation of new strategic relationships; but it is also an implosion in which the parties separated earlier by the machinations of power are brought together once again, so that earlier history can be rewritten.

Shakespeare constructs the action around a series of tensions between past and present, centrifugal and centripetal political forces, explosion and implosion, the well-known territories of the Mediterranean and the novel New-World Caribbean. It is significant that a marriage at Tunis would have worked to cement cooperative trading partnerships in the Mediterranean in a way, for instance, that Charles V's military campaign to capture Tunis three-quarters of a century before *The Tempest* did not;[73] yet Prospero's power is also built upon his coercion of the island's indigenous inhabitants in a manner typical of European conquest of the New World.[74] The ostensibly wrecked ship is carefully preserved by Ariel's skills as a mobile turning-point symbolically located at the junction of old and new, east and west, trade and colonization, negotiation and conquest:

> Safely in harbour
> Is the King's ship, in the deep nook where once
> Thou called'st me up a midnight to fetch dew
> From the still-vexed Bermudas, there she's hid;
>   ...

> And for the rest o'th' fleet,
> Which I dispersed, they all have met again,
> And are upon the Mediterranean float
> Bound sadly home for Naples,
> Supposing that they saw the King's ship wrecked
>
> (1.2.227–37)

As it transpires, it is a compromise between old and new which the play allows to develop: neither the re-establishment of the reigning hierarchies as they were at the beginning of the action, nor their destruction by plebeian revolt or by aristocratic coup, is achieved. In this way, the play mobilizes an inaugural rupture through the transgression of travel, only to recuperate that moment of instability in the denouement of the dramatic action, in a manner similar to that of *The Fair Maid of the West* and *The Sea Voyage*. This holds good, however, only as long as one considers the fictional world as a sealed-off whole.

Precisely this reification of the fictional world of *The Tempest* is swept away, however, by Shakespeare's unexpected finale. For Prospero's closing address to the audience ostentatiously draws attention to the theatrical character of the actions performed upon the stage. The transgression of travel has opened up a space in which alternative political scenarios can be rehearsed, a place between old and new, between the usurpation and restoration of a 'legitimate' political order. In pointing out the theatrical character of his peaceful coup, however, Prospero marks out in clear spatial terms the limits of power, thus admitting that the return to real political office in Milan is not yet achieved. The desired translation of political theatre into political power is expressed in geographical terms:

> Now my charms are all o'erthrown,
> And what strength I have's mine own,
> Which is most faint. Now 'tis true
> I must be *here confined by you*
> *Or sent to Naples*. Let me not,
> Since I have my dukedom got,
> And pardoned the deceiver, *dwell*
> *In this bare island* by your spell;
> But *release me from my bands*
> With the help of your good hands.
> Gentle breath of yours *my sails*
> *Must fill*, or else my project fails,
> Which was to please.
>
> (Epilogue, 1–13; my emphasis)

The theatrical fiction has rehearsed a set of alternative configurations of power, but without the approval of the audience, these spectacles of restored political legitimacy cannot be made reality. For Prospero's 'return' to be completed, and spectacle to be transposed back into the real world, Prospero is obliged to submit his theatricals to audience ratification. The theatre insists, in this way, upon its linkage to the real world of political meaning-making.

This linkage, however, is dependent not upon the drama's own capacities (so often admitted to be inadequate) but upon audience participation, as the travel drama never tires of repeating. The recurring trope of the limits of the stage takes on a new meaning in Prospero's meta-theatrical meditation upon political spectacle, because it transfers political responsibility back to the audience. The moment of rupture which inaugurated the dramatic narrative of travel in foreign parts is replicated at the level of the performance in its self-reflexive visibility as performance. This time, however, travel-as-transgression does not open up the alternative world sanctioned by stage fiction, but opens up the fiction to the real world, in which political fictions must be carried out in practice, a movement of travel-as-transposition. Thus the travel drama, by reversing the spatial terms of the inaugural *transgression* into that of closing *transposition* ('With the help of your good hands | Gentle breath of yours *my sails* | *Must fill*, or else my project fails'), points to its oscillating focus between fiction and real, between theatre and context, and thus, by means of an exemplary spatial *mise en abyme*, to its function within Jacobean society. Furthermore, in spatializing its capacity to compare reality-as-given to reality-as-constructable, the theatre implicates the audience as participants in the modelling process, a process which sometimes but not always entails a moment of critical comparison between what is, and what might be – a constantly operative (albeit often cautiously retracted) function of the travel drama. In the 'here'/'there' of the spectators' own position on the threshold between those two spaces, the drama of travel installs the dangerous potential for critique.

7
Local Thought: Intellectual and Subjective Mobility

Mobility of mind

If travel in the wider world was undergoing rapid transformation, the 'contracted world' of individual subjectivity was caught in a process of change no less significant. In Shakespeare's *Coriolanus*, Menenius admonishes the short-sighted and hypocritical old tribunes Brutus and Sicinius: 'O that you could turn your eyes towards the napes of your necks, and make but an interior survey of your good selves!' (2.1.37–9). Moments later, he refers to himself in similarly topographical terms, speaking of 'the map of my microcosm' (2.1.61). To refer to selfhood in spatial terms, as we saw in Chapter 1, was a common trope of the early modern age and should thus not overly surprise us. Of greater consequence, however, is the deviation between the two similes.

What is striking about Menenius's allusions is that he uses two quite distinct topographical paradigms in order to describe himself and his political opponents. On the one hand, the notion of self as a microcosmic part of the macrocosm situated selfhood within a larger order of things which defined the human subject as one link in the great chain of being, in accordance with Donne's figure of the individual as part of the continent.[1] It was this conception of the world which was inscribed in the Anglican homily on order, which we looked at earlier, first published in 1547 and reprinted under James and Charles:

Almightie God hath created & appointed al thynges, in heauen, yearth, and waters in a most excellent and perfect ordre. ... Euery degree of people, in the vocacion, callyng, & office, hath appoynted to them, their duetie and ordre. Some are in high degree, some in lowe, some kynges & princes, some inferiors and subiectes, priestes

215

and laimen, masters and seruantes, fathers and children, husbandes & wifes, rich and poore, and euery one hath nede of other, so that in al thinges, it is to be lauded & praised ye goodly ordre of God, without ye whiche, no house, no cite no common-wealth, can continue & endure.[2]

On the other hand, the contrasting notion of surveying the self was linked to novel notions of property ownership, which allowed the self to be figured as an acquisitive and essentially egotistical landowner, one who rejected a communal ethos of interdependence. Thus Milton's Satan, expelled from the community of the angels for self-interested plotting, consoles himself with the thought that 'The mind is its own place.'[3] The rise of surveying was directly linked to the notion of land as quantifiable, commodifiable, and to this end mappable; surveyors' maps, as equally reified and valuable images of landed wealth, could be sold in turn as representations 'whose subject [had] the same owner as itself.'[4]

The progressive interiorization of these new paradigms of commodifying cartography is evinced in pedagogic injunctions to the nobility to practice the drawing of maps, 'for the practice of the hand, doth speedily instruct the mind, and strongly confirme the memorie beyond any thing else.'[5] The identification of selfhood with land acquisition within accelerated changes of property relationships gave rise to expressions derived from the notion of copyhold tenancy, such as 'to change one's copy', meaning a change of style, behaviour, action, so extreme as to suggest that a person had assumed an entirely new character, or 'to make a copy of one's countenance', to describe imposture, dissembling, as the characteristics of selfhood became as unstable and exchangeable as the landed property inherited, possessed, bought or sold by that self.[6] In Menenius's image of an emergent survey cartography applied to one's own self, a picture forms of a subject slowly developing out of a recursive attention to its own empirical characteristics, at what Foucault has called the 'site of empirical-transcendental redoubling'.[7] It is by virtue of this recursive self-constitution that we can recognize this early modern self as a forerunner of modern subjectivity: 'Paradoxically, it is because the self is an object for the ... hero that the ... hero seems like a subject to us.'[8] This new topography of selfhood pays less attention to its position within the whole than to its own boundaries and limits as constitutive of a space of self-possession, to the exclusion of the larger community. This new space of selfhood is clearly a concomitant of changing property relationships through which the self's links to others within a hierarchical network of duties and responsibilities were jettisoned in the cause of self-interest and economic rationalization. The interiority mentioned by Menenius is meant, however, more as an index of inadequate self-knowledge than of a stable, inward subjectivity. The co-existence of the mutually antagonistic tropes of surveying, and of an organic microcosmic-macrocosmic universe is evidence of a transitional period in which the two conceptions of subjective space sit uneasily alongside each other, vying for dominance. In a period of shifting paradigms of subjective self-definition, several apparently contradictory models of selfhood are available to contemporaries to map their personal contours within the social whole. Whereas Greenblatt claims that self-fashioning in the Renaissance was always, if not exclusively, rooted in language, this chapter poses the counter-claim that the transformations of identity in that period were always, though not exclusively, grounded in the decisive spatial transformations of society.[9]

It is above all an element of fluidity which characterizes the emergent versions of selfhood. When Sir Anthony Sherley in Day, Rowley and Wilkins' *The Travels of the Three English Brothers* asks a Venetian gentleman friend, 'And now, dear friend, what tidings at St Mark?' he receives the reply, 'Like to men's minds, distract and variable' (9.2–3). Similarly, Drayton wrote: 'My verse is the true image of my mind, | Ever in motion, still desiring change.'[10] The new intellectual and subjective mobility evident in Renaissance England reflects a shift away from the immobile hierarchy of the great chain of being, towards a more fragmented and mobile view of selfhood and the self's place in the world. The 'rusting' of the links of the great chain of being was quite concretely the result of increased social mobility which had consequences for individuals' perception of their own identity.[11] Greenblatt links the unusual sensitivity of a number of Renaissance writers – More, Spenser, Marlowe, Wyatt, Shakespeare – to the construction of identity with the fact that 'they all embody, in one form or another, a profound mobility.'[12]

Several names in Greenblatt's group highlight the fact that the theatre was one principal locus of this loosening of social bonds and of the emergence of a new monadic subjectivity. Thus J. Cocke accused the player, mutable by virtue of his costume changes, of being 'a Motley: His mind observing the same fashion of his body: both consist of parcells and remnants: *but his minde hath commonly the newer fashion, and the newer stuffe: hee would not else hearken so passionately after new Tunes, new Trickes, new Devises*: These together *apparell his braine and understanding*, whilst he takes the materials upon trust, and is himself *the*

Taylor to take measure of his souls liking.[13] The actor, according to this conception, was a person constantly in search of novelty as a result of his profession, just as were his customers – the audience. By definition, the actors constantly had to embody new characters who acted in new stories set in new worlds, in the interests of their own economic survival: novel subjects were the player's principal wares, even when old subjects could still be performed profitably. The mobility encapsulated within the actor's selfhood rendered tangible the new fluidity in conceptions of subjectivity generalized across a society made mobile by the working of new economic forces, and summed up under the epithet of an 'histrionic calculus' – the lucrative employment of substitute identities.[14]

Alongside a certain stylized tradition of pessimism and a general belief that the world was in a process of decay,[15] the traditional cosmic order was being cast into question by the discoveries of Galileo and Copernicus, with ostensibly catastrophic results for the hierarchic and organic cosmos. Just as the individual, with 'al his partes, both within & without, as soule, harte, mynd and memory, vnderstanding, reason, speache, withall and syngular corporall membres of his body', formed 'a profitable, necessary and pleasaunt ordre'[16] which could be disturbed by disease, so wrote Shakespeare in *Troilus and Cressida*,

> ... when degree is shaked,
> Which is the ladder to all high designs,
> The enterprise is sick.
> ...
> Take but degree away, untune that string,
> And hark what discord follows.
> ...
> This chaos, when degree is suffocate,
> Follows the choking.
>
> (1.3.101–3, 109–10, 125–6)

Donne's *The First Anniversarie*, quoted above, lamented the dissolution of rank and degree: 'Prince, Subject, Father, Sonne, are things forgot, | For every man alone thinks he hath got | To be a Phoenix, and that then can bee | None of that kinde, of which he is, but hee.'[17] Once again, the hierarchical relationships of the cosmos, in which each element contributes to the good of the whole, thereby justifying paternalistic social degree, is said to cede to a new individualism and egotism. In 1623, Drummond of Hawthornden echoed Donne, writing that

> The element of fire is quite put out, the air is but water rarefied, the earth is found to move and is no centre of the universe, is turned into a magnet; stars are not fixed, but swim in ethereal space, comets are mounted above the planets; some affirm that there is another world of men and sensitive creatures … in the moon; the sun is lost. … Thus sciences, by the diverse motions of this globe of the brain of man, are become opinions, nay errors, and leave the imagination in a thousand labyrinths. What is all we know compared with what we know not.[18]

In Hawthornden's account of the new cosmology, the earth moves, rather than having a fixed place in the order of things, the stars appear to be cut loose from their secure emplacements in the spheres, the comets, rather than possessing cosmic significance as portents of future events, are reduced to mere physical objects in space; and the abrupt mobility of the earth, by virtue of a paradoxical left-over from an obsolete macrocosm, is reflected in the bewildering mobility of human imagination and conceptualization. The conviction of fixed truths about a fixed world are replaced by the sense of having erred regarding a highly mobile universe, and the observer, overwhelmed by the fragility and contingence of his knowledge, has the impression of wandering (etymologically, one meaning of error) in a labyrinth.

The dismantling of the *a priori* cosmic framework went hand in hand with a radical change in patterns of thought which was fundamental in the presentation of conceptualizing selfhood enacted by the Jacobean drama, a change in modes of thought epitomized by if not necessarily originating in Francis Bacon. If the disturbing atomization of society was closely connected with the emergence of an increasingly autonomous self, both of which were manifested in the drama, characterizations of the actor accurately pointed towards the locus of such changes. Cocke's description of the actor, cited above, locates that chameleon personality in its random collection of scraps of knowledge described as 'parcells and remnants', 'stuffe' and 'materials'.[19] The textile metaphors refer to ideas torn out of a broader framework, and taken on their own merits and for their pure utility – an apposite image of the new philosophy championed by Bacon.

Local thought

In his *Novum Organon*, Bacon suggested that 'There are and can only be two ways of searching into and discovering truth. The one flies from the senses and particulars to the most general axioms, and from principles, which it takes for *settled and immoveable*, proceeds to judgement and to the discovery of middle axioms. And this way is now in fashion. The other derives axioms from the senses and particulars, rising by a gradual and unbroken ascent, so that it arrives at the most general axioms last of all. This is the true way, but as yet untried.'[20] Bacon portrays on the one hand a mode of thought based on accepted authority, one which has no place for flexibility or mobility of thought. The three orders of axioms, not without a certain resemblance to the orders of social privilege, function so as to impose authoritarian dictates upon the 'middling sort'. On the other hand, in opposition to this time-honoured mode of thought which still holds sway, Bacon suggests an alternative, one which moves from the 'lower orders' of empirical experience upwards to the higher orders. This mode of 'democratic thought' has its bases in the pragmatic, artisanal experience of the here and now, what, following Geertz in a rather different context, one could call a 'craft of place', 'local knowledge'.[21]

Bacon, whose writings were only published after 1640, was not particularly original in these formulations, for he merely synthesized and formalized the attitude of a large number of vernacular, non-university scientists. The necessity of empirical experiment was well established among non-academic scientists communicating in the vernacular from the latter half of the sixteenth century. Examples of this often autodidactic trend in experimental enquiry included the mathematicians Robert Recorde and John Dee, or the astronomer Thomas Digges, whose work on the infinity of the universe was far more radical than that of Copernicus; other mathematicians such as Hariot and Wright proved better at solving the problem of 'Mercator's projection' than Mercator himself.[22] Scientific debates in England, in contrast to the Continent, were conducted in the vernacular, so that the influence of such debates permeated society particularly at the levels of merchants and artisans; empirical scientific research, starting from an intrinsic scepticism about over-arching cosmic theories and an emphasis upon individual testable experience, originated not surprisingly from the middling sort, and not from the upper echelons of society. Empirical experimentation was inherently pragmatic and operative and aimed at applied knowledge as an aid to action in the interests of economic gain. A helpful contrast is suggested by Helgerson between the epic text of the Portuguese poet Camões, which presents the world as a global whole, contained within the familiar Ptolemaic cosmos, and the travel chronicles of a Hakluyt, which conceive the world as a myriad of enterprises to be undertaken with the assistance of the corresponding parcels of local, incomplete knowledge relayed by many different mariners and traders.[23] This mode of knowledge is based upon 'the trial and error of craftsmen raised to a principle', driven by the conviction that 'reality could be changed by human effort'. Indeed, there was a strong link between anti-authoritarian Puritanism and the empirical tradition of scientific enquiry in sixteenth- and seventeenth-century England: 'The Baconian attitude of mind would be hostile to all mere authority which would not submit to the test of use and experience. Bacon, like Nicholas Hill, insisted that men should reexamine the things they took for granted, the apparently obvious and self-evident: with minds cleared of all prepossessions. A man steeped in Baconianism would, if he applied the method to politics at all, not be an unquestioning supporter of the status quo.'[24] From this point on, the organic cosmic hierarchy, in which individuals were seen as subordinate to their superiors and occupying a predetermined place within the whole, was increasingly superseded by a vision of space which placed individual knowledge in the here-and-now of empirical perception at the centre of the world.

Thus, whereas Malynes claimed in 1623 that 'Princes and Governors are to sit at the sterne of the course of Trade and Commerce', using their supreme authority to determine rates of exchange,[25] Misselden countered that only the merchant on the spot, possessing exact information about a market situation which was constantly in a state of flux, could calculate the factors best suited to promote economic advantage: 'For there is no Merchant of any experience, but as he hath one eye vpon the value of his Commoditie, so hath he the other eye vpon the money, both *Instrinsique*, in the inward value or finenes, and *Extrinsique*, in the outward denomination or account as it is currant in euery Countrey, together with the course of *Exchange*, whither he doth direct his trade.'[26] The extraordinary mobility and fluidity of the new economic reality necessitated a corresponding mobility and empiricity of modes of thought to deal with it. A huge amount of empirical information was necessary in order to act effectively with the local flux of trade. Lionel Cranfield received regular reports from the factor Rawstorm in Stade and pestered correspondents in Middelburg and Amsterdam, or even Danzig, for news; only in this way was it possible to keep track of the immense number of incalculable factors which needed to be taken into account in dealing in European trade: fluctuations in price, determined by the unexpected arrival of a cargo or delays in arrivals of shipments, internal changes in the producing country, exceptional foreign demand or fluctuations in availability of other goods, political crises – all this information needed to be passed back to London as rapidly as possible.[27]

The quantity and quality of empirical information generated in the new economic climate is encapsulated in the dialogue from *The Travels of the Three English Brothers* already cited above. A Venetian gentleman replies to the question, 'what tidings at St Mark?' with the quip 'Like to men's minds, distract and variable' (9.2–3). In this play, the variability and distraction of men's minds merely reflects the variable and aleatory character of their destinies, which in turn is immediately absorbed into the over-arching net of European information provision, sited in St Mark's, which corresponded, in the real London of the theatre, to St Paul's. Dekker compared the much-frequented Paul's Walk to a meeting place for people 'of all Countreyes' like 'the *Mediterranean Sea*',[28] a dense site of encounters between travellers from all parts, functioning to receive incoming information and distribute it to the capital and the rest of the country. Indeed, as Cust acidly remarks, 'the gossip of the "Paul's Walkers" was reproduced so widely and so precisely that one can find the same mistakes being repeated as far afield as Cambridge and Devon.'[29] Here, the drama functions self-reflexively as a similar condenser and transmitter of disparate information, in this case with regard to the fortunes of the Sherley family.[30] To this extent, the theatre can be seen as contributing to the global image of Europe which was gradually coalescing at this epoch based upon the increasing flow of local, regional information.

The erosion of an ordained cosmic hierarchy, with the concomitant opening-up of the infinity of space, was accompanied by the valorization of individual knowledge, and an infinitude of new discoveries based on concrete experience. Innovative artists and architects discovered that lines did not merely define the surfaces of objects, but could also be extended beyond into space so as to give it shape, thus creating concrete and measurable relationships between objects apparently far removed from one another and hitherto without connection.[31] Likewise, information emerged in the concrete experience of individuals and was transmitted across great distances through the development of linguistic innovation and new media.

Indeed, the vertiginously inventive language of English Renaissance drama was fuelled by novel empirical experiences. In his *Art of Reason* of 1573, Ralph Lever claimed that 'there are more things than there are words to express things by'; the language of the Elizabethan and Stuart periods was constantly minting new words to keep apace of new technological, scientific and geographical discoveries. Shakespeare alone created a myriad of new expressions to describe empirical experiences which were constantly outstripping the resources of language.[32] It was the new alliance between the concrete and the infinite which drove not only the emergence of the Renaissance theatre with its inventiveness and energy, but which provided the material of the dramas themselves.

The drama of the period consistently negated over-arching knowledge, privileging instead empirical knowledge anchored in the concrete place of the speaker. In *No Help, No Wit Like a Woman's*, Weatherwise is a clear figure of ridicule, for his views on the integrity of the universe clash with that of other more modern characters. Earlier, having witnessed the betrothal kiss between Lady Goldenfleece and the disguised Mistress Low-Water, which simultaneously signifies his own failure as a suitor, he announces: 'Nay, so my almanac told me there should be an eclipse, but not visible on our horizon but about the western inhabitants of Mexicana and California', to which Mistress Low-Water replies somewhat tartly, 'Well, we have no business there, sir' (2.3.204–7). This flat contradiction of the spatial relevance of the larger cosmic scheme constantly recurs in the texts of this period. This localized mode of thinking insists, likewise, upon the necessity of empirical testing. Brabantio, commenting the love of Desdemona for Othello, confidently claims that 'It is a judgement maimed and most imperfect, | That will confess perfection so could err | Against all the rules of nature'; on the basis of this biblically-authorized assumption that black is by definition imperfect, he then suggests that some supernatural force must have overridden the functioning of nature: 'I therefore vouch again, | That with some mixtures powerful o'er the blood, | Or with some dram conjured to this effect, | He wrought upon her.' The hierarchies of ethnic identity are immobile and apparently invulnerable. There is nothing particularly surprising about these assertions of the inherent evil of blackness. More striking, however, is the Duke's reply to this, where he sceptically asserts the primacy of empirical evidence over against *a priori* generalizations: 'To vouch this is no proof | Without more wider and more overt tests, | Than these thin habits' (*Othello* 1.3.99–108). Against such habitual mental reflexes, against the customary outward, convention-bound garb of phenomena, the Duke recommends experimentation capable of breaking out of the constrictions of traditional thought, displaying an empirical curiosity characterized by the breadth and openness of its enquiry.

With the loss of fixed, *a priori* structures of knowledge, it consequently became increasingly difficult to hierarchize apparently contradictory versions of experience. The doctrinal unity of Christendom had been shattered by the Reformation, and from that point on, it was possible for quite opposing beliefs to be held, without anyone definitively being able to say which practices and ideologies were right and which were wrong.[33] Empirically driven development of new ways of thinking about physical and geographical space, encapsulated in the rise of new cartographic methods, also generated a critical awareness of the difficulties involved in the representation of space. The Privy Council experienced initial problems in understanding the differences of scale used in Saxton's county maps of Britain, which led to the same tax burden being placed upon Pembrokeshire (which occupied one sheet in his atlas) as upon the other four Welsh counties (which also shared one sheet).[34] With the creation of the first globe (around 1490) the problematic question of representation of space arose. Mercator's projection drew attention to the conflicting character of the intrinsic structure of the various media, namely the unresolvable dilemma of transferring the curved three-dimensional space of the surface of the earth to the two dimensions of flat charts. This dilemma made it clear that there can be no true maps.[35]

The emergence of specific knowledge tended to stress the relativity of knowledge and the difficulty of incorporating localized knowledge into a ideal larger whole (although it should be added that this was Bacon's ultimate, albeit – significantly – unfinished project). Thus the philosopher Nicole Oresme posited that money was simply a valid convention, which allowed a centralized system of price equivalence, within a certain 'currency territory'. Money continued to carry the figure of the monarch, and was still minted by that monarch alone; however, Oresme claimed, the monarch was no longer absolute owner of that money, but simply the public figure acting as guarantee of the money's worth, an arbitrary but visible servant of a specific geographical community; the legitimacy of the monarch functions as a centralizing organizing principle for society, but one which is easily transferable to another place or another person, thus possessing only a spatially limited validity.[36]

Such relativity is dramatized on the stage by the exchangeability of roles of knowledge and ignorance, as, for instance, when Viola comments on Feste in *Twelfth Night*:

> This fellow is wise enough to play the fool,
> And to do that well craves a kind of wit.
> ...   This is a practice
> As full of labour as a wise man's art,
> For folly that he wisely shows is fit,
> But wise men, folly-fall'n, quite taint their wit.

(3.1.59–67)

Viola's chiastic inversion of the relationship between wit and folly relies upon far more than the traditional trope of the wise fool or the sacred knowledge partaken of by madmen.[37] Rather, the inversion of the places of wisdom and folly is based upon an exactly calculated appraisal of available information and entails a finely calibrated response to the flux of reality. The dramatic topos of the confusion of truth and appearance serves the larger topos of the primacy of empirical knowledge which precludes the priority of any one preordained site of knowledge, thus opening up mobility in what can be known where, and in consequence, what constitutes wisdom's opposite, ignorance.

Indeed, it is the trope of misrecognition, so important in a drama obsessed with costuming, disguises and cross-dressing, which Feste himself uses to destabilize all inner/outer relationships, not in order to make them fully arbitrary, but to open them up to operative logic. 'Misprision in the highest degree!' exclaims Feste: 'Lady, "*Cuculus non facit monachum*" – that's as much to say as I wear not motley in my brain. Good madonna, give me leave to prove you a fool' (1.5.51–4). Feste accuses Olivia of misprision, that is, of falling into the trap to which almost every character in the play is susceptible: that of misrecognizing outward appearances. Feste's accusation, moreover, is that his appearance of foolery, and in particular his fool's costume, do not affect his mental capacities, a statement reflected in Viola's succinct assessment of the skills of fine observation and precise calculation necessary to successful foolery. In requesting Olivia's permission to prove his mistress a fool, Feste suggests that not only does she not understand his own worth, but also that she is mistaken about her own relative identity, just as Cesario [Viola] tells her 'that you do think you are not what you are' (3.1.135). The assertion of the incongruence of inner and outer necessary to the very identity of foolery corresponds to Feste's displacement of the qualification of fool onto his mistress, in order to reassert *his own* position as Olivia's fool. In proving Olivia a fool, he will win back his own status as 'her' fool. Thus the label of 'fool' switches backward and forward between lady and jester, such that the displacement and the emplacement of the fool are interdependent. Feste thereby wields a tactical subversion of the hierarchy of lady and fool in order to guarantee his own employment. In this way he suggests that there is no inherent social place, no inherent identity of the knowing subject, but rather, an instrumental knowledge which allows the sites of knowledge and ignorance to be exchanged at will.

Feste's assertion of Olivia's foolishness depends upon his condemnation of her misguided mourning. She is wrong to mourn her brother's death, he suggests, for her brother has gone to paradise, a cause for celebration for a Christian believer: 'The more fool, madonna, to mourn for your brother's soul, being in heaven. Take away the fool, gentlemen' (1.5.66–8). Olivia's behaviour is out of place because it does not accord with her brother's place, and this confusion of place earns her the dubious honour of switching places with Feste – to the point where he can suggest that she be cast out rather than himself. Once again, it is the inversion of inner and outer which is used to re-establish the 'order of things'. Clearly, however, this is not a given, immutable order, but rather, a tactical, contingent constellation in which Feste determines what is good for him and operates accordingly. The 'misprision' committed by Olivia is to not realize that inner and outer are operative terms, not wantonly exchangeable, but subject to a chiastic operation according to a careful assessment of the conditions reigning at a given time and place.

No all-encompassing structure determines the meanings of words; their sense is fixed by local factors alone. Viola, jesting with Feste, enquires: 'So thou mayst say the king lies by a beggar if a beggar dwell near him, or the church stands by thy tabor if thy tabor stand by the church' (3.1.8–10). The hierarchy governing the relations between places – in which one place serves as prioritized reference point, in relation to which other subordinated places are situated – can readily be inverted. The examples chosen by Viola playfully place symbols of worldly authority (the monarch and the church) in subsidiary relation to a beggar and a musical instrument. This subversive order of places is not without hierarchy, as might initially appear. Rather, it takes the individual's perspective as the centre point of perception, rather than the immutable, transcendent hierarchy imposed from above by monarch or church. Kernodle links this shift of perceptual standpoint to Cusanus's notion 'that any point could be considered as a central point from which the rest might be considered', marking 'the turn from a theological view to a more realistic view of the world and of space'[38] (though the 'realism' of this new configuration of perception is perhaps something that might be queried today, as studies on the 'constructedness' of the emergent perspective mode of representation demonstrate[39]).

It should be asked, however, to what extent Feste's jocular rearrangement of socio-political geography genuinely represents a questioning of the traditional sites of theologically legitimized power. The fool, in turn, confirms Viola's appraisal of his tactics of subversion: 'A sentence is but a chevrel glove to a good wit, how quickly the wrong side may be turned outward' (3.1.11–13). Feste's reply confirms this mechanism of reversibility while holding fast to the principle of a right side and a wrong side, that is, to some sort of inherent order which can be contravened by inversion. This begs the question: where is the reference point for this right side/wrong side to be situated, and can this prior and founding hierarchy not also be contravened? The fact that it is Feste who utters such a thought, embodying in his identity as house jester the always recuperated fool's freedom to express subversive thoughts within a strictly constrained space of jest, underlines the possibility that Shakespeare's play toys with the modalities of subversion while displaying a deep seated reluctance to give up a notion of inherent order which underpins but finally banishes the very concept of subversion. If it is a shipwreck – the geographical displacement which throws Viola up on the coast of Illyria – which triggers the action of the play, it is none the less clear that notions of rightful home and places of belonging will finally be confirmed by the romance mode of drama. Given that the play as a whole appears, in the last analysis, to re-establish the larger orderly frameworks of society, it is possible that Feste's disturbance of the hierarchies of inner and outer merely constitutes a minor subset of the larger set of intact hierarchies. Or, conversely, it is also possible that Feste's juggling, as a subset capable of relativizing that inner/outer hierarchy, mischievously asserts that the encompassing and ordered set of the play as a whole is itself merely an operative subset of the larger set of contingent and reversible inner/outer relationships. The play, with its title 'What you will', accommodates local subversion to the frame of larger resolution in that both levels of the dramatic action, turbulent micro and stable macro, lead in the direction indicated by individual desire – with the disturbing exception of Malvolio, whose desires are plainly thwarted, and whose parting threat opens a breach in the apparent closure of the play's action.

The largely peaceful outcome of the play is in part a generic feature of comic romance. It is also, however, a sign that local individual and overarching collective consciousness coexisted in a sort of fluid cohabitation. Clearly, what was emerging at this period was an individual subjectivity possessed of an new interior sensibility (whence Menenius's 'interior survey') which did not yet mark it out as a stable 'person' equipped with a clearly defined depth of personal identity (exemplified in Hamlet's 'I have that within which passeth show' – 1.2.85). Rather, the emergent mode of selfhood appears to be characterized by a fluid and pragmatic functioning within a world in flux. As Graham notes, 'Although an individualist society and culture clearly does emerge from the period, and emphasis on the self in general grows, a *coherent* notion of self does not emerge uniformly. Notions of "self" and the social primacy of the individual self are formulated within divergent discourses and are variously inflected.'[40] The depth of subjectivity becoming increasingly visible on the Jacobean stage is less 'personality' than an operative assumption of an exterior persona protecting the calculating subject from the prying gaze of other competitors in a universally self-interested society. Thus, commented the poet John Hall, it is only 'in his retired and hid actions' that the man of business 'pulls off his disguise and acts openly'; here, we are much closer to the notion of a commodity self, a mercurial being whose contours are determined by what others are prepared to exchange or invest.[41]

This selfhood is thus still not so very distant from the notion of collective identity which preceded it, embedded in macrocosmic relationships of obligations and duties, and thus porous to society, for social pressures and impulses continue to define the emergent subjectivity, with the simple difference that these forces in turn are far more fragmented and fluid. Even the opaque depth of subjectivity heralded by Foucault's model of confessional subjectivity is produced by operational tactics of judicial torture and 'discovery of secrets' well before a self-determining confessional mode arises.[42] Burkhardt's notion of full-blown Renaissance individualism would appear to be less appropriate to early modern England than the more commonly cited models of individuality as an extraordinary flexible but artificial construction in the service of power, dictated by the necessities of political intervention and the pressures of the contingent historical moment – models to be found in Machiavelli and Castiglione.[43] Within this context, Bacon wrote, 'All practice is to discover, or to work. Men discover themselves in trust, in passion, at unawares, and of necessity, when they would have somewhat done and cannot find an apt pretext. If you would work any man, you must either know his nature and fashion, and so lead him; or his ends, and so persuade him; or his weaknesses and disadvantages, and so awe him; or those that have interest in him and so govern him.'[44] Bacon's aphorism bears out the connection between inward 'discovery' (with its multiple early modern inflexions) and 'work' – between subjectivity and empirical knowledge serving pragmatic ends. The pragmatic, operational image of individual subjectivity current on the Jacobean stage is thus a transitional being, still as driven by the impulses of social life as its predecessor, but cut loose from a unified cosmic community, caught up in the extraordinary flux of commodity exchange and as yet untrammelled by the substantial contours of the later Enlightenment individual.

Localized thought in the theatre

With the exception of the court theatre, the theatres of the Stuart period did not employ perspective scenery. Yet the functioning of the perspective mode of perception none the less offers a very apposite analogy for the dramatization of early modern subjectivity on the Jacobean stage. In the words of Panofsky, 'The decisive innovation of *focused perspective* epitomizes a situation … in which the work of art had become a segment of the universe as it is observed – or at least, as it could be observed – by a particular person from a particular point of view at a particular moment.'[45] The erosion of a cosmic hierarchy thrust the experience of the individual into the foreground, with the result however, that this experience could become foreign and opaque for others. The fragmentation of community under the pressure of self-interest leads to fragmentation of language, to the emergence of islands of the sort Donne so passionately denied.

Thus, in *The Revenger's Tragedy*, for instance, linguistic 'dialects' indicate radically incompatible views of the world anchored in distinct regions of human experience. Dondolo arrives with a missive for Castiza: 'Madona, there is one … that would very desirously mouth to mouth with you.' Here, communication is presented as an act of oral intercourse, embodied in the promiscuity of punning, where meanings link up with each other in unexpected and sometimes less than legitimate ways. Implicitly, this is the language of the court with its decadent sexual morals and corresponding innuendo. 'What's that?' asks the puzzled Castiza, and is granted only a further example of linguistic foreplay: 'Show his teeth in your company', a phrase which at once couples oral, verbal and aggressively sexual significance in a single corrupt embrace. 'I understand thee not', replies Castiza finally, thus signalling that she belongs to a different linguistic region, where meaning behaves in a chaste and monogamous manner: for her, one word possesses only one meaning. Dondolo, finally obliged to translate his intention into a speech intelligible to Castiza, is greeted with her reprimand, 'Why say so, madman, and cut off a great deal | Of dirty way; had it not been better spoke | In ordinary words, that one would speak with me?' Castiza speaks the language of Puritan plain speech, a mode of communication favouring the most direct route rather than the 'dirty ways' taken by the messenger; but Dondolo, scorning such economy of expression, converts the 'verbal hygiene', the 'propre' and 'propreté' of Puritan monosemic language, into a distinction of social milieu:[46] 'Ha, ha, that's as ordinary as two shillings, *I would strive a little to show myself in my place,* a gentleman-usher scorns to use the phrase and fancy of a serving-man' (2.1.10–23; my emphasis). Dondolo declines to place himself in the domain of the prosaic, pragmatic use of language in service of everyday commercial transaction (exemplified by the reliable plain-speaking for which Montaigne praised his servant, or by Bacon's 'men of plainer sort, that are like to ... report back again faithfully'[47]); for Dondolo's sophisticated language belongs to the ludic extravagance and corrupt sexual intrigues of the court. Statements of non-understanding in Jacobean comedy frequently stand as indicators of dramatic generic boundaries, where characters are confronted with language usages arising from another dramatic context than the one which they themselves inhabit.[48] The meta-linguistic punning in this episode is evidence of a similar confrontation of language-universes, where even the mode of contact itself is construed differently: as promiscuity and erotic aggression on the one hand; as (ideally) unhindered communication on the other. Under the pressure of self-interest, generic linguistic differences take on aggressive valences; the reciprocal opacity of individuals for each other becomes one aspect of a pre-emptive strike, communication as 'showing one's teeth'.

Ironically, it subsequently transpires that this confrontation between two modes of language, those of sensuality and morality, of convolution and plainness, between these two apparently mutually incomprehensible linguistic regions, is not imposed from without, but comes from within. Little does Castiza know that the intruder thus announced is her own brother Vindice, disguised as a henchman of Lussurio, who seeks to seduce her by appealing to the mother's venal instincts. Thus the apparently homogenous site of family unity splits into disparate language-domains motivated by conflicting interests. When a son provokes his mother to prostitute her own daughter in order to sound out her moral depths, inner and outer values, truth and falsehood, endogenous and exogenous languages become so entangled that it is no longer possible to adjudicate between them. Subjective opacity and family community, operative dissembling and the morally-driven extraction of truth, are superimposed with such density in a single social site that the truth and falsehood inhabiting the function of the 'player' become indistinguishable.

The drama enacts the place-specific character not only of sociolects, but of truth and falsehood, which, when overlaid within a single social unit, come to be a matter of perspective rather than absolute value. In Middleton's *A Mad World, My Masters*, to name only one of many plays which exemplify the phenomenon, truth and falsehood inhabit the space of the same utterance in such a way as to make a clear distinction between the two concepts impossible. Indeed, a large part of the comedy's appeal lies in the audience's relishing the cohabitation of truth and lies. Lord Owemuch (alias Follywit) has been attacked by thieves (alias Follywit and his companions) while visiting Sir Bounteous. Host and visitor discuss the identity of the thieves the following morning:

> *Follywit*: Can you not guess what they should be, Sir Bounteous?
> *Sir Bounteous*: Faith, Lincolnshire men, my lord.
> *Follywit*: Fie, fie, believe it not, sir; these lie not far off, I warrant you.
> (2.6.44–6)

Follywit's opinionated denial is part of the fiction in which he takes part as the spurious Lord Owemuch; and yet is also true, as the thieves of the previous night (himself and his friends) are indeed anything but far off; and at the very moment of telling the (concealed) truth about their whereabouts they 'lie' by virtue of their concealed identity.

The villains in these comedies often speak ambiguously, their words having one apparently innocuous meaning for the victims of their scheming, and another known to themselves and to the audience, which directly refers to their cozening of the victims. The overlapping of truth and falsehood is thus a matter of points of view, depending on which world, that of deception or that of shared, complicit knowledge, one occupies. These overlapping worlds do not result in a total indifference or relativity of truthfulness, for there is an implicit hierarchy of degrees of knowledge which privileges the audience/trickster-knowledge over the limited knowledge of the gulled victims, and upon which the success of comedies depends. None the less, within certain limits it is possible for a statement to be both true and false, according to the parameters of localized knowledge conditions. Truth, in the theatre, is not absolute, but governed by a hermeneutics of differing places which tend to intersect with each other, thus producing a performative topography of paradox. In this way the stage foregrounds its mode of dramatizing the immensely problematic character of secretive and duplicitous operative subjectivity, embodied in the actors themselves, those 'double dealyng Ambodexters', as Stubbes called them.[49] The audience is of course drawn into the phenomenon of the cohabitation of truth and falsehood, occupying as they do *one* of the sites from which a given situation can be regarded, but able to observe *other* possible places of enunciation. Indeed, it is precisely this experience which the audience pays to see; the pleasure gained arises from the possibility of taking up, as it were, several mutually contradictory perceiving-subject-positions simultaneously, in a manner isomorphic with the character duplication of the players themselves. Indeed, without knowingly complicit audience participation, the production of multiple and contradictory sites of truth would not be feasible. Thus the emergence of the theatre commodifies the heterogeneity of monadic subject positions, and by the same token, overcomes their mutual isolation.

Yet, as observed above, the fragmentation of the cosmic hierarchy which produces individual sites of subjective perception also opens up the boundaries of the Ptolemaic universe, creating by implication infinite possibilities of novelty which also exist within the everyday experience of individuals. Subjectivity itself becomes a site of novelty. Typically, the process of naming no longer exclusively denotes a place within a social order, but also points towards a pragmatic, intentional function, one which the drama constantly foregrounds. In replying to the inaugural question, Who is Follywit?, the opening lines of *A Mad World, My Masters* set the tone of the whole play, asserting an explicit orientation towards novelty and innovation rather than the maintenance of given structures. The play opens with the question of the mode of address appropriate to the arch-wit:

> *Maworm*: O captain, regent, principal!
> *Hoboy*: What shall I call thee? ... the life blood of society.
> *Follywit*: Call me your forecast, you whoresons.
>
> (1.1.1–4)

Follywit's self-christening looks into the future, not to what is established, but towards what is to come, to what is not yet preordained by existing social structures and hierarchies. Naming, one of the basic operations of thought, is responsible for moving forwards, rather than merely reiterating the already known. The obsequiously rehearsed titles of hierarchy ('captain, regent, principal') are abruptly displaced by a rougher tone and a new mode of address without precedent: 'your forecast'.

From being a place of repetition of extant hierarchies, the space of the stage is thus transformed into the locus of exploration of novelty, indeed, into the performative creation of the as-yet-inconceivable. Middleton's play preceded Harvey's public formulation of the circulation of the blood, which reduced the heart from its status as the seat of the soul to a mechanical pump, by a decade, but Hoboy's epithet ('the life blood of society') none the less forcefully connotes mobility and fluidity. Moreover, the plotting that is to make money for Follywit and his accomplices is isomorphic with the novel plots that are to make money for the actors; novel incidents are to produce wealth both at the *fabula* (dramatic construction of the story) and the *sujet* (performance) levels. At both levels, it is pragmatic ingenuity which holds the day. This mode of thought is not interested in a metaphysical appraisal of its location in the grand scheme of things, but rather, in an action-oriented response to the exigencies of a specific time and place. Savourwit says: 'Our knavery is for all the world like a shifting bankrupt; it breaks in one place and sets up in another; he tries all trades from a goldsmith to a tobacco seller; we try all shifts from an outlaw to a flatterer; he cozens the husband and compounds with the widow; we cozen my master and compound with my mistress; only here I turn o'th'right hand of him; he is known to live like a rascal, when I am thought to live like a gentleman' (*No Wit, No Help Like a Woman's* 2.2.186–92). Of particular significance is Savourwit's use of the word 'shift', at once a spatial and a pragmatic term, signifying practical knowledge applied to specific situations, and the restless motion of the wits driven by the necessity to deal inventively with the givenness of the new situation.

Mobility in a specific locality rather than inertia in the confident knowledge of a sure place in the larger universe is the starting-point for this form of operative thought. Thus the actor, in the very mode of performing operative subjectivity – through the mutable, pragmatic, constructed depth of the fictional character which the audience pays to see – enacts the operative subjectivity embodied in characters such as Follywit. The commodity offered to the audience in this transitional period is at once a reflection of their own mode of inhabiting the social world, as well as a confrontation with something that is radically other than traditional schemes of conceptualizing the universe which were still current if no longer exclusively hegemonic.

Operative thought and interiority in the theatre

If there emerges at this period the forerunner of a modern interiorized subjectivity, a notion which can only be accepted with some qualifications as suggested above, such an interiority is first and foremost a function of operative subjectivity. However, the Jacobean drama also offers glimpses of the ways in which a fluid, strategic subjectivity may be articulated upon a fledgling interiorized subjectivity. An example of such an articulation can be found in *Othello*, where Shakespeare explores these distinct aspects of emerging configurations of subjectivity in a theatrical mode of representation by exploiting the spatial operative trope *par excellence*: that of military conflict.[50]

The play, with its opening scenes of naval warfare between Turkey and Cyprus, is deeply concerned by space and its control. The military commanders and civil governors who make up a large part of the cast are constantly preoccupied with visibility: 'What from the cape can you discern at sea?' asks Montano, and Cassio cries: 'But hark, a sail' (2.1.1, 96). However, open space can signify not only territorial mastery but also exposure and potential destruction, as has been pointed out with reference to landscape poetry.[51] This the Turkish fleet learns to its peril, caught without shelter in a storm on its way to attack Cyprus, the scene of Shakespeare's drama: 'If that the Turkish fleet | Be not ensheltered and embayed, they are drowned. | It is impossible to bear it out' (2.1.17–19) – whence the importance, once again, of secrecy and duplicity in dealing with others, on the battlefield as at court or in the market-place.

These operative spaces of visibility and vulnerability govern the terms in which subjectivity is formulated within Shakespeare's play. Othello's openness is that of the seafarer or soldier, used to living in wide-open spaces:

> I would not my unhousèd free condition
> Put into circumscription and confine
> For the seas' worth …
>   I must be found.
> My parts, my title, and my perfect soul
> Shall manifest me rightly.

>   (1.2.26–32)

Othello's assumption is that visibility is a virtue in itself, that visibility will convey the subject's inherent nobility. But his confidence in the unassailable strength of his public standing, it would appear, is his greatest personal weakness, for it mistakenly assumes that the spaces of visibility are equally unambiguous for all the actors in the political arena. On the contrary, these spaces are heterogeneous and discontinuous, in no way the 'always similar and immovable' expanses of later Newtonian absolute space; rather, they are traversed by boundaries where the nature of space and the ways in which it is used alter radically: 'the *limits* where various spaces meet and clash are of crucial importance.'[52] Thus Iago notes that

The Moor is of a free and open nature
That thinks men honest that but seem to be so,
And will as tenderly be led by th' nose
As asses are.

(1.3.391–4)

Just as the openness of the sea rapidly becomes the downfall of the Turkish attackers, so the exposure of Othello's public persona can equally be harnessed to undermine the stability of the Moor's power.

Openness is outmanoeuvred by Iago's closeness, which is a function of tactical duplicity. Duplicity was a cardinal virtue espoused in the emerging discourse of operative mercantile subjectivity. Such recommendations are exemplified in the advice given by the Bristol merchant John Browne to his agent in Lisbon, to 'deale closelie and secretlie in all your affaires & busines. ... Also be earnest in noting and marking euery thing that you may, but bee your selfe as secret and silent as is possible.'[53] In contrast, the uncomplicated openness of the Moor and his accustomed terrain of movement is not conducive to guile. It is Othello's lack of critical faculties, his unawareness of other possibilities of spatial operation which leads to his downfall. The merchant William Scott warned against such naiveté: 'It is necessary, my Citizen defend himselfe, by this buckler, distrust, which is a great part of prudence; it is even the very sinew of wisdome ... a man must trust few, and those known by long experience, and distrust must be disguised; ... a professed trust then doth well with a concealed diffidence.'[54] For Iago, who perfectly embodies such principles, visibility in no way implies good faith; the open sea can equally well be governed by the tactical scheming of sea warfare: 'Yet for necessity of present life, | I must show out a flag and sign of love | Which is indeed but sign' (1.1.157–9). It is significant that Iago uses the imagery of signalling at sea to describe his own strategy, thus displaying to what extent an apparently homogenous arena of struggle, that of naval warfare, can conceal heterogeneous modes of vision, and thereby, heterogeneous modes of subjective agency.

Even a writer of as limpid morality as Scott thought in these terms, echoing Bacon's discourse on dealing with business partners in his espousal of a 'superficiall knowledge' combined with the ability to 'penetrate into the inside, and see things in themselves':

joyning both these together, it will be easy for him to profit, if according to the divers natures of the persons and affaires, he change

his stile, and manner of proceeding; as a wise Sea-man, who according to the divers state of the Sea, and change of winds, doth diversly
turne his sayles and rudder; knowing every mans nature and fash-
ions, hee may lead him; knowing his ends, he may perswade him;
knowing his weaknesse or disadvantage, he may awe him.[55]

Elsewhere, Iago justifies such duplicity in his meditations upon the
naiveté of unconsidered openness:

> For when my outward action doth demonstrate
> The native act and figure of my heart
> In compliment extern, 'tis not long after
> But I will wear my heart upon my sleeve
> For daws to peck at. I am not what I am.
>
> (1.1.61–5)

A clear continuity between inward subjectivity and outward manifestation, of which Othello is so proud, is transformed here into the scheming cynicism of tactical falsity. In a move not dissimilar to Hamlet's
creation of a mysterious persona as a means of defence within the
treacherous labyrinth of court politics at Elsinore, Iago also conceals his
true intentions.

But in *Othello*, there is more at work than simply the dialectic of openness and closure dictated by the heterogeneous fields of military conflict
and political intrigue. There is also the emergence of an interiorized subjectivity which appears to be driven by the complex machinations of
power. In one of the most lapidary couplets of the play, Iago announces:
'Were I the Moor, I would not be Iago. | In following him I follow but
myself' (1.1.57–8). Here he posits something which appears to be the
complement of the dissimulation of court intrigue, of the false signs
emitted by an ostensibly loyal underling, the 'flag and sign of love':
overtly following one's superior in actual fact serves one's own political
goals. Yet the spatial language has undergone a decisive shift. The language of false flags, and duplicity of 'outward action', 'native act and
figure of my heart' and 'compliment extern' all function within the par-
adigm of visibility and invisibility. These figures do not in any essential
way affect the social fabric of expansive public spaces in which social
actors pursue their aims with more or less transparency or honesty or
duplicity.

What emerges in Iago's statement is the splintering of a shared social
space (quite apart from questions of the unevenness of that space or of

folds within that field of visibility) in which self and other are explicitly posed against each other. In other words, whereas hanging out a false flag did not significantly alter the collective space of naval warfare, now the very possibility of following (or implicitly opposing) an other social actor is predicated upon the irreducible uniqueness of selfhood. Whereas the common ground previously offered the possibilities of political opposition, it is now the fabric of subjective opposition which appears to drive social activity (following, whether directed to self or other). It is evidence of the splitting of the social body, not by the mere force of political strife, but to form the individual by the hollowing out of the collective public sphere into an infinite number of implacably opposed private domains.

These two modes of experiencing the self are not always clearly to be distinguished from one another; the transitional moment in which emergent and residual modes of subjectivity are simultaneously expressed dictates Iago's formulations of his animosity:

> I hate the Moor,
> And it is thought abroad that 'twixt my sheets
> He has done my office. I know not if't be true,
> But I, for mere suspicion in that kind,
> Will do as if for surety. …
>   Let me see now,
> To get his place, and plume up my will
> In double knavery—

> (1.3.378–86)

Iago's intention 'to get his place' refers primarily to the reinstatement of the discredited Michael Cassio which is to be achieved with the help of Desdemona ('Importune her help to put you in your place again' prompts Iago – 2.3.311–12). Her assistance will subsequently be manipulated to arouse Othello's self-consuming jealousy. But 'in his place' also refers to Iago's strong sense of having been supplanted, 'replaced' as aspirant for Desdemona's love, by Othello. The intimacy of ''twixt my sheets' is clearly qualified by 'done my office', which transforms the privacy of sexual desire into some sort of public function – which sexuality, within the context of dynastic unions, of course to a large degree was. The bedchamber was not necessarily a particularly intimate place until, precisely, the period we are looking at in these dramas. The public character of this feud is corroborated by the fact that Iago shows no interest in verifying the truth of the rumour of Othello's act of usurpation. The fact of it being whispered in public appears to be sufficient grounds for his action. And yet what is also at play in this statement, particularly in so far as *''twixt my sheets* | He has done *my* office', is the confusion of selfhood and alterity, the intrusion of an other into the space of a self expressed as a complex stratification of elements differentiated from others.

This emergence of a self constituted in opposition to others rather than sharing the same space as them, is thus characterized by the fragility and contingence inherent in transitional processes of differentiation. This element of contingence perhaps goes some way to explaining the extraordinary animosity which motivates Iago's actions, until now habitually accounted for by recourse to notions of pure and unadulterated evil. Out of this bedevilled competitiveness between subjects whose identity rests upon only half-formed sentiments of individualism as opposition, arises the hatred driving Iago's actions. He confides that

> I do suspect the lusty Moor
> Hath leapt into my seat, the thought whereof
> Doth, like a poisonous mineral, gnaw my inwards;
> And nothing can or shall content my soul
> Till I am evened with him, wife for wife—
>
> (2.1.294–8)

Less than the apparently harmless occupation of 'my seat', it is the inward experience of the jealous lover which is emphasized. One almost has the impression that no inward space existed in Iago before it was scalloped out by the corrosive acids of jealousy. The denial of the self's uniqueness carves out a new space which is a peculiar private hell.

Significantly, Iago employs exactly the same mechanism to bring about the downfall of this intruder into his field of desire. Iago never states directly his implied suspicions of Desdemona's faithfulness, but awakes Othello's mistrust all the more effectively by his pretence of reluctance to express his fears. By appearing to withhold information, he creates a concealed space within himself. Othello raves: 'By heaven, thou echo'st me | As if there were some monster in thy thought | Too hideous to be shown! ... By heaven, I'll know thy thoughts' (3.3.110–12, 166). Iago defends himself by claiming his right to silence: 'I am not bound to that all slaves are free to. | Utter my thoughts? Why, say they are vile and false, | And where's that palace whereinto foul things | Sometimes intrude not' (3.3.140–3). Othello's accusation of echoing is accurate, but unbeknown to him, inverted. For it is Iago's strategy which will cause *Othello* to echo his ensign's jealousy, the subordinate's jealous words being repeated in a corroded inner space of the captain. Iago's closedness, suggesting depths which cannot be immediately sounded, produces in Othello a mirrored space of fertile apprehensions. The oft-cited opacity of Iago's motives generates a *subjected* interior subjectivity in his enemy, a subjectivity which is the *object* of Iago's operative subjectivity.

In this way, Shakespeare articulates two powerfully spatial modes of subjectivity at work in the Jacobean drama: on the one hand, the pragmatic empirical local knowledge of operative thought – and on the other, the monadic, hollowed-out subjectivity of the new selfhood increasingly distanced from its environment and involved in inner dialogue, a subjectivity we associate with Enlightenment individuality. Shakespeare's capacity to link these two modes of subjectivity to each other is a remarkable dramatic example of a 'dialectic image' of the sort evoked by Benjamin, not a 'frozen dialectic' but rather, one performed dynamically on the stage, showing distinct but connected facets of a history of spatialized subjectivity in emergence.[56]

Coda: Drama and the Appropriation of Social Space

The emergence of a localized mode of thought and of a form of subjectivity predicated upon operative, pragmatic action is the culmination of the diverse aspects of changing spatial experience considered in the preceding chapters: money as a catalyst for spatial transformation, social and demographic mobility, and overseas travel. In all these areas, it was the novel forces of economic change which progressively corroded the links of a previous traditional mode of organic social existence, triggering a new dynamism and space for movement. The stage constantly embodied and dramatized this new and disturbing fluidity while claiming to defend the old order of stability and organic place.

Typical of this paradoxical embodiment of fluidity and stability at the same time was Thomas Harman, the author of *A Caveat for Common Cursetors*, who gathered information about the vagrants roaming the English countryside during the Elizabethan period, ostensibly in the interests of social control and community security, but as Elizabeth Hanson suggests, no less in order to establish himself as a successful writer, in the sense Foucault gave to the 'author function' as an attribute of the work rather than its triumphant origin.[1] Harman's emergence as an identifiable persona rested upon the appropriation of the vagrants' voices, vagrants whose dispossession in the wake of changing relations of land-ownership forced them to appropriate ('illegally') the identities and property of respectable folk. Harman proudly touted his text as 'my bold beggars book', which captured, classified and commodified 'their lives, their language, their names as they be'.[2] Though a gentleman and heir to a local manor, and the guardian of traditional forms of 'neighbourliness' and communal cohesion which are repeatedly staged as the framing conditions of his accounts of vagrancy, Harman's authorial status was based upon the expropriation of the identities of the vagrant poor. His text blended the voices of the mobile poor with the voice of patriarchal and patrician authority, appropriating the identities of the expropriated in defence of private property. The immense circulation of his text on the nascent print market both emulated the mobility of the masterless men *and* simultaneously profited from the new forces of money economy whose effects the author was otherwise so eager to combat.[3]

Harman thus embodies the flagrant collision of two diametrically opposed impulses: on the one hand, the defence of traditional spaces of stable rural community governed by horizontal relationships of neighbourliness and vertical relationships of respect for one's betters and paternalist responsibility for the lower sort; on the other hand, a movement of appropriation of previously collective property which establishes an individualist identity emerging from new market forces. Conflicting social forms with their respective social spaces, conflicting modes of subjectivity, and conflicting modes of economic organization coalesced in the person of Thomas Harman, author. The entanglement of old and new, of stability and fluidity was exemplary for the period in question. The drama played a particularly important role in the articulation of such entanglements of tradition and transformation in that it arose out of their conflict and constantly enacted that conflict on the stage. The early seventeenth century possessed a social theory ill-equipped to deal with social mobility, and equally unfitted to take account of epistemological and subjective mobility.[4] Moreover, social theory tends to lag behind everyday uses of new epistemic notions, which have generally 'long been used by people in highly contingent and untheorized ways to negotiate myriad local crises and opportunities in economic, social and institutional life' before they attain sufficient currency to be taken up by philosophical discourse.[5] The theatre can thus be understood as offering a tangible, performed theory of the new subjective moment lived by the audience well before any comparable social analysis was available. As a 'concrete science', 'concrete philosophy' or 'material thought' (Lévi-Strauss, Deleuze, Jameson), the theatre offered a mode of understanding and articulating the transformations of subjective experience, without for all that extracting itself from that experience. It embodied the new mode of fluid subjectivity, and indeed profited from it, while offering the audience moments of lucid distance towards their own condition.

The theatre offered its audiences a partially explicative articulation of the bewildering phenomena of experienced space in an age in the throes of turbulent processes of transformation. Yet it did far more than merely reflect and thus explain the fluidity and mobility which marked Jacobean society. The theatre's principal mode of articulation of the tensions of the time was the one gestured at by Harman's *Caveat*: appropriation. Lefebvre's tripartite model of spatial production offers a useful way of understanding some of the resonances of 'appropriation' on the Jacobean stage. The first level described by Lefebvre's triadic model is that of spatial practices, the everyday material transactions and processes across space which guarantee the material production and reproduction of social relations. The second level is that of representations of space, representations which are usually controlled by the dominant class in a given society, and which regulate practices of space. The third category is that of spaces of representation, which Lefebvre defines as space as it is lived via symbols and images – and as it is reconfigured and rearticulated by space-users, as opposed to the controllers of space. Here we see the imagination trying to seize and modify dominated space. Lefebvre further describes these three forms of space as experienced, perceived and imagined, with these three modalities being linked by constant dialectical interaction.[6]

Social space was the object of strategies of control on the part of ruling groups, and equally the object of strategies of contestation on the part of users demanding new organizations of space and proposing new spatial representations in order to bring about spatial change. The early modern age in England saw increasing claims for the ownership of social space on the part of the smaller gentry and middling sort against the interests of the crown and the nobility. The stage constantly enacted and dramatized the appropriation of spaces of authority, through the use of cast-off aristocratic costume, through its usurpation of City or Guild pageantry, through its imitation of monarchy and its spectacles. This was a mode of appropriation which belongs to the spaces of representation (user contestation). Yet it also dramatized the interests of acquisitive individualism, the reassertion of order and stability, thus revealing itself to be complicit with the very representations of space (instances of domination and control) which it so often undermined and cast into question. However, the order enacted and enforced upon the stage did not necessarily serve the interests of the same group of power-holders as the order desired by the state, although these goals may have coincided on occasions. Rather, the theatre's operations frequently straddled the apparently opposed processes of controlling or regulating representations of space and appropriated spaces of representation, expropriating precisely in order to create a new order in the interests of a newly emergent group of political actors. Thus both processes may have overlapped in the theatre's own appropriation and reworking of social and political spatial representation, enacting the subversion of state spectacle in order to assert the rights of an acquisitive individualism which in turn aspired to a dominant position in defence of its newly acquired property, thereby anticipating the bourgeois revolution ratified by the Restoration.

Chapter 3 of this study moved beyond the reified universe of the court drama to examine the dramatization of space upon the stage under the influence of the novel money economy. Chapter 3's interrogation of the importance of money, both for the emergence of the theatre and for its thematics and functioning, is intimately linked to the last chapter, devoted to the spatial contours of a new early modern subjectivity acted out upon the Jacobean stage. The spaces colonized by new mercantile actors and the subjective spaces which characterized their novel sensibility are both reflected in the spatial operations of the Jacobean stage. Thus the broad span of the spatial themes treated in the second part of this study is linked by the ubiquitous activity of seizure of new social space through the agency of social actors rising to new prominence, and the counterforce of movements resisting the remodelling of social space. 'Here is my space' says Antony, in a passage cited in the opening lines of this book, by which he asserts not only his marginal place on the outskirts of the Roman empire as his new abode, but also foregrounds the theatre as the privileged site of a new form of subjectivity based upon the appropriation of urban space, aristocratic costume, prior literary discourse, and the surplus income of the theatre-going audience. The polysemic mode of reference (fictional place and real site of performance) embodied in Antony's '*Here* is my space' thus announces and is borne along by the ambivalent form of appropriation (both resistance to authority and egotistical, acquisitive occupation of space) dramatized in 'Here is *my* space.' In the new theatre, a new subject takes its place on the stage, and in so doing, seizes a place in an evolving society.

Notes

Introduction: Staging Space

1 The classic definition of deixis is to be found in Emile Benveniste, 'L'Appareil formel de l'énonciation', *Problèmes de linguistique générale 2* (Paris: Gallimard/Tel, 1980), 79–88.

2 See Edward W. Said, *The World, the Text and the Critic* (London: Faber, 1984).

3 A. J. Greimas, 'Pour une sémiotique topologique', in *Sémiotique de l'espace: Architecture, urbanisme, sortir de l'impasse*, eds Manar Hammad, Eric Proovost, Michel Vernin (Paris: Denoël/Gonthier, 1979), 11.

4 The two classics are Gaston Bachelard, *La Poétique de l'espace* (Paris: PUF/Quadrige, 1994), and Henri Lefebvre, *La Production de l'espace* (Paris: Editions Anthropos, 1974). Apart from Foucault's better-known book-length studies, the following shorter articles and interviews are of interest: 'Des espaces autres', *Dits et écrits 1954–1988*, eds Daniel Defert and François Ewald (Paris: Gallimard, 1994), IV: 752–62; 'Espaces, savoir et pouvoir', *Dits et écrits 1954–1988*, IV: 270–85; 'L'oeil du pouvoir', *Dits et écrits 1954–1988*, III: 190–207; 'Questions à Michel Foucault sur la géographie', *Dits et écrits 1954–1988*, III: 28–40.

5 Lefebvre, *La Production de l'espace*, 58.

6 Foucault, 'Questions à Michel Foucault sur la géographie', 34, and 'Des espaces autres', 752–3.

7 To name only a few representative titles in an extensive field, see, on socio-logical approaches to space, Derek Gregory and John Urry (eds.), *Social Relations and Spatial Structures* (London: Macmillan, 1985); on psychological approaches to space, Kathleen M. Kirby, *Indifferent Boundaries: Spatial Concepts of Human Subjectivity* (New York: Guildford Press, 1995); on spatiality in cul-tural history and cultural theory, Erica Carter, James Donald and Judith Squires (eds), *Space and Place: Theories of Identity and Location* (London: Lawrence and Wishart, 1993); on gender and space, Gillian Rose, *Feminism and Geography: The Limits of Geographical Knowledge* (Oxford: Polity Press, 1993); on the semiotics of space, Ernst W. B. Hess-Lüttich, et al. (eds), *Signs and Space, Zeichen und Raum: An International Conference on the Semiotics of Space and Culture in Amsterdam* (Tübingen: Gunter Narr, 1997); on the contribution

of postmodern thought to theorization of space, Edward W. Soja, *Postmodern Geographies* (London: Verso, 1989).

8   See for instance Lefebvre, *La Production de l'espace*, 10ff; Neil Smith and Cindi Katz, 'Grounding Metaphor: Towards a Spatialized Politics', in *Place and the Politics of Identity*, eds Michael Keith and Steve Pile (London: Routledge, 1993), 67–83.

9   See Una Chandhuri, *Staging Places: The Geography of Modern Drama* (Ann Arbor: University of Michigan Press, 1995); James Redmond (ed.), *The Theatrical Space* (Cambridge: Cambridge University Press, 1987); Hanna Scolnicov, *Women's Theatrical Space* (Cambridge: Cambridge University Press, 1994).

The most substantial contribution to the exploration of theatrical space has been made by theatre semiotics: Jean Alter, *A Socio-Semiotic Theory of Theatre* (Philadelphia: University of Pennsylvania Press, 1990); Elaine Aston and George Savona, *Theatre as Sign System: A Semiotics of Text and Performance* (London: Routledge, 1991); Marvin Carlson, *Theatre Semiotics: Signs of Life* (Bloomington: Indiana University Press, 1990); Keir Elam, *The Semiotics of Theatre and Drama* (London: Methuen, 1980); Erika Fischer-Lichte, *The Semiotics of Theater*, trans. Jeremy Gaines and Doris. L. Jones (Bloomington: Indiana University Press, 1992).

Important work has also been done on the sociology of theatrical space: Denis Bablet and Jean Jacquot (eds), *Le Lieu théâtral dans la société moderne* (Paris: Editions du CNRS, 1969); Marvin Carlson, *Places of Performance: The Semiotics of Theatre Architecture* (Ithaca: Cornell University Press, 1989).

Technical aspects of theatrical space have been explored principally by theatre practitioners: Peter Brook, *The Empty Space* (Harmondsworth: Pelican, 1972); William Faricy Condee, *Theatrical Space: A Guide for Directors and Designers* (Lanham, Md.: Scarecrow Press, 1995); Ronnie Mulryne and Margaret Shewring (eds.), *Making Space for Theatre: British Architecture and Theatre since 1958* (Stratford-upon-Avon: Mulryne and Shewring, 1995).

10   Alter, *A Socio-Semiotic Theory of Theatre*, 95–132.

11   Aston and Savona, *Theatre as Sign-System*, 101.

12   Elam, *The Semiotics of Theatre and Drama*, 18–19.

13   Elam, *The Semiotics of Theatre and Drama*, 16, 29, 26.

14   On space in literature see Trevor Barnes and James S. Duncan (eds), *Writing Worlds: Discourse, Text and Metaphor in the Representation of Landscape* (London: Routledge, 1992); Joseph Frank, 'Spatial Form in Modern Literature', in *The Widening Gyre* (Bloomington, Ind.: Indiana University Press, 1968), 3–62; Joachim Frenk (ed.), *Spatial Change in English Literature* (Trier: WWT, 1999); Gérard Genette, 'Espace et langage', *Figures I* (Paris: Seuil, 1966), 101–8; 'La littérature et l'espace', in *Figures II: Essais* (Paris: Seuil, 1969), 43–8; Leonard Lutwack, *The Role of Place in Literature* (Syracuse, NY: Syracuse University Press, 1984); Louis Marin, *Utopiques: Jeux d'espace* (Paris: Minuit, 1973); Cary Nelson, *The Incarnate Word: Literature as Verbal Space* (Urbana: University of Illinois Press, 1973); Jeffrey M. Smitten and Ann Daghistany (eds), *Spatial Form in Narrative* (Ithaca, NY: Cornell University Press, 1981); Sharon Spencer, *Space, Time and Structure in the Modern Novel* (New York: New York University Press, 1971).

For recent studies on Renaissance literature including a consideration of space see Richard Helgerson, *Forms of Nationhood: The Elizabethan Writing of*

England (Chicago: University of Chicago Press, 1992); James Turner, *The Politics of Landscape: Rural Scenery and Society in English Poetry 1630–1660* (Oxford: Blackwell, 1979); Don E. Wayne, *Penshurst: The Semiotics of Place and the Poetics of History* (London: Methuen, 1984).

15 See J. H. Andrews, 'Geography and Government in Elizabethan Ireland', in *Irish Geographical Studies in Honour of E. Estyn Evans*, eds N. Stephens and R. E. Glassock (Belfast: Department of Geography, Queen's University of Belfast, 1970), 178–91; Jerry Brotton, 'Mapping the Early Modern Nation: Cartography Along the English Margins', *Paragraph* 19:2 (July 1996), 139–55; Richard Helgerson, 'The Land Speaks: Cartography, Choreography and Subversion in Renaissance England', in *Representing the English Renaissance*, ed. Stephen Greenblatt (Berkeley: University of California Press, 1988), 327–61; Bernhard Klein, *Maps and the Writing of Space in Early Modern England* (London: Palgrave, 2000).

16 On time and space in literature see Mikhail Bakhtin, 'Forms of Time and of the Chronotope in the Novel', *The Dialogic Imagination: Four Essays*, ed. Michael Holquist, trans. Caryl Emerson and Michael Holquist (Austin: University of Texas Press, 1981). Hubert Wurmbach stresses the necessity of combining temporal and spatial analysis in the study of drama: *Christopher Marlowes Tamburlaine Dramen: Struktur, Rezeptionslenkung und historische Bedeutung: Ein Beitrag zur Dramenanalyse* (Heidelberg: Carl Winter Universitätsverlag, 1984), 51–2.

17 Steven Mullaney, *The Place of the Stage: License, Play and Power in Renaissance England* (Chicago: University of Chicago Press, 1988); Garrett A. Sullivan, *The Drama of Landscape: Land, Property and Social Relations on the Early Modern Stage* (Stanford: Stanford University Press, 1998).

18 See Alan C. Dessen, *Elizabethan Stage Conventions and Modern Interpreters* (Cambridge: Cambridge University Press, 1984), 19; Anne Ubersfeld, *Lire le théâtre* (Paris: Editions sociales, 1978), 153; John Styan, *The English Stage: A History of Drama and Performance* (Cambridge: Cambridge University Press/Canto, 1996), 138–9; Elam, *The Semiotics of Drama and Theatre*, 73.

19 Alan C. Dessen, *Elizabethan Drama and the Viewer's Eye* (Chapel Hill: University of North Carolina Press, 1977), 30–1.

Chapter 1: Stage-space in the Jacobean Age

1 See Frances A. Yates, *The Art of Memory* (London: Routledge and Kegan Paul, 1966).

2 John Willis, *The Art of Memory* (London, 1621), 1, 2, 8, 11.

3 Herbert Grierson (ed.), *The Poems of John Donne* (London: Oxford University Press, 1964), 295.

4 See Debora Kuller Shuger, *Habits of Thought in the English Renaissance: Religion, Politics and the Dominant Culture* (Berkeley: University of California Press, 1990), 258; Frances A. Yates, *Theatre of the World* (London: Routledge and Kegan Paul, 1969), 142.

5 See for example Elisabeth Bronfen, *Der literarische Raum: Eine Untersuchung am Beispiel von Dorothy M. Richardson's Romanzyklus Pilgrimage* (Tübingen: Niemeyer, 1986), 169.

6   Richard Mulcaster, *The First Part of the Elementary* (London, 1582), GiR; John Sanford, *An Entrance to the Spanish Tongue* (London, 1611).

7   John Hale, *The Civilization of Europe in the Renaissance* (London: Harper Collins, 1993), 34.

8   Albrecht Meier, *Certaine Briefe, and Speciall Instructions for Gentlemen, Merchants, Students, Souldiers, mariners, &c. Employed in Seruices Abrode*, trans. Philip Jones (London, 1589), B1r; Sir Thomas Palmer, *An Essay of the meanes how to make our Trauailes, into forraine Countries, the more profitable and honourable* (London, 1606), 1A–1B; Gerard Malynes, *The Center of the Circle of Commerce* (London, 1623), 8; John Barlow, *The Good Mans Refuge in affliction* (London, 1618), B1r–B1v.

9   Hugo Keiper, *Studien zur Raumdarstellung in den Dramen Christopher Marlowes: Daramaturgie und dargestellte Wirklichkeit* (Essen: Das Blaue Eule, 1988), 61, 62n.

10 Henry Peacham, *The Garden of Eloquence* (London, 1577), BiR; Abraham Fraunce, *The Arcadian of Rhetoric* (London, 1588).

11 George Steiner, *Language and Silence: Essays 1958–1966* (Harmondsworth: Pelican, 1969), 31.

12 From *CERTAYNE Sermons, or homilies, appoynted by the kynges Maiestie, to be declared and redde, nby all persones, Vicares, or Curates, euery Sondaye in their churches, where thei haue cure* (1547; reprinted under James I in 1623), KI–KIV. Quoted in John C. Meagher, *Method and Meaning in Jonson's Masques* (Notre Dame: University of Notre Dame Press, 1966), 164–5.

13 Peter Clark and Paul Slack, *English Towns in Transition 1500–1700* (London: Oxford University Press, 1976), 58.

14 Keith Wrightson, *English Society 1580–1680* (London: Routledge, 1993), 39; Jeremy Boulton, *Neighbourhood and Society: A London Suburb in the Seventeenth Century* (Cambridge: Cambridge University Press, 1987), 146–7.

15 James Turner, *The Politics of Landscape: Rural Scenery and Society in English Poetry 1630–1660* (Oxford: Blackwell, 1979), 5–6.

16 Lawrence Stone, *The Crisis of the Aristocracy 1558–1641* (Oxford: Clarendon Press, 1965), 28–9; Jeremy Boulton, *Neighbourhood and Society: A London Suburb in the Seventeenth Century* (Cambridge: Cambridge University Press, 1987), 147.

17 See Valerie Traub, *Desire and Anxiety: Circulations of Sexuality in Shakespearean Drama* (London: Routledge, 1992), 3; Linda Levy Peck, 'The Mental World of the Jacobean Court: An Introduction', in *The Mental World of the Jacobean Court*, ed. L. Peck (Cambridge: Cambridge University Press, 1991), 11; Norbert Elias, *Die höfische Gesellschaft: Untersuchungen zur Soziologie des Königtums und der höfischen Aristokratie* (Frankfurt/Main: Surhrkamp, 1983), ch. 3; Emannuel Le Roy Ladurie, *Montaillou, village occitan de 1294 à 1324* (Paris: Gallimard, 1975), ch. 2.

18 Robin Evans, 'Figures, Doors and Passages', *Architectural Design*, 4 (April 1978), 267.

19 Lawrence Stone, *The Family Sex and Marriage in England 1500–1800* (Harmondsworth: Penguin/Pelican, 1979), 69, 89.

20 See Keith Wrightson, *English Society 1580–1680* (London: Routledge, 1993), 45; J. A. Sharpe, *Early Modern England: A Social History 1550–1760*, 2nd ed. (London: Arnold, 1997), 40, 59, 60, 94–5.

21 James I, *Basilikon Doron* (Edinburgh: Robert Waldegrave, 1599) (facsimile) (Menston: The Scholar Press, 1969), 9; Margot Heinemann, *Puritanism and Theatre: Thomas Middleton and Opposition Drama under the Early Stuarts* (Cambridge: Cambridge University Press, 1980), 153; John Stow, *A Suruey of London* (London, 1603), 559.

22 A. J. Greimas, 'Pour une sémiotique topologique', in *Sémiotique de l'espace: Architecture, urbanisme, sortir de l'impasse*, eds Manar Hammad, Eric Proovost, Michel Vernin (Paris: Denoël/Gonthier, 1979), 15.

23 Herbert Grierson (ed.), *The Poems of John Donne* (London: Oxford University Press, 1964), 213–14; Keith Sturgess, *Jacobean Private Theatre* (London: Routledge and Kegan Paul, 1987), 5.

24 Michael Hattaway, *Elizabethan Popular Theatre: Plays in Performance* (London: Routledge and Kegan Paul, 1982), 97.

25 Keith Sturgess, *Jacobean Private Theatre* (London: Routledge and Kegan Paul, 1987), 13, 159.

26 Hattaway, *Elizabethan Popular Theatre*, 78, 88, 93.

27 Martin White, *Renaissance Drama in Action: An Introduction to Some Aspects of Theatre Practice and Performance* (London: Routledge, 1998), 24–6.

28 Alan C. Dessen, *Elizabethan Stage Convetions and Modern Interpreters* (Cambridge: Cambridge University Press, 1984), 96.

29 Douglas Bruster, *Drama and the Market in the Age of Shakespeare* (Cambridge: Cambridge University Press, 1992), 96.

30 Henri Fluchère, *Shakespeare, dramaturge élisabéthain* (Toulouse: Cahiers du Sud, 1948), 17 (my translation); for a critique of this attitude see André Helbo, *Les Mots et les gestes: Essai sur le théâtre* (Lille: Presses Universitaires de Lille, 1983), 14.

31 Sir William Davenant, *Preface to Gondibert* (1650), quoted in *Elizabethan-Jacobean Drama*, ed. G. Blakemore Evans (London: A. & C. Black, 1989), 59

32 See White, *Renaissance Drama in Action*, 29, 133ff; John Styan, *The English Stage: A History of Drama and Performance* (Cambridge: Cambridge University Press/Canto, 1996), 141.

33 See David Bradby, *Modern French Drama 1940–1990*, 2nd ed. (Cambridge: Cambridge University Press, 1991), 91.

34 Cited in White, *Renaissance Drama in Action*, 34 (my emphasis).

35 Keir Elam, *The Semiotics of Theatre and Drama* (London: Methuen, 1980), 66.

36 C. Walter Hodges, *The Globe Restored: A Study of the Elizabethan Theatre* (London: Ernest Benn, 1953), 78–80.

37 Francis Barker, *The Tremulous Private Body: Essays on Subjection* (London: Methuen, 1984); 22–6; Foucault, *Surveiller et punir: Naissance de la prison* (Paris: Gallimard, 1975), ch. 1; J. A. Sharpe, *Early Modern England: A Social History 1550–1760*, 2nd ed. (London: Arnold, 1997), 114–15.

38 See Mullaney, *The Place of the Stage* (Chicago: University of Chicago Press, 1988), 105ff.

39 Sturgess, *Jacobean Private Theatre*, 50.

40 Hattaway, *Elizabethan Popular Theatre*, 56–7, 40–1.

41 See Michael Issacharoff, 'Space and Reference in Drama', *Poetics Today* 2:3 (Spring 1981), 216.

42 Dessen, *Elizabethan Stage Conventions*, 77; Hattaway, *Elizabethan Popular Theatre*, 57; Elam, *The Semiotics of Theatre and Drama*, 29.

43 Peter Brook, *The Empty Space* (Harmondsworth: Penguin, 1972), 11.
44 Dessen, *Elizabethan Stage Conventions*, 96.
45 Dessen, *Elizabethan Stage Conventions*, 86, 88; Keiper, *Studien zur Raumdarstellung in den Dramen Christopher Marlowes*, 47–8.
46 Andreas Höfele, *Die szenische Dramaturgie Shakespeares. Dargestellt an Titus Andronicus, Romeo and Juliet und Macbeth* (Heidelberg: Quelle und Meyer, 1977), 145; Styan, *The English Stage*, 148.
47 Hayden White, *Tropics of Discourse: Essays in Cultural Criticism* (Baltimore: Johns Hopkins University Press, 1978), 128.
48 Jean Wilson, *The Shakespeare Legacy: The Material Legacy of Shakespeare's Theatre* (Godalming: Bramley, 1995), 46–7.
49 Antonin Artaud, *Le Théâtre et son double* (Paris: Gallimard/Idées, 1972), 52.
50 Fredric Jameson, *Postmodernism, or, The Cultural Logic of Late Capitalism* (London/New York: Verso, 1992), 128, 125, 129.
51 See Höfele, *Die szenische Dramaturgie Shakespeares*, 33–5; Keiper, *Studien zur Raumdarstellung in den Dramen Christopher Marlowes*, 61.
52 Sigmund Freud, *Die Traumdeutung* (Frankfurt/Main: Fischer, 1991), 318ff.
53 Claude Lévi-Strauss, *La Pensée sauvage* (Paris: Plon/Pocket, 1990), 11–49. English trans: *The Savage Mind* (Chicago: University of Chicago Press, 1968).
54 Elam, *The Semiotics of Theatre and Drama*, 88.
55 Jurij Lotman, *The Structure of the Artistic Text*, trans. Gail Lenhoff and Ronald Vroon (Ann Arbor: University of Michigan/Department of Slavic Languages and Literatures, 1977), 209–10.
56 Manfred Pfister, *Das Drama: Theorie und Analyse*, 8th ed. (München: Wilhelm Fink/UTB, 1994), 328.
57 See for instance Friedrich Nietzsche, *Die Geburt der Tragödie,* in *Werke in drei Bänden*, ed. Rolf Toman (Köln: Könemann, 1994), I: 54; Jean Alter, *A Socio-Semiotic Theory of Theatre* (Philadelphia: University of Pennsylvania Press, 1990), 10–11; Darko Suvin, 'Approach to Topoanalysis and to the Paradigmatics of Dramaturgical Space', *Poetics Today* 8:2 (1987), 324.
58 Cited in Styan, *The English Stage*, 98.
59 See Jean Wilson, *The Shakespeare Legacy*, 20–1.
60 See Michel Foucault, *Les Mots et les choses* (Paris: Gallimard, 1966), ch. 1.
61 Thomas Heywood, *An Apology for Actors* (London, 1612), A7r.
62 See R. B. Graves, 'Shakespeare's Outdoor Stage Lighting', *Shakespeare Studies* 13 (1980), 248; White, *Renaissance Drama in Action*, 132.
63 White, *Renaissance Drama in Action*, 119.
64 White, *Renaissance Drama in Action*, 115.
65 Chambers, *The Elizabethan Stage* (Oxford: Clarendon Press, 1923), II: 536–7.
66 Chambers, *The Elizabethan Stage*, II: 536n2.
67 Thomas Dekker, *The Guls Horn-Booke* (1609), in *The Non-Dramatic Works of Thomas Dekker*, ed. Alexander D. Grosart (New York: Russell and Russell, 1963), II: 248–50.
68 Lotman, speaking of the eighteenth-century Russian theatre, *The Structure of the Artistic Text*, 209.
69 Chambers, *The Elizabethan Stage*, II: 535n3.
70 Francis Beaumont and John Fletcher, *The Knight of the Burning Pestle, in The Works of Beaumont and Fletcher*, ed. Alexander Dyce (London: Edward Moxon, 1843), II: 133.

71   White, *Renaissance Drama in Action*, p. 174.

72   Edmund Gayton, *Pleasant Notes upon Don Quixot* (1654), quoted in *Elizabethan-Jacobean Drama*, ed. Evans, 34.

73   Robert Weimann, *Shakespeare and the Popular Tradition in the Theatre: Studies in the Social Dimension of Dramatic Form and Function*, trans. Robert Schwartz (Baltimore: Johns Hopkins University Press, 1978), 6ff, 208ff. A cogent critique of Weimann can be found in Brian Vickers, *Appropriating Shakespeare: Contemporary Critical Quarrels* (New Haven: Yale University Press, 1993), 386–93

74   Keiper, *Studien zur Raumdarstellung in den Dramen Christopher Marlowes*, 61n.

75   See Gottfried Krieger, 'Dramentheorie und Methoden der Dramenanalyse', in *Literaturwissenschaftliche Theorien, Modelle und Methoden*, eds Ansgar Nünning, Sabine Buchholz, Manfred Jahn (Trier: WWT, 1995), 82; Marvin Carlson, *Theatre Semiotics: Signs of Life* (Bloomington/Indianapolis: Indiana University Press, 1990), 75–91; Issacharoff, 'Space and Reference in Drama', 215; Anne Ubersfeld, *Lire le théâtre* (Paris: Editions sociales, 1978), 157, 153, 162, 164.

76   Jean Alter, *A Socio-Semiotic Theory of Theatre* (Philadelphia: University of Pennsylvania Press, 1990), 95–132.

77   See Rainer H. Schmid, *Raum, Zeit und Publikum des geistlichen Spiels: Aussage und Absicht eines mittelalterlichen Massenmediums* (München: tuduv, 1975), 50–1; Elie Konigson, *L'Espace théâtral médiéval* (Paris: Editions du CNRS, 1975), ch. 4.

78   See Sharon Tyler, 'Minding True Things: The Chorus, the Audience, and *Henry V'*, in *The Theatrical Space*, ed. James Redmond (Cambridge: Cambridge University Press, 1987), 69–79.

79   Elam, *The Semiotics of Theatre and Drama*, 11.

80   Anthony Brennan, *Onstage and Offstage Worlds in Shakespeare's Plays* (London: Routledge, 1989); Issacharoff, 'Space and Reference in Drama', 211–24; Dessen, *Elizabethan Stage Conventions*, 11–12, 36–7; Issacharoff, *Discourse as Performance* (Stanford: Stanford University Press, 1989).

81   Sir Philip Sidney, *Defence of Poesie*, in *The Complete Works of Sir Philip Sidney* (Cambridge: Cambridge University Press, 1923), III: 38.

82   Gottfried Krieger, 'Dramentheorie und Methoden der Dramenanalyse', 82.

83   Adorno appears to have something similar in mind when he writes that 'Art is the social antithesis of society' ('Kunst ist die gesellschaftliche Antithesis zur Gesellschaft'), in *Ästhetische Theorie* (Frankfurt/Main: Suhrkamp, 1990), 19. I am grateful to Tilman Höss for pointing out to me this aspect of Adorno's thought.

84   See the excellent article by Jonathon Haynes, 'The Elizabethan Audience on the Stage', in *The Theatrical Space*, ed. James Redmond, 60, 63–4.

85   See Lotman, *The Structure of the Artistic Text*, 211.

86   Alter, *A Socio-Semiotic Theory of Theatre*, 91.

87   George H. Cunningham, *London: Being a Comprehensive Survey of the History, Tradition and Historical Associations of Buildings and Monuments Arranged under Streets in Alphabetical Order* (London: Dent, 1927), 24, lists 'The Oliphant' and 'The Crane' at numbers 8–11 Bankside; John Stowe, *A Suruey of London* (London, 1603), 409, lists 'The Crane', but not 'The Elephant', as one of the Stewhouses on Bankside.

88 See Neil Carson, 'Some textual implications of Tyrone Guthrie's 1953 Production of *All's Well that Ends Well'*, *Shakespeare Quarterly* 25 (1974) 56; Thomas Pavel, *Univers de la fiction* (Paris: Seuil, 1988), 38–9.

89 Viktor Shklovsky, *Theory of Prose*, trans. Benjamin Sher (Elmwood Park, Ill.: Dalkey Archive Press, 1990), 94; Roland Barthes, 'En sortant du cinéma', *Communications* 23 (1975), 106–7.

90 Pfister, *Das Drama*, 327–9.

91 See Sturgess, *Jacobean Private Theatre*, 31–2, 52, 48.

92 See Elam, *The Semiotics of Theatre and Drama*, 64–5; see also Erika Fischer-Lichte, 'Spatial Signs', *The Semiotics of Theater*, trans. Jeremy Gaines and Doris. L. Jones (Bloomington: Indiana University Press, 1992), 100.

93 See Sturgess, *Jacobean Private Theatre*, 54; Elam, *The Semiotics of Theatre and Drama*, 67–8; William Faricy Condee, *Theatrical Space: A Guide for Directors and Designers* (Lanham, Md.: Scarecrow Press, 1995), chs 5 and 6, for modern confirmation of these experiences.

94 Henri Lefebvre, *La Production de l'espace* (Paris: Editions Anthropos, 1974), 191–3, 218.

95 Elam, *The Semiotics of Drama and Theatre*, 28–9.

96 Darko Suvin, 'Approach to Topoanalysis and to the Paradigmatics of Dramaturgical Space', 330–1.

97 Gregory Bateson, 'A Theory of Play and Fantasy', *Steps to an Ecology of Mind* (New York: Ballantine Books, 1974), 180, 182, 191–3.

98 Maurice Merleau-Ponty, *Phénoménologie de la perception* (Paris: Gallimard, 1945), 289, 325.

99 Valerie Pearl, *London and the Outbreak of the Puritan Revolution: City Government and National Politics, 1625–43* (Oxford: Oxford University Press, 1961), 15–16; Jeremy Boulton, *Neighbourhood and Society: A London Suburb in the Seventeenth Century* (Cambridge: Cambridge University Press, 1987), 152.

100 See Graham Holderness and Carol Banks, 'True Originall Copies', *European English Messenger*, 4:1 (1997), 23.

101 Douglas Bruster, *Drama and the Market in the Age of Shakespeare* (Cambridge: Cambridge University Press, 1992), 9–10.

102 Mullaney, *The Place of the Stage*, 31. See also Victor Turner, 'Liminal to Liminoid in Play, Flow and Ritual: An Essay in Comparative Symbology', *From Ritual to Theatre: The Seriousness of Human Play* (New York: PAJ Publications, 1982), 20–60.

103 Marvin Carlson, *Places of Performance: The Semiotics of Theatre Architecture* (Ithaca: Cornell University Press, 1989), 70.

104 Jerzy Limon, *Dangerous Matter: English Drama and Politics in 1623/24* (Cambridge: Cambridge University Press, 1986).

105 Chambers, *The Elizabethan Stage*, IV: 321.

106 Thomas Nash, *Pierce Peniless, His Supplication to the Divell* (London, 1592), 26v.

107 Philip Armstrong, 'Watching *Hamlet* Watching: Lacan, Shakespeare and the Mirror/Stage', in *Alternative Shakespeares Volume 2*, ed. Terence Hawkes (London: Routledge, 1996), 219.

108 Philip Stubbes, *The Anatomie of Abuses* (1584), in *Phillip Stubbes's Antanomy of the Abuses in England in Shakespere's Youth, A. D. 1583, Part I*, ed. Frederick J. Furnivall (1877) (Vaduz: Kraus Reprint Ltd, 1965), x. This 'Preface to the

Reader' is not included in all contemporary editions; see for instance the edition in STC Reel 1716.

109   Stephen Gosson, *Plays confuted in five actions* (1582), ed. Peter Davison (New York: Johnson Reprint Corporation, 1972), G4r.

110   Bacon, *Novum Organum* (1620), in *Elizabethan-Jacobean Drama*, ed. Evans, 322.

111   See Leeds Barroll, *Politics, Plague and Shakespeare's Theater: The Stuart Years* (Ithaca: Cornell University Press, 1991).

112   John Northbrooke, *A Treatise Against Dicing, Dancing, Play and Interludes. With Other Idle Pastimes* (1577) (London: Shakespeare Society, 1843), 97.

113   Both cited in Mullaney, *The Place of the Stage*, 34, 50.

114   Gervase Markham, *The English Arcadia* (London, 1607), 25v.

115   See Susan Melrose, *A Semiotics of the Dramatic Text* (London: Macmillan, 1994).

116   Christopher Hill, *A Nation of Change and Novelty: Radical Politics, Religion and Literature in Seventeenth-Century England* (London: Routledge, 1990), 106; Stephen Greenblatt, *Renaissance Self-Fashioning: From More to Shakespeare* (Chicago: University of Chicago Press, 1980), 162–8.

117   James I, *Basilikon Doron*, 121.

118   Thomas Heywood, *An Apology for Actors* (London, 1612), E3r.

119   Heywood, *An Apology for Actors*, G1v–G2v.

120   David Harris Willson, *King James VI & I* (London: Jonathon Cape, 1966), 124.

121   Lotman, *The Structure of the Artistic Text*, 350ff.

122   Elam, *The Semiotics of Theatre and Drama*, 121, 139, 143–4, 145.

123   Bruster, *Drama and the Market in the Age of Shakespeare*, 30.

Chapter 2: The Sun King: James I and the Court Masque

1   James I, *Basilikon Doron* (Edinburgh: Robert Waldegrave, 1599) (facsimile) (Menston: The Scholar Press, 1969), A3r.

2   See Jonathon Goldberg, *James I and the Politics of Literature: Jonson, Shakespeare, Donne and Their Contemporaries* (Baltimore and London: Johns Hopkins University Press, 1983), 62.

3   Cited in John C. Meagher, *Method and Meaning in Jonson's Masques* (Notre Dame: University of Notre Dame Press, 1966), 119, and Stephen Orgel and Roy Strong, *Inigo Jones: The Theatre of the Stuart Court* (London/Berkeley: Sotheby Parke Bernet/University of California Press, 1973), I: 206.

4   See David Harris Willson, *King James VI & I* (London: Jonathon Cape, 1966), 184; Pauline Croft, 'Robert Cecil and the Early Jacobean Court', in *The Mental World of the Jacobean Court*, ed. Linda Peck (Cambridge: Cambridge University Press, 1991), 137.

5   Linda Peck, 'The Mental World of the Jacobean Court: An Introduction', in *The Mental World of the Jacobean Court*, ed. Peck, 5.

6   See for instance John Savile, *King Iames his entertainment at Theobalds: With his welcome to London, together with a salutatorie Poeme* (London, 1603), C3v.

7   See David Morse, *England's Time of Crisis: From Shakespeare to Milton* (Basingstoke: Macmillan, 1989), 65ff.

8   Roy Strong, *Art and Power: Renaissance Festivals 1450–1650* (Woodbridge, Suffolk: The Boydell Press, 1984), 159–60.

9   See Anne Ubersfeld, *Lire le théâtre* (Paris: Editions sociales, 1978), 173–5, on paradigmatic and syntagmatic functioning of spatial images in the theatre.

10 Willson, *King James VI & I*, 162.

11 See Meagher's excellent chapter on 'Light' in his *Method and Meaning in Jonson's Masques*, 107–24.

12 See Jerzy Limon, 'The Masque of Stuart Culture', in *The Mental World of the Jacobean Court*, ed. Peck, 219, 334n30.

13 Stephen Orgel, *The Jonsonian Masque* (Cambridge, Mass.: Harvard University Press, 1965), 6–7; Orgel and Strong, *Inigo Jones: The Theatre of the Stuart Court*, I: 2; Strong, *Art and Power*, 155; David Lindley, 'Introduction', in Lindley (ed.), *The Court Masque* (Manchester: Manchester University Press, 1984), 1.

14 Orgel and Strong, *Inigo Jones: The Theatre of the Stuart Court*, I: 283.

15 Samuel Daniel, *Tethys' Festival* in *Court Masques: Jacobean and Caroline Entertainments 1605–1640*, ed. David Lindley (Oxford: Clarendon Press, 1995), 64.

16 John Orrel, *The Theatres of Inigo Jones and John Webb* (Cambridge: Cambridge University Press, 1985), 79; Orgel and Strong, *Inigo Jones: The Theatre of the Stuart Court*, I: 24.

17 Stephen Orgel, *The Illusion of Power: Political Theater in the English Renaissance* (Berkeley: University of California Press, 1975), 39, 117; John Peacock, *The Stage Designs of Inigo Jones: The European Context* (Cambridge: Cambridge University Press, 1995), 4.

18 Thomas Campion, *The Lord Hay's Masque* in *Court Masques*, ed. Lindley, 22.

19 See Limon, 'The Masque of Stuart Culture', 216.

20 See Emile Benveniste, 'L'Appareil formel de l'énonciation', *Problèmes de linguistique générale, 2* (Paris: Gallimard/Tel, 1980), 82.

21 Occasionally, as at the end of *Oberon*, the masquers did not totally relinquish their roles, but disappeared '*into the worke*', so that their transgression of the stage space of illusion was only temporary (356: 444).

22 See Orgel, *The Illusion of Power*, 50–2.

23 See Helen Cooper, 'Location and Meaning in Masque, Morality and Royal Entertainment', in *The Court Masque*, ed. Lindley, 144–5.

24 James I, *Basilikon Doron*, 'The Argument of the booke', A3r.

25 Orgel, *The Jonsonian Masque*, 138.

26 Orgel and Strong, *Inigo Jones: The Theatre of the Stuart Court*, I: 18.

27 Orrel, *The Theatres of Inigo Jones and John Webb*, 31–7.

28 Strong, *Art and Power*, 157.

29 Malcolm Smuts, 'Cultural Diversity and Cultural Change at the Court of James I', in *The Mental World of the Jacobean Court*, ed. Peck, 107.

30 See also Goldberg, *James I and the Politics of Literature*, 128

31 Sara Pearl, 'Sounding to Present Occasions: Jonson's Masques of 1620–5', in *The Court Masque*, ed. Lindley, 72.

32 David Lindley, 'Introduction', in *The Court Masque*, ed. Lindley, 5.

33 See Goldberg, *James I and the Politics of Literature*, 126–7.

34 See Pearl, 'Sounding to Present Occasions', 61–4.

35 See Lisa Jardine, *Worldly Goods: A New History of the Renaissance* (London: Macmillan, 1996).

Chapter 3: The Dumb God: Money as an Engine for Mobility

1 Lefebvre, *La Production de l'espace* (Paris: Editions Anthropos, 1974), 120.

2 Edward Misselden, *Free Trade, or, the Meanes to make Trade Flourish* (London, 1622), 25.

3 Pierre Dockès, *L'Espace dans la pensée économique du XVIe au XVIIIe siècle* (Paris: Flammarion, 1969), 10.

4 See Garrett A. Sullivan, *Staging Space: The Theatre and Social Relations in Early Modern England*, unpublished Ph.D. dissertation, Brown University, 1995, ch. 4; Christopher Hill, *Intellectual Origins of the English Revolution – Revisited* (Oxford: Clarendon Press, 1997), 211.

5 See Richard Hosley, 'The Playhouses and the Stage', in *A New Companion to Shakespeare Studies*, eds Kenneth Muir and S. Schoenbaum (Cambridge: Cambridge University Press, 1974), 15–16.

6 Richard Helgerson, *Forms of Nationhood: The Elizabethan Writing of England* (Chicago: University of Chicago Press, 1992), 13.

7 Lawrence Manley, *Literature and Culture in Early Modern London* (Cambridge: Cambridge University Press, 1995), 299–300.

8 F. J. Fisher, 'The Development of London as a Centre of Conspicuous Consumption in the Sixteenth and Seventeenth Centuries', *Transactions of the Royal Historical Society*, 4th series, 30 (1948), 47.

9 I.G., *A Refutation of the Apology for Actors* (1615), in *An Apology for Actors* by Thomas Heywood, 1612 and *A Refutation of the Apology for Actors* by I.G. [John Greene?], 1615, ed. J. W. Binns (New York: Johnson Reprint Corporation, 1972), 4.

10 Quoted in Muriel Bradbrook, *The Rise of the Common Player: A Study of Actor and Society in Shakespeare's England* (London: Chatto and Windus, 1964), 39–40.

11 Thomas Dekker, *The Guls Horn-Booke* (1609), *The Non-Dramatic Works of Thomas Dekker*, ed. Alexander D. Grosart (New York: Russell and Russell, 1963), II: 246.

12 See Lisa Jardine, *Worldly Goods: A New History of the Renaissance* (London: Macmillan, 1996).

13 John Wheeler, *A Treatise of Commerce, Wherein are shewed the commodies arising by a wel ordered and ruled trade, such as that of the Societie of Merchanest Adventures is proved to bee, written principallie for the better information of those who doubt of the necessarienes of the saide societie in the State of the Realme of Englande* (Middleburgh, 1601), 22–3.

14 Wheeler, *A Treatise of Commerce*, 3.

15 Jean-Christophe Agnew, *Worlds Apart: The Market and the Theater in Anglo-American Thought, 1550–1750* (Cambridge: Cambridge University Press, 1986), 42.

16 Joyce Oldham Appelby, *Economic Thought and Ideology in Seventeenth-Century England* (Princeton: Princeton University Press, 1980), 5.

17 Appelby, *Economic Thought and Ideology in Seventeenth-Century England*, 26.

18 Agnew, *Worlds Apart*, xi.

19 Douglas Bruster, *Drama and the Market in the Age of Shakespeare* (Cambridge: Cambridge University Press, 1992), 15–16.

20 Thomas Middleton, *Father Hubburd's Tales: Or, The Ant and the Nightingale*, in *The Works of Thomas Middleton*, ed. A. H. Bullen (New York: AMS Press, 1964), VIII: 74.

21 See Marshall McLuhan, *Understanding Media: The Extensions of Man* (London: Sphere, 1967), 146–7.

22 Martin Burkhardt, *Metamorphosen von Raum und Zeit: Eine Geschichte der Wahrnehmung* (Frankfurt/Main: Campus, 1997), 88, 82.

23 Edward Misselden, *The Circle of Commerce, or The Ballance of Trade, in defence of free Trade* (London, 1623), 93–4.

24 See Philipp Wolf, *Einheit, Abstraktion und literarisches Bewußtsein: Studien zur Ästhetisierung der Dichtung, zur Semantik des Geldes und anderen symbolischen Medien der frühen Neuzeit Englands* (Tübingen: Gunter Narr, 1998), 262.

25 John Hale, *The Civilization of Europe in the Renaissance* (London: Harper Collins, 1993), 177.

26 Thomas Mun, *A Discourse of Trade, from England unto the East Indies* (London, 1621), 52–3.

27 Bacon, 'Of Usury', *The Essays of Francis Bacon* (1625), ed. Mary Augusta Scott (New York: Charles Scribner's Sons, 1908), 187–8.

28 Lawrence Manley, *Literature and Culture in Early Modern London*, 90; Stephen Greenblatt, *Marvelous Possessions: The Wonder of the New World* (Oxford: Clarendon Press, 1991), 64.

29 Steven Mullaney, *The Place of the Stage: License, Play and Power in Renaissance England* (Chicago: University of Chicago Press, 1988), 47; Sir Thomas Culpeper, *A Tract against Usury* (London 1621), 4; Bacon, 'Of Usury', 188.

30 Brian Gibbons, *Jacobean City Comedy*, 2nd ed. (London: Methuen 1980), 20–1.

31 Gerard de Malynes, *Englands View, In the Unmasking of Two Paradoxes: With a replication unto the answer of Maister John Bodine* (London, 1603).

32 Gerard Malynes, *The Center of the Circle of Commerce* (London, 1623), 121. See also Thomas Milles, *The Customer's alphabet and primer* (London, 1608).

33 Misselden, *The Circle of Commerce*, 21.

34 John Norden, *The Surueyor's Dialogue* (London, 1607), 2–3.

35 William Harrison, *Description of England* (1577) (Ithaca: Cornell University Press, 1968), 115.

36 Cited in Manley, *Literature and Culture in Early Modern London*, 99.

37 Garrett A. Sullivan, *The Drama of Landscape: Land, Property and Social Relations on the Early Modern Stage* (Stanford: Stanford University Press, 1998), 6–7.

38 Lawrence Stone, *The Crisis of the Aristocracy 1558–1641* (Oxford: Clarendon Press, 1965), 76–7.

39 Conrad Russell, *The Crisis of Parliaments* (Oxford: Oxford University Press, 1971), 280–1.

40 See Raymond Williams, *The Country and the City* (London: Hogarth Press, 1985).

41 Dockès, *L'Espace dans la pensée économique du XVIe au XVIIIe siècle*, 10.

42 David Harvey, *The Condition of Postmodernity: An Enquiry into the Origins of Cultural Change* (Oxford: Blackwell, 1989), 227.

43 Greenblatt, *Marvelous Possessions*, 110.

44 Tzvetan Todorov, *Grammaire du Décameron* (The Hague: Mouton, 1969), 77–82.
45 Keir Elam, *The Semiotics of Theatre and Drama* (London: Methuen, 1980), 139, 143–4, 145.
46 'Money is my Master ...' Broadsheet ballad in two parts (London, [1635?]).
47 Manley, *Literature and Culture in Early Modern London*, 451.
48 Greenblatt, *Marvelous Possessions*, 69–71.
49 Lars Cassio Karbe, *Venedig, oder die Macht der Phantasie: Die Serenissima – ein Modell für Europa* (München: Diedrichs, 1995), 62.
50 Philipp Wolf, *Einheit, Abstraktion und literarisches Bewußtsein*, 272–3.
51 William Scott, *An Essay of Drapery: Or, the Compleate Citizen* (London, 1635), 106–7.
52 Appelby, *Economic Thought and Ideology in Seventeenth-Century England*, ch. 3.
53 Agnew, *Worlds Apart*, xi.
54 See R. H. Tawney, *Religion and the Rise of Capitalism* (Harmondsworth: Penguin, 1964), 155.
55 C. Walter Hodges, *The Globe Restored: A Study of the Elizabethan Theatre* (London: Ernest Benn, 1953), 48.
56 Cited in Agnew, *Worlds Apart*, 97.
57 Agnew, *Worlds Apart*, 37–50.
58 Gasparo Contarini, *The Commonwealth and Government of Venice*, trans. Lewes Lewkanor (London, 1599), 1.
59 Agnew, *Worlds Apart*, 60.
60 See Maud Ellmann, *The Hunger Artists: Starvation, Writing and Imprisonment* (Cambridge, Mass.: Harvard University Press, 1993).
61 Gamini Salgado (ed.), *Three Jacobean Tragedies* (Harmondsworth: Penguin, 1969), 362.
62 Manley, *Literature and Culture in Early Modern London*, 452.

Chapter 4: Mean Persons and Counterfeit Port: Social Mobility

1 See Agnes Heller, *Renaissance Man*, trans. Richard E. Allen (London: Routledge and Kegan Paul, 1978), 3–4; Lawrence Stone, *The Crisis of the Aristocracy 1558–1641* (Oxford: Clarendon Press, 1965), 35.
2 Cited in Douglas Bruster, *Drama and the Market in the Age of Shakespeare* (Cambridge: Cambridge University Press, 1992), 14.
3 Christopher Hill, *A Nation of Change and Novelty: Radical Politics, Religion and Literature in Seventeenth-Century England* (London: Routledge, 1990), 52.
4 See Christopher Hill, *Reformation to Industrial Revolution: A Social and Economic History of Britain 1530–1780* (London: Weidenfeld and Nicolson, 1967), 4; Lawrence Stone, 'Social Mobility in England 1500–1700', *Past and Present* 33 (April 1966), 33, 32, 45; *The Crisis of the Aristocracy 1558–1641*, 27; Alan Everitt, 'Social Mobility in Early Modern England', *Past and Present* 33 (April 1966), 66.
5 David Mathew, *The Jacobean Age* (Port Washington, NY: Kennikat Press, 1971), 6.
6 Stone, 'Social Mobility in England 1500–1700', 18–20.

7   Lawrence Manley, *Literature and Culture in Early Modern London* (Cambridge: Cambridge University Press, 1995), 93–5, 111–2.

8   Stone, 'Social Mobility in England 1500–1700', 20–1.

9   David Morse, *England's Time of Crisis: From Shakespeare to Milton* (Basingstoke: Macmillan, 1989), 103.

10 Lawrence Manley, *Literature and Culture in Early Modern London*, 75–6.

11 Raymond Williams, *The Country and the City* (London: Hogarth Press, 1985), 51, 53.

12 J. A. Sharpe, *Early Modern England: A Social History 1550–1760*, 2nd ed. (London: Arnold,1997), 179; Keith Wrightson, *English Society 1580–1680* (London: Routledge, 1993), 28.

13 Edward Bolton, *The Cities Advocate* (London, 1629), 47–8.

14 Bernhard Klein, 'English Cartographers and the Mapping of Ireland in the Early Modern Period', *Journal for the Study of British Cultures* 2:1 (1995), 123–4.

15 Victor Kiernan, *Eight Tragedies of Shakespeare* (London: Verso, 1996), 176.

16 See Gaston Bachelard, *La Poétique de l'espace* [1957] (Paris: PUF/Quadrige, 1994), 61.

17 Norbert Elias, *Die höfische Gesellschaft: Untersuchungen zur Soziologie des Königtums und der höfischen Aristokratie* (Frankfurt Main: Surhrkamp, 1983), 81; Don E. Wayne, *Penshurst: The Semiotics of Place and the Poetics of History* (London: Methuen, 1984), 85–6.

18 Donald Lupton, *London and the countrey carbonadoed and quartred into several characters* (London, 1632), 100–1, 103, 104.

19 Quoted in Bruce R. Smith, *Shakespeare and Masculinity* (Oxford: Oxford University Press, 2000), 29.

20 Thomas Middleton, *Father Hubburd's Tales: Or, The Ant and the Nightingale*, in *The Works of Thomas Middleton*, ed. A. H. Bullen (New York: AMS Press, 1964), VIII: 75.

21 See Georges Bataille, *L'Erotisme* (Paris: Minuit, 1957) and *La Part maudite précédé de La Notion de dépense* (Paris: Minuit, 1967).

22 James Turner, *The Politics of Landscape: Rural Scenery and Society in English Poetry 1630–1660* (Oxford: Blackwell, 1979), 143.

23 A. L. Beier, *Masterless Men: The Vagrancy Problem in Britain 1560–1640* (London: Methuen, 1985), 23.

24 Peter Clark and Paul Slack (eds), *Crisis and Order in English Towns 1500–1700: Essays in Urban History* (London: Routledge and Kegan Paul, 1972), 20–1, 26–7.

25 Richard Helgerson, 'The Land Speaks: Cartography, Choreography and Subversion in Renaissance England', in *Representing the English Renaissance*, ed. Stephen Greenblatt (Berkeley: University of California Press, 1988), 349.

26 See Lawrence Manley, *Literature and Culture in Early Modern London*, 102.

27 Richard Elton, *The Compleat Body of the Art Military* (1650), quoted in Turner, *The Politics of Landscape*, 6.

28 Stone, *The Crisis of the Aristocracy 1558–1641*, 28–9; Hill, *Reformation to Industrial Revolution*, 35.

29 Philip Stubbes, *The Anatomie of Abuses* (London, 1584), 8v–9r.

30 Quoted in Barry Taylor, *Vagrant Writing: Social and Semiotic Disorders in the English Renaissance* (Hemel Hempstead: Harvester Wheatsheaf, 1991), 4.

31 Cited in E. K. Chambers, *The Elizabethan Stage* (Oxford: Clarendon Press, 1923), IV: 255–6.
32 Cited in Chambers, *The Elizabethan Stage*, IV: 255–6.
33 John Earle, *Micro-Cosmographie, or, A Peece of the World Discovered* (London, 1628), D12r, D12v, D13v.
34 Earle, *Micro-Cosmographie*, E7r.
35 Stephen Gosson, *Plays Confuted in Five Acts* (1582) (New York: Johnson Reprint Corporation, 1972), E5r.
36 Michael Hattaway, *Elizabethan Popular Theatre: Plays in Performance* (London: Routledge and Kegan Paul, 1982), 71.
37 See Jonas Barish, *The Antitheatrical Prejudice* (Berkeley: University of California Press, 1981), ch. 4.
38 James I, *Basilikon Doron* (Edinburgh: Robert Waldegrave, 1599) (facsimile) (Menston: The Scholar Press, 1969), 121–2.
39 Elizabeth to Parliament: 'We princes are set upon stages in sight and view of all the world' (Christopher Hill, *A Nation of Change and Novelty: Radical Politics, Religion and Literature in Seventeenth-Century England* [London: Routledge, 1990], 106).
40 Heywood, *An Apology for Actors* (London, 1612), E3r.
41 James I, *Basilikon Doron*, 122.
42 Manley, *Literature and Culture in Early Modern London*, 431.
43 Manley, *Literature and Culture in Early Modern London*, 434.
44 Hill, *Reformation to Industrial Revolution*, 64; Standish, *The Commons Complaint* (1611), cited in Turner, *The Politics of Landscape*, 160; Clark and Slack (eds), *Crisis and Order in English Towns 1500–1700*, 19; Turner, *The Politics of Landscape*, 6–7; Hill, *Reformation to Industrial Revolution*, 54; John Walter and Keith Wrightson, 'Dearth and the Social Order in Early Modern England', in *Rebellion, Popular Protest and the Social Order in Early Modern England*, ed. Paul Slack (Cambridge: Cambridge University Press, 1984), 108–28; Christopher Hill, *A Nation of Change and Novelty: Radical Politics, Religion and Literature in Seventeenth-Century England* (London: Routledge, 1990), 206.
45 Henry Peacham, *The Compleat Gentleman* (London, 1627), 16; Stone, *The Crisis of the Aristocracy 1558–1641*, 120.
46 James I, *Basilikon Doron*, 49.
47 Stone, 'Social Mobility in England 1500–1700', 54–5.
48 Douglas Bruster, *Drama and the Market in the Age of Shakespeare* (Cambridge: Cambridge University Press, 1992), 35–6.
49 Stone, *The Crisis of the Aristocracy 1558–1641*, 120.

Chapter 5: Masterless Men and Shifting Knavery: Demographic Mobility

1 Christopher Hill, *Reformation to Industrial Revolution: A Social and Economic History of Britain 1530–1780* (London: Weidenfeld and Nicolson, 1967), 9.
2 Peter Clark, 'The Migrant in Kentish Towns 1580–1640', in *Crisis and Order in English Towns 1500–1700: Essays in Urban History*, eds Peter Clark and Paul Slack (London: Routledge and Kegan Paul, 1972), 146; Alan Everitt, 'Social Mobility in Early Modern England', *Past and Present* 33 (April 1966), 69–70.

3 Maurice Ashley, *Life in Stuart England* (London/New York: B. T. Batsford/G. P. Putnam's Sons, 1964), 159–60; Richard Cust, 'News and Politics in Early Seventeenth-Century England', *Past and Present* 112 (Aug. 1986), 69–71; Ann Hughes, 'The King, the Parliament, and Localities during the English Civil War', *Journal of British Studies* 13:2 (Spring 1984), 238.

4 Richard Helgerson, 'The Land Speaks: Cartography, Choreography and Subversion in Renaissance England', in *Representing the English Renaissance*, ed. Stephen Greenblatt (Berkeley: University of California Press, 1988), 327–61.

5 J. A. Sharpe, *Early Modern England: A Social History* 1550–1760, 2nd ed. (London: Arnold, 1997), 219; Keith Wrightson, *English Society 1580–1680* (London: Routledge, 1993), 41–3.

6 Wrightson, *English Society 1580–1680*, 126–7.

7 Christopher Hill, *Reformation to Industrial Revolution: A Social and Economic History of Britain 1530–1780* (London: Weidenfeld and Nicolson, 1967), 46; Alan Everitt, 'Social Mobility in Early Modern England', 57.

8 Philip Stubbes, *The Anatomie of Abuses* (London, 1584), 69r–69v.

9 Donald Lupton, *London and the countrey carbonadoed and quartred into several characters* (London, 1632), 107.

10 Lawrence Manley, *Literature and Culture in Early Modern London* (Cambridge: Cambridge University Press, 1995), 64, 68; Sharpe, *Early Modern England*, 138–9; Hill, *Reformation to Industrial Revolution*, 51; Wrightson, *English Society 1580–1680*, 137–8.

11 Peter Clark, 'The Migrant in Kentish Towns 1580–1640', 149; A. L. Beier, *Masterless Men: The Vagrancy Problem in Britain 1560–1640* (London: Methuen, 1985), 16–17; Margot Heinemann, *Puritanism and Theatre: Thomas Middleton and Opposition Drama under the Early Stuarts* (Cambridge: Cambridge University Press, 1980), 134–5; Hill, *Reformation to Industrial Revolution*, 40.

12 Manley, *Literature and Culture in Early Modern London*, 80.

13 Quoted in Conrad Russell, *The Crisis of Parliaments* (Oxford: Oxford University Press, 1971), 172.

14 Beier, *Masterless Men*, 40; Lawrence Stone, 'Social Mobility in England 1500–1700', *Past and Present* 33 (April 1966), 30–1; Brian Gibbons, *Jacobean City Comedy*, 2nd ed. (London: Methuen 1980), 22; Peter Clark and Paul Slack, *English Towns in Transition 1500–1700* (London: Oxford University Press, 1976), 9; Heinemann, *Puritanism and Theatre*, 4; Manley, *Literature and Culture in Early Modern London*, 269; Douglas Bruster, *Drama and the Market in the Age of Shakespeare* (Cambridge: Cambridge University Press, 1992), 20; Keith Sturgess, *Jacobean Private Theatre* (London: Routledge and Kegan Paul, 1987), 24; Valerie Pearl, *London and the Outbreak of the Puritan Revolution: City Government and National Politics, 1625–43* (Oxford: Oxford University Press, 1961), 20.

15 Beier, *Masterless Men*, 40; Heinemann, *Puritanism and Theatre*, 32; Clark and Slack, *English Towns in Transition 1500–1700*, 71–2; Pearl, *London and the Outbreak of the Puritan Revolution*, 23–44.

16 Clark, 'The Migrant in Kentish Towns 1580–1640', 140–1; Simon Shepherd, *Amazons and Warrior Women: Varieties of Feminism in Seventeenth-Century Drama* (Brighton: Harvester, 1981), 93.

17 See Wrightson, *English Society 1580–1680*, 169–70.
18 Simon Shepherd, *Amazons and Warrior Women*, 96.
19 Bruster, *Drama and the Market in the Age of Shakespeare*, 32.
20 Garrett A. Sullivan, *The Drama of Landscape: Land, Property and Social Relations on the Early Modern Stage* (Stanford: Stanford University Press, 1998), 20.
21 E. K. Chambers, *The Elizabethan Stage* (Oxford: Clarendon Press, 1923), IV: 337; see also IV: 270, 324.
22 Barry Taylor, *Vagrant Writing: Social and Semiotic Disorders in the English Renaissance* (Hemel Hempstead: Harvester Wheatsheaf, 1991), 5.
23 Philip Stubbes, *The Anatomie of Abuses* (London, 1584), 92r.
24 I.G., *A Refutation of the Apology for Actors* (1615), in *An Apology for Actors* by Thomas Heywood, 1612 and *A Refutation of the Apology for Actors* by I.G. [John Greene?], 1615, ed. J. W. Binns (New York: Johnson Reprint Corporation, 1972), 37.
25 See Beier, *Masterless Men*, 9.
26 Lupton, *London and the countrey carbonadoed*, 28.
27 Taylor, *Vagrant Writing*, 14.
28 Hill, *Reformation to Industrial Revolution*, 40.
29 John Northbrooke, *A Treatise Against Dicing, Dancing, Play and Interludes. With Other Idle Pastimes* (1577) (London: Shakespeare Society, 1843), 98.
30 Muriel Bradbrook, *The Rise of the Common Player: A Study of Actor and Society in Shakespeare's England* (London: Chatto and Windus, 1964), 40. Bradbrook does qualify this picture by claiming that by 1622, the date of Henry Peacham's *Compleat Gentleman*, the player was freed of the stigma of ideleness (66).
31 Beier, *Masterless men*, 27–8.
32 Stubbes, *The Anatomie of Abuses*, 92r.
33 Michael Hattaway, *Elizabethan Popular Theatre: Plays in Performance* (London: Routledge and Kegan Paul, 1982), 71.
34 I.G., *A Refutation of the Apology for Actors* (1615), 4.
35 Steven Mullaney, *The Place of the Stage: License, Play and Power in Renaissance England* (Chicago: University of Chicago Press, 1988), 47.
36 Bradbrook, *The Rise of the Common Player*, 74.
37 Stephen Orgel, *Impersonations: The Performance of Gender in Shakespeare's England* (Cambridge: Cambridge University Press, 1996), 64–5, 67.
38 Chambers, *The Elizabethan Stage*, IV: 322.
39 See for instance Thomas Harman, *A Caveat or Warening for Common Cursetors Vulgarely called Vagabones*, 3rd ed. (1567), in *Cony-Catchers and Bawdy Baskets: An Anthology of Elizabethan Low Life*, ed. Gaminin Salgado (Harmondsworth: Penguin, 1972), 111, 116.
40 Stubbes, *The Anatomie of Abuses*, 92r.
41 Cited in Chambers, *The Elizabethan Stage*, IV: 255–6.
42 Lawrence Stone, 'Social Mobility in England 1500–1700', *Past and Present* 33 (April 1966), 53–4.
43 Margot Heinemann, *Puritanism and Theatre*, 135n, 136; Leeds Barroll, *Politics, Plague and Shakespeare's Theater: The Stuart Years* (Ithaca: Cornell University Press, 1991), 9; Jean E. Howard, *The Stage and Social Struggle in Early Modern England* (London: Routledge, 1994), 74–5.
44 Peter Ure, Introduction to *Richard II* (London: Methuen, 1962), lix.

45 Sir Francis Bacon, 'A Declaration of the Practices and Treasons attempted and committed by Robert late Earl of Essex and his complices against Her Majesty and her Kingdoms ...' (1601), in *The Works of Lord Bacon* (London: Henry G. Bohn, 1850), I: 424.

46 Cited in Beier, *Masterless Men*, 7.

47 Chambers, *The Elizabethan Stage*, IV: 321–2 (my emphasis).

48 Jean Wilson, *The Shakespeare Legacy: The Material Legacy of Shakespeare's Theatre* (Godalming: Bramley, 1995), 27.

49 Chambers, *The Elizabethan Stage*, IV: 341.

Chapter 6: Travelling Thoughts: Travel on the Stage

1 Régis Debray, *Contre Vénise* (Paris: Folio/Gallimard, 1995), 23–4.

2 Anthony Pagden, *European Encounters with the New World: From Renaissance to Romanticism* (New Haven: Yale University Press, 1993), 3.

3 Thomas Platter d.J., *Beschreibung der Reisen durch Frankreich, Spanien, England und die Niederlande 1595–1600*, ed. Rut Keiser (Basel/Stuttgart: Schwabe, 1968), II: 791 (my translation).

4 E. K. Chambers, *The Elizabethan Stage* (Oxford: Clarendon Press, 1923), I: 296; II: 121, 370; IV: 312, 368.

5 John Taylor, *The True Cause of the Watermen's Suit concerning Players, and the reasons that their playing on the London side is their extreame hindrances*, in *All the workes of J. Taylor the Water Poet* (London, 1630), 172.

6 Donald Lupton, *London and the countrey carbonadoed and quartred into several characters* (London, 1632), 22.

7 Lisa Jardine, *Worldly Goods: A New History of the Renaissance* (London: Macmillan, 1996), xxiv.

8 Platter, *Beschreibung der Reisen* ..., II: 794–5 (my translation).

9 See Anthony Parr, 'Introduction', in *Three Renaissance Travel Plays: The Travels of the Three English Brothers; The Sea Voyage; The Antipodes*, ed. Parr (Manchester: Manchester University Press, 1995), 1–2.

10 Ania Loomba, *Gender, Race, Renaissance Drama* (Manchester: Manchester University Press, 1989), 136.

11 Richard Hakluyt, 'Epistle Dedicatory to the First Edition, 1589', *The Principall Navigations, Voyages, Traffiques and Discoveries of the English Nation* [London, 1589; 1598–1600] (London: Everyman, 1913), I: 1–2.

12 See George H. Cunningham, *London: Being a Comprehensive Survey of the History, Tradition and Historical Associations of Buildings and Monuments Arranged under Streets in Alphabetical Order* (London: Dent, 1927), 24.

13 Jurij Lotman, *The Structure of the Artistic Text*, trans. Gail Lenhoff and Ronald Vroon (Ann Arbor: University of Michigan/Dept of Slavic Languages and Literatures, 1977), 231–9.

14 Peter Holland, ' "Travelling Hopefully": The Dramatic Form of Journey in English Renaissance Drama', in *Travel and Drama in Shakespeare's Time*, eds Jean-Pierre Maquerlot and Michèle Willems (Cambridge: Cambridge University Press, 1996), 160–1.

15 The edition used contains no line numbers; references indicate pagination.

16 Michael Issacharoff, 'Espaces mimétiques, espaces diégétiques: Pour une sémiotique des *Mouches'*, in *Sartre et la mise en signe*, eds Michael Issacharoff and Jean-Claude Vilquin (Paris: Kleincksieck/Lexington: French Forum, 1982).

17 Samuel Y. Edgerton, *The Renaissance Rediscovery of Perspective* (New York: Basic Books, 1975), 133–4.

18 Alexandre Koyré, *Du monde clos à l'univers infini* (Paris: Gallimard/Tel, 1973); Max Jammer, *Concepts of Space: The History of Theories of Space in Physics* (New York: Harper and Row, 1960), 88, 98–9; Bernhard Jahn, *Raumkonzepte in der Frühen Neuzeit: Zur Konstruktion von Wirklichkeit in Pilgerberichten, Amerikareisebeschreibungen und Prosaerzählungen* (Frankfurt/Main: Peter Lang, 1993), 34–49; Oswald Spengler, *Der Untergang des Abendlandes: Umrisse einer Morphologie der Weltgeschichte* (München: dtv, 1997), 234.

19 See J. A. Sharpe, *Early Modern England: A Social History 1550–1760*, 2nd ed. (London: Arnold,1997), 141; Robert Brenner, *Merchants and Revolution Commercial Change, Political Conflict and London's Overseas Traders, 1550–1653* (Princeton, NJ: Princeton University Press, 1993), 32–3.

20 Louis B. Wright, 'Colonial Developments in the Reign of James I', in *The Reign of James VI and I*, ed. Alan Smith (London: Macmillan, 1973), 123–39; R. H. Tawney, *Religion and the Rise of Capitalism* (Harmondsworth: Penguin, 1964), 170; Joyce Oldham Appelby, *Economic Thought and Ideology in Seventeenth-Century England* (Princeton: Princeton University Press, 1980), 27.

21 Kenneth R. Andrews, *Trade, Plunder and Settlement: Maritime Enterprise and the Genesis of the British Empire, 1480–1630* (Cambridge: Cambridge University Press, 1984), 1–2, 12–13, 17–18, 357–60.

22 Andrews, *Trade, Plunder and Settlement*, 37.

23 Graham Parry, *The Golden Age Restor'd: The Culture of the Stuart Court, 1603–42* (Manchester: Manchester University Press, 1981), 84–5.

24 See David Morse, *England's Time of Crisis: From Shakespeare to Milton* (Basingstoke: Macmillan, 1989), 76.

25 Samuel Purchas, *Hayklvtvs Posthumus or Purchas His Pilgrimes* (London, 1625), 4.

26 Christopher Hill, *A Nation of Change and Novelty: Radical Politics, Religion and Literature in Seventeenth-Century England* (London: Routledge, 1990), 209.

27 Sir Thomas Palmer, *An Essay of the meanes how to make our Trauailes, into forraine Countries, the more profitable and honourable* (London, 1606).

28 Justus Lipsius, *A Direction for trauailers taken out of Ivstvs Lipsius and enlarged for the behoofe of the right honourable Lord, the yong Earle of Bedford*, trans. Sir John Stradling (London, 1592), A4r, C3r.

29 See Pagden, *European Encounters with the New World*, 10ff.

30 Richard Hakluyt, 'Epistle Dedicatory to the First Edition, 1589', *The Principall Navigations*, I: 1.

31 Christopher Hill, *Intellectual Origins of the English Revolution – Revisited* (Oxford: Clarendon Press, 1997), 264.

32 Purchas, *Hayklvtvs Posthumus or Purchas His Pilgrimes*, 3.

33 Andrews, *Trade, Plunder, Settlement*, 30; John Gillies, *Shakespeare and the Geography of Difference* (Cambridge: Cambridge University Press, 1994), 41.

34 Andrews, *Trade, Plunder, Settlement*, 29.

35 Gillies, *Shakespeare and the Geography of Difference*, chs 1 and 2.

36 Andrew Hadfield, *Literature, Travel and Colonial Writing in the English Renaissance 1545–1625* (Oxford: Clarendon Press, 1998), 17–68.

37 Richard Marienstras, *New Perspectives on the Shakespearean World*, trans. Janet Lloyd (Cambridge: Cambridge University Press, 1985), 163.

38 A. J. Greimas, 'Pour une sémiotique topologique', in *Sémiotique de l'espace: Architecture, urbanisme, sortir de l'impasse*, eds Manar Hammad, Eric Proovost, Michel Vernin (Paris: Denoël/Gonthier, 1979), 14.

39 Tzvetan Todorov, *La Conquête de l'Amérique: La question de l'autre* (Paris: Points/Seuil, 1991); see also Francis Barker and Peter Hulme, 'Nymphs and Reapers Heavily Vanish: The Discursive Con-texts of *The Tempest*', in *Alternative Shakespeares*, ed. John Drakakis (London: Methuen, 1985), 191–205; Jonathon Dollimore and Alan Sinfield, *Political Shakespeare: New Essays in Cultural Materialism* (Manchester: Manchester University Press, 1985); Stephen J. Greenblatt, *Learning to Curse: Essays in Early Modern Culture* (New York/London: Routledge, 1990); Stephen Orgel, 'Shakespeare and the Cannibals', in *Cannibals, Witches and Divorce: Estranging the Renaissance*, ed. Marjorie Garber (Baltimore/London: The Johns Hopkins University Press, 1987), 40–66; Alden T. Vaughan and Virginia Mason Vaughan, *Shakespeare's Caliban: A Cultural History* (Cambridge: Cambridge University Press, 1991).

40 Albrecht Meier, *Certaine Briefe, and Speciall Instructions for Gentlemen, Merchants, Students, Souldiers, mariners , &c. Employed in Seruices Abrode*, trans. Philip Jones (London, 1589), A2v.

41 Robert Harcourt, *A Relation of a Voyage to Guiana* (London, 1613), B2v, B3r.

42 John Hale, *The Civilization of Europe in the Renaissance* (London: Harper Collins, 1993), 33.

43 See Peter Stallybrass, 'Patriarchal Territories: The Body Enclosed', in *Rewriting the Renaissance: The Discourses of Sexual Difference in Early Modern Europe*, eds Margaret W. Ferguson, Maureen Quilligan, Nancy J. Vickers (Chicago: University of Chicago Press, 1986), 129; Roy Strong, *Portraits of Queen Elizabeth I* (Oxford: Clarendon Press, 1963), 15; Jeffrey Brotton, 'Mapping the Early Modern Nation: Cartography Along the English Margins', *Paragraph* 19:2 (July 1996), 139–55; Richard Helgerson, 'The Land Speaks: Cartography, Choreography and Subversion in Renaissance England', in *Representing the English Renaissance*, ed. Stephen Greenblatt (Berkeley: University of California Press, 1988), 327–61.

44 Laura Hunt Yungblut, *Strangers Settled Here Amongst Us: Policies, Perceptions and the Presence of Aliens in Elizabethan England* (London: Routledge, 1996); Marienstras, *New Perspectives on the Shakespearean World*, ch. 5.

45 Andrews, *Trade, Plunder and Settlement*, 36.

46 Richard Knolles, *The Generall Historie of the Turkes*, 2nd ed. (London, 1610), A4r–A6v.

47 Mikhail Bakhtin, *Rabelais and his World*, trans. Helene Iswolsky (Cambridge, Mass.: MIT Press, 1968).

48 See Andrews, *Elizabethan Privateering*, 233–4.

49 William Morrell, *New England, or a Briefe Enarration of the Ayre, Earth, Water, Fish and Fowles of that Country, with a Description of the Natures, Orders, Habits and Religion of the Natives; in Latin and English Verse* (London, 1625), 13–14.

50 Harcourt, *A Relation of a Voyage to Guiana*, 2–3.

51 See Wright, 'Colonial Developments in the Reign of James I', 129–30.

52 See Linda Woodbridge, *Women and the English Renaissance: Literature and the Nature of Womankind, 1540–1620* (Brighton: Harvester, 1984).

53 Sir John Mandeville, *The Voyages and Trauailes of Sir John Mandeuile Knight* (London, 1625), L2v.
54 Francis Bacon, 'Of Travel', *The Essays of Francis Bacon* (1625), ed. Mary Augusta Scott (New York: Charles Scribner's Sons, 1908), 81–2.
55 Georges Balandier, *Anthropo-logiques* (Paris: Livre de poche, 1985), 82.
56 See for instance Hanna Scolnicov, *Women's Theatrical Space* (Cambridge: Cambridge University Press, 1994).
57 Jeanne Addison Roberts, *The Shakespearean Wild: Geography, Genus and Gender* (Lincoln: University of Nebraska Press, 1991), ch. 3.
58 Michael Hattaway, ' "Seeing Things": Amazons and Cannibals', in *Travel and Drama in Shakespeare's Time*, eds Maquerlot and Willems, 179–80.
59 See Catherine Belsey, 'Cleopatra's Seduction', in *Alternative Shakespeares Volume 2*, ed. Terence Hawkes (London: Routledge, 1996), 42–6.
60 George Sandys, *Relation of a Journey begun anno Dom. 1610* (London, 1615), pp. 100–1.
61 Sabine Schülting, *Wilde Frauen, Fremde Welten: Kolonisierungsgeschichten aus Amerika* (Reinbek: Rowohlt, 1997), 54, 57.
62 Ania Loomba, 'Shakespeare and Cultural Difference', in *Alternative Shakespeares Volume 2*, ed. Hawkes, 177.
63 Catherine Belsey, *The Subject of Tragedy: Identity and Difference in Renaissance Drama* (London: Methuen, 1985), 35.
64 See Andrews, *Trade, Plunder and Settlement*, p. 6; Loomba, 'Shakespeare and Cultural Difference', 164–91.
65 Gillies, *Shakespeare and the Geography of Difference*, 65, 204n56.
66 See Pagden, *European Encounters with the New World*, 4–5.
67 Andrew Hadfield, *Literature, Travel and Colonial Writing in the English Renaissance 1545–1625*, 231.
68 Urs Bitterli, *Die 'Wilden' und die 'Zivilisierten': Grundzüge einer Geistes- und Kulturgeschichte der europäisch-überseeischen Begegnung*, 2nd ed. (München: C. H. Beck, 1991), 87; Christopher Hill, *Intellectual Origins of the English Revolution – Revisited*, 347; Stephen Greenblatt, *Renaissance Self-Fashioning: From More to Shakespeare* (Chicago: University of Chicago Press, 1980), 187; Thomas Saunders, *A True Discription and breefe Discourse, Of a most lamentable Voiage, made lately to Tripolie in Barbarie* (London, 1587), B4r, C2r; Lois Potter, 'Pirates and "Turning Turk" in Renaissance Drama', in *Travel and Drama in Shakespeare's Time*, eds Maquerlot and Willems, 129.
69 See also A. E. H. Swaen's edition of *A Christian turn'd Turk*, in *Anglia* 20 (NF 8) (1898), 226–7.
70 Stephen Greenblatt, *Marvelous Possessions: The Wonder of the New World* (Oxford: Clarendon Press, 1991), 135.
71 See Erwin Panofsky, *Meaning in the Visual Arts: Papers in and on Art History* (Garden City, NY: Doubleday Anchor, 1955), 51; Panofsky, *Perspective as Symbolic Form*, trans. Christopher S. Wood (New York: Zone Books, 1991), 67; Kathleen M. Kirby, 'Re: Mapping Subjectivity: Cartographic Vision and the Limits of Politics', in *BodySpace: Destabilizing Geographies of Gender and Sexuality*, ed. Nancy Duncan (London: Routledge, 1996), 45.
72 Hadfield, *Literature, Travel and Colonial Writing in the English Renaissance 1545–1625*, 47; Christopher Hill, *A Nation of Change and Novelty: Radical Politics, Religion and Literature in Seventeenth-Century England* (London: Routledge, 1990), 40.

73 See Jardine, *Worldly Goods*, 386–90.

74 See Paul Brown, ' "This Thing of Darkness I Acknowledge Mine": *The Tempest* and the Discourse of Colonialism', in *Political Shakespeare: New Essays in Cultural Materialism*, eds Dollimore and Sinfield, 48–71.

Chapter 7: Local Thought: Intellectual and Subjective Mobility

1 See Arthur O. Lovejoy, *The Great Chain of Being: A Study of the History of an Idea* (Cambridge, Mass.: Harvard University Press, 1957).

2 *CERTAYNE Sermons, or homilies, appoynted by the kynges Maiestie, to be declared and redde, nby all persones, Vicares, or Curates, euery Sondaye in their churches, where thei haue cure* (1547), quoted in John C. Meagher, *Method and Meaning in Jonson's Masques* (Notre Dame: University of Notre Dame Press, 1966), 164–5.

3 John Milton, *Paradise Lost*, I, 253, in *Poetical Works*, ed. Douglas Bush (Oxford: Oxford University Press, 1979), 218.

4 J. H. Andrews cited in Bernhard Klein, 'English Cartographers and the Mapping of Ireland in the Early Modern Period', *Journal for the Study of British Cultures* 2:1 (1995), 122.

5 Henry Peacham, *The Compleat Gentleman* (London, 1627), 65.

6 Jean-Christophe Agnew, *Worlds Apart: The Market and the Theater in Anglo-American Thought, 1550–1750* (Cambridge: Cambridge University Press, 1986), 58.

7 Michel Foucault, *Les Mots et les choses: Une archéologie des sciences humaines* (Paris: Gallimard, 1966), 329.

8 Linda Bamber, *Comic Women, Tragic Men: A Study of Gender and Genre in Shakespeare* (Stanford: Stanford University Press, 1982), 7.

9 Stephen Greenblatt, *Renaissance Self-Fashioning: From More to Shakespeare* (Chicago: University of Chicago Press, 1980), 9, 256.

10 Cited in Richard Helgerson, *Forms of Nationhood: The Elizabethan Writing of England* (Chicago: University of Chicago Press, 1992), 14.

11 Lawrence Stone, *The Crisis of the Aristocracy 1558–1641* (Oxford: Clarendon Press, 1965), 36.

12 Greenblatt, *Renaissance Self-Fashioning*, 7–9.

13 Cited in E. K. Chambers, *The Elizabethan Stage* (Oxford: Clarendon Press, 1923), IV: 255–6 (my emphasis).

14 Agnew, *Worlds Apart*, 106–7.

15 See David Morse, *England's Time of Crisis: From Shakespeare to Milton* (Basingstoke: Macmillan, 1989), ch. 6.

16 *CERTAYNE Sermons ...* , quoted in Meagher, *Method and Meaning in Jonson's Masques*, 164–5.

17 Herbert Grierson (ed.), *The Poems of John Donne* (London: Oxford University Press, 1964), 213–14.

18 Cited in Christopher Hill, *Intellectual Origins of the English Revolution – Revisited* (Oxford: Clarendon Press, 1997), 9.

19 Cited in Chambers, *The Elizabethan Stage*, IV: 255–6.

20 Francis Bacon, *Novum Organum* (1620), the second part of the *Instauration Magna* (1620), quoted in the English translation of 1860 in

Elizabethan-Jacobean Drama, ed. G. Blakemore Evans (London: A. & C. Black, 1989), 319 (my emphasis).

21   See Clifford Geertz, *Local Knowledge: Further Essays in Interpretive Anthropology* (New York: Basic Books, 1983), 167.

22   Hill, *Intellectual Origins of the English Revolution – Revisited*, ch. 2.

23   Helgerson, *Forms of Nationhood*, 165, 174–5.

24   Hill, *Intellectual Origins of the English Revolution – Revisited*, 62, 99.

25   Joyce Oldham Appelby, *Economic Thought and Ideology in Seventeenth-Century England* (Princeton: Princeton University Press, 1980), 43.

26   Edward Misselden, *The Circle of Commerce, or The Ballance of Trade, in defence of free Trade* (London, 1623), 16–17.

27   R. H. Tawney, *Business and Politics under James I: Lionel Cranfield as Merchant and Minister* (London: Russell and Russell, [1958], 1976), 41–4, 50–1.

28   Thomas Dekker, *The Dead Tearme* (1608), *The Non-Dramatic Works of Thomas Dekker*, ed. Alexander D. Grosart (New York: Russell and Russell, 1963), IV: 51.

29   Richard Cust, 'News and Politics in early Seventeenth-Century England', *Past and Present* 112 (Aug. 1986) 70.

30   See Anthony Parr, 'Introduction', *Three Renaissance Travel Plays: The Travels of the Three English Brothers; The Sea Voyage; The Antipodes* (Manchester: Manchester University Press, 1995), 7–9.

31   See Pierre Francastel, *Peinture et société: Naissance et destruction d'un espace plastique: De la renaissance au cubisme* (Lyon: Audin, 1951), 23.

32   Martin White, *Renaissance Drama in Action: An Introduction to Some Aspects of Theatre Practice and Performance* (London: Routledge, 1998), 2.

33   Lawrence Stone, *The Family Sex and Marriage in England 1500–1800* (Harmondsworth: Penguin/Pelican, 1979), 146, 409.

34   Victor Morgan, 'The Cartographic Image of "the Country" in Early Modern England', *Transactions of the Royal Historical Society* 5th Series, 29 (1979), 138.

35   Fredric Jameson, *Postmodernism, or, The Cultural Logic of Late Capitalism* (London/New York: Verso, 1992), 52.

36   Martin Burkhardt, *Metamorphosen von Raum und Zeit: Eine Geschichte der Wahrnehmung* (Frankfurt/Main: Campus, 1997), 97–100.

37   See Michel Foucault, *Histoire de la folie à l'âge classique* (Paris: Gallimard, 1972), 31–2.

38   George R. Kernodle, *From Art to Theatre: Form and Convention in the Renaissance* (Chicago: University of Chicago Press, 1944), 47.

39   See for instance Samuel Y. Edgerton, *The Renaissance Rediscovery of Perspective* (New York: Basic Books, 1975) and Erwin Panofsky, *Perspective as Symbolic Form*, trans. Christopher S. Wood (New York: Zone Books, 1991).

40   Elspeth Graham, 'Women's Writing and the Self', in *Women and Literature in Britain 1500–1700*, ed. Helen Wilcox (Cambridge: Cambridge University Press, 1996), 213.

41   Agnew, *Worlds Apart*, 97, 13.

42   See Michel Foucault, *Histoire de la sexualité, 1: La Volonté du savoir* (Paris: Gallimard, 1976); Elizabeth Hanson, *Discovering the Subject in Renaissance England* (Cambridge: Cambridge University Press, 1998), in particular ch. 1.

43   Jonathon Dollimore, *Radical Tragedy: Religion, Ideology and Power in the Drama of Shakespeare and His Contemporaries* (Brighton: Harvester Wheatsheaf, 1984), 175, 179.

44 Francis Bacon, 'Of Negotiating', *The Essays of Francis Bacon* (1625), ed. Mary Augusta Scott (New York: Charles Scribner's Sons, 1908), 226–7.

45 Erwin Panofsky, *Meaning in the Visual Arts: Papers in and on Art History* (Garden City, NY: Doubleday Anchor, 1955), 278.

46 Deborah Cameron, *Verbal Hygiene* (London: Routledge, 1995).

47 Michel de Montaigne, *Oeuvres complètes*, eds Albert Thibaudet and Maurice Rat (Paris: Gallimard/Pléiade, 1962), 202–3; Bacon, 'Of Negotiating', 225.

48 Lawrence Manley, *Literature and Culture in Early Modern London* (Cambridge: Cambridge University Press, 1995), 453.

49 Philip Stubbes, *The Anatomie of Abuses* (London, 1584), 78v–79r.

50 See Michel Foucault, 'Questions à Michel Foucault sur la géographie', *Dits et écrits 1954–1988*, eds Daniel Defert and François Ewald (Paris: Gallimard, 1994), III: 28–40; Yves Lacoste, *La géographie, ça sert, d'abord, à faire la guerre* (Paris: Maspero, 1976); Paul Virilio, *Bunker Archeology*, trans. George Collins (Paris: Les Editions du Demi-cercle, 1994); *Vitesse et politique* (Paris: Galilée, 1977).

51 Barbara Korte, 'English-Canadian Perspectives of Landscape', *International Journal of Canadian Studies/Revue internationale d'études canadiennes* 6 (Autumn 1992), 9–24.

52 Darko Suvin, 'Approach to Topoanalysis and to the Paradigmatics of Dramaturgical Space', *Poetics Today* 8:2 (1987), 312.

53 I.B., [John Browne?], *The Marchants Avizo* (London, 1607), 2–3.

54 William Scott, *An Essay of Drapery: Or, the Compleate Citizen* (London, 1635), 137, 138, 139.

55 Scott, *An Essay of Drapery*, 127–8.

56 Walter Benjamin, *Das Passagen-Werk* in *Gesammelte Schriften*, ed. Rolf Tiedmann (Frankfurt/Main: Suhrkamp, 1982), V.1/V.2: 575–8.

Coda: Drama and the Appropriation of Social Space

1 Michel Foucault, 'Qu'est-ce qu'un auteur', *Dits et écrits 1954–1988*, eds Daniel Defert and François Ewald (Paris: Gallimard, 1994), I: 789–821 [abbreviated English version: 'What is an Author?', in *Textual Strategies: Perspectives in Post-Structuralist Criticism*, ed. Josué Harari (London: Methuen, 1979), 141–60].

2 Thomas Harman, *A Caveat for Common Cursitors* (1567), in *Cony-Catchers and Bawdy Baskets: An Anthology of Elizabethan Low Life*, ed. Gamini Salgado (Harmondsworth: Penguin, 1972), 153 (my emphasis).

3 Elizabeth Hanson, *Discovering the Subject in Renaissance England* (Cambridge: Cambridge University Press, 1998), 97–106.

4 Theodore B. Leinwand, *The City Staged: Jacobean Comedy, 1603–1613* (Madison: University of Wisconsin Press, 1986), 37.

5 Hanson, *Discovering the Subject in Renaissance England*, 3.

6 Henri Lefebvre, *La Production de l'espace* (Paris: Editions Anthropos, 1974), 48–9.

Index